PUBLIC HEALTH LAW AND POLICY

PUBLIC HEALTH LAW AND POLICY

AMIT KUMAR
Max Planck Fellow
M.A (JNU), LL.M (ILI)
Assistant Professor of Law
Maharashtra National Law University, Mumbai

PHI Learning Private Limited
Delhi-110092
2025

In fond memory of ***Shri Asoke K. Ghosh*** *(October 1942 – February 2024), Founder Chairman and Managing Director of PHI Learning, whose vision endlessly inspires.*

The Legacy Continues....

Published by Pushpita Ghosh, PHI Learning Private Limited, Rimjhim House, 111, Patparganj Industrial Estate, Delhi-110092 and Printed by Syndicate Binders, A-20, Hosiery Complex, Noida, Phase-II Extension, Noida-201305 (N.C.R. Delhi).

₹ 655.00

PUBLIC HEALTH LAW AND POLICY
Amit Kumar

ISBN-978-93-5443-955-1 (Print Book)
ISBN-978-93-5443-991-9 (e-Book)

The export rights of this book are vested solely with the publisher.

For

Juba, who pilots deftly the vessel of happiness

Family, the ocean which keeps the vessel afloat

Contents

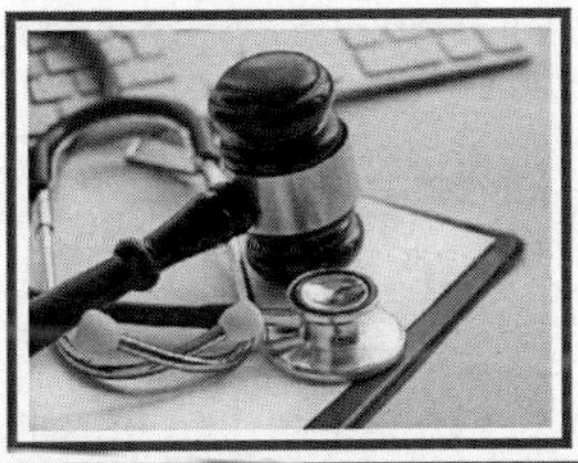

Prologue

Health occupies a singularly pivotal position in the evolving narratives and churning discourses of rights, governance, and human development. It is a prerequisite for individual well-being and correspondingly an undisputable benchmark to measure social progress. This book discusses the intricate interconnections between health, law, and policy elucidating how these domains coalesce to shape lived experiences of individuals and communities. Health in its most holistic sense, implies physical, mental, and social well-being, but its realization as a universal right is still characterized by problems, such as disparities, governance gaps, and socio-political as well as economic differentials.

At the heart of this discourse lie constitutional frameworks including the Indian one, which enshrines health as an aspirational directive. The framers of the Constitution envisioned a nation where equitable access to healthcare would form the bedrock of social justice. Over decades, this vision has been nurtured by judicial interventions that have sought to interpret and expand the scope of the right to health to fashion it as a justiciable right. This book begins by charting the foundational principles of health, its definitions, ethical considerations, and its entanglement with justice and rights. These foundational aspects provide a theoretical lens through which the subsequent discussions are framed.

The book also explores contemporary debates that challenge traditional notions of health and ethics. It discusses gender and health, euthanasia, surrogacy, and the rights of non-binary individuals in terms of their legal and ethical implications. These debates demonstrate how health governance need to evolve to meet the changes in society and keep abreast of the technological innovations of the times.

Moreover aside from the domestic health governance landscape, the broader framework of global health governance is also another important issue in this regard particularly in the wake of a sharp rise in emerging transboundary infectious diseases. Addressing the interconnected nature of health during pandemics and other infectious diseases which remind us of our shared vulnerabilities thus becomes quintessential. This book in this context also analyses how institutions, international health treaties, conventions any other legal of policy frameworks work towards facilitating global health solidarity and what are the challenges they confront.

Overall this book and the content it encapsulates calls out to a wide audience transcending the confines of academia. Hence the book shall be useful not only for students and teachers of health law but also policymakers, practitioners, and citizens in general. It invites readers to reflect on the challenges and possibilities of realizing health as a universal right by providing a comprehensive analysis of health law and policy in India and beyond. But contained within the pages an endeavour more than academic can also be discerned, call for vigilance, for advocacy, and for sustained efforts to make health a lived reality for all.

I shall be grateful to the readers for suggestions/feedback to further improve the contents of the book. Readers can reach me at **thinkverito@gmail.com** and **https://www.linkedin.com/in/amit-kumar-a43041352/**

AMIT KUMAR

PART I

Health: Foundational Aspects

CHAPTER

1

Health Concept and Definitions

INTRODUCTION

In the conventional understanding of the term, health has been framed in contrast to illness or as merely the absence of a disease. This is a reductive, mono-dimensional projection of health which implies a binary relationship between health and illness. This perspective has its roots in the biomedical model of health, which focuses primarily on the biophysical aspects of health and disease.

However, this perspective has been increasingly viewed as being limited and insufficient in capturing the complexities human health entails. Health is not merely the absence of disease but encompasses a broader spectrum of physical, mental, and social well-being. This perspective aligns closely with and is reflected in the World Health Organization's definition of health as "a state of complete physical, mental, and social well-being and not merely the absence of disease or infirmity."[1]

The WHO definition presents health as a positive state of well-being rather than merely the absence of illness. This framing emphasizes the promotion of health and well-being as proactive endeavours, focusing on enhancing the overall quality of life rather than just treating diseases. It encourages a shift from a disease-centric approach to healthcare to one that prioritizes health promotion, prevention, and the promotion of positive health outcomes. This understanding of health provides a comprehensive framework that recognizes health as a multidimensional concept encompassing physical, mental, and social dimensions of well-being. It emphasizes the importance of promoting holistic health and well-being and emphasizes the need for a broad and inclusive approach to healthcare that addresses the diverse needs of individuals and communities.

A more relevant conceptualization of health therefore requires capturing different dimensions of well-being. In addition to the absence of physical disease or pain it also highlights the importance of soundness in body, mind, and spirit. This perspective acknowledges the holistic nature of health, suggesting that true well-being encompasses not only physical fitness but also mental and spiritual vitality. Another dimension of health focuses on the functional

1. https://www.who.int/about/accountability/governance/constitution

aspect of health, stressing on the ability to perform daily tasks and engage in activities without impairment. It suggests that health is achieved when the body and mind function optimally, allowing individuals to lead productive and fulfilling lives.

Another perspective, articulated as "a series of successful and continuous adaptations to a continuously changing environment," portrays health as a dynamic process of adaptation. This definition emphasizes the ongoing interaction between individuals and their environment, suggesting that health is not a static state but rather a state of resilience and flexibility. It implies that maintaining good health involves continually adjusting to various physical, social, and environmental stressors. Additionally health can also be perceived as "a state of relative equilibrium of body, form, and function". This understanding dwells on the dynamic interaction between the body and its environment. It suggests that health is achieved through active responses to internal and external forces, leading to a state of balance and harmony. This perspective focuses on the body's innate capacity to adapt and self-regulate, promoting overall well-being.

The various definitions and perspectives analysed above offer complementary perspectives on health, highlighting its multifaceted nature. They emphasize the importance of considering physical, mental, and social aspects of health and emphasize on the need for ongoing adaptation and resilience in maintaining well-being.

Nevertheless, the World Health Organization's definition of health has also faced criticism for being overly idealistic and rigid. Critics argue that the term "complete" implies an unrealistic standard of health, as it suggests a state free from all worries and ailments, which is unlikely to be achievable throughout one's life[2]. Furthermore, some critics contend that the emphasis on "complete physical, mental, and social well-being" blurs the distinction between health and happiness, two distinct aspects of human experience. They argue that while health encompasses physical, mental, and social well-being, happiness is a subjective emotional state that may not always align with one's health status. Additionally, critics highlight the dynamic nature of health needs, which vary with age and individual circumstances, emphasizing the importance of personal responsibility in maintaining well-being. Critics argue that the WHO definition may not adequately capture the complexities and nuances of health as experienced by individuals in different contexts.

In response to such critique in contemporary discourse therefore, newer approaches have emerged which seek to look at health through a different lens by aligning health with social and rights based dimensions. According to this perspective, health is seen as an inherent human right and has distinctive social dimensions fundamental to leading a productive life while also reducing the need for excessive medical expenses. Rather than existing in isolation, health is viewed as intricately linked to various sectors of society and is considered a crucial component of social development. In this framework, health becomes the focal point of measuring quality of life, transcending individual concerns to become a shared responsibility of both governments and the international community. Investing in health is therefore seen as an investment in

2. Daniel Callahan points out that the most specific complaint about the WHO definition is that its very generality, and particularly its association of health and general well-being as a positive ideal, has given rise to a variety of evils.
See, https://academic.oup.com/phe/article/16/3/210/7232444

societal progress and development. This philosophy recognizes health as a global phenomenon, highlighting the interwoven nature of health outcomes across nations and emphasizing the need for collaborative efforts on a worldwide scale to address health challenges effectively.

Summing up the ideas, perspectives and critique outlined above, health can be seen as a dynamic and holistic concept that involves multiple dimensions which can be discussed as follows:

1.1 PHYSICAL HEALTH

The physical dimension of health is intricately tied to the optimal functioning of the body's cells and organs. However, defining what constitutes "optimal" functioning can be ambiguous, as perspectives on physical health vary among individuals. Some individuals perceive physical health in terms of outward physical characteristics such as skin colour, height, body weight, and other features. This perception often equates physical health with attributes such as moderate body weight, a robust appetite, sound sleep, the ability to engage in strenuous activity without fatigue, and the efficient operation of the body's various organs and senses etc. Moreover, physical health encompasses biomedical attributes like a normal pulse rate, appropriate blood pressure levels relative to age and sex, and the overall well-functioning of bodily systems. It's evident that physical health extends beyond mere appearance and encompasses the intricate workings of the body's internal mechanisms. In essence, physical health refers to the holistic state of the body, including its composition, development, functions, and the maintenance of vital organs. Given the integral connection between health and the proper functioning of bodily organs, physical health becomes an important attribute in the overall determination of health and its constituent parameters.

1.2 MENTAL HEALTH

Mental health encompasses emotional well-being, efficient cognitive function, and psychological resilience. It involves the ability to cope with stress, maintain positive relationships, and experience a sense of purpose and fulfilment in life. Mental health issues, such as depression, anxiety, and stress, can significantly impact overall well-being. Mental health transcends the mere absence of mental illness; it encompasses the capacity to navigate life's diverse experiences with adaptability and purpose. In recent years, mental health has been redefined as a state of equilibrium, reflecting a harmonious relationship between oneself, others, and the environment. Formerly perceived as independent entities, the mind and body are now understood as being aligned with psychological factors influencing various physical conditions, such as hypertension, peptic ulcers, and asthma, alongside mental illnesses like depression and schizophrenia. This recognition points to the complexity of mental health, where behavioural, psychological, and biological factors intersect to maintain or disrupt the functional equilibrium.

Despite its significance, the scientific understanding of mental health is still evolving. It still lacks precise assessment tools akin to those available for physical health. Psychologists have outlined key attributes characterizing mental health, including internal harmony, interpersonal adeptness, resilience in the face of criticism, identity formation, robust self-esteem, self-awareness, emotional regulation, problem-solving skills, and effective coping mechanisms. A mentally healthy individual demonstrates an absence of internal conflict, harmonious interactions with others, openness to feedback, a quest for self-understanding and purpose, emotional stability, and a proactive approach to addressing challenges.

In essence, mental health encompasses a dynamic balance between internal and external forces, influencing an individual's psychological well-being and adaptive functioning. While mental health remains complex and multifaceted, efforts to promote mental well-being entail strengthening resilience, self-awareness, interpersonal skills, and effective coping strategies. By recognizing mental health as an integral component of overall well-being, society can strive towards nurturing environments that support individuals in achieving and maintaining optimal mental health.

1.3 SOCIAL HEALTH

Social health relates to one's interactions with others and the quality of relationships. It involves having a support network of friends, family, and community members, as well as a sense of belonging and connectedness. Social isolation and loneliness can have detrimental effects on both mental and physical health.

Human beings are inherently social creatures. They are a part of an intricate network of social relationships that fulfil various needs within society. These relationships are reciprocal, facilitating the exchange of ideas, emotions, and cultural practices among individuals. Despite the diversity of cultures within society, these cultural norms and practices are shared among community members, cultivating a sense of unity and belonging. The interaction and sharing of cultural traits contribute to building a positive image and enhancing interpersonal communication skills, essential for active participation in both community and society at large.

Active engagement in the process of cultural integration is crucial for social cohesion and individual well-being. The social dimension of health encompasses the level of social skills, social functioning, and an individual's sense of belonging within society. As individuals participate in familial, societal, and broader community contexts, they contribute to and benefit from the collective social fabric. Moreover, the social dimension of health extends beyond interpersonal relationships to encompass broader social and economic factors that influence overall well-being.

A positive human and material environment is essential for supporting individuals' social connections and well-being. This includes access to supportive social networks, as well as favourable economic and material conditions. The social dimension of health is thus intricately linked to the quality of social relationships and the broader socio-economic context within which individuals live. By nurturing positive social environments and addressing socio-economic disparities, society can promote the holistic well-being of its members and inculcate a sense of belonging within the community.

1.4 EMOTIONAL AND SPIRITUAL HEALTH

The spiritual dimension of health, in conjunction with the emotional aspect, forms an integral part of a holistic approach to well-being. Beyond mere social interactions, spiritualism provides individuals with a deeper sense of purpose and direction in life. By setting personal goals and beliefs, individuals find meaning and fulfilment, transcending mere existence. Unlike objective measures, spiritualism is inherently subjective, rooted in one's inner self and understanding of existence. This pursuit of meaning and purpose not only enriches personal well-being but also positively impacts physical health. The intrinsic worth derived from spiritual fulfilment contributes to overall physical well-being, highlighting the alignment of mind, body, and spirit in achieving holistic health.

Turning to the emotional dimension of health, it is essential to acknowledge the profound influence of emotions on human well-being. As emotional beings, individuals experience a wide range of feelings, from joy and contentment to hopelessness and anxiety. Emotional well-being encompasses the ability to cope with these feelings effectively, enhancing resilience in the face of adversity.

Emotions are inherent to human nature; unaddressed emotional distress can lead to mental illness and negatively impact overall health. Therefore, it is crucial for individuals to be aware of their emotional strengths and weaknesses, seeking support when needed to address emotional challenges constructively. Building strong relationships with family, peers, and community members serves as a vital buffer against emotional distress, providing a support network for individuals to lean on during difficult times.

In contemporary perspectives on health, the distinction between emotional and mental aspects is increasingly recognized. While mental health focuses on cognition and knowledge, emotional health revolves around feelings and interpersonal dynamics. Addressing both dimensions separately yet holistically can enhance resilience, emotional well-being, and overall health and vitality.

1.5 ENVIRONMENTAL HEALTH

Environmental health is a multifaceted domain that encompasses a broad range of factors, all of which exert significant influence on human well-being. At its core, environmental health addresses the interaction between individuals and their surrounding environment, encompassing various dimensions such as air and water quality, access to green spaces, exposure to pollutants and toxins, and the overall conditions in which people live, work, and engage in recreational activities.

Air and water quality for instance are fundamental determinants of environmental health. Poor air quality, resulting from pollutants emitted by vehicles, industries, and other sources, can lead to respiratory illnesses, cardiovascular diseases, and other adverse health outcomes. Similarly, contaminated water sources pose significant risks to public health, contributing to the spread of waterborne diseases and compromising overall well-being. Access to green spaces, including parks, forests, and recreational areas, is essential for promoting physical activity, reducing stress, and improving mental health. Green spaces offer opportunities for exercise, relaxation, and social interaction, thereby enhancing overall quality of life and contributing to psychological well-being. Exposure to toxins and pollutants in the environment can have profound impacts on human health. Chemical contaminants found in air, water, soil, and food can accumulate in the body over time, leading to various health problems, including cancer, neurological disorders, and reproductive issues. Additionally, exposure to environmental hazards such as hazardous waste sites, industrial pollutants, and pesticides can disproportionately affect marginalized communities, exacerbating existing health disparities. The conditions in which people live, work, and play also play a crucial role in environmental health. Factors such as housing quality, access to sanitation facilities, and neighbourhood safety can significantly impact individuals' health outcomes and overall well-being. Social and economic factors, including income inequality, employment opportunities, and access to healthcare, further shape individuals' exposure to environmental risks and their ability to mitigate potential health hazards.

In analysing environmental health, it is essential to consider the complex interplay between environmental factors, social determinants, and individual behaviours. Addressing environmental health challenges requires a comprehensive approach that integrates scientific research, public policy, community engagement, and individual empowerment. By promoting sustainable environmental practices, ensuring equitable access to resources, and promoting healthy living environments, societies can safeguard and enhance the health and well-being of present and future generations.

It is therefore evident that health is a multifaceted concept and encompasses many dimensions. Acknowledging these multiple dimensions of health, can pave the way for a more comprehensive and inclusive approach to promoting health well-being can be adopted rather than simply focusing on the absence of disease. Such an approach advocates examining and assessing all aspects of health to achieve a state of overall wellness and flourishing. This broader perspective not only empowers individuals to take an active role in their health but also highlights the importance of addressing social determinants and inequalities that impact health outcomes.

1.6 BACKWARD AND FORWARD LINKAGES IN HEALTH

An analysis of the dimensions outlined above demonstrates the interrelatedness of various factors that influence individual and population health outcomes. These dimensions operate at different levels and stages and can been seen as backward and forward linkages, they are inherently linked and can significantly impact each other.

- **Upstream Dimension:** In contrast, the upstream dimension of health encompasses the broader social, economic, and environmental determinants that shape individual health outcomes. These determinants include factors such as socio-economic status, education, employment, housing, environmental conditions, and access to resources and opportunities. Upstream interventions aim to address the root causes of health disparities and inequities by targeting social, economic, and environmental factors that influence health outcomes. For example, policies and programs focused on poverty reduction, improving educational attainment, ensuring access to affordable housing and nutritious food, and reducing environmental pollution are all upstream interventions aimed at promoting health at the population level.
- **Downstream Dimension:** The downstream dimension of health refers to the immediate and proximal factors that directly affect individual health outcomes. This includes factors such as lifestyle behaviours, access to healthcare services, and biological factors. Downstream interventions typically focus on treating diseases, managing symptoms, and promoting changes at individual and community levels to improve health outcomes.

For example, providing medical treatments for diseases like diabetes or hypertension, promoting healthy eating and physical activity habits, and offering access to preventive healthcare services are all downstream interventions aimed at addressing immediate health concerns.

The key concept underlying the upstream-downstream framework is that upstream factors have a profound impact on downstream health outcomes. Social, economic, and environmental conditions shape people's opportunities and constraints, influencing their ability to make healthy choices and access healthcare services. Addressing upstream determinants of health is essential for reducing health inequities and promoting health equity, as it tackles the root causes of disparities rather than simply treating symptoms.

Moreover, there is a bidirectional relationship between upstream and downstream dimensions of health. While upstream factors influence downstream health outcomes, downstream interventions can also have upstream effects by addressing immediate health needs and mitigating the impact of upstream determinants on individual health. For instance, improving access to healthcare services through downstream interventions can help individuals better manage chronic conditions and prevent complications, thereby reducing the overall burden of disease and improving population health. This perspective addresses the importance of addressing both immediate and underlying determinants of health to achieve better health outcomes and promote health equity. By recognizing the interlinkages between these dimensions, policymakers, healthcare providers, and communities can develop comprehensive strategies to improve health and well-being at individual and population levels.

SUMMARY

From the foregoing description it is clear that the definitional as well as conceptual understanding of health has progressively evolved. A contemporary understanding of health is not premised only upon the biomedical aspect but has expanded to become multidimensional in its scope. The changing conceptual paradigm is more comprehensive, this holistic approach integrates elements from the biomedical, ecological, and psychosocial frameworks, acknowledging the profound impact of social, economic, political, and environmental factors on health. It is characterized as a unified or multidimensional approach that considers the overall well-being of individuals within their environmental context. The holistic perspective suggests that all sectors of society influence health, with particular emphasis on agriculture, animal husbandry, food production, industry, education, housing, public infrastructure, communication, and healthcare. This approach prioritizes health promotion and protection.

By moving beyond traditional medical paradigms, recognizing the interdependence of various factors influencing health and factoring in social, economic, political, and environmental influences, the contemporary perspective offers a comprehensive understanding of health and well-being. Additionally, the appreciation of the various social and community dimensions leads to the formulation of law and policy in this area. It also signifies the importance of collaborative efforts beyond the healthcare system alone in promoting and safeguarding public health. Such perspectives have contributed to the evolution of public health as a distinct approach in health and healthcare service delivery. This shall be discussed in detail in the following Chapter.

CHAPTER

2

Public Health Meaning and Salient Aspects

INTRODUCTION

The biomedical model of health, which emerged predominantly in the 19th and 20th centuries, revolutionized medical science by framing health and disease through the lens of biology and the germ theory of disease. This model emphasizes the diagnosis and treatment of physical ailments caused by pathogens or physiological dysfunctions. While highly successful in advancing medical treatments and significantly reducing mortality from infectious diseases, the biomedical approach has notable limitations in providing a holistic understanding of health and well-being.

2.1 EVOLUTION OF THE PUBLIC HEALTH PARADIGM

One of the key limitations of the biomedical model is its reductionist view of health. It tends to isolate health issues into distinct biological components, focusing primarily on identifying specific pathogens or physiological abnormalities responsible for disease. This reductionist perspective often overlooks the broader social, psychological, and environmental factors that also influence health outcomes. For instance, while antibiotics effectively target bacterial infections, they do not address the social determinants of health such as poverty, access to healthcare, or education, which are crucial in shaping overall health outcomes.

Moreover, the biomedical model tends to prioritize reactive rather than proactive approaches to health. It is predominantly concerned with diagnosing and treating diseases after they have already manifested clinically. While this approach has been essential in managing acute illnesses and emergencies, it may not adequately address preventive measures and health promotion strategies aimed at reducing the incidence of diseases in the first place. For example, while vaccines are effective in preventing certain infectious diseases, they do not address underlying factors contributing to disease susceptibility, such as nutrition, lifestyle, or environmental exposures.

The biomedical model's emphasis on individual pathology often sidelines the importance of community and population-level factors in health. It does not fully account for how social determinants, such as income inequality, social support networks, or environmental policies, shape health outcomes at a population level. Public health issues like obesity, substance abuse, and mental health disorders are increasingly recognized as consequences of a complex interplay of biological, social, economic, and environmental factors that require multifaceted approaches beyond medical interventions alone.

Critics argue that the biomedical model's exclusive focus on disease and treatment can perpetuate a reactive healthcare system that is costly and unsustainable in the long term. Addressing chronic diseases, which are often rooted in lifestyle choices and broader socio-economic determinants, requires a shift towards holistic health promotion strategies that encompass prevention, education, and community-based interventions. Integrative approaches that combine medical treatments with social determinants of health interventions have shown promise in improving health outcomes and reducing healthcare disparities.

- **Reductionism:** The biomedical model tends to reduce health to the absence of disease or the presence of specific biological abnormalities. This reductionist view overlooks the complex interactions between biological, environmental, social, and psychological factors that influence health outcomes. Furthermore, by solely focusing on disease and biological abnormalities, the biomedical model often neglects the broader determinants of health that can significantly impact individuals and communities. Social factors such as income, education, employment, and access to healthcare services play crucial roles in shaping health outcomes. For instance, individuals from lower socio-economic backgrounds may face greater barriers to accessing quality healthcare, leading to disparities in health outcomes compared to their more affluent counterparts. Moreover, environmental factors such as air and water quality, housing conditions, and exposure to pollutants can profoundly affect health, contributing to conditions like respiratory illnesses or chronic diseases. Psychological factors such as stress, social support networks, and mental health also exert a powerful influence on overall well-being, yet these are frequently overlooked in a purely biomedical framework. Therefore, a comprehensive understanding of health requires integrating these diverse factors by adopting an inclusive holistic approach that acknowledges their mutual interdependence and impact on individual and population health outcomes.
- **Neglect of Social Determinants:** In the context of health disparities, the social determinants mentioned, socio-economic status, education, employment, housing, and healthcare access are critical. Individuals with higher socio-economic status generally have better access to healthcare services, can afford healthier lifestyles, and may live in environments that are less stressful and more conducive to health. Conversely, those with lower socio-economic status often face barriers such as limited access to healthcare facilities, higher exposure to environmental risks, and increased stress due to financial instability or unsafe living conditions. These disparities contribute significantly to differences in health outcomes across populations. For example, studies consistently show that individuals with lower education levels or income tend to have higher rates of chronic diseases, shorter life expectancies, and poorer overall health compared to their more affluent counterparts. Furthermore, within the biomedical model, there is often an implicit assumption that health issues can be primarily addressed through medical interventions targeting biological factors. While medical treatments are crucial, they

may not effectively mitigate the impact of social determinants on health outcomes. For instance, prescribing medication for a chronic condition may be ineffective if the patient lacks stable housing or cannot afford nutritious food. Recognizing and addressing these social determinants requires a broader approach that includes policies aimed at reducing income inequality, improving educational opportunities, ensuring fair employment practices, and enhancing access to safe housing and healthcare. By integrating these elements into healthcare practices and policies, it becomes possible to create more equitable and effective strategies for improving population health and reducing disparities.

- **Individualistic Focus:** The biomedical model's emphasis on individual pathology and treatment often disregards the significant influence of social networks, community support systems, and cultural factors on health outcomes. Social networks and community ties can provide crucial emotional support, access to resources, and opportunities for health-promoting behaviours such as exercise or healthy eating. Moreover, cultural beliefs and practices shape health behaviours and attitudes towards healthcare, impacting treatment adherence and health-seeking behaviours. Neglecting these community and cultural influences can limit the effectiveness of healthcare interventions and preventive measures, as well as hinder efforts to address health disparities at the population level. Therefore, a comprehensive approach to healthcare must acknowledge and integrate these broader community and cultural factors to better promote health and well-being across diverse populations.
- **Overemphasis on Medical Interventions:** The biomedical model tends to prioritize medical interventions, such as pharmaceutical treatments and surgical procedures, over preventive measures and health promotion strategies. This emphasis on treating symptoms rather than addressing underlying determinants of health can lead to overmedicalization and unnecessary healthcare expenditures. By focusing solely on biological mechanisms of disease, the biomedical model neglects the holistic nature of health, which encompasses physical, mental, emotional, and social well-being. This narrow perspective may result in fragmented care that fails to address the synergistic nature of various aspects of health.
- **Population Health Dynamics:** The biomedical model does not focus adequately on the macro aspect of health, the health of communities and populations. Understanding the complex dynamics of population health is also crucial for effective healthcare delivery. For example, the context of infectious diseases, requires consideration of various factors beyond individual pathology. These include transmission routes, population dynamics (such as demographics and migration patterns), environmental reservoirs (where pathogens persist in the environment), and socio-economic determinants (like access to clean water, sanitation, and healthcare). Infectious diseases can spread rapidly in densely populated areas or communities with inadequate sanitation, regardless of individual health status. Addressing these broader aspects is crucial for developing effective disease control and prevention strategies that not only treat individual cases but also mitigate the spread of infections within communities and across populations, better target interventions and allocate resources to reduce the burden of infectious diseases on society.

Therefore, while the biomedical model has made significant contributions to medical science and treatment approaches, its limitations highlight the need for a more comprehensive and holistic approach to health that considers the broader determinants of well-being and prioritizes preventive measures and health promotion strategies. The appreciation of the broader and multidimensional nature of health has engendered a shift away from the individual and pathogen centric framing of health to a more inclusive, social and rights-based perspective on health. This understanding invariably highlights the importance of adopting a more communitarian and public orientated approach to health. The concept of public health assumes significance in this context.

Public health focuses on promoting and protecting the health of populations and communities, rather than just individuals. It is a collective responsibility that involves many stakeholders. The concept of public health has evolved over time, shaped by changes in population health and the broader determinants of health.

This definition of public health is closely connected to the broader understanding of health outlined in the preamble of the World Health Organization's constitution from 1948 discussed in the previous chapter. According to this definition, health is not merely the absence of disease but rather encompasses complete physical, mental, and social well-being. This broader view of health emphasizes the importance of addressing the broader determinants of health, such as social, economic, and environmental factors, in order to achieve optimal health outcomes for populations and communities.

As our understanding of health and its determinants continues to evolve, so too does the concept of public health. It remains an essential framework for addressing the health needs of populations and promoting health equity, with a focus on prevention, health promotion, and addressing the underlying determinants of health to improve the well-being of communities worldwide.

Definitions of public health abound in various sources, including textbooks, academic journals, government websites, and professional organizations. The concept of public health is not only widely recognized but is also practically significant across society. Even individuals unfamiliar with its formal definition can grasp how different aspects of our environment impact health positively or negatively. Moreover, public health is not just an abstract concept it requires specialized expertise and competencies. Its importance is understood by the fact that it constitutes a core function and responsibility of government.

Given the prevalence and practical importance of public health, one might wonder why there is a need to define it explicitly. However, despite its widespread recognition, clarifying its definition serves several analytical purposes. It helps delineate the scope of activities undertaken within the field, guides the development of policies and interventions, facilitates communication among professionals and stakeholders, and ensures accountability in addressing health challenges at the population level. Therefore, while the concept of public health may seem self-evident, articulating its definition remains essential for advancing understanding, practice, and governance in this critical domain.

One of the most popular definitions of public health comes from Winslow who states that:

Public Health is the science and the art of preventing disease, prolonging life, and promoting physical health and efficiency through organized community efforts for the sanitation of the environment, the control of community infections, the education of the individual in principles of personal hygiene, the organization of medical and nursing services for the early diagnosis and preventive treatment of disease, and the development of the social machinery which will ensure to every individual in the community a standard of living adequate for the maintenance of health[1].

A more recent definition of public health has been attempted by Detels and Breslow[2] who define public health as:

The biologic, physical, and mental well-being of all members of society regardless of gender, wealth, ethnicity, sexual orientation, country, or political views.

This definition signifies the importance of equity and acknowledges that public health encompasses a wide range of interests beyond solely physical and biological aspects, extending to the mental well-being of society. Both the World Health Organization (WHO)[3] and Detels' definitions portray public health as concerned with more than just eradicating disease. Achieving the WHO's goal of 'health for all' necessitates the integration of diverse disciplines, including the physical, biological, and social sciences, to attain optimal health outcomes.

The field of public health has embraced and applied these disciplines to combat disease, promote health, and achieve its overarching goals. Analysing this statement, we recognize a shift in focus from the traditional notion of public health solely as disease prevention towards a more comprehensive approach that encompasses broader aspects of well-being, including mental health. The mention of equity highlights the importance of addressing health disparities and ensuring that all individuals have equal access to health resources and opportunities. Moreover, the definitions emphasize the interdisciplinary nature of public health, highlighting the need for collaboration across various fields to tackle complex health challenges effectively. This interdisciplinary approach allows for a more holistic understanding of health determinants and facilitates the development of comprehensive interventions that address the diverse needs of populations.

The evolving definition of public health reflects a broader understanding of health that goes beyond disease eradication to encompass the promotion of overall well-being and the reduction of health inequities. It also emphasizes on the field's adaptability and its capacity to integrate diverse disciplines in pursuit of its goals. A cursory examination of this definition reveals the complexity inherent in the term "public health." This complexity necessitates a more thorough analysis. Such an analysis can be enriched by incorporating perspectives from critical public health and the philosophy of public health.

This definition points to the multifaceted nature of public health, encompassing not only the scientific aspects of disease prevention and life prolongation but also the broader societal endeavours aimed at promoting health and well-being. Delving deeper into this concept requires considering critical perspectives that scrutinize power dynamics, social inequalities,

1. See, Winslow, Charles-Edward Amory (1920), The Untilled Field of Public Health, Modern Medicine, 2:183–191.
2. Detels R, Breslow L. Current scope and concerns in public health. In Oxford Textbook of Public Health, 4 ed., Vol. 1, pg. 3–20, 2006.
3. https://www.who.int/about/governance/constitution

and structural determinants of health. Additionally, philosophical inquiries into the underlying principles and values guiding public health interventions can provide insights into the ethical implications and moral imperatives inherent in public health practice.

In the light of the foregoing analysis the following ingredients of public health can be delineated. These ingredients point to the need of a more inclusive and comprehensive approach and a community orientation to health and the corresponding need for legal and policy interventions by the government and other stakeholders which shall be discussed in subsequent Chapters.

- **Emphasis on Social Determinants:** Public health offers an understanding of health as influenced by a multitude of factors beyond just microbial agents or pathogens. It highlights the critical role of social determinants such as socio-economic status, education, employment, housing, and access to healthcare of communities and societies as a whole. These factors have significant impacts on health outcomes at both individual and community levels. Thus, addressing health disparities and promoting health equity requires collective efforts that extend beyond medical interventions to encompass social and economic policies aimed at improving the overall well-being of communities.
- **Holistic Health Promotion:** A communitarian approach to public health emphasizes holistic health promotion strategies that address not only the treatment of diseases but also the promotion of overall well-being. This includes initiatives focused on preventive healthcare, health education, lifestyle modifications, and the creation of supportive environments that promote healthy behaviours. An active engagement with communities in health promotion activities and empowering individuals to take ownership of their health, can lead to more sustainable improvements in population health outcomes.
- **Community Engagement and Empowerment:** Recognizing health as a collective responsibility encourages active community participation in decision-making processes related to healthcare planning, implementation, and evaluation. Involving community members in identifying their own health needs, priorities, and solutions can tailor public health interventions to meet the unique needs and preferences of diverse populations. This cultivates a sense of ownership, solidarity, and empowerment among community members, leading to more effective and sustainable health outcomes.
- **Intersectoral Collaboration:** A communitarian orientation of health promotes collaboration across different sectors, including healthcare, education, housing, transportation, urban planning, and social services. Recognizing that health is influenced by a wide range of social, economic, and environmental factors requires coordinated efforts across multiple sectors to address the underlying determinants of health and promote population well-being. Though concerted collaboration towards common goals, stakeholders can leverage their respective resources, expertise, and influence to create healthier communities and reduce health inequities.

2.2 THE GOALS OF PUBLIC HEALTH

Public health plays a pivotal role in safeguarding and promoting the health and well-being of communities, both locally and globally. It encompasses a diverse range of functions and responsibilities aimed at preventing diseases, promoting healthy behaviours, addressing health disparities, and ensuring access to essential healthcare services. From disease surveillance and outbreak response to health policy formulation and environmental protection, public health initiatives touch every aspect of society, shaping the conditions in which people live, work, and thrive. Although the range of objectives and functions of public health is very broad some of the major functions can be discussed as follows:

- **Preventing Disease and Injuries:** Public health endeavours aim to prevent the occurrence and progression of diseases and injuries within communities. This involves implementing strategies such as vaccination campaigns, promoting safe behaviours, and implementing safety regulations to minimize risks and protect public health. For instance, public health agencies conduct vaccination campaigns to prevent the spread of infectious diseases such as measles, polio, and influenza. They also implement injury prevention programs, such as promoting seatbelt use, installing safety barriers, and enforcing speed limits, to reduce the risk of accidents and injuries on roads and in workplaces.
- **Promoting Healthy Lifestyles and Good Health Habits:** Public health initiatives work to promote healthy behaviours and habits among individuals and communities. This includes campaigns to encourage regular exercise, balanced nutrition, smoking cessation, and responsible alcohol consumption, among other health-promoting activities. For example, public health campaigns educate the public about the harmful effects of smoking and implement policies such as tobacco taxes, smoke-free laws, and anti-smoking advertisements to reduce tobacco use and promote smoking cessation. Additionally, public health efforts promote healthy eating habits by providing nutrition education, supporting access to fresh fruits and vegetables, and regulating food labelling to help individuals make informed dietary choices.
- **Identifying, Measuring, Monitoring, and Anticipating Community Health Needs:** Public health professionals conduct thorough assessments of community health needs through data collection, analysis, and surveillance. Identification of health trends, monitoring disease outbreaks, and anticipating emerging health threats, can proactively address public health challenges and allocate resources effectively. For instance, public health agencies establish disease surveillance systems to monitor the incidence and prevalence of infectious diseases within communities, enabling early detection of outbreaks and timely implementation of control measures. Additionally, public health professionals periodically conduct community health assessments to identify priority health needs, assess health disparities, and allocate resources effectively.
- **Formulating, Promoting, and Enforcing Essential Health Policies:** Public health agencies play a vital role in formulating, advocating for, and enforcing policies that safeguard public health. This includes regulations on food safety, sanitation standards, tobacco control, and environmental protections, among others, to create environments conducive to health and well-being. For example, public health policies such as clean indoor air laws regulate smoking in public places to protect non-smokers from second-hand smoke exposure and reduce the overall prevalence of smoking-related diseases. Similarly, public health policies mandating seatbelt use in vehicles aim to reduce the risk of injuries and fatalities in motor vehicle accidents.

- **Collaborating with Stakeholders and Partners:** Effective public health practice often requires collaboration among various stakeholders, including government agencies, healthcare providers, community organizations, and private sector entities. These actors can leverage their respective expertise and resources to address complex public health challenges comprehensively by working in collaboration. For example, public health agencies collaborate with healthcare providers to deliver immunization services, conduct disease screenings, and provide clinical care for individuals with infectious diseases. They also partner with community organizations to implement health promotion programs, address social determinants of health, and engage with marginalized populations to ensure equitable access to healthcare services.
- **Responding to Health Emergencies and Disasters:** Public health agencies play a critical role in responding to health emergencies and disasters, such as natural disasters, infectious disease outbreaks, and bioterrorism incidents. They develop preparedness and response plans, conduct drills and exercises, and coordinate emergency response efforts with other agencies and organizations to mitigate the impact of emergencies on public health. For instance, public health departments lead efforts to contain outbreaks of infectious diseases by conducting contact tracing, isolating cases, and implementing community-wide measures such as quarantine and social distancing. They also provide essential healthcare services and humanitarian aid to affected populations during emergencies, ensuring continuity of care and support for those in need.
- **Advocating for Health Equity and Social Justice:** Public health professionals advocate for policies and initiatives that address health inequities and promote social justice, aiming to ensure that all individuals have the opportunity to attain their highest level of health. This involves addressing underlying social determinants of health, such as poverty, discrimination, and lack of access to healthcare, which contribute to health disparities among different population groups. For example, public health advocacy efforts may focus on improving access to affordable healthcare services, advocating for policies that reduce income inequality, and addressing systemic racism and discrimination in healthcare delivery. With a focus on health equity and social justice, public health initiatives strive to create healthier and more equitable communities for all.

SUMMARY

The functions of public health as outlined above are closely linked with health in law, justice, and rights frameworks. Public health endeavours aim to prevent diseases and injuries, promote healthy lifestyles, identify community health needs, formulate essential health policies, collaborate with stakeholders, respond to emergencies, and advocate for health equity. To effectively fulfil these objectives public health needs to be understood from a justice and rights-based perspective. Correspondingly adequate legal safeguards and regulatory provisions must be effectuated which accord positive recognition to the right to health, promote justice and equity, and mandate the formulation and state led enforcement of health policies to safeguard public health. This shall be discussed in the next chapters.

CHAPTER

3

Health Law, Ethics, Justice and Rights

INTRODUCTION

In medicine and health, ethics are pivotal. They guide all crucial aspect related to health including practice, research, and policy-making. Unlike many other fields, the consequences of ethical decisions in healthcare can be immediate and profound, directly impacting human lives and well-being. This importance stems from the fundamental principle that healthcare providers and researchers hold a position of immense trust and responsibility towards their patients, participants, and the broader community. This foundational role is not incidental but intrinsic to the very essence of healthcare provision, research endeavours, and policy formulation.

3.1 HEALTH ETHICS

Ethical dilemmas in medicine and healthcare are complex and multifaceted, they often involve question of trust, integrity and are very closely connected to human dignity. Ethical considerations also extend beyond the patient-provider relationship to encompass broader societal implications. Issues such as healthcare access, resource allocation, and the use of emerging technologies like genetic testing or artificial intelligence demand careful ethical scrutiny. For instance, while genetic testing offers potential benefits in diagnosing and treating diseases, ethical concerns arise regarding privacy, consent, and the potential for discrimination based on genetic information.

Ethics in health and medicine are not merely moral guidelines but imperatives that intersect consistently with law, policy and research. Upholding ethical principles ensures that healthcare remains patient-centred, equitable, and grounded in integrity and compassion. As the field continues to evolve, maintaining a robust commitment to ethical standards will be essential in navigating the complexities and uncertainties of modern healthcare systems while prioritizing the well-being and dignity of every individual.

The domain of health ethics is extensive and interdisciplinary. However, for the sake of clarity of understanding, ethical issues in the domain of health are broadly divided into two sub domains namely bioethics and medical ethics. While these disciplines often overlap and share foundational principles, they each focus on distinct areas of ethical inquiry and application within the realm of healthcare.

Bioethics encompasses a broader scope, addressing ethical issues that arise at the intersection of biology, medicine, technology, and society. It delves into the moral implications of advancements in biotechnology, genetics, reproductive medicine, and other areas where scientific innovation intersects with human life. Bioethics often grapples with questions of moral boundaries, such as the ethics of genetic manipulation, cloning, stem cell research, and the use of emerging technologies like artificial intelligence in healthcare.

A key characteristic of bioethics is its interdisciplinary nature. It draws on insights and perspectives from various fields including philosophy, law, social sciences, theology, and healthcare practice. Bioethicists aim to provide ethical guidance and policy recommendations that balance scientific progress with ethical considerations, aiming to ensure that research and technological advancements are conducted responsibly and in alignment with societal values.

Medical ethics, on the other hand, focuses more narrowly on the ethical dilemmas and principles that arise within the context of clinical practice and healthcare delivery. It is concerned with the ethical responsibilities and obligations of healthcare providers, institutions, and patients in the clinical setting. Medical ethics examine issues such as patient autonomy, confidentiality, informed consent, end-of-life care, resource allocation, and the physician-patient relationship.

Unlike bioethics, which often addresses futuristic or cutting-edge ethical challenges posed by scientific advancements, medical ethics tends to be more grounded in the everyday ethical dilemmas faced by healthcare professionals. These dilemmas may include decisions about treatment options, conflicts of interest, conscientious objection, and the ethical implications of healthcare policies and practices.

One distinctive feature of medical ethics is its practical orientation towards guiding ethical decision-making in clinical settings. It provides frameworks and ethical principles that healthcare providers can apply directly to navigate complex situations and ensure that patient care is delivered ethically and with compassion.

However, to reiterate, together, bioethics and medical ethics form a comprehensive framework for ethical decision-making in biomedical practice, research, and policy. They collaborate to address ethical challenges across the healthcare spectrum, ensuring that ethical considerations are integrated into medical research, clinical practice, healthcare policy development, and public health initiatives.

Combining these two ethical subdomains health certain principles of biomedical ethics have been developed. One of the most prominent is the framework of biomedical ethics developed by Beauchamps and Childress in their seminal work principles of biomedical ethics[1]. This has also been termed as principalism. Principalism is an ethical framework that is widely used in bioethics and medical ethics to guide ethical decision-making. It is based on the idea that there are several fundamental ethical principles that should be considered when evaluating ethical issues in healthcare and biomedical research. These principles provide a structured

1. Beauchamp, T.L. and Childress, J.F. (2019a), *Principles of Biomedical Ethics*, New York: Oxford University Press.

approach to analysing and resolving ethical dilemmas. Four of the core ethical principles enunciated in this framework can be discussed as follows. Many allied ethical principles are also derived from these basic principles. They can be discussed as follows:

- **Autonomy:** Autonomy, deriving from the Greek words 'autos' (self) and 'nomos' (law), denotes the capacity of individuals to self-determine their actions and make decisions aligned with their own values and preferences. This concept transcends healthcare, encompassing moral, political, and social dimensions, as various philosophers have explored. Autonomy holds a profound significance in healthcare ethics. In recent decades, its relevance in biomedical ethics has been pivotal, marking a shift from traditional paternalistic models of healthcare towards a more collaborative approach where patients actively participate in decision-making regarding their health. In conventional medical practice **paternalism** has traditionally characterized the doctor-patient relationship, with physicians assuming a dominant paternalistic role where decisions were made on behalf of patients, often without their full consent or involvement. This model positioned doctors as authoritative figures, guiding healthcare choices based on their expertise and judgment and patients just being passive recipients of medical decision making.

  However, societal changes and evolving ethical standards have challenged this paternalistic approach, advocating instead for patient autonomy and collaborative decision making between the doctors and the patients for better health outcomes. In healthcare ethics, autonomy is a crucial component. It ensures that patients have the right to make informed decisions about their treatment options. Autonomy in healthcare necessitates that patients understand the risks, benefits, and alternatives to proposed treatments, enabling them to participate actively in decisions that affect their health outcomes.

  Consent and capacity are integral components intertwined with autonomy in healthcare ethics. These are pivotal ethical parameters that underpin the principles of autonomy, respect, and patient-centred care. Consent, fundamentally, embodies the principle that individuals have the right to make informed decisions about their medical treatment and interventions. It requires that patients provide voluntary agreement based on a comprehensive understanding of relevant information, including potential risks, benefits, alternatives, and consequences. This ethical principle not only respects patients' autonomy but also promotes transparency and trust in the healthcare relationship. Healthcare providers are tasked with ensuring that consent is freely given, without coercion or undue influence, and that patients have the capacity to understand and make decisions about their care. Consent mandates that medical procedures cannot proceed without the explicit agreement of the patient, based on their understanding of the information provided. It emphasizes the ethical imperative that patients' decisions must be voluntary and devoid of external pressure or influence.

  Capacity, closely linked to consent, indicates the ability of individuals to comprehend relevant information, weigh the risks and benefits of their treatment options, appreciate the consequences of their decisions, and communicate their choices effectively. Assessing capacity is essential to determine whether patients can provide valid consent for medical treatment. This evaluation involves assessing patients' understanding of their medical condition, treatment options, and implications, as well as their ability to weigh information rationally and make decisions in line with their values and preferences. Capacity assessments are particularly critical in cases involving minors, individuals with cognitive impairments, or those facing temporary incapacitation due to illness or treatment. Healthcare professionals have a duty to assess and respect patients' capacity to make decisions, ensuring that they are supported in exercising their autonomy effectively.

- **Non-maleficence:** Non-maleficence is a foundational principle in medical ethics that emphasizes the obligation of healthcare providers to avoid causing harm to their patients. The principle of non-maleficence is encapsulated in the Latin phrase "*primum non nocere*," which translates to "first, do no harm." Non-maleficence requires healthcare professionals to refrain from intentionally or unintentionally inflicting harm, whether through actions or negligence. This principle highlights the ethical responsibility to prioritize patient safety and well-being above all else.

  Intentional harm refers to situations where harm is knowingly inflicted upon a patient. An example is when a nurse fails to change a patient's bandage despite knowing the increased risk of infection. This deliberate neglect breaches the duty of care owed to the patient and violates the principle of non-maleficence by putting the patient at foreseeable risk.

  Unintentional harm, on the other hand, occurs due to negligence or carelessness. For instance, a physician administering the wrong medication to a patient due to a mix-up in prescriptions could unintentionally cause harm. Despite the lack of malicious intent, such actions still contravene the principle of non-maleficence because they result in harm that could have been prevented through diligent practice and attention to detail.

  In determining non-maleficence certain conditions are examined such as a duty of care towards patients which posits that there must be an established duty of care owed to the affected party, which forms the basis of the professional relationship between the healthcare provider and the patient. Secondly it also must be determined that the healthcare professional has breached this duty, either through an act of commission (doing something that directly causes harm) or omission (failing to do something that prevents harm). The third criterion to be determined is harm to the patient, the patient must suffer harm, which can be physical, emotional, or both, as a direct result of the breach of duty by the healthcare professional. Moreover, a direct causation must also be determined as the fourth criterion. Causation implies that the harm under question suffered by the patient must be causally linked to the breach of duty. This establishes the professional's responsibility for the harm incurred by the patient. The principle of non-maleficence is also used to determine medical negligence and these four conditions act as guiding factors. These will be dealt with in detail in the chapter on medical negligence.

- **Beneficence:** The principle of beneficence is another core principle of biomedical ethics emphasizing the obligation of healthcare providers and researchers to act in ways that promote the well-being and welfare of their patients and research participants. This ethical principle is rooted in the moral imperative to do good and to actively seek the benefit of others, reflecting a commitment to enhancing the health, quality of life, and overall flourishing of individuals. There are certain key elements of beneficence healthcare providers and researchers towards promoting patient welfare and well-being. First among them is acting in the best interests of patients. This obligates healthcare professionals to prioritize the best interests of their patients when making clinical decisions, carefully weighing potential benefits and risks to maximize positive outcomes. This includes addressing physical ailments as well as considering the emotional, psychological, and social aspects of health to alleviate suffering and enhance overall quality of life.

Another core aspect of beneficence is alleviating suffering and promoting well-being. Healthcare professionals are tasked with providing compassionate care that not only addresses physical ailments but also considers the emotional, psychological, and social aspects of health. This includes managing pain, improving comfort, and supporting patients' overall quality of life. Balancing risks and benefits are also essential under beneficence, ensuring that medical interventions justify potential harms with expected benefits, thereby ensuring a positive net outcome for the patient. Moreover, beneficence respects patient autonomy, allowing individuals to make informed decisions aligned with their values and preferences through shared decision-making processes. In the realm of biomedical research, beneficence extends to ethical conduct, requiring researchers to prioritize participant well-being, minimize risks, and maximize potential benefits. This involves obtaining informed consent, maintain. One very important point to understand is that beneficence must be applied with sensitivity to cultural differences and diverse ethical perspectives. What constitutes "benefit" and "good" can vary significantly across cultures and belief systems, requiring healthcare providers to engage respectfully and inclusively with patients from diverse backgrounds.

- **Justice and Rights:** The concept of justice is another foundational principle in biomedical ethics. It is also inextricably linked to the concept of health as a human right. Health justice pertains to the fair distribution of healthcare resources, benefits, and burdens within society. It involves ensuring that all individuals have equal access to healthcare services, treatments, and opportunities for health, regardless of factors such as socio-economic status, race, ethnicity, gender, or age. Justice as a principle in biomedical ethics aims to promote equity and fairness in healthcare delivery and research practices. Health justice and rights shall be elaborated separately later in this chapter.
- **Confidentiality:** Confidentiality is a very significant ethical principle in healthcare that addresses the privacy and protection of patients' personal and medical information. It is an important part as well as a derivative of non-maleficence. Confidentiality itself has many dimensions such as legal obligations, ethical standards, and professional norms aimed at safeguarding sensitive data shared between patients and healthcare providers. At its core, confidentiality ensures that healthcare providers maintain the privacy of patients' medical records and personal information. This includes details such as medical history, diagnoses, treatments, test results, and any other information disclosed during consultations or examinations.

  The ethical imperative of confidentiality also necessitates legal compliances, however more than that it also facilitates trust and transparency in the patient-provider relationship. When patients trust that their sensitive information will be kept confidential, they are more likely to disclose relevant details about their health, symptoms, and concerns without fear of stigma or repercussions. This open communication is crucial for accurate diagnosis, effective treatment planning, and collaborative decision-making between healthcare providers and patients. Confidentiality also serves to protect patients from potential harm or discrimination that could arise from unauthorized access to their health information. Breaches of confidentiality can lead to breaches of trust, compromised medical care, and even legal consequences for healthcare providers. Therefore, maintaining confidentiality is not only an ethical duty but also a legal and professional responsibility that healthcare professionals must uphold to ensure the well-being and rights of their patients.

- **Solidarity:** Solidarity emphasizes collaboration, mutual support, and collective responsibility in addressing healthcare challenges and promoting health equity. It involves healthcare providers, institutions, and civil society working together to address disparities, advocate for vulnerable populations, and advance public health initiatives. Solidarity promotes a shared commitment to social justice, inclusivity, and the common good in healthcare practice and policy. Solidarity within healthcare ethics emphasizes the shared nature of responsibilities and cooperative efforts among healthcare providers, institutions, and the broader community to confront healthcare challenges effectively and promote equitable health outcomes. It enables healthcare institutions to develop comprehensive approaches to healthcare delivery that are inclusive and responsive to the diverse needs of their patient populations.

  Solidarity in healthcare ethics extends beyond local contexts to encompass international dimensions, emphasizing global collaboration, mutual support, and collective responsibility in addressing complex healthcare challenges and promoting health equity worldwide. At its core, international solidarity in healthcare emphasizes the shared commitment to advancing the well-being of all individuals, irrespective of geographical boundaries. Global health solidarity becomes even more relevant in case of transboundary health hazards including infectious diseases such as epidemics and pandemics and humanitarian crises which impact vulnerable populations such as the poor and the marginalized, refugees, migrants and indigenous populations. International solidarity supports initiatives to improve access to healthcare services, reduce inequities in health outcomes, and advocate for social justice in healthcare policy and practice across different countries and regions. Global solidarity calls for concerted efforts to address health disparities on a global scale. Solidarity as a critical ethic in health has led to the creation of global health institutions such as the WHO and other international legal instruments dealing with various aspects of global health. This shall be discussed in detail in a separate chapter.

It is also important to note that the different ethical parameters discuss above do not operate in isolation. Health ethics principles such as autonomy, beneficence, non-maleficence, justice, confidentiality, and solidarity often intersect and sometimes conflict in healthcare decision-making and practice. These intersections and conflicts arise because each principle emphasizes different ethical values and considerations, which may not always align perfectly in every clinical scenario or healthcare policy. For instance, while autonomy respects patients' decisions it may come in conflict with healthcare providers' goals of promoting beneficence or patient well-being if complete autonomy is given to the patient in taking decisions pertaining to his health. Similarly, justice demands fair distribution of healthcare resources, which can conflict with considerations of individual autonomy or prioritizing beneficence. Confidentiality is vital for patient privacy but can conflict with the duty to disclose information that could prevent harm or protect public health. Healthcare providers face ethical dilemmas when deciding whether to maintain confidentiality or breach it in the interest of preventing harm to others. Solidarity, while promoting collaboration and collective responsibility in addressing healthcare challenges, may also intersect with other principles like justice and beneficence. However, conflicts can arise when determining priorities or allocating resources among competing needs and interests

Resolving conflicts between these health ethics principles requires careful ethical reasoning, dialogue among stakeholders, and considering the specific circumstances of each case. Ethical decision-making frameworks, such as principalism or casuistry[2], can guide healthcare professionals in balancing conflicting principles by prioritizing the most relevant ethical considerations based on the particular context and values at stake. Furthermore, clear policies, guidelines, and training in ethics can help healthcare providers navigate ethical dilemmas effectively. Interdisciplinary collaboration and consultation with ethics committees or peers can also provide valuable perspectives and insights in resolving complex ethical conflicts.

Attempts have been made to incorporate these ethical principles in the form of medical ethics codes to guide doctors and medical service providers. The first such attempt was the ancient Hippocratic oath[3]. Subsequently other codes of ethics have been developed internationally and also in India. Some prominent modern code of ethics and their salient aspects can be discussed below:

3.2 NUREMBERG CODE OF MEDICAL ETHICS[4]

The Nuremberg Code, established in 1947 in the aftermath of the Nuremberg Trials, is a foundational document in medical ethics and research involving human subjects. Its development was a direct response to the unethical medical experiments conducted by Nazi physicians during World War II. The code consists of ten principles aimed at protecting individuals from unethical

2. Casuistry is an approach to ethical reasoning that focuses on the analysis of particular cases or situations rather than applying general ethical principles or theories. It involves examining the specific details and circumstances of individual cases to determine the morally appropriate course of action. In casuistry, ethical decision-making is guided by comparing the case at hand with similar past cases where ethical judgments have been made. This method emphasizes practical reasoning and aims to find relevant precedents or analogies that can help in making ethical judgments about complex or ambiguous situations.
3. See, https://www.bu.edu/arion/files/2010/03/Arenas_05Feb2010_Layout-3.pdf
The ancient Hippocratic Oath, attributed to the Greek physician Hippocrates (circa 5th century BCE), outlines ethical principles and professional conduct expected of physicians. The oath binds the physician to use their knowledge and skills for the benefit of their patients, emphasizing the primacy of patient welfare above personal gain or harm. Hippocratic Oath serves as a timeless ethical framework for physicians, emphasizing principles of altruism, integrity, and patient-centered care. It continues to influence medical ethics and professional standards, guiding physicians worldwide in their commitment to healing and the well-being of those they serve.
4. https://research.unc.edu/human-research-ethics/resources/ccm3_019064/#:~:text=The%20Nuremberg%20Military%20Tribunal's%20decision,medical%20experimentation%20on%20human%20subjects.

experimentation and ensuring that research involving human subjects upholds fundamental ethical standards.

The Nuremberg Code consists of ten principles that outline the ethical principles and guidelines for conducting medical research involving human subjects. At its core is the principle of voluntary consent, emphasizing that individuals must willingly participate in research without coercion or duress. This consent must be informed, meaning participants must be fully aware of the risks, benefits, and purposes of the research before agreeing to participate. Researchers are obligated to provide comprehensive information in a language understandable to the participant, ensuring they can make an informed decision. The Code also emphasizes the importance of minimizing risks and ensuring that the benefits of research outweigh any potential harms. It prohibits experiments that may result in unnecessary physical or mental suffering and stresses the need for procedures that avoid all unnecessary physical and mental suffering and injuries. The code also mandates that researchers have the expertise and qualifications necessary to conduct research and ensures that they protect the participants from harm during the study.

3.3 DECLARATION OF GENEVA[5]

The Declaration of Geneva, also known as the "Modern Hippocratic Oath," was adopted by the World Medical Association (WMA) in 1948 and has been subsequently revised up to its latest version on 2006. The declaration articulates the ethical responsibilities of physicians globally. It serves as a guiding principle for medical professionals, emphasizing their commitment to patient welfare and the highest standards of medical practice. The declaration begins with a solemn pledge to honour the dignity and autonomy of patients, recognizing their right to receive compassionate and competent medical care. Physicians vow to prioritize the health and well-being of their patients above all else, striving to alleviate suffering and promote health through their knowledge and skills.

Central to the Declaration of Geneva is the principle of professional integrity. Physicians pledge to uphold the utmost standards of honesty, transparency, and ethical conduct in their interactions with patients, colleagues, and society. They commit to maintaining patient confidentiality, safeguarding sensitive medical information, and respecting the privacy of individuals under their care. This ethical framework highlights the importance of trust between physicians and patients, essential for effective medical treatment and shared decision-making.

The declaration also highlights the physician's commitment to lifelong learning and professional development. Physicians acknowledge their responsibility to continually update their medical knowledge and skills to ensure they provide the most current and effective treatments for their patients. Collaboration and respect for colleagues are also emphasized, recognizing the collective effort required to deliver comprehensive and compassionate care.

Beyond individual patient care, the Declaration of Geneva calls on physicians to advocate for public health initiatives and policies that promote equitable access to healthcare and improve health outcomes for all. This advocacy reflects a broader commitment to advancing the well-being of communities and addressing systemic healthcare challenges worldwide.

---

5. https://www.wma.net/policies-post/wma-declaration-of-geneva/

3.4 THE WORLD MEDICAL ASSOCIATION (WMA) INTERNATIONAL CODE OF MEDICAL ETHICS[6]

The WMA code of medical ethics builds further on the Geneva Declaration. It was first adopted in 1949 and been revised many times including the latest revision in 2022. This code serves as a comprehensive guide outlining the ethical duties and responsibilities of physicians worldwide. Developed as a canon of principles for the medical profession, it is closely aligned with the WMA Declaration of Geneva and other policies of the association. The code emphasizes that physicians must adhere to national and international ethical, legal, and regulatory norms while ensuring that these standards do not compromise the ethical principles outlined in the code itself.

The International Code of Medical Ethics is structured to be read and applied as a cohesive whole, with each paragraph informing and complementing the others. It is directed specifically at physicians but encourages all healthcare stakeholders to adopt its ethical principles. Fundamental to the code are the general principles that emphasize the physician's primary duty to promote the health and well-being of individual patients through competent, compassionate, and timely care. This duty extends to contributing to the health of populations and society as a whole, while always respecting human life, dignity, autonomy, and patient rights.

The code mandates fair and just medical practice, free from discrimination based on various factors, and emphasizes responsible stewardship of healthcare resources. It requires physicians to uphold conscience, honesty, integrity, and accountability in their practice, exercising independent professional judgment and avoiding conflicts of interest. Collaboration with other healthcare professionals is encouraged, respecting patient confidentiality and ensuring comprehensive care.

Regarding patient care, the code outlines specific duties such as respecting patient autonomy, providing care in the patient's best interests, and obtaining informed consent before any medical intervention. It addresses situations where patients may have limited decision-making capacity, emphasizing the involvement of trusted representatives when necessary. In emergencies, where immediate action is required and consent cannot be obtained, interventions must be justified in the patient's best interests.

Physicians are also obligated to maintain patient confidentiality, even after death, and to disclose information only when absolutely necessary and with minimal disclosure. The code prohibits intrusive advertising, ensures physicians remain free from commercial influences, and promotes environmentally sustainable medical practices.

As members of the medical profession, physicians are called to continuous learning, supporting healthcare equity, advocating for public health, and upholding the highest standards of professional conduct. They must actively prevent practices or policies that undermine ethical responsibilities and support fellow physicians in upholding these duties against undue influences or abuses.

---

6. https://www.wma.net/policies-post/wma-international-code-of-medical-ethics/
The International Code of Medical Ethics, established by the World Medical Association (WMA), outlines ethical principles that guide healthcare professionals globally. Aligned with the WMA Declaration of Geneva, known as The Physician's Pledge, and complemented by its broader policies, the code defines the responsibilities of physicians towards patients, fellow healthcare providers, themselves, and society at large.

3.5 CODE OF MEDICAL ETHICS REGULATIONS (INDIA)[7]

The Code of Medical Ethics Regulations, 2002 (amended in 2016), issued by the Medical Council of India, outlines fundamental ethical guidelines for physicians practicing in the country. It mandates high standards of professional conduct, emphasizing integrity, honesty, and ethical behaviour in all doctor-patient interactions. Central to the regulations is the principle of patient welfare, requiring physicians to prioritize the health and well-being of patients above personal interests. This includes confidentiality, respecting patient autonomy and ensuring informed consent for medical decisions. This code shall be discussed in detail in a subsequent chapter on India.

3.6 JUSTICE AND RIGHTS IN HEALTH

Justice is a multidimensional concept and encompasses a wide array of perspectives and principles that shape ethical and fair practices in society, particularly in domains such as healthcare. In the Rawlsian[8] framework distributive justice is understood as being synonymous with fairness or equity, ensuring equal opportunities and distribution of resources tailored to individual needs or the needs of the most vulnerable individuals or social groups.

Health justice within the broader framework of justice addresses the fair distribution of healthcare resources, opportunities, and outcomes within societies particularly in public health contexts. The idea of health justice is premised upon ethical principles and frameworks aimed at ensuring that all individuals have equal access to necessary healthcare services, regardless of their social or economic circumstances. At its core, health justice seeks to rectify disparities in health outcomes and access to healthcare by addressing underlying social determinants of health such as income, education, and living conditions. A justice-oriented approach to health acknowledges that different individuals and communities may require differing levels of support to achieve optimal health outcomes, and thus advocates for tailored interventions to address these disparities. Health justice also involves considerations of fairness in healthcare delivery, ensuring that decisions regarding resource allocation, treatment options, and healthcare policies are made transparently and without bias or discrimination.

Health justice is not an isolated concept confined only to health or healthcare service delivery. In application and practice it extends beyond the healthcare system itself to encompass the social determinants of health. These are broader societal factors that influence health, such as economic and environmental conditions, access to education, employment opportunities, and social support networks. Health justice therefore emphasizes the importance of addressing structural inequalities and systemic barriers that contribute to health disparities among different populations. This comprehensive approach recognizes that achieving health justice requires

7. https://www.nmc.org.in/rules-regulations/code-of-medical-ethics-regulations-2002/. The regulations have been made In exercise of the powers conferred under Section 20A read with Section 33(m) of the Indian Medical Council Act, 1956. The Code is intended to provide guidance to the Members as regards their conduct and interactions inter se, with patients/ end users, and with Third Parties. The purpose of the Code is to offer guidance to its members concerning their behaviour and interactions among themselves, with patients or end users, and with third parties.
8. See, https://plato.stanford.edu/entries/justice-distributive/

collaboration across multiple sectors, including healthcare providers, law and policymakers, community organizations, and individuals themselves, to advocate for policies and practices that promote equitable health outcomes for all.

Moreover, health rights and health justice are deeply intertwined, with health rights often serving as a foundational principle within the broader framework of health justice. The concept of health rights asserts that every individual has a fundamental entitlement to the highest attainable standard of health, encompassing access to healthcare services, essential medicines, and facilities. This entitlement is grounded in international human rights law and ethical principles, affirming that health is not merely a privilege but a universal right that should be upheld and protected by governments and societies.

Health rights form a critical component of health justice by establishing a legal and ethical basis for demanding equitable health outcomes and healthcare access. They provide a framework for accountability, enabling individuals and communities to hold governments and institutions responsible for ensuring that healthcare services are accessible, affordable, and of high quality for all. Rights and justice perspectives to health recognize the intersectionality of factors that influence health, including race, gender, socio-economic status, disability, and geographic location. They also emphasize the importance of taking a comprehensive approach to address these intersecting inequalities and ensure that healthcare systems are inclusive and responsive to the diverse needs of individuals and communities.

The right to health has been considered as a fundamental human right and therefore has been incorporated in domestic legislations, judicial interpretations as well as in some of the most prominent international human rights documents. These shall be dealt with in detail in specific chapters. However, for the sake of analytical and conceptual clarity the juxtaposition of the paradigms of rights-justice in health and medicine can be better appreciated in terms of the following salient aspects.

- **Availability** refers to the presence of functioning healthcare facilities, essential medicines, and necessary healthcare services that meet the population's needs in terms of both quantity and quality. This includes ensuring that hospitals, clinics, and health centres are adequately equipped with medical infrastructure and staffed by qualified healthcare professionals capable of delivering essential services effectively.
- **Accessibility** emphasizes that healthcare services should be physically reachable, economically affordable, and geographically accessible to all individuals without discrimination. This dimension considers factors such as spatial or geographical proximity to services, transportation infrastructure, financial barriers, and the availability of health insurance or financial protection mechanisms to mitigate costs for vulnerable populations.
- **Acceptability** entails that healthcare services must respect medical ethics, cultural norms, and the preferences of individuals and communities seeking care. Services should be culturally appropriate, respecting diverse beliefs and practices, and ensuring confidentiality, informed consent, and patient autonomy. Gender sensitivity is also crucial, ensuring that healthcare delivery addresses specific health needs and challenges faced by different genders effectively and respectfully.
- **Quality** ensures that healthcare services are safe, effective, patient-centred, timely and efficient. It requires adherence to clinical guidelines and best practices to deliver effective

treatments and interventions. Safety measures include infection control, medication safety, and overall patient safety protocols. Patient-centred care involves respecting patient preferences, promoting shared decision-making, and providing compassionate and respectful interactions. Timeliness ensures timely access to healthcare services to prevent delays in diagnosis and treatment, while efficiency optimizes resource use to maximize health outcomes without unnecessary waste.

Availability, Accessibility, Acceptability, and Quality is collectively also referred to as the AAAQ approach or framework. It offers a robust framework for assessing and promoting health rights and health justice. AAAQ approach provides a holistic framework for evaluating healthcare systems. It ensures that assessments are not limited to just one aspect (e.g., availability of services or quality of care) but encompass multiple dimensions critical to effective healthcare delivery. This framework serves as a valuable tool for policymakers and healthcare planners to assess the strengths and weaknesses of healthcare systems. It informs strategic planning efforts by highlighting areas needing investment or intervention to achieve universal health coverage and improve population health.

- **Non-Discrimination:** Non-discrimination and equality are foundational principles of human rights and essential elements of the right to health. Discrimination refers to any distinction, exclusion, or restriction based on various characteristics that undermines the enjoyment of human rights and freedoms. It often leads to the marginalization of specific groups within society and perpetuates deep-rooted structural inequalities. Consequently, these marginalized groups often face higher levels of poverty and poorer health outcomes. For instance, ethnic minorities and indigenous populations in many societies encounter barriers such as limited access to healthcare, inadequate housing, unsafe drinking water, and higher rates of child mortality and malnutrition compared to the general population. Most major human rights instruments specifically prohibit discrimination on certain various non-exhaustive grounds such as race, colour, sex, language, religion, political or other opinion, national or social origin, property, disability, birth or other status.[9]

Discrimination becomes more severe when individuals experience intersecting forms of discrimination, such as gender and racial or age-based discrimination. For example, indigenous women in some regions may receive fewer health services and face heightened risks of physical and sexual violence, highlighting the compounded effects of discrimination. Non-discrimination and equality principles also require states to acknowledge and address the specific health needs of groups that are particularly vulnerable to health disparities or diseases. States have an obligation to implement measures that prevent discrimination and promote equal access to healthcare and health services. This includes adopting specific health standards tailored to address the unique challenges faced by groups such as women, children, and persons with

9. See, Article 2 of The International Covenant on Economic, Social and Cultural Rights. https://www.ohchr.org/en/instruments-mechanisms/instruments/international-covenant-economic-social-and-cultural-rights. Also Article 2 of the International Covenant on Civil and Political Rights. https://www.ohchr.org/en/instruments-mechanisms/instruments/international-covenant-civil-and-political-rights. Both covenants incorporate almost identical grounds for prohibiting discrimination.

disabilities. Positive measures are essential to counteract historical patterns of discrimination and ensure that marginalized groups receive equitable healthcare and protection. This proactive approach is crucial in upholding human rights standards and achieving health equity across diverse populations.

- **Equity:** Equity is also a fundamental aspect of health justice and rights and very closely relates to the AAAQ framework. As a component of the right to health emphasizes the fair distribution of healthcare resources and opportunities to ensure that all individuals have equal access to necessary healthcare services. It is rooted in the principle that achieving health equity is essential for realizing the broader human right to health. Equity in healthcare acknowledges that different individuals and communities may have varying healthcare needs due to social determinants such as income inequality, education level, access to clean water and sanitation, housing conditions, and employment opportunities. These factors significantly influence health outcomes and access to healthcare services. Equity requires that healthcare systems recognize and address these disparities by providing targeted interventions and resources to populations with greater health needs or barriers to access. Furthermore, equity in healthcare is closely linked to social and distributive justice principles, emphasizing the ethical imperative to promote fairness and reduce disparities in health. It requires healthcare systems to adopt inclusive practices, such as culturally competent care, language services, and community engagement, to better meet the diverse needs of all individuals and communities.
- **Universal Health Coverage (UHC)** is intricately linked to the concept of the right to health, which asserts that every individual should have access to necessary healthcare services without facing financial hardship. UHC aims to provide coverage for a wide range of essential health services, ensuring that these services are accessible, affordable, and of high quality for all people, regardless of their socio-economic status or other factors. Furthermore, Universal Health Coverage (UHC) aims to address the financial aspect of healthcare access by urging or obligating the state to ensure that all individuals and communities have access to essential health services without suffering financial hardship. This involves designing healthcare systems that provide coverage for a wide range of services, including preventive, curative, rehabilitative, and palliative care, regardless of an individual's ability to pay. This helps prevent catastrophic health expenditures that can push households into poverty, thereby promoting economic stability and social well-being. Achieving UHC involves not only expanding coverage but also improving the quality and acceptability of healthcare services. Quality healthcare under UHC means services that are effective, safe, and respectful of patient dignity and preferences. This approach ensures that healthcare is not only accessible but also meets the highest standards of clinical effectiveness and patient satisfaction.

  On a global scale, UHC is supported by international frameworks such as the Sustainable Development Goals (SDGs), particularly Goal 3[10], which aims to ensure healthy lives and promote well-being for all at all ages. Many countries have committed to advancing UHC as part of their national health policies, recognizing its role in achieving health equity and fulfilling the right to health.

10. See, https://www.un.org/sustainabledevelopment/health/

However, challenges exist in implementing UHC, including ensuring financial sustainability, strengthening health systems, and addressing disparities in healthcare infrastructure and workforce capacity. Overcoming these challenges requires coordinated efforts from governments, healthcare providers, civil society, and international organizations to build robust health systems that can deliver UHC effectively and sustainably. Recognizing UHC as a critical component of the right to health consistently exhorts the states to work towards its progressive realization.

3.7 HEALTH AS A PUBLIC GOOD

A justice focused and rights-based analysis of health shall not be complete without understanding the conceptualization of health as a public good. A public good is as a commodity or service that benefits society as a whole, rather than benefiting only individuals or specific groups. These goods typically involve benefits that cannot be easily restricted to those who pay for them and are often provided collectively through government or community efforts. Examples include clean air, national defence etc. The appreciation of health as a public good is fundamental to understanding how healthcare should be structured and accessed within societies. Viewing health as a public good implies several key principles and implications that shape policies and practices in healthcare systems locally as well as globally. The idea of health as a public good suggests that access to healthcare services and resources should not be limited to those who can afford them but should be universally available to all members of society. This aligns with principles of social justice and human rights, ensuring that everyone has the opportunity to attain the highest possible standard of health.

Besides, the public good nature of health emphasizes the collective responsibility of governments and societies to invest in and prioritize public health initiatives. This includes funding for preventive measures, health promotion campaigns, and the development of healthcare infrastructure that benefits the entire population. By pooling resources and distributing them equitably, societies can better protect and improve the health of their citizens as a shared responsibility. Also, recognizing health as a public good signifies the interdependence of health outcomes within a community or society. Improved health for individuals contributes to broader societal benefits such as increased productivity, economic stability, and social cohesion. Conversely, neglecting health disparities or failing to address public health threats can lead to widespread negative consequences affecting everyone.

From a rights-based perspective, framing health as a public good supports the notion that healthcare is not merely a commodity but a fundamental right. It requires governments to prioritize health as a public policy goal and allocate resources accordingly, guided by principles of equity, non-discrimination, and accessibility. This approach is crucial for advancing health justice, where every individual has the right to access timely, affordable, and quality healthcare services based on their health needs rather than their ability to pay.

Health as a public good incorporates two major characteristics. They are Non-Excludable and Non-Rivalrous in consumption[11]. Non-Excludability implies that health as a public good is non-excludable, meaning that individuals cannot be easily excluded from its benefits. In other

11. See, Cowen, Tyler, and Lincoln Anderson. "Public Goods". Econlib, February 25, 2021. https://www.econlib.org/library/Enc/PublicGoods.html#abouttheauthor.

words, once health interventions are made available, it is challenging to prevent individuals from accessing them, regardless of their nationality or socio-economic status. This idea is also extended across national borders which further strengthens the idea of health as a global public good. For example, efforts to control infectious diseases like Ebola or COVID-19 require a collective response that benefits all members of society, transcending even national boundaries.

Another significant feature is the non-rivalrous consumption of health as a common good. This in essence means that one person's consumption of health benefits does not diminish the availability of those benefits for others. Unlike rivalrous goods, such as food or clothing, where consumption by one individual reduces the amount available for others, investments in health interventions can benefit multiple individuals simultaneously without diminishing their effectiveness. For example, vaccination campaigns protect entire populations from infectious diseases, regardless of the number of people who receive the vaccine.

Viewing health as a common good for humankind and societies strengthens the ethical framework surrounding healthcare and bolsters the concept of health interdependence. When health is considered a common good, it emphasizes that health outcomes and access to healthcare are not solely individual concerns but collective responsibilities shared by communities and nations worldwide. This perspective promotes solidarity and mutual support in addressing health challenges, transcending national boundaries and cultural differences to prioritize human well-being on a global scale.

Furthermore, recognizing health as a common good enhances the ethical imperative to ensure equitable access to healthcare services and resources. It shifts the focus from viewing health as a commodity or privilege to understanding it as a fundamental human right that should be universally protected and promoted. This ethical framework guides policies and actions aimed at reducing health disparities, promoting health equity, and encouraging collaboration among countries to tackle global health issues collectively. It reinforces the idea that investing in public health infrastructure, disease prevention, and healthcare systems benefits not only individuals but also contributes to the overall resilience and stability of societies, thereby reinforcing the concept of health interdependence. In essence, viewing health as a common good encourages a shared commitment to advancing health as a foundational aspect of human dignity and social justice worldwide.

SUMMARY

It is crucial to understand that the various aspects of the right to health discussed above do not operate in isolation. They are integrated and interdependent. They together provide a comprehensive framework to understand health as a holistic concept that encompasses not only access to healthcare services but also the conditions necessary for individuals and communities to lead healthy lives. Analysing these aspects together can help assess their collective impact on health outcomes and societal well-being. A deficiency in any one component can undermine the overall effectiveness of healthcare systems and impede progress towards achieving universal health coverage and health equity. By integrating these aspects, policymakers and healthcare providers can identify gaps, prioritize interventions, and strengthen healthcare systems to better meet the diverse needs of populations. This approach not only supports the fulfilment of the right to health as a fundamental human right but also contributes to broader goals of justice, equality, and social inclusion within societies.

Looking at health through the lenses of ethics, justice, and rights is essential for translating these principles into effective legal and policy instruments that safeguard and promote public health. Legislation and regulatory framework are crucial in translating ethical guidelines into specific rules governing healthcare practices, clinical research, pharmaceuticals, medical devices, and public health interventions. These regulations ensure adherence to ethical standards and uphold public health safeguards. Ethical principles, considerations of justice, and rights-based approaches inform the drafting of health-related laws. Laws establish norms for healthcare delivery, lay down patient rights, and outline the responsibilities of healthcare providers and institutions.

Health policies too are framed based on ethical analyses and justice considerations to address healthcare priorities, allocate resources effectively, and strengthen health systems. Policies often target reducing health disparities, promoting preventative care, and improving access to essential services. International commitments to human rights and health provide a global framework informed by ethical principles and justice considerations. These agreements guide countries in international collaborations, establishing funding mechanisms, and developing strategies to achieve shared global health objectives. The legal and policy aspects are thus invariably grounded in principles of justice and rights and are derived from them.

QUESTIONS FOR PART I

Q.1 Discuss the concept of health as a dynamic state rather than a fixed condition. How does this perspective change our approach to health promotion and disease prevention?

Q.2 Compare and contrast different models of health (e.g., biomedical, holistic, and biopsychosocial). Which model do you believe most effectively addresses individual and community health needs?

Q.3 What is public health, and how does it differ from individual healthcare? Provide examples of public health initiatives and their impacts.

Q.4 Analyse the interplay between health and human rights. How do legal and ethical considerations influence access to healthcare?

Q.5 Examine the World Health Organization's (WHO) definition of health. Discuss the concept of health as a dynamic state rather than a fixed condition. How does this perspective change our approach to health promotion and disease prevention?

Q.6 Reflect on a case study where justice or ethics played a critical role in public health. How were the principles of justice and ethics applied or challenged in the situation?

PART II

Health: Constitutional, Legal and Judicial Perspectives

CHAPTER 4

Health in the Indian Constitution

INTRODUCTION

In the previous part it has been discussed that health is not a static mono dimensional concept but is multifaceted in its nature and scope involving both individual and public health dimensions. The concept of Health involves distinct ethical, rights, justice and public good aspects. It is also closely linked to the notion of national security as well as national and social development. At its core, health reflects an individual's physical, mental, and social well-being, each of which interacts in intricate ways to determine overall quality of life. Furthermore, health as a public good underscores its importance beyond individual benefits. Public health initiatives aim to protect and promote the health of entire populations through preventive measures, health education, and policy interventions. This collective approach not only improves population health outcomes but also enhances societal resilience and economic productivity. Health is also therefore related to social and economic development.

The rights-based perspective of health emphasizes that equal healthcare is a right which must be respected to live a worthy life. At the same time, from a developmental standpoint, the consideration of health as one of the basic components of the human development contributes to the general well-being and quality of life. Issues such as, health facilities, availability of safe drinking water, hygiene practices, and adequate nutrition are some of the key markers of health outcomes particularly for the vulnerable and the marginalized. These social determinants not only contribute to enhancing health or organic well-being of the people, but intervention in these areas also promotes equity and social inclusion, thus allowing individuals or communities to realize their full potential. Integrating health into social and economic development agendas is therefore essential for achieving sustainable development goals and promoting inclusive growth

However, despite the importance of the conceptual and philosophical analysis of such ideas to discuss issues such as human right to healthcare, equity in access together with ethical principles of medical decision-making it is crucial to recall that such a discussion in abstraction does not guarantee the implementation of the principles in the real-world scenario unless they are translated into constitutional and legal entitlements which would provide tangible protections and healthcare entitlements for people.

When such principles are incorporated in law, it can be ensured that there is a legal requirement of ethical behaviour and justice in the provision of healthcare services as well as protection of the rights of the users. All these can only be practically defended through legal provisions and concrete measures supported by the constitutional and legal systems. Constitutional provisions can also establish healthcare as a fundamental right, which is the basis of the subsequent tangible legal action and implementation.

This formal recognition thus constitutionalizes and legalizes health entitlements making them more immune to encroachment by the state. It is important to understand that legal systems are the instruments in relation to which these constitutional provisions become operational rights and responsibilities. They prescribe specific duties to healthcare providers, outline rights for the patients, and provide guidance to resolve ethical challenges.

Including ethics in the health legislations is important to realize equal opportunities in access to healthcare, for patients' privacy as well as to set standards for medical profession in medical practice. However, such legal frameworks should evolve to accommodate changes in medical technology or changes in the social values. For example, laws regarding the patient's consent, the privacy and security of the data, and the withdrawal of life-sustaining treatment, etc. may require adaptation for creating relevant and effective mechanisms for the protection of healthcare entitlements.

This is the reason why health as a rightful entitlement of the people finds expression directly or indirectly in many constitutions of the world and India is no exception. At the outset it is important to mention that the right to health is not explicitly enumerated as a standalone constitutional right within the Indian Constitution. However, in its essence health-related ideals, aspirations and provisions permeate India's constitutional framework, which is fundamentally rooted in the principles of equity, welfare and justice. Health therefore finds mention at many places in the Indian constitutional scheme. In the light of the above discussion, a detailed analysis of the health-related provisions in the Indian constitutional scheme can be undertaken.

4.1 HEALTH IN THE PREAMBLE

The Preamble of our Constitution serves a dual role, firstly, it identifies the foundational authority from which the Constitution derives its legitimacy; and secondly, it outlines the fundamental objectives and aspirations that the Constitution seeks to uphold and promote. It does not confer specific powers but rather provides a guiding direction and purpose to the entire constitutional framework. The goals articulated in the Preamble, such as justice, liberty, equality, and fraternity, are further elucidated and given practical form through the substantive provisions of the Constitution, including Part III on Fundamental Rights and Part IV on Directive Principles of State Policy. These operative parts serve to clarify, strengthen, and operationalize the overarching principles laid out in the Preamble, ensuring that they are translated into tangible rights, duties, and policies that govern the Indian polity. By integrating these foundational ideals into the constitutional fabric, India endeavours to establish a just, equitable, and harmonious society where the welfare and rights of all citizens are safeguarded and promoted.

The Preamble of our Constitution serves a dual purpose. Firstly, it recognizes the source from where constitution derives its legitimacy and the second, it also signals the most important objectives and aspirations contained in the Constitution. Even though it does not confer any specific power or special prerogatives the preamble does provide a guiding direction and purpose to the entire constitutional arrangement.

The aim and objects listed in the preambular part of the Constitution such as justice, liberty, equality, and fraternity are further elucidated and given concrete manifestation through the provisions of Part III of the Constitution containing Fundamental Rights and Part IV containing the Directive Principles of State Policy. All these operative parts aim at explaining, clarifying and giving practical effect to overarching principles outlined in the preamble so as to establish concrete rights and duties that would govern our polity. When these tenets are incorporated into the constitutional fabric, the country strives to achieve a just, equitable, and harmonious society where the welfare and rights of all citizens are safeguarded and promoted.

In the Preamble to the Constitution of India, health, has not been set out as an enumerated objective but a careful analysis of the principles set out in preamble unequivocally identifies health as a paramount concern for the welfare of its citizens. The preamble of India evokes the ideals of justice, liberty, equality, and fraternity as critical components of democracy.

For example, *Justice* in the context of health encompasses social, economic, and political justice, which implies that healthcare equity and eradication of inequalities in health is an integral part of attaining a just society. Equal provision of healthcare signifies that people ought not to be denied provision of health services on account of socio-economic status thus making the society inclusive with everybody a chance to live a healthy life.

Liberty, another key ideal included in the Preamble extends beyond freedom in the personal sense only and also implies the ability of people to fully exercise rights and capabilities. Health plays a pivotal role in this regard as it enables individuals to pursue their aspirations without the hindrance of preventable health issues. A healthy population is better equipped to participate actively in civic life, contributing to the nation's overall progress and development.

Likewise, equality which means equal status, rights and opportunities for all citizens as proclaimed in the Preamble also definitely includes health equity. It means that every citizen of the country should have equal opportunity to access healthcare services and resources irrespective of their socio-economic status. Healthcare legislation and policies that will address health disparities not only uphold the constitutional mandate of equality but also helps in building a more cohesive and harmonious society where the health needs of all citizens are met fairly.

Finally, measures oriented towards the enhancement of people's health and disease prevention are also the manifestations of *fraternity* as it means solidarity and collective and shared responsibility of the people as well as state-citizen cooperation for their health and well-being.

It therefore becomes clear that the Preamble of the Indian Constitution is the foundation on which the health principles are embedded in other parts of the Constitution. The Preamble lays the moral and philosophical base which finds more concrete expression in the subsequent provisions of the Constitution. This includes health-related rights and responsibilities in Part III (Fundamental Rights) and Part IV (Directive Principles of State Policy). These references not only spell out the specific entitlements of individuals to health and well-being but also the duty of the state to provide healthcare services and public health programmes. So, the Preamble's aspirational goals set in motion a narrative that directs the constitutional mandate to ensure that the people of India get their right to health as a constitutional entitlement.

4.2 HEALTH AS A FUNDAMENTAL RIGHT

While health is not explicitly listed as a fundamental right under Part III of the Indian Constitution, a contextual and specific interpretation of several key rights within this part can lead to the inference of health as a fundamental entitlement. The Constitution of India guarantees a range of rights under Part III, the right to equality (Articles 14–18), the right to life and personal liberty (Article 21), the right against exploitation (Articles 23–24) etc. Interpreting the essence of rights through a health-focused lens establishes a close connection of these rights with both individual and public health. Judiciary has also played a very significant and laudable role in further enriching the content of these rights by expansively and liberally interpreting many of the textual constitutional provisions under Part III to secure the health rights of the people of this country. The judicial interpretation of the right to health shall be dealt with in a separate chapter. A brief analysis of some of the most important fundamental rights and their interrelationship with law can be undertaken as follows:

Article 14 of the Constitution of India guarantees equality before the law and equal protection of laws to all persons within the territory of India. This fundamental right is bedrock of India's constitutional framework. It ensures that no one is discriminated against on arbitrary grounds. All citizens are treated equally under law. In the context of health as a fundamental right Article 14 plays a crucial role. It ensures equal access to healthcare services and amenities for al

Article 14 aligns with affordability principles by preventing discriminatory pricing and promoting policies that make healthcare affordable for economically disadvantaged individuals. It advocates for just allocation of healthcare resources, prioritizing those in greatest need by promoting equitable healthcare access. Courts have interpreted Article 14 broadly to uphold the right to health, ensuring access to affordable treatments and medicines, particularly for economically disadvantaged groups. Article 14 of the Constitution of India guarantees equality before the law and equal protection of laws to all persons within the territory of India. This fundamental right is the bedrock of India's constitutional framework, so that no one is discriminated against on arbitrary grounds and all citizens are treated equally under the law. In the context of health as a fundamental right, Article 14 plays a crucial role in ensuring equal access to healthcare services and amenities for all citizens.

This "equality" right of the constitution also intersects with key ethical principles in healthcare like equity, access, affordability among others. Article 14 of the Indian Constitution aims to promote equity in healthcare by prohibiting discrimination and ensuring fair distribution of healthcare resources based on need rather than socio-economic status. It supports efforts to reduce health disparities and improve access for marginalized groups. Equity in access comes out as an important incidence of Article 14 which aims to secure timely and non-discriminatory access to healthcare services, to remove financial barriers and enhance physical accessibility. This promotes inclusivity in healthcare.

Article 15 of the Indian Constitution applies the general principle of equality enshrined in Article 14 to specific instances by prohibiting based on religion, race, caste, sex, place of birth, or any combination thereof. Non-discrimination is also a fundamental ethical principle in health and healthcare service delivery, so that individuals receive equal treatment regardless of their socio-economic status, gender, caste, religion or other characteristics. This principle means fair access to healthcare services and facilities, free from prejudice or bias. By upholding non-discrimination in healthcare and societal contexts, Article 15 mandates reinforcing the ethical imperative to protect individual rights and promote equality, contributing to a more just and inclusive healthcare system in India.

Article 21 of the Constitution of India is arguably the most relevant article in the Constitution of India as far as the right to health is concerned. This Article guarantees the fundamental right to life and personal liberty. It states that no person shall be deprived of their life or personal liberty except according to procedure established by law. This constitutional provision has been interpreted expansively by the Indian judiciary to include the right to live with dignity, which inherently encompasses the right to health.

The right to health is considered an integral part of a life that is lived with dignity. It by implication means that individuals have the right to access timely, affordable, and quality healthcare services, essential medicines, and adequate nutrition. Without adequate health, individuals cannot fully enjoy their right to life and consequently even personal liberty. Therefore, Article 21 imposes a positive obligation on the state to ensure the availability and accessibility of healthcare facilities, services, and infrastructure necessary to protect and promote the health of its citizens.

The judiciary in India has consistently recognized the inalienable connection between the right to life and the right to health. Judicial decisions have affirmed that denial of healthcare or inadequate healthcare services that endanger an individual's health can violate their right to life under Article 21. This interpretation stresses upon the state's duty not only to refrain from directly taking life or liberty without lawful justification but also to proactively provide conditions to ensure individuals can lead a life of dignity which undeniably includes access to healthcare. Moreover, the right to health under Article 21 extends beyond mere absence of illness to encompass positive elements such as the right to healthcare information, the right to participate in health-related decision-making, and the right to access essential public health goods and services. This holistic understanding aligns with international human rights standards, where the right to health is recognized as essential for the enjoyment of other rights and for overall human development.

Another fundamental right whose enforcement has a direct bearing on the right to health is Article 23. Article 23 of the Indian Constitution prohibits trafficking in human beings, begar (compulsory work without payment), and forced labour. This constitutional provision protects individuals not only from state-enforced practices but also from exploitation by private citizens. Trafficking in human beings, which involves the buying and selling of individuals as commodities, is completely abolished under the Constitution due to its detrimental effects on human health, including the heightened risk of sexually transmitted diseases among those involved. Many legislative enactments directly flow from this fundamental right.

The Immoral Traffic (Prevention) Act of 1956 complements Article 23 by criminalizing brothel keeping and intermediary roles in human trafficking. Forced labour, as defined under Article 23, encompasses practices akin to trafficking and begar. The Constitution mandates stringent measures against forced labour, supported by legislative frameworks such as the Minimum Wages Act of 1948, which ensures fair remuneration, and the Contract Labour (Regulation and Abolition) Act of 1970, aimed at eradicating exploitative practices in contract labour.

Moreover, the Bonded Labour System (Abolition) Act of 1976 plays a crucial role in eliminating bonded labour arrangements, which ensnare individuals into exploitative conditions of labour. These legislative measures collectively uphold the dignity and fundamental rights of individuals, ensuring they are not subjected to degrading or coercive labour practices. By prohibiting trafficking, begar, and forced labour, Article 23 reinforces India's commitment to human rights and equitable treatment of all its citizens.

4.3 HEALTH IN DIRECTIVE PRINCIPLES OF STATE POLICY

Articles 36 to 51 of the Indian Constitution outline the Directive Principles of State Policy, reflecting India's commitment to the welfare of its people. These principles set socio-economic objectives that governments must strive to achieve. While not enforceable by courts (as per Article 37), they guide legislators and executives on how to exercise their powers to promote the welfare and economic democracy of the nation. The state is duty-bound to incorporate these principles into law, underscoring their fundamental role in governance. Health is a crucial measure of social welfare and a significant goal for any welfare state. It is prominently highlighted in several instances within the directive principles of our state policy, emphasizing its importance in governmental objectives. Following is a brief discussion on some important directive principles and their interrelationships with health.

Article 38: Article 38 of the Indian Constitution imposes a duty on the state to secure social order for the promotion of the welfare of the people. This includes maintaining public health as a cornerstone of societal stability and progress. Public health initiatives such as disease prevention, sanitation, and healthcare infrastructure are essential for fostering a healthy population. A healthy society is more productive, resilient, and capable of achieving overall welfare goals. By prioritizing public health, the state ensures that its citizens can lead fulfilling lives free from preventable health risks, thereby contributing to a more prosperous and harmonious society.

Article 39(e): Article 39(e) exhorts the state to protect the health of workers, recognizing it as a fundamental right essential for societal well-being and economic productivity. Ensuring safe working conditions, access to healthcare services, and occupational safety measures are crucial aspects of fulfilling this directive. Healthy workers are more productive, contribute effectively to economic growth, and are better equipped to support their families. By safeguarding workers' health, the state not only upholds their rights but also strengthens the foundation of a prosperous and equitable society.

Article 41: Article 41 mandates the state to provide public assistance, especially to those who are sick, disabled, or otherwise in need of care. This provision ensures that vulnerable populations have access to essential healthcare services and support systems. It encompasses measures such as healthcare subsidies, disability benefits, and rehabilitation programs. By offering comprehensive public assistance, the state addresses socio-economic disparities and promotes inclusive growth. This enables individuals facing health challenges to regain their well-being, participate actively in society, and contribute to its overall development. A number of India's social welfare acts such as the Persons with Disabilities (Equal Opportunities, Protection of Rights and Full Participation) Act, Rastriya Swasthya Bima Yojana (RSBY) etc. have been enacted in pursuance of the directives contained in this Article.

Article 42: Article 42 highlights the primary responsibility of the state in protecting the health of mothers and infants. It emphasizes maternity benefits, healthcare provisions for expectant mothers, and childcare facilities essential for early childhood development. This directive acknowledges the critical role of maternal and child health in shaping the future of society. By ensuring access to quality healthcare during pregnancy, childbirth, and early childhood, the state promotes healthier families and reduces maternal and infant mortality rates. Investing in maternal and child health not only improves individual outcomes but also strengthens the social fabric and economic potential of the nation. Maternity benefits Act, 1961 has been promulgated to fulfil this objective.

Article 47: Article 47 places a duty on the state to improve nutrition levels and raise the standard of living of its people. It recognizes that adequate nutrition and living standards are essential components of achieving optimal health outcomes and overall well-being. The state's responsibility under Article 47 includes initiatives such as food security programs, nutritional support schemes, and measures to enhance living conditions. By prioritizing nutrition and living standards, the state aims to eradicate hunger, reduce malnutrition, and improve the quality of life for all citizens. This holistic approach contributes to building a healthier, more resilient population capable of realizing its full potential.

Article 48(A): Article 48(A) is another directive principles which has a close nexus with human health. This principle casts responsibility on the state to actively strive towards the preservation of our environment, and the protection of forests, wildlife and natural habitat. This constitutional commitment has been given further legislative weightage by the enactment of several environmental laws such as the Environment Protection Act of 1986, the Air Act of 1981, and the Water Act of 1974, among others. These legislative measures are pivotal not only in safeguarding our natural heritage but also in promoting public health. Laws and mandate provisions for clean air, safe water, and overall a sustainable ecosystem, contribute significantly to the well-being and vitality of our communities. Thus, they play a crucial role in protecting human health and enhancing the quality of life for all citizens.

These directive principles have been often read in conjunction with fundamental rights by the legislature and the courts to argue and create a framework for governance based on democratic principles, constitutional protections, and human rights that ensures both individual liberties and societal welfare. These protections enshrined in the constitution have mandated the state to promulgate legislations and create institutional and regulatory frameworks to safeguard the right to health. Some of the statutory provisions related to health can be discussed in in this light.

4.4 OTHER CONSTITUTIONAL PROVISIONS RELATED TO HEALTH

Fundamental Rights and Directive principles provide a compelling basis on which legislations covering various aspects of health have been framed. In addition to this health-related provisions have also been articulated at various other places in the constitution. A few important constitutional provisions outside Part III and Part IV can be discussed as follows:

Article 242 of the constitution authorizes the state legislatures to confer the necessary powers and authority to the municipalities to enable them to function as institutions of self-governance and to implement any schemes as may be entrusted to them. This provision read in conjunction with Twelfth Schedule item 6 of the constitution which deals with public health, sanitation conservancy and solid waste management' becomes relevant for health. A similar provision exists with respect to panchayats under Article 243 G of the constitution read with item 23 of the 11th Schedule. These two constitutional provisions also make provision of health and sanitation the responsibility of local self-governance institutions. Such responsibilities may include provisions for safe water and sanitation, establishment and maintenance of dispensaries, preventing disease outbreaks etc. In case the local authorities fail in their constitutional obligations, citizens can pursue legal remedies through the courts of law.

4.5 INDIA'S FEDERAL SCHEME AND HEALTH

India follows a federal structure where powers and responsibilities are distributed between the centre and its constituent units, the states. This federal framework, envisaged in the Indian Constitution, delineates these roles through three distinct lists: the Union List, the State List, and the Concurrent List. Along similar lines health as a functional domain also follows the federal scheme. The **Union List** includes subjects on which only the central government can legislate. This includes public health and sanitation, regulation of drugs and poisons, and quarantine measures etc. These provisions in the union list aims to establish a standard and unified approach in managing public health crises and preventing the spread of infectious diseases within the country and also transboundary health hazards like pandemics.

The **State List** grants state governments exclusive authority over matters such as public health and hospitals, local government institutions' health-related functions, and the provision of healthcare services. This autonomy allows states to tailor healthcare policies and services according to local needs, demographics, and epidemiological trends, thereby promoting effective delivery of healthcare within their jurisdictions.

Concurrent List, contains entries where both the Union and State governments have the authority to legislate. This list includes areas like healthcare infrastructure, preventive and social medicine, and regulation of food and drugs. Collaboration under this list ensures a coordinated effort between the central and state authorities in addressing common health challenges, promoting uniform standards, and enhancing healthcare accessibility and quality nationwide.

India's federal setup aims to ensure a coordinated health governance by leveraging the strengths of both central and state governments. While the Union government formulates broad policies and guidelines, state governments have been entrusted with the role to execute, implement and manage healthcare services provincial and grassroot levels. For a vast country like India, this decentralized approach has been adopted with the objective of ensuring responsiveness to local health needs and encouraging innovation and provide flexible and adaptable solutions to health challenges faced by diverse populations across the country.

4.6 ISSUES AND CHALLENGES IN INDIA'S HEALTHCARE DOMAIN

The above discussion highlights that Indian Constitution's provides a significant place to health within its federal structure. Significant progress has also been made after independence with respect to some of the health indicators and outcomes. The life expectancy has surpassed 67 years, infant and under-five mortality rates are declining as is the rate of disease incidence. Many diseases, such as polio, guinea worm disease, yaws, and tetanus, have been eradicated.

However, in spite of these constitutional pronouncements and the progress achieved India's healthcare domains still faces enormous challenges. These issues weaken the ability to provide adequate and equitable healthcare to India's vast population that is also demographically diverse. Limited access to healthcare services, particularly in rural and remote areas is a major challenge India is struggling with. Many people in these regions lack access to basic healthcare facilities such as primary health centres, hospitals, and clinics. Infrastructure deficiencies pose another significant challenge. Despite recent improvements healthcare facilities, equipment and manpower are still remain in short supply. Consequently, the Quality of care gets severely impacted and contributes to disparities in healthcare access between urban and rural areas as well as between the rich and the poor. A NITI Ayog[1] report has brought these disparities into sharp relief by highlighting disparities and varying progress made by the states on various health indicators including the Sustainable Development Goals SDGs. Different states in India vary in their progress towards achieving the Sustainable Development Goals (SDGs). Some states have made significant advancements in meeting specific SDG targets. For instance, Kerala and Tamil Nadu have already achieved the SDG target of reducing neonatal mortality rate (NMR) to 12 deaths per 1,000 live births by 2030. Similarly, Punjab and Maharashtra are close to meeting this goal as well. However, several other states and Union Territories (UTs) still lag far behind. This differential progress is the direct result of unequal healthcare infrastructure, inconsistent policy design and implementation along states and socio-economic factors which have a bearing on the health outcomes. Continued focus on healthcare reforms, equitable access to healthcare services, and targeted interventions will be crucial in ensuring that all states in India can achieve the SDGs related to health and well-being by 2030[2].

Financial barriers also negate healthcare access for millions of Indians. Affordability of healthcare services still remains with a large proportion of the population unable to afford out-of-pocket expenses for medical treatment. Health insurance coverage in India is limited, particularly among low-income and rural populations. The healthcare workforce shortage is another significant challenge. India faces a severe scarcity of trained healthcare professionals, including doctors, nurses, and specialists. This shortage is particularly acute in rural and remote areas, where healthcare professionals are reluctant to work due to limited infrastructure, lower salaries, and inadequate career development opportunities. The uneven distribution of healthcare workforce further widens the healthcare access gap between urban and rural populations.

Public health challenges, including infectious diseases and the burden of non-communicable diseases (NCDs), add to the complexities of India's healthcare sector. Communicable diseases such as tuberculosis, malaria, and now, the challenges posed by emerging infectious diseases such as COVID-19, highlight the need for strengthening public health infrastructure and preparedness for disease outbreaks. Additionally, the rising prevalence of non-communicable diseases such as diabetes, cardiovascular diseases, and cancers requires sustained management and access to specialized care, which is often limited in many parts of the country.

1. See, https://social.niti.gov.in/uploads/sample/health_index_report.pdf.
2. Ibid. Key Results, para 5.

Addressing these challenges requires concerted efforts from policymakers, healthcare providers, civil society, and the private sector. It calls for comprehensive reforms aimed at enhancing healthcare infrastructure, expanding healthcare workforce capacity, improving healthcare financing mechanisms, and bringing about accountability in the public healthcare system.

4.7 HEALTH AS AN ENUMERATED FUNDAMENTAL RIGHT IN THE CONSTITUTIONAL FRAMEWORK

In this context it is often debated whether health should be made a specific enumerated fundamental right in the Indian constitution. Advocates for this position argue that recognizing health as a fundamental right would provide stronger legal protection to healthcare entitlements for all citizens. By elevating health to the status of a fundamental right, individuals could legally demand and enforce their entitlement to healthcare services. It is also contended that a step in this direction would also sit well with India's commitment at the international level and its compliance with the global standards on public health as a human right.

In September 2019, a High-Level Group constituted under the aegis of the 15th Finance commission[3] submitted a report suggesting to accord Right to health the status of a specifically enumerated fundamental Right to the citizens in order to strengthen their access to healthcare as a constitutional entitlement. In addition to this, another recommendation made was to transfer health sector from the state list to concurrent list of the Indian constitution.

As it stands today, "Public health and sanitation; hospitals and dispensaries" come in the state list of the seventh schedule of the Indian constitution. It is thus primarily within the power of state legislatures, to legislate and regulate health policies and laws. Moving health to the concurrent list would imply that both the central and state governments are able to make laws on these matters at the same time. Although this change might help bring efficiency in decision-making process and standardization of health policies across the region, it does not seem to be compatible with the concept of cooperative federalism envisaged in the Indian constitution. It is worth noting that while centralising public health management may bring about some policy level uniformity, it may also create bureaucratic hurdles and coordination issues between the centre and states which may slow down implementation processes at grass root level.

A recent NITI Aayog report[4] has also reiterated these concerns. The report highlighted that the disparities in healthcare delivery systems and infrastructure among states in terms of variables such as technical expertise and financial wherewithal. Moving health to the concurrent list might exacerbate these problems which can hinder states' ability to address local health issues and concerns. Furthermore, there is a possibility that a centralized model of health policymaking can obscure the state's particular need and peculiarities with respect to healthcare provisioning. Due to a lack of consideration of the varied regional and demographic health contexts. Despite the fact that a national framework might provide consistency such approach might not cover all the needs of the demographic differences of the country and diverse terrains.

3. See, Report of the High Level group of Health Sector https://www.im4change.org/siteadmin/tinymce/uploaded/High%20Level%20group%20of%20Health%20Sector.pdf

4. See, Healthy States Progressive India: Report on the Ranks of States and Union Territories http://social.niti.gov.in/uploads/sample/health_index_report.pdf

However, this must be kept in mind that while declaring health a specific fundamental right in India and shifting it to the concurrent list may hold some advantages it must be approached cautiously. This is due to the fact that India faces a lot of challenges in terms of healthcare infrastructure, budgetary provisions, and human resources. Recognizing health as a fundamental right without provision of matching resources could further strain the already burdened healthcare system and pose financial challenges for the government. Moreover, declaring health as a specific fundamental right could open floodgates of litigation leading to apprehensions of excessive judicial interference in health policy making which in turn could lead to decisions that are impractical or unsustainable in the longer run. Irrespective of the advantages and disadvantages of making health a distinct fundamental right one thing is certain from the foregoing analysis. The drafters of the constitution have done a remarkable job in situating health as a prominent constitutional and legal rights. Indian judiciary has also played a complementary but pivotal role in giving meaning and effect to some of the fundamental rights (most notably Article 21) through creative and liberal interpretation and reading health into them. The judicial interpretation of the right to health shall be discussed in the following chapter.

SUMMARY

The chapter provides a comprehensive exploration of the constitutional framework of health and public healthcare delivery in India. It examines the various dimensions, from foundational principles to specific provisions and federal arrangements relating to the right to health. The chapter begins by analysing the Preamble of the Indian Constitution, which sets out the overarching goals and aspirations of justice, liberty, equality, and fraternity. While health is not explicitly stated in the preamble, its exalted principles imply a commitment to create a society where the well-being of all citizens, including their health, is paramount.

Moving to the Fundamental Rights chapter, the discussion focuses on the specific provisions relevant to health. In the absence of a specific and stated right to health in the Indian constitution, Article 21 acts as a bulwark and guarantees the right to life and personal liberty. This right has been interpreted expansively by judiciary to also include the right to health and healthcare. This interpretation recognises the fundamental nature of health as an inherent dimension of a dignified life under the Indian Constitution. The Directive Principles of State Policy notably Articles 39, 41, 42, and 47 also highlight the state's obligation to secure the right to work, education, and public health. Although they are non-justiciable in nature, they have a strong persuasive effect on the state. It also demonstrates a commitment to promoting social and economic justice through healthcare initiatives in the Indian constitutional scheme.

The chapter then explores other constitutional provisions related to health, this includes legislative powers and the roles of central and state governments in healthcare administration. It discusses the challenges and opportunities presented by India's federal scheme and the complex distribution of powers, jurisdiction and responsibilities between the Union and the states in matters of health. Lastly, the chapter addresses the debate around the question of recognising health as an enumerated fundamental right in the Indian constitutional framework and its pros and cons. Overall, the chapter looks into the evolving nature of health rights within India's constitutional framework, and consequent legislative actions as well as policy initiatives in realizing the constitutional mandate to ensure health as a fundamental entitlement for all citizens.

CHAPTER

5

Judiciary and the Right to Health

INTRODUCTION

The previous chapter has examined the legal and constitutional status of the right to health. The foregoing analysis shows that health has not been accorded the status of a specific fundamental right in the Indian constitution. Although there are significant provisions pertaining to health in the Directive Principles of State Policy, they are non-justiciable which implies that the entitlements of these rights and any violations or deficiencies with respect to their availability or enjoyment can't be directly remedied through the courts of law. This serves as a limitation because it deprives people to assert their right to health through the judicial means and processes.

5.1 JUDICIARY'S ROLE IN SECURING HEALTH RIGHTS

Courts in India have endeavoured to overcomes these limitations of justiciability by adopting various approaches often innovative. For by instance referring to and expanding the equality provisions in Part III courts have mandated that state should provide equitable, non-discriminatory and affordable access to healthcare to citizens irrespective of their socio-economic status or positions. The most significant judicial intervention however has happened with respect to the right to life under Article 21 of the Constitution. In a plethora of judgements courts particularly the supreme court has liberally construed the term life to encompass the right to health and a dignified life and all the necessary elements that enable us to lead a healthy and dignified life. Many of these interventions have come while adjudicating public interest litigations (PILs) which themselves are a judicial innovation in the judicial processed developed by the Indian judiciary. Public Interest Litigations (PILs) have been instrumental in advancing these judicial interpretations. PILs dilute the principle of *locus standi* (the principle applies that one someone who is directly aggrieved can seek legal remedy) and allow any individual or organization to approach the court on behalf of those whose rights are affected, even if they are not directly involved in the case. This innovative judicial mechanism has enabled the judiciary to address systemic issues affecting public health, such as inadequate healthcare infrastructure, lack of medicines, and environmental pollution to name a few. Courts through such mechanism have cast the net wide and have been able to intervene in cases where health-related issues jeopardize an individual's fundamental rights, thereby compelling state action to address healthcare deficiencies and ensure access to essential services.

After this general overview of the role played by the Indian judiciary, some landmark cases on health as a rightful entitlement of people can be discussed as illustrative examples. This will enable a better understanding the proactive role played by the judiciary in advancing the right to health as a rightful entitlement.

It would only be apt to illustrate the role played by the judiciary in so far as the right to life and concomitantly health is concerned is the landmark *Maneka Gandhi* v. *Union of India*[1]. This case brought about a seminal shift in the discourse around the right to life and liberty jurisprudence in India. In this case the Court moved away from the earlier restrictive interpretations of Article 21 notably in A.K Gopalan[2], which took a restrictive and literal view of the constitutional guarantees of life and personal liberty by confining it to mere absence of physical restraint. Instead, the Court undertook a liberal reconstruction and reinvigorated the concept. The Court's reinterpretation emphasized that "personal liberty" should not be narrowly conceived and must include attributes other than those explicitly listed in Article 21.

Such a reinterpretation of Article 21 had a definitive impact on the subsequent development of the right to health jurisprudence in India. The determination by the Court that life and personal liberty is comprised of many interrelated rights necessary for a dignified life, the Court established implicitly that healthcare is integral to the broader concept of life and the freedoms it entails. Health is thus established as being of utmost importance for personal well-being and the ability to pursue a dignified life.

Hence in judicial view in the expanded interpretation of Article 21, access to healthcare services and facilities becomes not just a policy goal but a constitutional imperative. This case put onus on the state to protect and promote the health of its citizens. Even after decades this judgement has continued to shape legal discourse and has provided legal backing and impetus to advocacy efforts aimed at ensuring comprehensive healthcare access and quality for all individuals in India.

Another landmark judgement which came shortly after the Maneka judgement was *Francis Coralie* v. *Union Territory of Delhi*[3], a case on the right of an undertrial prisoner to meet her family members and consult her lawyer. The Supreme Court in this instance observed that the denial of such rights is violative of both Article 14 (equality) and Article 21 (life). The Supreme Court further expanded the Right to life to imply a life with dignity. In the course of this case the Court observed.

"While arriving at the proper meaning and content of the right to life, the attempt of the court should always be to expand the reach and ambit of the fundamental right rather than

1. AIR 1978 SC 597
2. AIR 1950 SC 27. A.K. Gopalan case adopted a literal and textual approach to interpreting Article 21 and interpreted liberty to mean a mere absence of physical restraint . It focused narrowly on the language of the provision and did not consider broader principles of human dignity, social justice, or the evolving nature of fundamental rights.
3. AIR 1981 SC 746

to attenuate its meaning and content. A constitutional provision must be construed, not in a narrow and constricted sense, but in a wide and liberal manner...This principle applies with greater force in relation to a fundamental right enacted by the Constitution. The fundamental right to life which is the most precious human right and which forms the ark of all other rights must therefore be interpreted in a broad and expansive spirit so as to invest it with significance and vitality which may endure for years to come and enhance the dignity of the individual and the worth of the human person."

These observations of the Apex Court are salient. They clearly indicate the judicial intent to allow a liberal and overarching interpretation of the right to life with the objective of enhancing the vitality as well as dignity of life. The Court went on to delineate that the Right under Article 21 cannot be restricted to mere animal existence and physical survival. It noted further...

"*...The right to life includes the right to live with human dignity and all that goes along with it, namely, the bare necessaries of life such as adequate nutrition, clothing and shelter and facilities for reading, writing and expressing oneself in diverse forms, freely moving about and mixing and commingling with fellow human beings.*"

Likewise in the case of *LIC of India* v. *Consumer Education and Research Centre*[4], the Supreme Court undertook a combined reading of the right to equality and the right to life. The LIC case highlights how constitutional principles of equality and the right to life intersect in the context of public health services. In this case, the Life Insurance Corporation (LIC), a statutory body, introduced a life insurance scheme under which only a certain class of individuals, those in government or semi-government service, or from reputed commercial firms were deemed to be eligible. The Supreme Court declared such a classification unconstitutional on account of breach of Article 14 of the Constitution, which guarantees the right to equality.

LIC argued that the classification was justified as it made health conditions experienced by a certain (salaried) class of individuals as the basis for determining eligibility, hence fulfilling the criterion of intelligible differentia for extending a differential treatment.

However, the Supreme Court countered this argument, emphasizing that the classification based on employment in chosen sectors would result in the exclusion of individuals engaged in unorganized or self-employed sectors from accessing life insurance. This exclusion squarely goes against Article 14 which prohibits discrimination on grounds such as socio-economic status in letter and spirit. Referring to multiple provisions enshrined in international covenants as well as its own previous judgements the Supreme Court made the following salient observations which crucial to appreciate the Court's reasoning as to the interconnected nature of life and health is concerned.

"*...Interpreting Article 19(e) vis-a-vis Article 25(2) of the Universal Declaration of the Human Right and Article 7 of the International Convention of Economic, Social and Cultural Rights, one of us (K. Ramaswamy, J.) in C.E.S.C. Ltd.* v. *Subhash Chandra Bose, (1992)1 SCC 441 at p. 462 in para 30, held that the right to social justice is a fundamental right. Right to livelihood springs from the right to life guaranteed under Article 21. The health and strength of*

4. AIR 1995 SC 1811

a worker is an integral facet of right to life. Right to human dignity, development of personality, social protection, right to rest and leisure are fundamental human rights to a common man"

The foregoing lines demonstrate that Court's decision stresses on the importance of equitable application in provisioning health facilities or services by the state. Selective determination of eligibility in providing life insurance implied that the scheme effectively restricted access to essential health protections for a significant portion of the population. This restriction was deemed unconstitutional as it impinged on the right to life under Article 21, which as the previous cases have demonstrated includes the right to live with dignity, encompassing access to adequate healthcare and social security measures.

It is amply evident from such observations that that "life" as expounded by the highest judicial authority of the country transcends a minimalistic understanding. On the contrary the term life is closely interconnected with dignity, self-expression livelihood, nutrition among other things. All of these are also necessary concomitants of our physical and mental health and well-being. The right to health therefore is clearly coopted with the right to life and cannot be separated from it.

Consumer Education and Research Centre v. *Union of India*, represents another instance where the Apex Court made references to several directive principles and synthesized them with the right to life. More specifically Articles 21, 38, 42, 43, 46, and 48A, were read together to assert that the right to health is a fundamental right. This landmark judgement emphasized that the protection of health and medical aid for workers both during their service and post-retirement is an integral part of their right to life.

Article 21 of the Indian Constitution guarantees the right to life and personal liberty, which has been expansively interpreted by the Supreme Court to include the right to live with dignity. This interpretation forms the foundation for recognizing the right to health as an integral part of the right to life. The court has consistently held that the right to health encompasses the right to medical care, treatment, and health facilities necessary to lead a meaningful life.

In the *Consumer Education and Research Centre* case, the Supreme Court undertook a holistic view of these constitutional provisions to pronounce that state's responsibility to ensure access to healthcare and medical aid is not merely a directive principle or a policy goal, but a right that must be honoured by the State. This includes the responsibility to provide adequate health infrastructure, facilities, and services to protect the health and well-being of worker and any denial of healthcare would violate the dignity and right to life guaranteed under Article 21. The Court *inter alia* declared.

"*...right to health to a worker is an integral facet of meaningful right to life and have not only a meaningful existence but also robust health and vigour without which worker would lead life of misery. Lack of health denudes his livelihood. Compelling economic necessity to work in an industry exposed to health hazards due to indigence to bread-winning to himself and his dependents, should not be at the cost of the health and vigour of the workman. Facilities and opportunities, as enjoined in Article 38, should be provided to protect the health of the workman. Right to human dignity, development of personality, social protection are fundamental rights to the workmen. Medical facilities to protect the health of the workers are fundamental rights to workmen. It was, therefore, held that "the right to health, medical aid and to protect the health and the vigour of a worker while in service or post-retirement is a fundamental* *right under Article 21 read with Articles 39(e), 41, 43, 48-A of the Constitution of India and fundamental human right to make the life of workmen meaningful and purposeful with dignity of persons.*"

This judicial interpretation paved the way for health as a fundamental right under the Indian Constitution by reiterating the State's responsibility to promote equal access to health services for the workers, especially the vulnerable ones. It brought out the relationship between various provisions of the constitution in as much as the protection of the health of the public and recognized the judiciary as the guardian of these rights as it declares its interpretation of the provision.

5.2 MEDICO LEGAL CASES

Similar reasoning has been extended by judiciary in medico legal cases as well which often involve emergency care. For example, *Parmanand Katara* v. *Union of India*[5] further opened up the right to life and health jurisprudence in India by extending it to the right to receive immediate and appropriate medical care for victims of emergencies such as road accidents etc. The case reached the Supreme Court through a public interest litigation concerning the death of a scooterist who was hit by a speeding car owing to refusal of medical attention and treatment. The jurisprudence involved interpretation of Article 21 of the Constitution, in conjunction with clauses 12 and 13 of The Code of Medical Ethics, 1970. Article 21 ensures the right to life, while clause 12 mandates doctors and practitioners to fulfil their duty to treat and serve the injured to the best of their abilities, without avoiding their professional responsibilities. Clause 13 prohibits practitioners from engaging in wilful negligence. The Supreme Court while adjudicating on the matter once again stressed on the sanctity of life and the foremost requirement to preserve it by adverting as follows:

"*Article 21 of the Constitution casts the obligation on the State to preserve life...There can be no second opinion that preservation of human life is of paramount importance. That is so on account of the fact that once life is lost, the status quo ante cannot be restored as resurrection is beyond the capacity of man...... Every doctor whether at a government hospital or otherwise has the professional obligation to extend his services with due expertise for protecting life.... No law or State action can intervene to avoid/delay the discharge of the paramount obligation cast upon members of the medical profession. The obligation being total, absolute and paramount, laws of procedure whether in statute or otherwise which would interfere with the discharge of this obligation cannot be sustained and must, therefore, give way*".

These observations of the Supreme Court are of immense significance. In holding that the right to life is inalienable and sacrosanct the Court has cast specific obligations on doctors serving in both public as well as private hospitals to save the life of the victim to the best of his ability and expertise. It further clarified that any state Laws or actions that hinder medical professionals from carrying out their duty to preserve life must yield to this overriding obligation.

5. 1989 AIR 2039

In *State of Punjab & Ors* v. *Mohinder Singh Chawla*[6] as well as in *State of Punjab & Ors* v. *Ram Lubayna Bagga*[7] both cases pertaining to medical reimbursements, the Supreme Court insisted that right to health is a fundamental right by virtue of a meaningful and purposive interpretation of Article 21. The Court in *Bagga* said "…*(M)an's Life should be meaningful, worth living. Pith and substance of life is the health, which is the nucleus of all activities of life including that of an employee or other viz. the physical, social, spiritual or any conceivable human activities. If this is denied, it is said everything crumbles.*"

Paschim Banga khet Mazdoor Samity v. *State of West Bengal*[8] is another significant judgement where the Supreme Court unequivocally reminded the state of its duty to provide medical treatment to the victims in case of emergency. In this case a person suffered serious injuries after falling off a train and was denied admission by a number of state hospitals on account of unavailability of beds or lack of facilities etc. The case hence involved the question whether denial of emergency medical treatment violated the patient's right to life. The Court in this judgement declared that safeguarding the right to health is one of the most important responsibilities of a welfare state. The Court observed.

"*The Constitution envisages the establishment of a welfare state at the federal level as well as at the state level. In a welfare state the primary duty of the Government is to secure the welfare of the people. Providing adequate medical facilities for the people is an essential part of the obligations undertaken by the Government in a welfare state. The Government discharges this obligation by running hospitals and health centres which provide medical care to the person seeking to avail those facilities. Article 21 imposes an obligation on the State to safeguard the right to life of every person. Preservation of human life is thus of paramount importance. The Government hospitals run by the State and the medical officers employed therein are duty bound to extend medical assistance for preserving human life. Failure on the part of a government hospital to provide timely medical treatment to a person in need of such treatment results in violation of his right to life guaranteed under Article 21.*."

It was hence reiterated that the right to life enshrined in the Indian Constitution (Article 21) imputes a corresponding duty on the State to safeguard the right to life of every person since preservation of human life sacrosanct and has to be the primary interest of the state. Denial of timely medical treatment particularly in emergencies is a gross infringement of this constitutional guarantee. Constraints of financial resources cannot be cited as a ground to evade this responsibility. The Court asked the Government of West Bengal to pay the petitioner compensation for the loss suffered. It also directed the Government to formulate a blue print for primary healthcare with particular reference to treatment of patients during an emergency.

5.3 CASES INVOLVING HEALTH AND ENVIRONMENT

Judiciary in India has played a stellar role in enriching the environmental law jurisprudence in India often by adjudicating on the public health implications of environmental pollution or

6. AIR 1997 SC 1225
7. AIR 1998 SC 1703
8. AIR 1996 SC 2426

degradation. Again, the instrumentality of Public Health Litigation has been put to effective use by the Courts in dealing with such cases as well. Public Interest Litigation has been a powerful tool in environmental litigation. It allows concerned citizens, environmental activists, and non-governmental organizations (NGOs) to petition the courts on behalf of affected communities or to highlight violations of environmental laws and their deleterious impact on public health. Some of the seminal cases can be discussed as follows:

As far back as 1980 the Supreme Court in *Ratlam Municipal Council* v. *Vardhichand*[9] held the civic body liable for its failure to ensure proper maintenance of the public drainage system in the municipal limits of Ratlam city which invariably had the impact of negatively impacting the health of the public at large. The Supreme Court also rejected the contention of the municipal corporation that it could not provide the sanitary facilities due to lack of funds. The Court held;

"*A responsible municipal council constituted for the precise purpose of preserving public health and providing better finances cannot run away from its principal duty by pleading financial inability. Decency and dignity are non-negotiable facets of human rights and are a first charge on local self-governing bodies. Similarly, providing drainage systems not pompous and attractive, but in working condition and sufficient to meet the needs of the people-cannot be evaded if the municipality is to justify its existence....The state will realise that Art. 47 makes it a paramount principle of governance that steps are taken for the improvement of public health as amongst its primary duties. The municipality also will slim its budget on low priority items and elitist projects to use the savings on sanitation and public health*".

After the Vardhichand judgement, Indian Judiciary has on multiple occasions adapted the existing constitutional provisions and also came up with innovative doctrines and interpretations on matters of environment and health. This has led to significant rulings such as the recognition of environmental rights as fundamental rights, the principle of sustainable development, and the "polluter pays" principle. Additionally, doctrines like Public Trust Doctrine and Precautionary Principle have been invoked to protect environmental and health. Such activism is exemplified in numerous petitions filed by prominent activist M.C. Mehta. In the *Oleum gas leak*[10] case for example an incident of oleum gas leak in a Delhi industrial plant in 1985 resulted in fatalities and raised significant public health concerns. The Supreme Court introduced the doctrine of 'Absolute Liability[11], departing from the earlier principle of 'strict liability.' This new doctrine imposed complete responsibility on industries handling hazardous substances, eliminating any potential defences to deflect or pass on their liability when it is a question of danger to public health.This doctrine indicated a radical shift from the set principles of tort law, making industries absolutely liable for any harm caused without exceptions or defences. The ruling laid a "no-fault" liability standard and enjoined upon the industries to treat the waste

9. AIR 1980 SC 1622.

10. *M.C. Mehta* v. *Union of India*, AIR 1987 SC 1086

11. Absolute liability signifies that if a person, industry or enterprise is engaged in an inherently dangerous activity he assumes "full legal responsibility for damages or for an injury, without the need for proof and regardless of the degree of negligence or fault." Source: https://www.collinsdictionary.com/dictionary/english/absolute-liability.

adequately. The Court required the creation of the first-stage treatment facilities and held local authorities responsible for prevention. The M.C. Mehta case had a cascading impact for both legislative action and future rulings. It became a precursor for Public Liability Insurance Act 1991 which established a legal framework to account for liability and subsequent compensation in industrial accidents.

This judgement also served as a precedent for future cases. In *Visakhapatnam Gas Leak Case*[12]. In this case the National Green Tribunal while granting to the victims of a gas leak at a factory in Vizag noted.

"If on account of hazardous commercial activity of any enterprise any person is affected, principle of absolute liability is attracted in view of M.C Mehta & Anr v. *Union of India, (1987) 1 SCC 395. It is not necessary to prove negligence.*"

Following the Oleum gas leak incident, which occurred in 1985 at the Shriram Food & Fertilizer Industries plant in Delhi, there was a significant judicial response that underscored the critical interconnections between environmental protection and public health. The Supreme Court's intervention in the aftermath of this disaster, through in a catena of related judgements many of which were filed as PILs by activists M.C. Mehta, greatly enriched the environment-health jurisprudence. The case brought to light the devastating impact of industrial pollution on human health and the environment, prompting a series of Public Interest Litigations (PILs) filed by M.C. Mehta that continue to shape environmental policy and law in India.

Subsequent PILs filed by M.C. Mehta have further emphasized the interconnectedness of environmental degradation and public health concerns. Cases addressing issues such as air and water pollution, deforestation, and hazardous waste management have consistently brought to the forefront the adverse effects of environmental deterioration on human well-being. These legal battles have compelled authorities to implement stricter regulatory frameworks and adopt sustainable practices aimed at mitigating environmental risks and protecting community health.

In the case *Vellore Citizen Welfare Forum* v. *Union of India & others*[13] as well the Supreme Court dealt with the issue of untreated industrial effluents being released into the river Palar which served as the primary water source for the residents of Vellore, Tamil Nadu. The court invoked the 'polluter pays' principle, ruling that industries must bear the cost of environmental damage and consequent public health implications engendered by their activities. This decision extended the 'absolute liability' principle beyond compensating pollution victims to encompass the expenses required for restoring environmental degradation. Attribution of corporate responsibility for environmental harm was a pivotal development in environment and health jurisprudence wherein the Court aimed to safeguard public health as well as the ecosystem's integrity. The Court in the course of the hearing proceeded to invoke Article 21of the Constitution of India which guarantees protection of life and personal liberty in conjunction with directive principles Articles 47, 48A and held as follows:

12. See, Original Application No. 448/2022 In re : News item published in Hindustan Times dated 03.06.2022 titled "178 women workers fall ill after gas leak in Andhra's Visakhapatnam." Available at: https://greentribunal.gov.in/gen_pdf_test.php?filepath=L25ndF9kb2N1bWVudHMvbmd0L2Nhc2Vkb2MvanVkZ2VtZW50cy9ERUxISS8yMDIzLTAxLTE4LzE2NzQxMTQxNTQyOTQxMTA2MDc2M2M4ZjQ2YWExNjI3LnBkZg==
13. AIR 1996 SC 2715.

"Consequently the polluting industries are "absolutely liable to compensate for the harm caused by them to villagers in the affected area, to the soil and to the underground water and hence, they are bound to take all necessary measures to remove sludge and other pollutants lying in the affected areas". The "Polluter Pays" principle as interpreted by this Court means that the absolute liability for harm to the environment extends not only to compensate the victims of pollution but also the cost of restoring the environmental degradation. Remediation of the damaged environment is part of the process of "Sustainable Development" and as such polluter is liable to pay the cost to the individual sufferers as well as the cost of reversing the damaged ecology."

Indian Council for Enviro-legal Action and others (Petitioners) v. *Union of India*[14], was brought forward by the Indian Council for Enviro-Legal Action aimed to address severe pollution caused by chemical industrial plants in Bichhri village, Udaipur District, Rajasthan. These plants operated without permits, releasing toxic substances contaminating water sources and soil, and reportedly causing illnesses and deaths among nearby residents. From 1989 to 1992, the Court issued orders to control and manage the pollution, which were largely disregarded by the respondents. A 1994 report by the National Environmental Engineering Research Institute (NEERI) confirmed the environmental damage. In 1996, the Court conducted a final hearing. The Court invoked the principle from the Oleum Gas Leak Case II, holding that enterprises engaged in hazardous activities are liable for harm caused, irrespective of fault. It endorsed the "polluter pays" principle, where the financial burden of pollution prevention and remediation falls on the polluters. Moreover, under Sections 3 and 5 of the Environment (Protection) Act, 1986, the Central Government was empowered to take action to safeguard the environment. It was determined that the respondents must pay for the remedial measures employed to mitigate the impact of river pollution. Describing the respondents as "rogue industries," the Court ordered the closure of all their facilities in Bichhri village and allowed villagers to seek damages through civil courts.

The discussion on judiciary's intervention shall not be complete without referring *to Ganga River Pollution Case* also commonly referred to as the *Kanpur Tanneries Case*.[15] This petition was also filed in public interest in the Supreme Court for the prevention of nuisance caused due to the pollution of the River Ganga caused by tanneries and soap factories on the banks of the river, at Kanpur. The Court in allowing the petition ruled that widespread and indiscriminate water pollution was a public nuisance and Mr. Mehta was well within his rights to file a public interest litigation. The pollution, a consequence of inadequate management of industrial waste resulted in increased incidences of water-borne diseases among communities relying on the water source. Regarding responsibility for pollution, the Court held that industries must treat their waste before discharge, and licenses should only be granted if adequate treatment provisions are demonstrated. Existing industries found responsible for pollution should face legal consequences. The Court also held statutory bodies accountable, directing immediate actions to implement pollution control schemes and sewage treatment policies.

The Court observed that the Central Government was mandated to prevent pollution and enhance environmental awareness. It also instructed the government to distribute educational

14. 1996 AIR 1446.

15. *M.C. Mehta* v. *Union of India* (Kanpur Tanneries), 1988 AIR 1115.

materials promoting environmental studies free of charge. Additionally, the Court prohibited the High Court from staying criminal proceedings initiated by State Boards against industrialists for environmental violations. The Supreme Court also directed that the decision should be applied *mutatis mutandis* to all municipal corporations having jurisdiction over areas along the Ganga River, emphasizing nationwide implications for pollution control and environmental protection.

5.4 JUDICIAL PRONOUNCEMENTS ON WORKERS AND VULNERABLE SECTIONS

In numerous seminal judgements judiciary has taken up the cause of the vulnerable sections of the society such as women children and workers and safeguarded their right to life, health and well-being. Besides legal interpretations, the judiciary's proactive stance is demonstrative of a broader societal commitment to inclusivity and equity. In standing up for the marginalized groups, courts have catalysed social change and promoted a culture of respect for human rights and fundamental freedoms. Judicial activism not only interprets laws in the interest of justice for the marginalized but also shapes the moral and ethical fabric of the nation, reinforcing the constitutional ideals of justice, equality, and dignity for all citizens.

Bandhua Mukti Morcha (BMM), a non-governmental organization working for the abolition of bonded and child labour. The organization has been instrumental in advocating for the rights of vulnerable labourers who are trapped in exploitative and often illegal employment practices. BMM has also filed a series of PILs and brought to focus the prevalence of bonded and child labour and their horrible working conditions which negatively impacts their right to health and life. Two of the most prominent case merit a discussion here.

Bandhua Mukti Morcha v. *Union of India*[16] gave voice to the longstanding yet unaddressed issue of bonded labour in India. The NGO while conducting a survey of stone quarries in Faridabad district near Delhi unravelled inhuman and intolerable working conditions faced by migrant workers from many states. The organisation wrote a letter to Justice P. N. Bhagwati detailing the plight of workers, including imprisonment, fatal injuries, respiratory diseases from stone dust, poor drinking water, inadequate sanitation, low wages, and exploitation of women. The petitioners contended that the working condition of the labourers was in utter violation of several labour legislations including the Mines Act of 1952, the Inter-State Migrant Workmen Act of 1979, the Contract Labour Act of 1970, the Bonded Labour System Abolition Act of 1976, and the Minimum Wages Act of 1948. The Supreme Court, recognizing bonded labour as a violation of fundamental rights, delivered a landmark judgment in favour of the petitioners, addressing the pervasive issue of bonded labour in India.

The Court thus held:

"It is the fundamental right of every one in this country, assured under the interpretation given to Article 21 by this Court in Francis Mullen's Case, to live with human dignity, free from exploitation. This right to live with human dignity enshrined in Article 21 derives its life breath from the Directive Principles of State Policy and particularly clauses (e) and (f) of Article 39 and Articles 41 and 42 and at the least, therefore, it must include protection

16. (1984) 3 SCC 161

of the health and strength of workers, men and women, and of the tender age of children against abuse, opportunities and facilities for children to develop in a healthy manner and in conditions of freedom and dignity, educational facilities, just and humane conditions of work and maternity relief".

The Supreme Court's landmark judgment in *Bandhua Mukti Morcha* v. *Union of India* & proved to be a milestone in India's fight against bonded labour which has a severely detrimental impact on the physical as well as mental health of workers which come from some of the most marginalized sections and communities of the country. Upon careful consideration of the arguments presented, the Supreme Court issued a series of directives aimed at addressing the pervasive issue of bonded labour. These directives included the immediate identification and release of all bonded labourers, effective implementation of the Bonded Labour Act and other relevant labour laws, and the establishment of rehabilitation programs to support freed labourers. Additionally, the Court mandated the creation of vigilance committees to monitor labour conditions and ensure compliance with legal protections.

From a public health perspective, the Supreme Court's ruling in *Bandhua Mukti Morcha* had profound implications. Bonded labourers typically endure harsh working conditions that make them susceptible to health hazards such as respiratory diseases from dust and pollutants, injuries from unsafe working environments, and nutritional deficiencies due to inadequate wages and living conditions. These conditions not only compromise the immediate health of labourers but also contribute to long-term health disparities and vulnerabilities within affected communities.

The directive for comprehensive rehabilitation programs was crucial in addressing these health concerns by providing freed labourers with access to healthcare services, nutritious food, and opportunities for vocational training. By focusing on rehabilitation and reintegration, the Court aimed to mitigate the health impacts of bonded labour and to improve the overall well-being of individuals who had suffered under exploitative conditions.

Another case in which Bandhua Mukti Morcha was instrumental was related to child labour. In this instance the BMM petitioned the Supreme Court to seek its intervention in the pervasive issue of employment and exploitation of children in the carpet industry of Uttar Pradesh. The case brought to light disturbing findings from a court-appointed committee which brought to light the gruesome reality of widespread exploitation of children. Many children were under the age of 14 and victims of trafficking. They endured hazardous working conditions and physical abuse. These practices flagrantly violated fundamental rights enshrined in the Constitution and international human rights standards.

In its landmark judgment, the Supreme Court stressed on the imperative to safeguard children's rights to education, health, and development, crucial for India's democratic progress. The Court did acknowledge the pragmatic economic realities that made immediate abolition of child labour difficult. Nevertheless, Court advocated steps to protect vulnerable children in impoverished segments of society. It invoked several constitutional provisions, including Article 21 (Right to life and personal liberty), Article 24 (Prohibition of child labour in hazardous industries), and Directive Principles like Article 39(e) and (f), which outline the State's duty to prevent exploitation and ensure children's healthy development. Additionally, Article 45's mandate for compulsory education below 14 years was also outlined in the judgement.

The Court observed

"Child of today cannot develop to be a responsible and productive member of tomorrow's society unless an environment which is conductive to his social and physical health is assured to him....Therefore, while exploitation of the child must be progressively banned, other simultaneously alternatives to the child should be evolved including providing education, healthcare, nutrient food, shelter and other means of livelihood with self-respect and dignity of person. Immediate ban of child labour would be both unrealistic and counter-productive. Ban of employment of children must begin from most hazardous and intolerable activities like slavery, bonded labour, trafficking, prostitution, pornography and dangerous forms of labour and the like."

Courts stirred the governments of Uttar Pradesh and Bihar to devise policies aimed at progressively eliminating child labour, ensuring compulsory education for affected children, providing nutritional support, and conducting regular health check-ups. These measures were intended to be monitored through periodic reports submitted to the Court, emphasizing accountability and enforcement of the orders. Another significant outcome of the case was the establishment of the National Commission for Protection of Child Rights (NCPCR) in 2006. This body was entrusted with the responsibility of monitoring compliance with international child rights conventions and undertake efforts to progressively eradicate child labour along with ensuring universal access to primary education.

5.5 CASES INVOLVING PUBLIC HEALTH AND INFECTIOUS DISEASES

The recent waves of the COVID-19 pandemic have put the issue of public health in the spotlight. The pandemic has demonstrated how infectious diseases impact different sections of the populations differentially in terms of access to healthcare and health service delivery. Socio-economic factors exacerbated these disparities, with lower-income and marginalized groups experiencing greater barriers to healthcare due to financial constraints, lack of insurance, and limited transportation. Vulnerable populations, including the elderly and those with pre-existing conditions too suffered disproportionately, revealing systemic gaps and the need for resilient healthcare systems. Some of these issues were also addressed in the course of judicial proceedings.

In Re: Distribution of Essential Supplies and Services during Pandemic[17], the Supreme Court of India took Suo motu cognizance of to oversee the proper and effective distribution of essential supplies and services during the COVID-19 pandemic across India. The Court took note of the widespread impact of COVID-19 infections across the nation and intervened to address critical issues. In a series of substantive orders posed questions to the government and gave directions and recommendations on various aspects related to COVID-19 management such as the supply of medical oxygen, keeping buffer stocks of oxygen, prohibition on clampdown on social media, essential drugs and vaccines, etc. The Court also directed the Centre to formulate a national policy on admission in hospitals and ordered that no patient shall be denied hospitalisation or essential medicines merely for want of identity proof, etc.

17. See, Suo Motu Writ Petition (Civil) No.3 of 2021. https://main.sci.gov.in/supremecourt/2021/11001/11001_2021_35_301_27825_Judgement_30-Apr-2021.pdf

In RE: Contagion of Covid 19 Virus in Prisons[18], In this Suo motu petition, the Supreme Court attempted to address the right to life and health of prisoners and undertrials. The Court took notice of the issue of overcrowding in prisons during the COVID-19 pandemic and directed states and Union Territories to form High Powered Committees tasked with evaluating if certain categories of detainees and prisoners could be granted parole or interim bail. Another significant directive was to stop the requirement of physical presence requirement for undertrial prisoners in court proceedings. Additionally, the Court mandated the development of state-specific readiness and response plans for prisons, and established state-level monitoring teams to ensure compliance with these directives.

Suo Motu Writ Petition (Civil) No. 7/2020. This case related to the right to health as well as public delivery and access to healthcare services during pandemics. It addressed the abominable conditions faced by patients admitted in various COVID-19 dedicated hospitals and the appalling state of wards in Delhi and other states. The Court pointed to the deficiencies and lapses in different hospitals with the objective of taking remedial action in order to alleviate the suffering of COVID-19 patients and other related individuals. While asserting that State, entrusted with the duty to safeguard the health of its citizens, cannot avoid its responsibility which is to ensure that all hospitals, including government facilities, adequately care for COVID-19 patients, the Supreme Court issued a series of directives aimed at improving the management of COVID-19 patients across hospitals in India.

The Ministry of Health was instructed to form committees of senior doctors to supervise hospitals weekly and conduct surprise visits to assess hospital readiness and submit reports to Delhi and state governments for necessary actions. Delhi hospitals were also directed to provide CCTV footage for continuous monitoring of patient care, and to install CCTV cameras in all COVID-19 hospitals within the city. States were also instructed to enhance COVID-19 testing efforts and not to deny testing facilities based on technicalities. The Court proposed uniform guidelines for setting reasonable rates for COVID-related facilities and tests across states with a view to standardize costs associated with COVID-19 care and testing, promoting equitable access to healthcare services throughout the country.

SUMMARY

This chapter has discussed with the help of illustrative cases how Indian judiciary has played a role in giving life to the oftentimes dormant letter of law. However, the cases referenced above are only illustrative and not exhaustive. In fact, in many more cases judiciary has closely examined issues covering a plethora of social, economic, environmental and gender dimensions and their impact on the rightful enjoyment of the constitutionally ordained twin rights of life and health.

The contribution of the higher judiciary in propelling the right to health to the centre of law and policy agenda through a conjoint reading with the right to life has been remarkable. Through landmark decisions pertaining to diverse allied facets of health, the judiciary has consistently interpreted these rights expansively. Such progressive rulings have often had the effect of compelling the state to provide enforce existing laws and also on occasions enact new

18. Suo Motu Writ Petition (C) NO. 1/2020.

legislations to provide accessible and adequate healthcare services to all citizens. Additionally, a proactive and sensitive judiciary has also acted as a check on executive and legislative actions that could jeopardize these rights. Through its interventions, the courts have reviewed and called into question laws and policies that infringe upon the right to life and health and have deleterious consequences particularly for the poor and the marginalised.

However, despite this, significant challenges persist. The implementation of court rulings remains uneven. This is even more stark in rural and marginalized communities where access and affordability issues continue to persist. Judicial pronouncements establish legal principles, however, translating these into practical improvements in healthcare delivery encounters numerous hurdles with shortages of facilities, medical personnel, and essential supplies particularly in remote and underserved areas. Economic and social disparities further complicate the realization of these rights. The poor and marginalized communities, already burdened by poverty and limited access to education, bear the brunt of ineffective policies and resource allocation. They continue to incur high out-of-pocket expenses for healthcare pushing them further into poverty. Moreover, the judiciary's intervention although significant is not without limitations. An overburdened judiciary, backlogs and consequent delays in adjudication can hinder timely justice and enforcement of healthcare rights particularly when it endeavours to address broader social and systemic rights. Addressing the root of such issues such as strengthening judicial capacity, enhancing access to justice, and collaboration between judicial, executive, and civil society stakeholders can help remedy some of the issues outlined and bridge the gap between judicial pronouncements and practical improvements in healthcare access and quality for all citizens.

QUESTIONS FOR PART II

Q.1 Which provisions in the Indian Constitution address health as a fundamental concern?

Q.2 How do the Directive Principles of State Policy (DPSP) emphasize health and well-being?

Q.3 Explain the connection between Article 21 (Right to Life) and the concept of health in India.

Q.4 Analyse key judicial pronouncements that have interpreted the right to health under Article 21.

Q.5 How has the judiciary addressed the intersection of health and social justice in India?

Q.6 Discuss the role of Public Interest Litigations (PILs) in ensuring access to healthcare.

PART III

Health Policy in India

CHAPTER

6

Public Health Policy

INTRODUCTION

Public policy in general is described as the ensemble of laws, decisions, and activities taken by governments and other institutions with an eye towards solving problems or issues within society. As an activity it involves designing, implementing, and evaluating policies as well as resource allocation, and distribution, and the regulation of public life. This may comprise a broad range of social policies that have quite close interlinkages among domains of economic, social and environmental, and health policy.

Health policy, within this context, focuses on strategies and interventions which aim at improving health outcomes for the population as a whole as well as its various demographic segments such as women, children, elderly and specially-abled just to name a few. Such policy initiatives or orientations may include improving healthcare delivery systems, implementing effective public health initiatives and studying and considering social determinants of health such as education, housing, and income disparity.

Formulating effective public health policies and ensuring their implementation is extremely crucial to secure public health. A good public health policy and governance system can contribute much to the prevention and control of diseases, protection of vulnerable groups from potential threats, promotion of healthy environments, and ensuring equity in distributing health resources. Systematic and holistic design characterizes public health policy making. It integrates legislation, regulation, and voluntary practices. The ultimate object of such an exercise is to promote overall population health improvements and support sustainable health outcomes where healthy choices are encouraged and are accessible to all.

Constitutional provisions, legislation, and other regulatory frameworks form the backbone of public health policy. They provide the legal basis that shapes as well as supports decision-making processes and governance structures. Laws provide the legal framework within which health policies are conceived, implemented, and enforced. Constitutional provisions for example may establish fundamental rights related to health which mandate the government to frame laws and formulate policies with an aim to guarantee provisioning and access to healthcare services. This is insured by a legal and policy framework that secures uniformity, accountability and respect for established norms and rights in the provision of healthcare and public health management. Moreover, it is the health policy that operationalizes the legal mandate into feasible, operational measures with direct bearings on the health of the public. The policies, based on laws and constitutional provisions, have well-defined objectives and strategies to achieve health-related goals. Such policies define not only the scope and implementation of healthcare services but also the roadmap towards their achievement on the ground.

Policy formulation is closely linked to policy research, it plays a crucial role in shaping effective public health policies by providing insights into the many variables of public health such as demographic trends, health disparities, social determinants etc. This analysis needs to be based on evidence. This would, then adequately inform the formulation of policies, their implementation, and review and ensure that decisions are based on data relevant to meet the diverse needs of various populations. Notably, frequent policy review and reformulation in the light of research can enable public health systems to respond effectively to emerging health needs and optimize community outcomes.

Public health policies materialize through various programs and services that are developed and carried out at the community level to address certain health needs within their respective jurisdictions. The activities in this category range from vaccination programs to health education campaigns, and other specific policies at the local level. These programs help improve the general health status and well-being among residents by way of specific interventions and easily accessible services. It requires, therefore, the collaboration of various stakeholders at the local, state, and federal levels including community, policymakers, legislators, and healthcare providers who work in collaboration to establish and implement policies that respond to these diversified needs and priorities of their respective populations.

6.1 CONSTITUENTS OF HEALTH POLICY

Health policy, as a subject is multifaceted. It comprises a number of elements which work together to shape and guide public health and healthcare systems. They comprise policy objectives and goals that set directions and targets for improvements in health. These constituents ensure that health policies are well designed and contain effective implementation strategies to achieve the intended health outcome. These constituents can be discussed in detail as follows:

- **Policy Objectives and Goals:** Policy objectives and goals refer to the outcome and results health policies seek to achieve. They are broad in nature and, therefore, offer directions and general guidelines for health policymaking. They can embrace a variety of aims such as a reduction in the incidence of certain diseases, improving access to healthcare services, or promotion of health equity among different population groups. For health policies to be effective and executable, the objectives need to be broken down into specific actionable targets, clearly set out and aligned with the national and regional health priorities. This allows policy measures to deal properly with the most important health problems of people. In general, the formulation of objectives should follow the SMART criteria: Specific, Measurable, Achievable, Relevant, and Time-bound. For instance, where there is a general aim of "improving public health," a SMART objective will be "achieve a 20% reduction in Type 2 diabetes by five years in adults through targeted public health campaigns and increased access to preventive care." This specific nature gives one the opportunity to plan, execute, and then determine the impact of the policy in an effective manner.

- **Policy Framework and Structure:** The policy framework and structure detail the organizational setup and processes for the formulation, implementation, and evaluation involved in health policy. It also explains the roles, duties, and relationships between the different entities involved in policy making. Broadly at the apex of such a structure are ministries and departments followed by special legislatives and regulatory bodies. These agencies are liable for drafting, reviewing, and approving policies. The framework also offers guidance on stakeholder engagement, which consults healthcare providers, patients, community organizations, and others to assure that varied perspectives and needs are taken into consideration in the process. The policy structure should also stipulate procedures for the drafting and approval of policies for transparency and accountability in the entire process of policy development. Effective frameworks ensure good coordination of policies and congruence with broader health system goals.
- **Policy Instruments and Tools:** Policy instruments and tools are specific means and mechanisms to implement health policies. These instruments translate policy objectives into action points that are very vital in the achievement of desired results in health. The common types of policy instruments are regulations, legal requirements and standards enforced by law. Regulations enable compliance and enforcement and stipulate mandatory requirements for conduct of behaviour and practices. In addition to regulations and laws, guidelines too offer evidence-based recommendations of best practices to be followed. Guidelines have a major role in standardizing care and ensuring that different healthcare professionals apply tried or proven methods to healthcare challenges. For instance, clinical practice guidelines on hypertension management would provide general guidance on how such patients should be treated based on the latest research. Incentives are another set of tools built in policy initiatives. These are rewards given to individuals to carry out certain behaviours or achieve some results. They may be financial in nature, such as subsidies for preventive health services or tax credits for a healthy lifestyle, or non-financial, like public recognition given to organizations or entities for meeting specific quality benchmarks in healthcare. Similarly funding programs envisage sources of funds for health activities and services. Funding programs may include grants for research, subsidies for reduced health insurance for the poor, or funds for community health projects.
- **Policy Development:** A policy development process refers to a sequence of activities that a health policy goes through from the early research work to the final approval and adoption. The process typically commences with research and cumulation and processing of data and evidence. From the information received, effective policies are drafted, keeping in view the current needs and best practices. This is followed by stakeholder engagement, comprising consultation with varied groups such as healthcare providers, patients, community leaders, etc., in order to get input or build consensus. This step ensures that policies are inclusive and take into consideration the needs and views of those concerned. Drafting involves writing a clear policy document, outlining objectives, strategies, and plans on how to implement them. After the policy has been

drafted, it undergoes approval and adoption, whereby it is reviewed and approved by the relevant legislative or governing bodies. This formal process gives the policy legal and institutional recognition.

- **Implementation and Execution:** The implementation and execution involve the actual steps to put a policy into action in a tangible way through particular programs, services, and procedures This step involves effective operationalization or making available the required fiscal, human, and infrastructural resources. It involves developing and launching certain programs or services that have clear links with the objectives of the policy. For instance, a policy aimed at raising vaccination rates could include provisions for community vaccination clinics and education campaigns. Coordination is indeed an important element that has to be there to ensure the policy is integrated into current systems without any glitches and that the various stakeholders in the process work in harmony. This may demand collaboration at all levels between the government, NGOs, and local communities to have it completely and cohesively implemented.
- **Monitoring and Evaluation:** Monitoring and evaluation involve the assessment of the effectiveness of health policy towards its objectives, as well as the making of necessary adjustments to have such a course met. Monitoring is the initial process in data collection, providing information on policy outcomes, indicators of performance, and process efficiency. Such data is used to assess whether or not the policy achieves its goals. Monitoring and evaluation involve an analysis of this data to establish the extent of success and point out certain shortcomings that require improvements. This may include evaluation of health outcomes, performance of programs, or compliance with laws and regulations. Feedback and adjustment are important for continuous improvement. Policies will, therefore, be adjusted or fine-tuned based on evaluation findings in a manner that makes them more effective and averts any new issues or problems that have cropped up.
- **Communication and Advocacy:** Communication and advocacy involve the process of disseminating information and engaging members of the public and stakeholders on health policies and their intended benefits to ensure its wide acceptance and effective implementation. Public awareness campaigns are organized with the aim of sensitizing members of the public about new policies or change in policy and health intervention and benefits. These campaigns may also involve information diffusion through different media, outreach in the community, and distribution of educational materials targeting different audiences. Stakeholder engagement is systematic communication with major stakeholders in terms of keeping them informed, managing concerns, and building support for the policy, sustained over the course of policy action. This would, in turn, assure that the stakeholders are committed and remain engaged throughout the entire lifecycle of the policy. Advocacy efforts are activities like lobbying or teaming with associated groups to gain wider support. Effective advocacy can drive quicker policy adoption and effective implementation to ensure adequate backing for the successful operation of health policies.

SUMMARY

Health policy is a dynamic and complex field that deals with shaping and improving public health through a coordinated approach. Its core components—policy objectives and goals, framework and structure, instruments and tools, development process, implementation and execution, monitoring and evaluation, and communication and advocacy—work in concert to ensure that policies are well-conceived, effectively executed, and responsive to diverse health needs. Policy objectives provide clear, measurable targets for health improvements, while the framework and structure outline the organizational setup and processes required for policy development and implementation. Policy instruments, including regulations, guidelines, and incentives, translate these objectives into actionable measures that drive tangible health outcomes.

The development process involves evidence gathering, stakeholder consultation, and policy drafting, ensuring that policies are based on solid data and community needs. Implementation requires resource allocation, program development, and stakeholder coordination to translate policies into practice. Monitoring and evaluation assess the effectiveness of policies and facilitate necessary adjustments, ensuring continuous improvement. Effective communication and advocacy are vital for informing and engaging the public and stakeholders, garnering support, and facilitating successful policy adoption. Collectively, these components form a comprehensive framework that addresses health challenges, promotes equity, and fosters sustainable improvements in population health. Through systematic and evidence-based strategies, health policies can drive meaningful progress and significantly enhance community well-being. These constituents need to act in sync to deliver a comprehensive health policies aimed at engaging and addressing complex health challenges by promoting health equity and supporting sustainable improvements in population health. Systematic and evidence-based health policies can drive meaningful progress and enhance well-being for communities.

CHAPTER

7 Social Determinants of Health

INTRODUCTION

Social Determinants of Health refers to a wide range of social, economic, and environmental factors that have a key bearing on the health outcome of individuals and populations. It refers to the totality of structural determinants and conditions in which we live our lives. These determinants are important indicators of health disparities and health quality. It is therefore crucial to address and incorporate them while designing policies related to public health. Understanding the factors that influence health beyond a clinical setting helps implement actions aimed at decreasing health inequity and generally improving public health.

WHO defines social determinants of health as those non-medical factors that influence health outcomes. They are the conditions in which people are born, grow, work, live, and age, and the wider set of forces and systems shaping the conditions of daily life. These include economic policies and systems, development agendas, social norms, social policies and political systems[1]. Social determinants of health are powerful drivers of health outcomes.

7.1 SOCIAL CONDITIONS INFLUENCING HEALTH

The social, economic, and environmental conditions in which we live our everyday lives have a shaping health status of an individual and community and an unfavourable set of social condition can create deep health inequities. Although not exhaustive WHO has also listed a few crucial social indicators which impinge on individual and community health outcomes. They can be analysed as follows:

Income and Social Protection

Income and social protection are central to health equity, particularly because they form the very basis for the very accessing all other services and opportunities including health. Higher income is closely associated with better health outcomes. This makes sense because when

1. See, https://www.who.int/health-topics/social-determinants-of-health#tab=tab_1.

people have more resources, they can afford good healthcare, decent food, and a safe place to live, each of which will significantly contribute to being healthy and well. Lower incomes, on the other hand, reduce access to these very important resources and thereby result in poor health. Indeed, people from low-income categories often have to bear inadequate housing, insufficient healthcare, and lack of proper nutrition, all factors detrimental to their health.

The negative impact of low income can be reduced through appropriate social protection mechanisms, such as social safety nets, insurance and other welfare programs. These programs therefore help cushion the risk of economic hardship by giving financial support or facilitating access to essential services. In that sense, social safety nets can be represented by unemployment benefits, housing assistance, and other means of financial support that allow a person and his family to enjoy at least a minimum standard of living. This can be instrumental in minimizing health disparities since even the poorest can get access to essential health services and health-related resources.

However, health inequities often persist due to the disparities in income and social protection. Lower socio-economic positions are more likely to bear poor health outcomes since they have lesser number of resources as well as less accessibility to health services. It is also clear how much these health inequities are reinforced by the lack of adequate income and efficient social protection, trapping people into a cycle of disadvantage and poor health. Policies and interventions can reduce income inequality and extend social protection to ensure that everybody has fair access to resources and services necessary for good health.

Education

Educational level is a key determining factor in ensuring health equity. Attaining high levels of education is positively correlated with positive health outcomes. Generally, people with higher levels of education do enjoy good health because they have the capability of understanding health information and apply it effectively. Relatively speaking they are also more likely to make informed choices and understand the result of their actions. This knowledge enables them to engage in safer health practice and make sound decisions about their well-being.

Education also affects other major determinants of health, such as work and income. Higher education most often results in better employment and income, providing higher access to healthcare, good living conditions, and healthier food. On the other side, less educated people may be exposed to insufficient job opportunities with low wages, and thus have a reduced capacity to afford and acquire necessary health resources. This in fact perpetuates a recurring cycle by which lower education levels is the cause of inferior health, and poor health leads to reduced educational and economic opportunities. This cycle can only be broken if universal access to quality education is ensured. Societies can reduce health inequalities by improving health outcomes if they can reduce educational disparities and increase access to education in all. This perspective adopts a health lens founded upon the recognition that education has direct effects on individual health but also interacts with the other determinants of health, highlighting the need for educational equity and its evident role in the advancement of health and well-being.

Unemployment and Job Insecurity

Unemployment and job insecurity play a significant role in determining an individual's health outcomes. Secure employment provides not only a stable financial foundation but also access to health benefits, such as health insurance, which are crucial for maintaining and improving health. The financial stability that comes with secure employment allows individuals to afford necessary healthcare services, nutritious food, and safe housing—key factors that contribute to better health. In contrast, unemployment and job insecurity can have detrimental effects on health. Financial hardships resulting from job loss or insecurity often lead to reduced access to essential healthcare services and can exacerbate existing health conditions. The stress and uncertainty associated with unemployment or unstable employment contribute significantly to mental health issues, such as anxiety and depression. This stress, combined with the financial strain, can deteriorate overall health and diminish quality of life.

Furthermore, the lack of job security can create a persistent state of worry and stress, which negatively impacts both physical and mental health. Chronic stress from job insecurity can lead to a range of health problems, including cardiovascular diseases and weakened immune function. The psychological impact of unemployment and job insecurity often results in reduced social participation and a diminished sense of purpose, further affecting well-being.

Addressing unemployment and job insecurity is therefore essential for reducing health inequalities and promoting health equity. By ensuring stable employment and job security, societies can help mitigate the adverse effects on health, improve access to healthcare, and enhance overall quality of life. Tackling these issues is crucial for achieving broader health equality and improving health outcomes for all individuals.

Working Life Conditions

The conditions at the workplace have a very great effect on the health condition of the employee. A safe, properly managed workplace that is supportive in terms of policies promotes both physical and mental health. At a safe workplace, employees are less prone to injuries and risks to health due to unsafe working conditions. Moreover, a supportive work environment would lessen stress levels and increase job satisfaction, thus enhancing mental health.

On the other hand, poor working conditions lead to adverse health effects. Hazardous materials and chemicals, faulty equipment, and poor safety measures will lead to physical harm, long-term health problems, and even death. It also comprises mental health problems caused due to high levels of job-related stress, mainly from job insecurity, heavy workload, lack of support, and many more. Continual mental stress has been related to a range of health problems, which include cardiovascular diseases, anxiety disorders, and depression.

Women and children often encounter far worse and less fair working conditions and environments than men. This is usually manifested in a number of ways, such as lower wages, less secure employment, and more dangerous working conditions. Women may additionally be exposed to discriminatory practices that stifle their chances at getting better-paid and safer jobs, thereby leaving them in work with poorer conditions and less protection. This inequity begets further physical and mental health problems and can also perpetuate economic disparities.

Children are also often employed in hazardous and labour-intensive industries due to chronic poverty, run a very serious risk. They are more prone to exploitation since they lack any bargaining power and legal protection. Work conditions for children are frequently perilous and unhealthy, putting them at heightened risks and ruining development and education. This exploitation not only harms their immediate health but has long-term consequences for their future opportunities and well-being.

Improving working conditions and workers' rights can thus effectively contribute to health equity. A safe working environment and sufficient support at work promote overall health of workers. This involves efficient measures for the enforcement of safety provisions, mental health protection, and wage security.

Food Security

Food security fundamentally revolves around access to adequate, safe, and nutritious food which will sustain healthy active living. It is a critical aspect of health and well-being, for it offers an individual the chance to consume adequate and wholesome food for good health. In its absence, malnutrition may set in and cause serious and potentially lifelong damage to health. Malnutrition can further lead to a long list of other secondary health issues, including stunted growth in children, weakened immune systems, and vulnerability to a variety of chronic diseases, such as diabetes and heart conditions.

Nutritionists have stressed upon the strong link existing between food insecurity and socio-economic factors, especially poverty and joblessness. When people live in poverty or without jobs, they cannot afford or access sufficient healthy food. Under these circumstances, the chance of malnutrition and its associated health complications becomes very high, resulting in a cycle of poor health and economic disadvantage. Therefore, the same socio-economic disparities that cause food insecurity are intensified, hence a priority in health equity efforts.

Food security entails more than just availability; it also means the availability of nutritious food at reasonable prices to all populations. Accessibility and affordability of healthy food are major factors for good health and health equity. Evidence suggests comprehensive interventions to improve availability of food and remove economic barriers are warranted. In other words, policies and programs that will improve food security have an important bearing on public health. For example, subsidized healthy food programs, local agriculture promotion, and food distribution systems can all improve the reduction in prevalence of nutritional deficiencies and associated disease burdens.

Reduction of food insecurity also leads to a corresponding lowering of mortality rates by reducing diseases resulting from a lack of proper nutrition. In laying the foundation for public health policy, addressing the root causes of food insecurity and ensuring that people have access to food that will support active health can improve societies' health outcomes and reduce health disparities. Food security is an intrinsic part of public health policy and one of the leading promoters of health equity. All people deserve access to adequate, safe, and nutritious food—integral components of better health for all and health equity..

Housing, Basic Amenities and the Environment

Adequate housing conditions, basic amenities, and a healthy environment are major determinants of health. They influence a wide array of divergent physical and mental health outcomes. Proper housing provides a stable and safe living environment essential for physical health and mental well-being. Poor living conditions on the other hand engender a host of health problems such issues include overcrowding and lack of proper sanitation. For example, overcrowding can easily contribute to infectious diseases such as respiratory infections and tuberculosis by raising the level of exposure to the pathogen with individuals in close proximity. Poor general sanitation and waste management lead to gastrointestinal diseases and many other conditions associated with contaminated water and unsanitary living conditions.

Moreover, housing quality and basic amenities have farther-reaching effects that extend into the mental health domains. Poor housing conditions can contribute to chronic stress, which is an established risk factor for a wide range of mental health disorders. Poor and cramped housing conditions may deepen feelings of anxiety and depression, particularly when combined with factors like noise pollution and a lack of privacy. Such conditions are leading to deep impacts on psychological effects when living under such conditions, hence affecting the quality of life, therefore leading to social inequalities.

Of these, environmental conditions are particularly associated with health inequities. The inhalation of air pollutants, mainly particulate matter and gases, is known to be injurious to health; the most common health effects are respiratory illnesses, such as asthma and chronic obstructive pulmonary disease. Similarly, contaminated water can range from acute illness caused by diarrheal diseases to long-term effects including cancer, depending on the nature of the contaminant. The harmful effects of environmental pollution are mostly felt in marginalized communities because they reside in parts of the city that are more prone to pollution due to socio-economic factors.

A safe, decent, and clean environment is significant in health equity. Good housing conditions, access to basic amenities, and a pure environment are important for health equity. Ensuring that everyone has safe and adequate housing aids in preventing the spread of diseases and mental health issues. Basic facilities, such as access to clean drinking water, proper sanitation, and adequate waste management systems, would prevent much of the health fallout from environmental contamination. Indeed, any policies or programs that improve environmental quality reducing pollution, increasing green space, and so forth generally tend to create more healthful circumstances for all concerned.

Early Childhood Development

Early childhood Development is fundamentally important in the shaping health outcomes across the life course. The early years are a very critical period of rapid physical, cognitive, and socio-emotional growth. Supportive conditions during this formative phase form the backbone for better health and educational outcomes that are sustain throughout one's life. This includes ensuring proper nutrition, providing nurturing care, and creating enriching environments. Such supportive conditions allow children to grow older with better educational and health outcomes . At the same time, adverse circumstances in childhood occasioned by neglect, abuse, or poor living conditions lead to severe or even long-lasting effects on health. The normal brain development may be altered which can result in children being susceptible to physical and mental health disorders. For example, chronic stress from neglect or poor care can lead to developmental delays and behaviour problems with lifelong physical health consequences, such as obesity and chronic diseases. Moreover, adverse early experiences can set cycles of disadvantage that pave the way for inequities in health, thereby limiting opportunities later in life.

Effective programs in early childhood development play a critical role in helping address these issues and achieving long-term health equity. Most often, such programs include high-quality early education for better cognitive development and preparation for schooling. The nutrition supplement measures assure that the child gets the necessary nutrients for proper growth. Parental support and education ensure that, children grow up in nurturing home environments. Good healthcare services, such as regular screenings, check-ups and vaccination programs, play a vital role in preventing or detecting health problems at an early stage. Moreover, mental health and emotional support in development help to offset the impact of negative experiences, enhance a person's resilience to them, and foster positive growth.

The bottom line is that the quality of early childhood development is an extremely strong determinant of health outcomes throughout the course of life. Early childhood environments that are enabling set the course for better health and achievement in education. On the contrary, poor or adverse experiences expose one to health inequities, which may sometimes cascade down the generations. In a nutshell, investments made in comprehensive early childhood development programs are very important in promoting health equity so that all children could have an opportunity to thrive.

Social Inclusion and Non-Discrimination

The achievement of health equity dependents greatly on inclusion and non-discrimination because these address systemic barriers hindering access to health resources and opportunities. Discrimination, often based on race, gender, or socio-economic status, worsens health inequities by further limiting access of health resources to some sections. For instance, discrimination may cause psychological stress, lower self-esteem, and other mental health problems, all of which can contribute negatively to physical health. Moreover, it can also impose practical barrier and reduced access to quality healthcare services thereby fuelling health inequalities further.

Systemic discrimination is present at all levels and affects both individuals and the broader health systems. One consequence of such discrimination might be poor access to appropriate and timely care, which may subsequently complicate further deterioration of health conditions that otherwise could have been controlled or regulated with better access to care. Discriminatory practices can also leave a systemic legacy that perpetuates poor health across generations due to inequitable access to health resources and opportunities.

Social inclusion refers to the process of addressing these inequities by ensuring that all, regardless of background, have equal access to resources and services. It consists of dismantling barriers to participation and opening equal opportunities for all. It signifies making healthcare accessible and equal for all and serving those who have been historically left out. The object of social inclusion is to provide a level playing field so that everyone in society has a fair chance to quality healthcare, decent housing, food, and education.

There are a number of advantages that go with social inclusion. It improves access to resources by ensuring that everybody gets to access services that keep them healthy. It creates equality in health outcome as it decreases disparities between the various socio-economic segments in the society. For example, culturally competent healthcare provision tends to improve the outcome for diverse populations since their needs and preferences are put into consideration. Besides, social inclusion empowers the marginalized group because it provides a feeling of belonging and engagement that motivates them to take part in health-enhancing activities and seek medical care when need be.

Strategies and interventions that uphold social equity through combating discrimination need to be intentionally designed. Protective laws and policies are responsible for preventing acts meant to discriminate against any person in health, employment, and education. Sensitization of healthcare providers assures that care provided is appropriate to the needs and sensibilities of diverse backgrounds. Participation of marginalized communities in terms of their specific needs and challenges is what informs the development of inclusive health programs and services. This would be possible through monitoring and evaluation of the health disparities and the strategies of inclusion in terms of their effectiveness to identify any gaps and make improvements where necessary.

Structural Conflict

Structural conflicts, such as political instability and systemic inequality, profoundly impact health outcomes and contribute significantly to health inequities and have been recognized as one of the social determinants of health. This includes structural conflicts such as political instability and systemic inequality which impacts health in really very profound ways and is actually responsible for large amounts of health inequity. In many instances, political instability jeopardizes crucial services like health and education, which significantly diminishes the potential and possibilities for people to acquire the resources necessary for them to be healthy. In many places where there have been conflicts, infrastructure in health is greatly damaged or destroyed, and health professionals who could offer these services are either displaced or cannot perform their duties effectively. This further deteriorates the availability and quality of health services, thus fostering health inequalities within the affected populations.

This is then systemically exacerbated by the prevailing inequality that creates and entrenches barriers to getting access to these health services. Consequently, poor health is disproportionately borne by marginalized communities. These disparities have been fanned by discriminatory policies, unequal economic opportunities, and low social protection. If anything, in both political instability and systemic inequality together induce a multiplier effect that stands in the way of promoting health equity, therefore creating a challenge towards better health outcomes for all. Political stability, good governance and conflict reduction can thus go a long way in dismantling the structural barriers.

Access to Affordable Health Services of Decent Quality

Access to affordable and quality healthcare is itself one of the social determinants of health listed by the WHO. It implies that people need to have equal opportunity to avail quality and affordable healthcare. When care is affordable, there will be less delay or refusal to avail treatment just because of the prohibitive cost. This is particularly relevant for preventive care, which in the long-term can prevent severe health issues from developing. High-quality care gives surety of most treatments being evidence-based, safe, and effective. The importance of affordable and quality healthcare extends beyond individual's health. It has a broader impact on public health social equity. When people can afford the requisite care without any financial hardship, they are better equipped to keep their chronic conditions under control and recover from illness or injury, and thus enjoy better health. The burden on the entire healthcare system is, in turn, lessened by reduced need for emergency care and hospitalization. Additionally, affordable healthcare lowers the treatment gaps between socio-economic groups, something that has grown mostly due to differential accessibility to healthcare. A more inclusive and just pathway to healthcare would be one in which everyone receives equal opportunities for obtaining quality medical services, regardless of their financial situation. It would require commitments on improving healthcare policies, cutting costs, and improving the quality of healthcare provided to all communities. This includes systemic issues such as insurance coverage gaps, inadequate healthcare infrastructure, and poor care quality that is associated with either geographic or socio-economic status.

SUMMARY

Social determinants of health are a crucial component of the overall health ecosystem. These determinants are non-medical factors that have an equally and in many cases a more profound impact on health outcomes and can induce health inequity. They encompass a broad range of conditions that influence the capacity of a person to lead a healthy life, including economic stability, education, social and community context, access to healthcare, and living environment.

It's important to appreciate that social determinants of health, economic stability, education, social support, healthcare access, and environment etc. are not independent or working in isolation. They are rather closely intertwined and interrelated. This would also mean that changes or disparities in any one of these determinants would impact another, hence having compounding effects on overall health outcomes. This further implies that no single determinant can be taken and worked upon in isolation with the rest, if inequalities are to be eliminated. What is required is an integrated approach that takes into consideration the multifaceted interactions between economic stability, education, social support, access to healthcare, and environment etc. It is through understanding and acting on these interrelated determinants that a more just and healthy society can be achieved.

CHAPTER

8 Health Policy in India

INTRODUCTION

India's diverse demography and social determinants create a complex landscape. The interplay of these manifold social and demographic determinants in India point to a pressing need for appropriate health policy interventions. It may be said without any exaggeration that of all countries, India is possibly the most varied in its landscape, a complex its mosaic of social, economic, and cultural factor each of which influences health outcomes in distinct ways. Education, income, employment, and living conditions vary immensely along with immense regional diversity

Demographic diversity in India adds to this complexity. The country has a wide array of ethnic groups, languages, and cultural practices, each with its characteristic health needs and practices. For example, nutritional practices differ a lot across different areas, thereby affecting the malnutrition or obesity rates as either high or low in the region. Secondly, distribution of health resources is not even since facilities in urban regions are relatively well compared to those in the rural areas. As such, healthcare policies need to be flexible to the local level and address the geographical issues in different communities.

8.1 ISSUES INFLUENCING HEALTH POLICY

- **Urban-Rural Divide:** Another critical factor in the health policy is the urban-rural divide. Infrastructure and healthcare facilities are relatively better in urban areas, but urbanization also ushered in problems like overcrowding and pollution, which fast-tracked chronic health problems such as respiratory diseases. This is contrasted by the rural areas, often contending with limitations to access healthcare facilities, medical personnel, and health infrastructure. It is therefore incumbent on health policies to bridge this gap by enhancing healthcare delivery in relatively unserved rural areas while attending to the peculiar health challenges of urban populations.
- **Socio-economic Inequality:** Thirdly, there is also a need for targeted health policies to address socio-economic inequalities. Income and wealth disparity leads to differences

in access to and quality of healthcare. For example, poor people may not access health services, preventive measures, and access to medications. This causes increased burden of disease among the poorer segments of society. Health policies should be directed at reducing these gaps through measures aimed at improving access to affordable healthcare services and health cover while ensuring health services are equitable and inclusive.

- **Cultural and Linguistic Barriers:** Cultural and linguistic diversity also challenges the formulation of health policy. People might not get access to health information and services due to the language barrier, mainly if there are several languages spoken in the area. Some cultural beliefs and practices also influence the health behaviours of individuals and attitude towards medical treatments. For this reason, policies should embed culturally sensitive approaches and health information available in different languages in order to reach and engage diverse populations effectively. In summary, the setting of such a complex health landscape within India has been particularly perturbing to various social and demographic variables. In an open framework, engaging with these challenges would, at the very least, require an approach that takes into consideration educational, economic, regional, and cultural variables. Health policies should, therefore, be designed in ways that would bridge gaps in healthcare accessibility, rise up to the challenges of inequalities in the socio-economic parameters, and answer the diverse needs of different communities. This will help in working towards greater health achievement and healthcare equity for a very heterogeneous population like India.

8.2 EVOLUTION OF HEALTH POLICY IN INDIA

Health policy in India has undergone significant evolution in the decades after Independence. The first systematic effort in formulating was done in 1943 in the Health Survey and Development Committee Report, popularly known as Bhore Committee report[1], suggested a blueprint for National Health Service with Universal and Free Healthcare coverage through an integrated and comprehensive state managed system. Such a well-documented and argued plan for health services has not been matched in Independent India. The Bhore Committee's recommendations envisaged considerable structural changes in the existing system to provide for adequate and active promotion of general health, in conjunction with curative and preventive medical care. Key recommendations of the committee can be listed as follows:

- **Primary Healthcare:** The need for an integrated system of primary healthcare was emphasized, and the committee recommended a three-tier system—care primary, secondary, and tertiary—that would provide universal coverage.
- **Health Infrastructure:** The committee recommended to create a well-organized health infrastructure comprising definite roles for different tiers, along with a network of rural health centres and community health services, district, and regional hospitals.

1. https://nihfw.ac.in/Doc/Reports/bhore%20Committee%20Report%20VOL-1%20.pdf

- **Public Health, Preventative Care:** The committee looked at possible ways of employing public health and preventive care. The emphasis was on health promotion through preventive measures and health education to enhance the health of the community, which will therefore reduce diseases.
- **Medical Education and Training:** The committee also recommended opening more medical colleges and training facilities to further expand the breadth of medical education and training. It also recommended better training of medical practitioners and health workers.
- **Integration of Health Services:** Integration of health services with other sectors, such as agriculture, education, and sanitation, was recommended to address the broader determinants of health.
- **Community Participation:** The Bhore Committee highlighted the importance of community involvement in healthcare services, advocating for the establishment of local health committees to ensure that health services were tailored to the needs of the community.

8.3 EARLY HEALTH INITIATIVES AND THE FOCUS ON EPIDEMIC CONTROL

In post-independence India, until the formal adoption of a National Health Policy, in 1983, India's health efforts governed primarily by Five-Year Plans and recommendations by several committees. In the early years particularly during the initial decades post-independence, emphasis was placed on management and control of epidemics through mass campaigns. The campaigns targeted diseases of immediate public health importance at that time, namely, malaria, smallpox, tuberculosis, and leprosy. To a great extent, this approach was saddled by past colonial-era practices and the dominant belief in modern medicine that public health can be improved by the elimination of pathogens. This strategy overlooks the wider social conditions and determinants of health such as inadequate nutrition, bad housing conditions, and environmental factors that are really the basis of preventing disease and promoting health.

The National Malaria Eradication Program (NMEP), started in 1953, was among the first efforts in controlling vector-borne diseases with large-scale international support. It was remarkable for its introduction of DDT spraying and gained technical and financial support from international agencies such as the Technical Cooperation Mission of the United States and WHO. Vertical programs like NMEP were conceived to address single diseases through vertical interventions. Although these programs showed some success in reducing the incidence of certain diseases, they were often at the cost of comprehensive improvements in the health system. For instance, rural areas continued to suffer a shortage of health resources, including medical facilities and personnel, as compared to the urban areas. This disparity in resource distribution meant that the benefits of disease control programs were not equally shared across different regions.

8.4 COMMUNITY DEVELOPMENT AND HEALTH INFRASTRUCTURE

Much greater emphasis was given to agriculture during the earlier Five-Year Plans, for it was thought to be the prime moving force for the advancement of the country and for economic stability. Among the several objectives of the Community Development Program, started during these Five-Year Plans, was the improvement of living conditions and health in rural areas. But despite the comprehensiveness of its objectives, the CDP gave more prominence to increasing agricultural productivity than to the improvement of health in rural areas. This led to a narrow health outcome view, with a little improvement in the rural health infrastructure. For instance, in terms of PHUs and hospitals, there was a huge inadequacy in comparison to urban areas. This represented a systemic oversight of rural health infrastructure and services.

In 1959, the **Mudaliar Committee** was set up to carry out an exhaustive assessment of the health system and brought out many critical deficiencies in its report. While the disease control programmes had been quite successful in bringing down the incidence of a number of epidemic diseases, it was found that basic health infrastructure was still grossly inadequate. These included measures for improving working conditions for health personnel so that more staff may be attracted and retained, increasing the number of medical professionals, etc. Even with all these recommendations, the focus was still on increasing the number of doctors rather than really developing an oversight of needs for other health personnel, in particular nurses, midwives, and community health workers. This narrow focus has continued to contribute to imbalances in the health workforce and delivery of services. The committee's findings pointed out a number of critical gaps:

- **Infrastructure and Facilities:** On an overview note, the committee observed that despite successes in controlling diseases, basic health facilities were still inadequate. Most rural areas had poor infrastructural facilities and this hindered the effective discharge of health services.
- **Health Personnel:** The committee proposed the need to improve health personnel working conditions in order to enhance attracting staff and keeping them. This included better working remunerations packages, good housing, and opportunities for advancing their careers. This would make health positions attractive and sustainable for the long term.
- **Medical Colleges Expansion:** The committee, in principle agreed to the increase in the number of doctors, but there should not be a compromise on the availability of other necessary health personnel. An isolated expansion of medical colleges has resulted in imbalances in health service delivery.
- **Training and deployment:** The recommendations included the need to improve the training of health personnel and their deployment to underserved areas. On the other hand, it has also been emphasized that balanced distribution of health professionals between urban and rural areas was necessary.

Among others, the recommendations by the committee also included the improvement of working conditions for health personnel to attract and retain staff, increasing the number of medical professionals. The focus, however, remained mainly on the increase in the number of doctors instead of heeding the needs on other health personnel like nurses, midwives, community health workers, etc. This contributed to an ongoing imbalance in both the health workforce and the delivery of services.

The Third Five-Year Plan (1961-66) first recognized serious deficiencies in rural healthcare, such as the shortage of doctors and the very poor coverage of health services in rural areas. Training medical assistants was, therefore, suggested as a remedial measure to the shortage of doctors. The idea behind this plan was to come up with an early, realistic solution for the dearth of medical personnel in deprived areas. This proposal had no effect on the plan, which went on emphasizing the increase in the number of medical colleges and doctors. The question of mere numbers of doctors did not pay due attention to the requirement of other categories of health personnel, like auxiliary health workers, who are an integral part of healthcare delivery.

The 1960s were certainly a watershed decade in health policy. International pressures and the perception of what appeared to be an urgent need for population control fuelled the increasing interest in family planning. This culminated in the formation of a separate department for family planning. This focus was oriented mainly by the recommendations of the **Mukherjee Committee** in 1966, where it particularly called for a vertical approach to family planning and the introduction of incentives for sterilization procedures and intrauterine contraceptive device insertions. These measures were adopted in order to enhance the acceptability of family planning methods. This emphasis was further pursued in the Fourth Five-Year Plan of 1969, with added directions that not only continued to set family planning apart from other health services but also distinctly separated water supply and sanitation from healthcare, in keeping with a more sectorized view of health policy.

Kartar Singh Committee established in 1973 identified that there was a need to revamp the health workforce which existed at that time to tackle rural health problems. The committee suggested converting uni-purpose workers, like auxiliary nurses, midwives, into multi-purpose workers. The aim was to reorient these workers to provide more comprehensive services and eventually integrate various vertical health programs that were often fragmented and inefficient in their operations into an integrated primary healthcare system. This reorientation of services was expected to bring about a more cohesive and easily accessible rural healthcare system where health services were poorly developed and under-resourced. Several reforms in the sphere of rural health services were recommended by the Kartar Singh Committee:

- **Multi-purpose Workers:** The committee recommended the conversion of uni-purpose workers like ANMs to multi-purpose workers. This entailed retraining of staff for a larger content of services and integrating the different vertical health programs into an integrated primary healthcare system.
- **Integration of Services:** This was based on the fact that health services were fragmented with the objective of setting up a more integrated and functional rural health system. It focused on enhancing the efficiency of health service delivery at the rural level.
- **Resource Allocation:** Better allocation of resources was recommended in order to achieve adequate support of rural health services and to manage them more efficiently.

Kartar Singh Committee was followed up by the Shrivastava Committee, 1975. It was set up in 1975 by the Government of India under the chairmanship of Dr. S.R. Shrivastava. It had the mandate to evaluate the medical education system in India and also recommend improvements in the health services infrastructure. These were meant to fill up the gaps in medical education and health services and promote primary healthcare as the basic unit of the health system. Some salient Recommendations of the Shrivastava Committee can be listed as follows:

- **Emphasis on Primary Healthcare:** The committee emphasised that PHC should be strengthened as the foundation of the Indian health system. It recommended that PHC should be accessible, affordable and provided at the community level.

  The committee's recommendation was to establish Primary Health Centres and Sub-Centres to deliver primary health services, preventive care, and health education for rural and underserved populations.
- **Integration of Medical Education with Primary Healthcare:** It recommended that medical schools should be closely linked to rural health centres to provide students with practical experience in community settings. This included curriculum development with community health components, and it encouraged students to work in rural areas and unserved parts as part of their training.
- **Development of a Community Health Worker Cadre:** The committee recommended the establishment of a cadre of trained community health workers to bridge the gap between formal healthcare system and the community for delivering basic health services and health education. To this end it proposed training and deployment of auxiliary nurse midwives, health assistants, and local health workers at the grassroots level for giving services.
- **Decentralization and Strengthening of the Local Health System:** The committee recommended that health services should be decentralized to local levels and that the local health system be strengthened for better delivery of services at the district and block levels.
- **Strengthening Health Infrastructure:** The committee called for improving health infrastructure, not only in regard to the building and upgrading of health facilities but also to essential medical equipment in the institutions, better transportation, and communication facilities. It recommended increasing the investments in the rural health infrastructure so that health facilities would be well equipped and accessible.
- **Improvement in Health Personnel Training:** The committee stressed on the need to reform the training and education of health personnel in keeping with the needs of primary healthcare.
- **Promotion of Preventive and Promotive Health Services:** The Committee underlined the importance of preventing and promoting health services including immunization, maternal and child health, and sanitation. It called for the strengthening of disease prevention, health promotion, and health education programs for better health generally.

The emerging health policy of India was very much influenced by the recommendations of the Shrivastava Committee. These recommendations prepared the groundwork for the first National Health Policy. These influentially emphasized the concern for primary healthcare, community health workers, and integration of medical education with primary health services in shaping India's health system reforms and currently influence health policy and practice.

8.5 FAMILY PLANNING POLICIES AND THEIR IMPACT

Within the period of National Emergency (1975-77), the Indian government launched an intensified family planning drive, which degenerated into coercive measures like compulsory sterilization. This aggressive stance was reflected in the National Population Policy, 1976, which aimed at controlling population growth through stringent measures. Such policies were very much criticized, and after the Emergency, most of these extreme steps were withdrawn. Notwithstanding the massive investment in family planning during this period, it brought out the inherent dichotomy between population control and broader health needs of the people. While family planning continued to be a large recipient of attention and resources, many other vital areas of healthcare were consequently sidetracked, thus creating an imbalanced approach to health policy.

The Fifth Five-Year Plan (1974) acknowledged that while there had been measurable improvements in major health indicators, including a reduction in infant mortality rates and a gain in life expectancy, there were wide disparities in the quality of rural health services. Indeed, addressing these gaps, the plan had to provide healthcare in rural areas, develop better referral systems, and improve the quality of training for health personnel. Some notable initiatives were the MNP, the minimum needs program that aimed at improving the basic health and social needs in rural areas, and the training of multipurpose health assistants. These attempts were made to meet the rural health needs and in order to give more equitable distribution of health resources and facilities.The Fifth Five-Year Plan (1974) also paid considerable attention to improved water supply and sanitation because these were accepted as the basics of public health. These problems were addressed, and substantial funds were allocated to solve them and provide safe drinking water to the rural areas. But the progress was very slow, and at the end of the Fifth Plan, in many areas the water and sanitation services were not adequate.

The **Sixth Five-Year Plan, 1980** was clearly influenced by the Alma Ata Declaration with its focus on "Health for All" through community-based healthcare. A few strategic shifts had been suggested in this plan, chief among them being the restructuring of health services in favour of rural health and training of community health workers. It also recommended that there should be a restriction on the expansion of urban curative facilities and instead integrate health programs horizontally and vertically to improve coordination across different health sectors. Much emphasis on preventive and promotive care in the plan marked a radical departure from the curative-centric model; it sought to create a comprehensive and more equal healthcare system that better addressed underserved populations.

8.6 NATIONAL HEALTH POLICY OF 1983

The National Health Policy 1983 was the first comprehensive policy document introduced by the Government of India to address the health needs of the Indian population and guide the country's healthcare system. It was expected to provide an integrated framework for the betterment of healthcare delivery, improvement in the quality of services, and action on the broader determinants of health. The Policy was brought against the backdrop of the Shrivastava Committee's recommendations and there was a felt need for a more structured and comprehensive approach towards healthcare in the country. This policy sought to focus attention on primary healthcare and outlined strategic objectives for dealing with preventive and curative healthcare. Better access to health services, especially in rural and under-served areas, and strengthening of general health infrastructure of the country, were the other objectives.

8.6.1 Distinctive Features of the National Health Policy of 1983

The policy reiterated the commitment to primary healthcare as the mainstay of the system, as enunciated by the Alma-Ata Declaration of 1978. It envisaged the expansion of the already existing network of PHCs and Sub-Centers, upgradation of infrastructural facilities, and making certain that the aforementioned facilities were functioning in an effective way so as to cater to the requirements of the rural and marginalized groups of people. The salient features of the policy are discussed as follows:

- **Critique of the Curative-oriented Western Model:** The 1983 health policy was critical of the curative west-centric approach to health. This model is primarily focused on interventions aimed at treating diseases after they occur which is both cost-intensive and requires advanced medical facilities. The critique stems from a recognition that this approach has often proved to be costly, inaccessible, and incapable of addressing the root causes of health issues. It suggested a more holistic perspective that takes into consideration all the broad determinants of health, including socio-economic factors and prevention of illness rather than curing it after onset.
- **Preventive, Promotive, and Rehabilitative Care:** NHP 1983 stressed on the principles of preventive, promotive, and rehabilitative dimensions of healthcare. Preventive care focuses on preventing the occurrence of disease through vaccination or health education. Promotive care ensures that people enjoy good health and promotes healthy living. Rehabilitative care enables one to recover and readjust after falling ill or getting injured. As opposed to the curative model, which responds to sickness after it has occurred, this model insists that intervention should precede the problem and ensure recovery and long-term health.
- **Decentralized System of Healthcare:** Another important principle of the 1983 policy was that of decentralization of healthcare services. This approach was set in motion in order to ensure that health services are accessible and suited to healthcare needs of the local communities by involving the people in the planning process for health interventions. This involved achieving low-cost healthcare by utilizing community-based resources and employing volunteers and paramedics instead of highly trained personnel wherever suitable. Community participation and a paramount interest in local ownership and responsiveness to health needs were impliedly meant to improve the quality-of-service delivery and sustainability.
- **Expansion of the Private Curative Sector:** The policy had provided for the expansion of the private curative sector to reduce pressure on the government. The policy allows for growth in the private sector of health services, hence providing supplementary resources and easing pressure on public health facilities. Such a strategy was meant to offer more diversified options for curative care, spur competition, and improve quality while allowing the government to focus on primary healthcare and preventative measures.
- **Demographic Targets for Achievement:** The policy also set demographic targets to serve as measures and indicators of health achievements. These were mainly based on measurable outcomes such as reductions in mortality rates, improvements in life

expectancy, or other population-based indicators. This therefore gave clear direction of progress and intended to evaluate the effectiveness of the working of the policy in bringing about tangible improvement in public health through health interventions.

After the NHP in 1983, a lot of importance was given to rural healthcare as well, and that led to developments in terms of primary healthcare facilities during. The targets were to establish PHCs subcentres to cater to the healthcare needs of the rural populations. Though, by and large, this objective has been fulfilled, deficiencies exist in the sector of rural primary healthcare. In most places, even though infrastructure is there, it is not being put to use, since there are no facilities, supplies are inadequate, inadequate effective working hours and no proper monitoring and evaluation mechanisms are in place. Moreover, the health system, heavily loaded with family planning and immunization programs, resulted in unequal distribution, thus enhancing disparities between rural and urban health services. Also, emphasis on private provision for curative care, on the other hand, really exacerbated financial burdens on the population, specifically burdening those within lower-income brackets.

8.7 NATIONAL HEALTH POLICY 2002

The NHP 2002 was brought out in India in the wake of considerable socio-economic and political changes. At the turn of the new millennium, India had adopted economic liberalization and had achieved considerable growth. However, which also brought to the fore many social inequalities including disparities in healthcare accessibility and quality. This was also accompanied by a growing population, rapid urbanization, and rising expectations of better health services, which further emphasized the need for a comprehensive review of the health policy framework. Far-reaching economic reforms in the 1990s set the economy on a high growth and modernization track. This also brought into sharp relief deep inequities in health services and laid bare the inability of the then-existing infrastructure for healthcare to meet new emerging challenges to health. Moreover, weak funding, inefficiency in service delivery, and increased burden of communicable and non-communicable diseases plagued the public health system. Pressures on health infrastructure increased and there was no coherent strategy for tackling the various health needs of the population.

The National Health Policy, 2002, of India was launched with the purpose of meeting the changing health needs of the nation and to build on the foundation laid by earlier policies. It contains features that point towards a shift towards more comprehensiveness and integration in healthcare. The salient features of NHP 2002 are as follows:

- **Integrated Health Services:** Focused on the need for a more unified healthcare system drawing on and coordinating primary, secondary, and tertiary care. NHP 2022 sought to improve coordination and quality of health services between different levels of healthcare
- **Infrastructure:** The policy noted the requirement for renovation and strengthening of existing health infrastructure, comprising hospitals and clinics, to satisfy population requirements more suitably.
- **Primary Healthcare:** The policy reaffirmed primary healthcare as the cornerstone of the health system, focused on preventive, promotive, and basic curative services. It

also proposed functional improvements in PHCs and CHCs so that they become more effective and responsive to local needs.

- **Healthcare Financing and Equity:** The policy called for increased public investments in health to improve the delivery and coverage of health services, recognizing that both the public and private sectors have a role in financing and delivering healthcare.
- **Non-Communicable and Lifestyle Diseases:** The policy also took into consideration the surge in the burden of non-communicable diseases such as cardiovascular diseases, diabetes, and cancer. It proposed strategies for prevention and management of these through lifestyle changes and improved health services.
- **Healthcare Quality and Standards:** The Policy recommended measures to enhance the quality of care in health services setting standards for care, enhancing patient safety, and better management practices in health facilities. It also proposed the establishment of mechanisms for accrediting and regulating healthcare providers and institutions for high standard cares.
- **Public Health and Prevention:** The policy focused on public health programmes to address the priorities identified to health, including Maternal and Child Health, Immunization, and Communicable Diseases. The policy targeted strengthening disease surveillance and response mechanisms.
- **Health Education:** This involved health education and raising awareness on healthy lifestyles and preventive practices among the population
- **Research and Development:** The policy emphasized that research and development was necessary to deliver good health amidst emerging health-related challenges. More support had to be given to research in various aspects of health and medicine
- **Cross-Sectoral Approach:** NHP 2002 a link between health policy and other sectors like education, environment, sanitation, and others to address the social determinants of health and promote a holistic approach towards health and well-being,

The National Health Policy 2002 was a significant initiative towards strengthening the healthcare system. It was a major step towards prioritizing primary healthcare to achieve accessibility and equity in health services. The policy envisaged reorienting focus more towards preventive and primary care from the initial heavy emphasis on curative care. It was also meant to bring in an inclusive health system that would benefit every part of the population, including the underserved and marginalized communities. There is also the advocacy for decentralization as it recommended that health services should be managed at the local levels to ensure that they are responsive to the specific needs of different regions. The NHP 2002 aimed at increasing the efficiency and effectiveness of healthcare delivery by promoting local governance and community involvement.

Despite these objectives, the implementation of the policy was sullied by a host of problems. One of the significant challenges during the implementation process was funding. Although the policy had proposed an increase in public expenditure on health, the financial resources were not forthcoming to see such ambitious goals to fruition. This funding shortfall actually limited adequate implementation of the policy. Disparities in access, predominantly in rural and remote areas continued to exist. Consequently, rural as well as poor and marginalized communities could not gain fully and equitably from the policy, particularly in terms of their access to essential health services. The focus on expanding services did not always translate into improved quality of care, which remained a critical issue. Nevertheless, the National Health Policy 2002 laid important groundwork for subsequent health policy developments, particularly the National Health Policy 2017. The NHP 2017 built upon the principles established in 2002 but aimed to address many of the shortcomings identified during the earlier period.

8.8 NATIONAL HEALTH POLICY 2017

The 2017 National Health Policy of India was introduced against the backdrop of changing healthcare needs and challenges. The country was undergoing a change in the landscape of diseases—from communicable to non-communicable ones like CVDs, diabetes, and cancer—thereby requiring a policy that would address the increased burden of chronic diseases while ongoing challenges with infectious diseases remained to be tackled. Also, a number of other challenges such as rapid urbanization, including demographic changes such as an aging population, among others. The growing urban population faced different health challenges compared to rural areas. This called for a more nuanced approach to health policy.

The policy was thus formulated to address some serious imbalances in access to healthcare that existed amidst economic growth. People in rural and underserved areas continued to find it difficult to access quality healthcare services. A key policy priority for NHP 2017 therefore was universal health coverage, wherein all people, irrespective of socio-economic status, get access to required health services without financial hardship. This objective was aligned with initiatives such as the Ayushman Bharat program, which was conceived to provided health insurance coverage to low-income families.

It was an opportune time when rapid advances were made in telemedicine, electronic health records, and health information systems, radically changing healthcare delivery. Building on these, NHP 2017 sought to leverage this progress for improving healthcare system through interventions that facilitate access to care, improve quality, and increase efficiency. Modernization of healthcare infrastructure, especially in notified backward districts and imperative health structures at sub-centre, primary, and secondary levels, was included to enable the introduction of new technologies and improve service delivery all over the country.

Global and national epidemiological scenario was also changing. New and emerging health threats of Antimicrobial Resistance (AMR) and pandemics were proving to be potent global threats. The main objective of the NHP 2017 was to strengthen the mechanisms of surveillance, preparedness, and response to such new threats more effectively. Preventive health measures, health promotion, and early detection were also given much more attention to reduce the burden of diseases and improve population health outcomes.

The process of formulation of NHP 2017 underwent wide consultations across different stakeholder groups, from health professionals and policymakers to regional representatives and civil society organizations. This made it an inclusive process for many diverse perspectives and needs to find a place. The policy was reviewed and approved by some of the key bodies, the Central Council of Health and Family Welfare and a Group of Ministers..

The policy was also sought to be aligned with the commitment of India to the United Nations Sustainable Development Goals, particularly those related to health and well-being. It had the goal of contributing to global health targets and frameworks while at the same time attending to priorities in health at the national level. By considering trends in health globally and best practices, NHP 2017 aimed at ensuring that strategies health-wise in India were aligned to international standards and recommendations. Some of the key policy priorities contained in the NHP 2017 can be understood in this backdrop.

NHP 2017 outlines certain key objectives oriented towards overhauling and improving the health system in India. These are explained below:

- **Increased Public Health Expenditure:** One of the primary objectives of NHP 2017 is to increase the expenditure of public health considerably, aiming at an increase of 2.5 percent of GDP by the year 2025. This increased funding aims at enabling the expansion and improvement of healthcare services in the country as well as to bridge the existing gaps in healthcare infrastructure, improve the quality of care, and decrease out-of-pocket expenses for most people with an augmented budget, thus working towards a more equitable and accessible healthcare system.
- **Augmentation of Primary Healthcare:** The policy accords primary importance to primary healthcare by advocating the creation of Health and Wellness Centres. These centres will provide an integrated package of primary healthcare and will thus act as the initial contact points for all patients. Two-thirds or more of this budget for health will be spent at the primary healthcare level. The aim is to reinforce health promotion and disease prevention and to get better health indices in the community, to ensure basic health services reach every section of society, especially in deprived rural areas.
- **Improved Access to Healthcare:** The policy has set a target regarding accessibility, with at least two beds per 1,000 population, strategically distributed to ensure access within the critical "golden hour." The policy will also initiate the use of health cards linked to primary care facilities for easier access to a defined health services package anywhere in the country. This card system is conceived to facilitate easy and efficient dispensation of healthcare in this country, helping people get necessary care without having to navigate the complex health delivery system.
- **Patient-centric Approach:** The NHP 2017 visualizes a patient-centric approach by the formation of an empowered medical tribunal. The said tribunal has the mandate to resolve through a fast-track process, the disputes relating to the standards of care, price of services, and other negligent acts. The policy equally allows for a streamlined regulatory framework that will oversee laboratories and imaging centres, ensuring that diagnostic and treatment services offered in all centres are of high standards and uniform. This move will protect patients' rights and increase the confidence expressed in the health system in general.
- **Combating Micronutrient Deficiency:** Another critical policy target is to fight micronutrient deficiency, which is so widespread in many areas. Reduction of malnutrition and ensuring adequate intake of micronutrients through targeted interventions based on regional needs, as envisaged in NHP 2017, would help iron out inequalities and improve the nutritional scenario throughout the country for better health and development.
- **Enhancing Quality of Care:** Concerns regarding quality of care lie at the heart of NHP 2017, which envisages periodic evaluation and certification of public hospitals and

healthcare facilities for the quality of services rendered to patients. Through a uniform mechanism of regulation and enforcement of standards for the health sector, it intends to reduce the risk of inappropriate care by laying down standards of diagnosis and treatment reflective of high standards of care. This assurance about quality is bound to improve safety practices among patients and bring effectiveness to healthcare services.

- **Promote Localized Manufacturing:** In sync with the Make-in-India initiative, this policy espouses more local manufacture of healthcare products. Encouraging indigenous products means catering to the needs of the Indian populace and reducing imports through incentives. It will foster innovation, job opportunities, and ensure that more affordable and customized health solutions are made available within the country.
- **Engaging Digital Health:** The policy reiterates that digital health tools could accelerate reform in the healthcare system. In its pursuit to deploy digital technologies extensively, NHP 2017 builds efficiency and quality in healthcare delivery. An integrated health information system would bring in transparency, lessen hassle, and result in better experiences of the patient and the healthcare professionals alike.
- **Engaging the Private Sector:** It equally recognizes that the private sector has potential to fill critical gaps in healthcare systems. Through strategic engagement, the NHP 2017 aims at harnessing their strengths in support of national health goals and improvement in service delivery. Such engagement shall complement efforts by the public sector and increase the coverage and effectiveness of healthcare services.

8.8.1 A Critical Examination of NHP 2017

NHP 2017 marked a significant step towards restructuring India's approach to healthcare. However, a closer scrutiny would reveal that several crucial areas of concern remain unaddressed. One pressing issue is the proposed increase in health expenditure from 2.5 percent of GDP from the present levels. This is much less than the 4-5 percent range that the policy itself acknowledges for making any significant impact on the health sector.

The policy also seems to ignore the critical thrust area of strengthening family welfare programmes. Family welfare programs are meant to be oriented towards reproductive health, child health, and preventive care. A more coherent approach is needed to assimilate and build upon the currently fragmented programs to strengthen family welfare. Similarly, there is also no coherent strategy in the policy to improve medical education. With the rapid strides that have been made in medical sciences and technologies, the quality of medical education would need to be enhanced so that quality medical professionals could be groomed to take care of the contemporary challenges to human health.

The other glaring gap is the lack of emphasis on school health education. Health education at the school age is a critical aspect in developing healthy practices and promoting good health throughout life. The policy also does not accord enough attention to the special needs of the elderly people. India is facing a vital demographic change with the ticking bomb of a rapidly greying population; hence specific programmes for the care of the elderly like geriatric health and support services become necessary.

The policy also appears to be not very vocal on mental health, which has been a growing concern. Mental healthcare needs a comprehensive approach in view of the increasing prevalence of mental disorders.

Another major omission is that of the assessment of health manpower. Good healthcare delivery requires proper training and an adequate number of professionals, for which in-depth assessment needs to be carried out in order to see that the workforce is sufficient to meet the needs of the population. The policy also fails to discuss putting in safeguards to bring about improvement in the efficiency of management at all levels of health management. Better management practices and the improvement of operational efficiencies are very essential for the health system to optimize its resources and delivery services.

Moreover, this policy does not talk much about the interstate and intrastate disparities in health services. The need for bridging such gaps assumes prime importance regarding the requirement to have equal access to healthcare in different regions and amongst the varied populations.

On the basis of the foregoing analysis, it can be concluded that even though the NHP 2017 lays down a basic framework for taking further strides in the healthcare sector in India, it remains deficient in several critical aspects. The policy needs to be more ambitious, both in terms of financial outlays and detailing associated aspects of healthcare like family welfare, medical education, mental health, care for the elderly, and health management. Policy in such aspects could then fathom a more inclusive and efficient health system design that would capably meet the diverse needs of the Indian population.

SUMMARY

This chapter provides an overview of the evolution of health policy in India. It examines how these policies have shaped the health system in India and looks at the development of health policies from the early days of independent India, examining the contribution of important committees and the evolution of key policies, including the National Health Policy (NHP) of 1983, 2002, and 2017. India's health policy has been evolving in a series of strategic shifts that have attempted to address the diversified and growing health needs of the country. Therefore, early health policies mainly focused on basic healthcare delivery and disease control. Over the years, the strategy changed to include the broader aspects associated with health, including preventive healthcare, health system strengthening, and building equity.

Important in this evolution was the constitution of influential committees that set about the task of laying down the bases for providing the foundational frameworks for comprehensive health policy frameworks. In particular, the Bhore Committee contributed immensely to early health policy, with some of its important recommendations being the development of a primary healthcare system and the integration of health services. Later, the historical "Alma Ata Declaration" on Primary Healthcare, expressed these views more concretely and was endorsed by the Srivastava Committee (1978), emphasizing strongly upon the community-based approach to preventive and promotive care.

The National Health Policy of 1983 was a landmark in the history of health policy development in India. It aimed to provide a comprehensive framework for health services in the country and aimed, at the same time, to reiterate the emphasis on primary healthcare services and community health services in an equitable and distributive manner. The policy envisioned enhancing access to healthcare, especially in the rural and underserved areas.

NHP 2002 built upon the background prepared by the earlier policy, dealing with both the existing and emerging health concerns. It also sought to incorporate the learnings from the implementation of past policies. It stressed on the need for a more comprehensive strategy in health as it envisaged effective integration of traditional and modern medicines into the healthcare system for the promotion of public health, to strengthen health delivery mechanisms, and to provide affordable healthcare infrastructure. It also placed emphasis on how taking social determinants of health into consideration is important in the provision of health services.

National Health Policy, 2017 was introduced to address the preexisting challenges as well as to respond to contemporary issues and priorities. The policy sought to further the objective of access and quality to healthcare through focusing on universal health coverage, health system strengthening, and moving towards a more strategic, outcome-oriented approach. It advocated increasing the health spending and improving the delivery of healthcare through schemes such as the Ayushman Bharat which aims to provide financial protection to the poorer sections of society and also to strengthen the primary and secondary healthcare systems.

Despite these advancements, critical assessments of the NHP 2017 reveal several areas that need to be improved upon. The most glaring policy gap is the underfunding of health sector which impedes many crucial reforms. Additionally, this policy does not fully address family welfare programs, medical education, school health education, the care of the elderly, mental health, and assessing the health manpower. The other area that received less attention was the intra-state and inter-state disparities and improving general health management efficiency.

To conclude, health policy reformation in India is a journey of progressive change in phases, meant to tackle emerging health demands from a consistently growing population. While notable development has been made in the health landscape of the country through these policies, critical gaps still remain. Political will and adequate investments are therefore crucial to fill existing gaps and ensure more fair and effective results from the health system.

CHAPTER

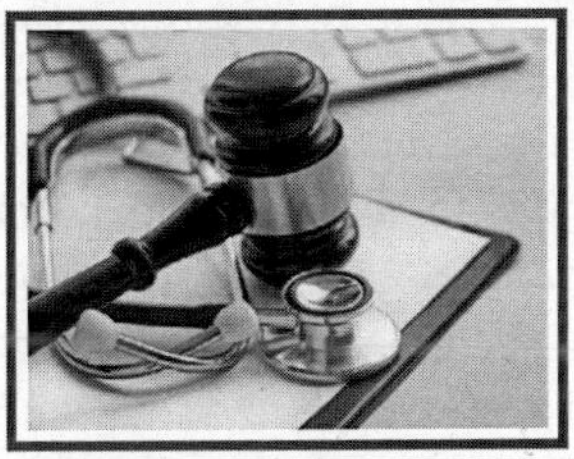

9 Health Governance and Stakeholders

INTRODUCTION

Universal healthcare coverage and improvement in critical health indicators, are at the core of many five-year plans and health policies. However, despite ambitious policy goals Indian healthcare system and governance suffers from multiple issues and challenges. One of the major deficiencies that continue to plague the overall functioning of healthcare delivery in India has been the lack of comprehensive Primary Healthcare (PHC). Primary healthcare is a critical segment of healthcare delivery in India since it is often likely to be the first point of contact of people seeking healthcare. PHC thus has to be accessible, inexpensive, and comprehensive and incorporate preventive, curative, as well as rehabilitative services.

In India, despite several initiatives for developing PHC, the system has remained fragmented and underdeveloped in most parts of the country. This means that on most occasions, rural and underserved areas lack proper facilities, trained human resources, and minimum essential drugs. Even in urban areas such services are not easily accessible to the poor and the marginalized due to economic barriers, inadequate public healthcare facilities, systemic inefficiencies and quality of Care and trust Issues This insufficiency leads to underutilization of the primary healthcare segment resulting in dependency and consequent overload on secondary and tertiary care for basic health needs, which burdens such healthcare facilities leading to health disparities. What follows is a health system where so many, notably the economically disadvantaged and those living in remote areas, are deprived of easy access to essential health services, thus defeating the universal health coverage goal.

The uncontrolled private health sector is another important challenge that India faces. While the private sector has made a significant contribution to health service provision, its growth has not been guided by effective regulation or oversight. This has led to an increase in private clinics and hospitals adhere to any sort of standardized practice or quality control. Patients, as a result, often face enormous variations in quality care, inflated costs, and sometimes even exploitative practices. Equally absent, in the lack of regulation, is accountability sufficient for malpractice and substandard care. This situation creates a parallel system of healthcare with variable quality and affordability, increasing still further the gap between those who afford high-quality private care and those who are forced to rely on the overburdened public health system. Inaccessibility and inequities in the healthcare system of India are multi-faceted and deeply anchored in socio-economic, geographical, and systemic factors. Access to healthcare has huge disparities between urban and rural areas, with the latter usually facing extreme shortfalls in infrastructure and personnel. Moreover, socio-economic inequities translate into healthcare access barriers amongst poor, women, and the lower caste populations. These inequities get further exacerbated due to lack of transportation and low health insurance coverage. Systemic biases impinge upon the quality of care received amongst various social groups, inequities further extend to health outcomes and eventually result in a cycle of disadvantage and ill-health in vulnerable groups.

For meeting such heterogeneous and complex challenges, a multi-stakeholder collaborative approach is required. The government needs to take the lead by investing and increasing the size of primary healthcare infrastructure, bringing stringent regulations in the private sector, and addressing systemic inequities through specially designed policies and programs. The private sector has to accept and maintain set standards, with full involvement in the development of affordable quality care. NGOs and community-based organizations have a role in advocacy for the underserved population and in providing support at lower levels. This involves ensuring health interventions are culturally and contextually appropriate.

Furthermore, academia and research institutions can contribute through well-researched data-driven insights and evidence-based recommendations in the formulation of policies and practices. International organizations and donors can commit technical assistance, funding, and expertise to strengthen health activities at all levels. Partnership among these very diverse stakeholders can ultimately tie into a more unified and equitable system for healthcare delivery, ensuring that all have access to comprehensive and good-quality healthcare, irrespective of their socio-economic background and geographical location. This multi-stakeholder approach shall be key to surmounting the complex challenges facing India's healthcare system and achieving meaningful health outcomes across the country.

These goals require a multifaceted approach involving coordinated efforts from a diverse group of stakeholders. Their achievement requires an integrated approach that involves collaborative efforts of a various stakeholders. In India many stakeholders are involved in the health policy landscape. It includes the public sector, autonomous organizations, donor and aid organizations, NGOs, private sector, professional organizations, research institutions and universities, think tanks, communities, and civil society organizations. All these stakeholders are vital in responding to the multifaceted challenges that healthcare service delivery in India faces. An analysis of the major policy can be undertaken as follows.

9.1 PUBLIC SECTOR

State or the public sector forms the backbone of health in India. It plays a vital role which range from policy formulation to service delivery and regulation. This sector is fundamental in shaping the country's health landscape and in ensuring the availability and access to healthcare services to all sections of the population, especially the disadvantaged groups in society and those in rural areas. It is the apex institutional mechanism for policy formulation on health matters and various programmes related to healthcare services. At the Centre, the Ministry of Health and

Family Welfare (MoHFW) sets health priorities, designs health schemes, and allocates budgets. Among the major national programmes on health that MoHFW administers are the National Health Mission with the objectives of strengthening health infrastructure, improving access to quality healthcare, and bridging the health inequities. The other major initiative is the National Health Policy, 2017, enunciating a vision of health systems in India: universal health coverage, preventive healthcare, and quality improvement.

At the state level, the implementation is entrusted to the Health Departments, which are responsible for implementing health policies and managing public health services. These departments look after the implementation of various national health programs and adapt them according to local needs. They manage state-run hospitals, clinics, and primary health centres to ensure that health services are provided appropriately in varied geographical and socio-economic milieus.

The public sector also drives major health initiatives improving health outcomes. Government works on vaccination programs, such as those for polio and measles, in order to avoid the origin or resurgence of infectious diseases into the system. For example, the Intensified Mission Indradhanush is one such focused vaccination drive for increasing immunization coverage in backward areas. There are also several disease control programs run by the public health authorities, with an objective to take control of the spread of diseases and reduce the cases, such as those for TB and malaria. For example, the Revised National Tuberculosis Control Program (RNTCP) is one of these programs oriented towards diagnosing, treating, and preventing TB. The other priority area includes maternal and child health services. Pradhan Mantri Matru Vandana Yojana (PMMVY) and similar programs provide monetary assistance to pregnant women and lactating mothers with a view to improving the health of mothers and infants. National Rural Health Mission has also been working towards making healthcare delivery better in rural areas for mothers and children.

One of the most significant initiatives taken by the state for strengthening the health systemin India and to make it more accessible is the Ayushman Bharat Mission. India, with its diverse population and vast geographical expanse, has long been faced with the challenge of delivering equitable healthcare to all its citizens. The burden of healthcare costs, especially for the economically disadvantaged, has led to many individuals and families being pushed into poverty due to exorbitant medical bills and out of pocket expenses. Recognizing the need to address these challenges, the Government of India launched Ayushman Bharat mission in 2018. It is an ambitious initiative aimed at providing accessible, affordable, and high-quality healthcare services to the underserved populations across the country..

Ayushman Bharat, often regarded as one of the largest health protection schemes in the world, is a comprehensive initiative aimed at universal health coverage (UHC) for all citizens, especially those from economically vulnerable and underserved sections of society. It is designed to address the twin challenges of accessibility and affordability of healthcare. This policy initiative has twofold objectives; financial protection through health insurance and the strengthening of healthcare infrastructure, Ayushman Bharat seeks to make healthcare services available to millions of people who have long been excluded from quality healthcare systems.

The mission is rooted in two key components, Pradhan Mantri Jan Arogya Yojana (PMJAY), a health insurance scheme aimed at providing financial protection for secondary and tertiary care, especially for families living below the poverty line and Health and Wellness

Centres (HWCs) which is a network of primary healthcare centres designed to provide comprehensive primary healthcare services, including preventive, diagnostic, and treatment services, close to where people live.

Pradhan Mantri Jan Arogya Yojana (PMJAY)

In this context the most notable initiative has been the Pradhan Mantri Jan Arogya Yojana (PMJAY). It is a flagship health insurance scheme launched by the Government of India in 2018. It aims to provide financial protection to low-income families by covering medical expenses for secondary and tertiary hospitalizations. The scheme is part of the broader Ayushman Bharat mission, which seeks to improve the accessibility and quality of healthcare services for vulnerable populations.

PMJAY offers a coverage of up to ₹5 lakh per family per year for hospitalization costs. The scheme covers over 10.74 crore poor and vulnerable families (approximately 50 crore beneficiaries), making it the world's largest publicly funded health insurance scheme. The scheme provides cashless treatment across a network of empanelled public and private hospitals. This ensures that beneficiaries do not need to pay for healthcare services upfront, reducing financial barriers to accessing quality care. PMJAY covers a wide range of medical services, including pre-hospitalization, hospitalization, post-hospitalization, surgery, daycare treatments, and diagnostics. It covers over 1,350 medical procedures across 23 specialties, including critical care, cardiovascular, cancer treatment, and maternity benefits.

The scheme targets the economically weaker sections of society, with beneficiaries identified based on the Socio-Economic Caste Census (SECC) 2011 data. This includes marginalized groups such as Scheduled Castes (SCs), Scheduled Tribes (STs), and other disadvantaged communities. PMJAY also offers portability, meaning beneficiaries can avail of treatment in any empanelled hospital across India, even if they are outside their home state or region. This feature ensures accessibility, especially for migrant labourers and people who move between states for work. The scheme leverages digital platforms for beneficiary identification, hospital empanelment, and claims processing. This reduces administrative burdens, ensures transparency, and speeds up service delivery.

PMJAY has the potential to significantly reduce out-of-pocket expenditures for healthcare, which is a leading cause of financial distress in India. It can prevent impoverished families from being burdened with massive medical bills thus improving access to healthcare, especially for rural populations and people in remote areas who may otherwise face difficulties in affording quality medical care. While previous schemes were more limited to primary healthcare, PMJAY focuses on secondary and tertiary care, addressing the more significant health challenges faced by families, such as surgeries, critical illness treatment, and cancer care.

However, while PMJAY has a broad coverage, the lack of awareness is a challenge for its uptake. Awareness campaigns are crucial to ensure that eligible families know about the scheme and how to access it. Many rural families may still be unaware of the benefits and procedures. Also the success of the scheme can be inconsistent, with differences in implementation between states. Variability in hospital quality and timely claims processing can affect the overall experience of beneficiaries. Moreover, like any large-scale public program, PMJAY has faced challenges related to fraudulent claims and leakages in some cases, where ineligible people might attempt to take advantage of the scheme. Stringent monitoring and auditing mechanisms are required to prevent misuse. To further strengthen the PMJAY scheme, enhancing beneficiary awareness, expanding the hospital network, improving claims settlement processes, and ensuring effective monitoring are essential steps. Incorporating data-driven insights to track health outcomes and identify emerging health trends will also improve the scheme's efficacy.

Health and Wellness Centres (HWCs)

Whilc PMJAY addresses the financial barriers to healthcare, Ayushman Bharat also aims to improve the primary healthcare infrastructure through the establishment of Health and Wellness Centres (HWCs). These centres serve as the first point of contact for healthcare, offering comprehensive health services that include maternal and child health, immunization, non-communicable disease management, mental health services, and basic curative care.

HWCs are designed to provide preventive healthcare and to address a wide range of health needs at the community level. They focus on early detection and management of diseases, reducing the burden on higher-level hospitals and ensuring that healthcare services are accessible and affordable to the underserved and rural populations. These centres are part of the primary health system, which is the foundation for a strong and resilient healthcare infrastructure. HWCs also provide preventive care programs such as health check-ups, disease screening, and health education, which play a critical role in improving overall health outcomes and reducing the incidence of preventable diseases. By prioritizing primary care and wellness, HWCs aim to keep communities healthier, reducing the need for hospitalization and intensive care services.

9.1.1 Challenges and the Way Forward

The implementation of Ayushman Bharat has encountered several challenges despite its success in improving healthcare access. One significant issue is the lack of awareness about the scheme, particularly in remote areas, which limits its reach and effectiveness. Many eligible families are unaware of the benefits they are entitled to, hindering the scheme's overall impact. Moreover, while substantial investments have been made in healthcare infrastructure, gaps still exist in rural regions, where limited connectivity and low internet penetration continue to affect the delivery of services. Furthermore, ensuring consistent quality standards across the large network of empanelled hospitals is a challenge, with concerns about both accessibility and the effectiveness of services. The scale of PMJAY also opens up the risk of fraudulent claims, necessitating the implementation of real-time auditing and electronic verification mechanisms to maintain the integrity of the system.

To strengthen Ayushman Bharat, focused efforts are needed. Raising awareness through targeted campaigns for remote and underserved communities will ensure that all eligible families are informed about their entitlements and how to access services. Continued investments in healthcare infrastructure, particularly in rural areas, along with improvements in digital connectivity, are crucial for expanding access to healthcare services. Strengthening quality assurance for both public and private hospitals under PMJAY is necessary to ensure consistent, high-quality care for all beneficiaries. Additionally, greater integration with the National

Digital Health Mission (NDHM) can enhance the efficiency, accountability, and transparency of the healthcare system. Addressing these challenges will allow Ayushman Bharat to truly revolutionize healthcare in India, ensuring that healthcare becomes more equitable, accessible, and affordable for every citizen, irrespective of their socio-economic status. Through continued investment and innovation, Ayushman Bharat has the potential to create a healthier and more resilient India.

9.2 NON-GOVERNMENTAL AND CIVIL SOCIETY ORGANIZATIONS

NGOs are one of the major stakeholders in the health landscape since they address peculiar challenges in health and address the gaps in public healthcare service delivery. Their contributions range from providing direct medical care, extension and outreach to underserved communities to advocacy and community-based programs that have a bearing on improved health outcomes and social equity. NGOs are major players in many specific health challenges not fully covered under government programs. through Doctors Without Borders (MSF) for example, carries out its activities in various parts of India, including isolated or conflict affected areas, by rendering crucial health services where access is poor. Such interventions consist of emergency medical care, provision for maternal and child health, treatment of diseases such as tuberculosis and malaria, among others. They often set up temporary clinics and mobile medical units, to reach out to and addressing pressing health needs which have been unaddressed by formal institutional health mechanisms thus benefitting the most vulnerable in society.

Another important contribution that NGOs make in India is improving health and educational outcomes through integrated programs. Organizations such as Akshaya Patra Foundation for example supplement the government midday meal programs by providing nutritious meals to school-going children.

NGOs in India are also actively engaged in advocacy and grassroots-level intervention, especially in family planning, reproductive health, and gender equality. Among organizations that have focused their attention on these issues, one of the most important is the Population Health Foundation of India. The foundation works on changing policies, conducting public awareness campaigns, and engaging in community-based programs to promote family planning and reproductive health. These are initiatives aimed at empowering people with knowledge and resources so they can make an informed decision about their reproductive health.

NGOs are usually successful in reaching people inadequately served by the mainstream healthcare system. Specialized services, like mental health support, addiction treatment, and chronic disease management, are usually not easily available through the public health channels or mainstream services. NGOs fill this gap by bringing both expertise and resources. Establishing community health centres, arranging health camps, and running education programs are some of the initiatives through which NGOs ensure that access to at least to some extent such services also reach the poor and the disadvantaged. The ability of NGOs to adapt to local contexts, responsiveness to specific community needs enables them to fill gaps within healthcare systems and improve the overall health landscape. Another role taken by NGOs is promoting community engagement and empowerment; without this, attaining long-term health improvements cannot be possible. By engaging local communities in health program design and delivery, NGOs engender trust and ensure that interventions are culturally appropriate and relevant. Such participatory approaches, where community members are involved in various stages of the projects, improve effectiveness and inculcate a sense of ownership and responsibility among community members.

Communities and the civil society organizations also act as advocates for health rights, mobilize communities and promote grassroots initiatives outside the conventional framework of public and private healthcare delivery. This makes them address specific health needs, support policy reforms, and work towards addressing the healthcare needs of all segments in society.

With respect to health rights, civil society organizations in India have played a very important role in terms of advocacy and ensuring that healthcare services are accessible to the underserved and the most disadvantaged groups of society. Jan Swasthya Abhiyan (JSA) is an example to understand such initiatives. JSA is a network of civil society organizations working on promoting issues of equitable healthcare and influencing health policy. It works to address the systemic inequities in the healthcare system by engaging in dialogues on policy and lobbying for reforms to address priorities of marginalized communities. Campaigns and advocacy are organized regarding issues such as poor infrastructure, inordinately high out-of-pocket spending, and inequity in access to healthcare, among others, with a view towards moving towards a more inclusive and fair health system.

Community-based organizations too play a major role in the execution of health programs at the local level. One such organization is the Self-Employed Women's Association, SEWA, based in Gujarat. It integrates health and economic development in its endeavour to enhance the general well-being of women in that region. SEWA runs community health programs that include access to primary healthcare services, maternal and child healthcare, and preventive health measures. Such programs are aimed at specific health challenges: malnutrition, reproductive health problems, and inaccessibility of basic medical services that women and their families face. SEWA integrates health with economic support and advocacy to ensure better health outcomes, thus empowering women.

Many of the pressing health-related issues at the grassroots level are addressed by local civil society initiatives that mirror the diversity of needs across communities in India. These include maternal and child health, sanitation, preventive care, and others responding to health challenges faced by local populations. These efforts are central to filling gaps in healthcare provision and taking care that health interventions at the community level are relevant and effective.

The role of civil society organizations in health education and empowerment is also paramount in encouraging healthy behaviours and the contribution of better health outcomes. These initiatives relate to issues such as nutrition, disease prevention, reproductive health etc. and help people make informed decisions about their own health. They often leverage community outreach methods to engage heterogeneous populations through workshops, health fairs, and peer education programs. Empowerment of communities with knowledge and the relevant tools allows people to participate in decisions about their health and well-being. This action contributes to improved health at all levels within society. Civil society also becomes involved in supporting systemic change within the healthcare system. Such organizations forge partnerships through activism around common issues and shape health policies that are inclusive and responsive to the needs of different communities. They bring out the lacunae and inequities in healthcare and work towards ensuring that there is better access to services, especially to the most vulnerable groups within society.

9.3 DONOR AND AID ORGANIZATIONS

Donor and aid organizations are also crucial stakeholders in advancing the country's health sector, especially to supplement areas where government resources and infrastructure may be lacking. These organizations operate in various areas of healthcare delivery landscape and make important contributions at different levels, bridging gaps in healthcare delivery and addressing specified challenges to public health. Provisioning of financial resources is one of the key contributions of these organizations. This funding is to address resource gaps in large-scale health interventions, particularly in areas that are either underserved or economically challenged. For example, funding provided by the Bill and Melinda Gates Foundation, allows procurement and supply of vaccines needed to carry out immunization coverage in remote and rural districts. This financing is not only utilized for procurement of medical supplies but also for infrastructure creation and maintenance such as clinics and laboratories, that consequently assist in the delivery of health services.

Besides financing, donor or aid agencies provide technical assistance for enhancing the capacity of the local health system. Technical assistance includes lending expertise in design and implementation of health programs, improvement of health service delivery, and development of creative solutions to health challenges. USAID, for example, provides technical support for strengthening Health Information Systems, which enhances data collection and management for appropriate health planning and policy action. Technical assistance also encompasses capacity-building activities which would include training of health workers and strengthening of medical protocols so that health interventions are delivered efficiently and effectively.

Donors and aid agencies are also instrumental in shaping health policy to guide strategic priorities. These organizations work in close collaboration with governments and local stakeholders to identify critical health needs and engage in advocacy for evidence-based policies to respond to the needs. Some institutions, such as the Global Fund, do a lot more than just providing finances but also participate in policy dialogue to ensure that programs against diseases such as HIV/AIDS and tuberculosis are brought up to global standards and best practices. Their work at times involves policy analysis, recommending reforms, and assisting in the implementation of health policies that are most likely to bring systemic changes in healthcare delivery.

Collaborative efforts of donor and aid organizations assume special meaning in tackling certain public health challenges. For instance, in India, this would mean dealing with infectious diseases, improvement of health of mothers and children, and access to quality healthcare services, reducing child mortality and improving the health outcomes for mothers by operating a number of specific programs and research initiatives. In the case of malaria, tuberculosis, and HIV/AIDS, it involves comprehensive work with strategies that mean a package of services in prevention, treatment, and care. In such critical areas, the involvement by donor and aid organizations has resulted in improvements of health outcomes and reduced disease burden. These agencies have contributed to narrowing the gaps in health access, promoting health education, and empowering communities to take charge of their health.

9.4 AUTONOMOUS INSTITUTIONS AND PROFESSIONAL BODIES

Autonomous organizations in India play an important work on the development and maintenance of health quality through their independence and specific focus. Unlike the public sector which is managed and controlled directly by the government, these organizations carry out their mission with relative independence and with a specific focus in one area of competence. They are often engaged in setting and enforcing standards, regulations, and best practices. Such operational independence is provided to ensure flexibility and innovation in their respective domains. For example, organizations such as the National Accreditation Board for Hospitals & Healthcare Providers set rigorous quality standards for hospitals and clinical establishments and provide accreditation to those who meet such criteria. This enhances the quality of healthcare and ensures that patients receive care that meets or exceeds benchmarks set for safety and effectiveness.

Furthermore, independent organizations are also indispensable for the advancement of biomedical research and innovation to meet emergent health challenges and improve medical practices. Medical research in the country for instance is promoted and coordinated by the Indian Council for Medical Research (ICMR) at the Centre. Its autonomy allows it to conduct research without unnecessary political or bureaucratic interference. This enabling environment is conducive to scientific inquiry and evidence-based policy development which makes these organizations instrumental in setting of priorities for research, financing research studies, and disseminating research findings. Autonomous organizations also contribute significantly to the development of treatments, diagnostic tools, and public health interventions. Their work supports continuous evolution in health practice, making sure that advancements are harnessed by rigorous research and scientific evidence.

Professional organizations in India are also essential pillars in the healthcare sector. They performing multifarious roles in support, regulation, and advancement of the medical and health-related professions. Such organizations attempt to ensure maintenance of high standards of practice and also support the rights and development of all health professionals, contribute to health policy formulation, and allow opportunities for continuing education and training. Professional bodies in the health sector are entrusted with the regulation and licensing in healthcare practice to ensure ensuring that healthcare professionals meet proper educational and professional standards. For instance, the National Medical Commission, which came into existence through the National Medical Commission Act, 2019, acts as the apex regulatory body for medical education and practice. It oversees the accreditation of medical colleges, maintains the national register of medical practitioners, and ensures compliance with ethical standards. These organizations also establish professional standards and guidelines on the quality and safety of health and medical services. Similarly, the Indian Nursing Council sets the standards of nursing education, training, and practice. The Nursing Council accredits the nursing colleges and institutions after ascertaining that they adhere to the stated educational and professional norms. Likewise, the Pharmacy Council of India regulates pharmacy education and practice by laying down the guidelines on qualification of pharmacists, approval of pharmacy institutions, and following ethical practices in the profession of pharmacy.

Professional bodies also advocate the interests of members and other affiliated healthcare communities. They engage in policy dialogue, represent their profession in legislative matters and work to address issues affecting healthcare professionals. The Indian Medical Association for example is the largest body of doctors in India. It represents their interest, provides a forum for airing professional grievances, and influences healthcare policymaking and legislation. IMA also undertakes continuing medical education and professional development programs for its members in order to keep up with the challenge of developments in medical science and technology. To this end workshops, seminars, and training programs are often organized by such professional bodies. Professional organizations have the responsibility to ensure the ethical standards are followed and handle disciplinary matters. An example of this is the code of ethics framed by the Indian Medical Association for its members and o handle issues related to professional misconduct. Similarly, the Indian Nursing Council has devised a code of ethics and conduct for nurses and midwives, and also looks into complaints related to breach of the ethical code or any other misconduct and takes disciplinary action whenever necessary. Many of these professional organizations are also support and influence research and contribute to policy development in their respected areas. For example, the Pharmacy Council of India (PCI) undertakes looks into matters related to pharmaceutical practice and suggests policies with the objective of ensuring safety and efficacy of drugs, etc.

9.5 RESEARCH INSTITUTIONS, UNIVERSITIES, AND THINK TANKS

Research Institutes, Universities and Think Tanks play a pivotal role in advancing medical science as well as shape and improve of public health policies and healthcare systems in India. Their contributions help in addressing continuous and emerging health-related challenges by providing the impetus for innovation, policy information, and training a new cadre of healthcare professionals

Research Institutions and think tanks are at the forefront of medical research pushing the boundaries of scientific knowledge and technological advancement. Besides, institutions such as the All-India Institute of Medical Sciences (AIIMS) undertake cutting-edge research in the different streams of medicine, such as cardiology, oncology, and infectious diseases. This research finally ends up developing new diagnostic tools, therapeutic methods, and treatment protocols. Research carried out by these institutions in critical areas including epidemiology, prevention, and management of diseases provide the basic data that goes into the formulation of public health strategy and intervention. For instance, institutions such as the Indian Institute of Public Health (IIPH) works with a mandate towards handling critical public health issues using innovative research and analysis Similarly, think tanks such as the Centre for Policy Research's (CPR) work in health policy analysis contributes to a deeper understanding of the challenges facing the healthcare system and helps in formulating effective policy responses. Evidence-based recommendations from these organizations are thus generated to guide policymakers in designing and implementing health reforms by ensuring that policies are well-grounded in research and tailored to suit the needs of the population.

Educational institutions in India, including those affiliated with research bodies, offer specialized training and education that are crucial for developing a skilled healthcare workforce. The Indian Institute of Public Health (IIPH) offers advanced degrees and professional development programs related to public health, management, and epidemiology. This helps train a skilled workforce to handle complex health issues.

Existing and emerging health challenges demand consistent changes as well as adaptation. Research institutions and think tanks keep tab on new health threats and developing innovative solutions. Inter-institutional collaboration between research institutions, universities, and think tanks has great potential to improve the quality and practice of healthcare. Such organizations often work together on interdisciplinary projects combining their respective areas of expertise in different applied fields to respond to the multidisciplinary requirements of complex health issues. To that end, joint research initiatives, academic partnerships, and policy analysis enhance the effectiveness of health interventions and promote the sharing of best practices. For instance, during the COVID-19 pandemic Indian research institutions collaborated to study the virus, develop vaccines, and assess public health measures. The response was instrumental in pandemic management and mitigation

9.6 PRIVATE SECTOR

The private sector has a significant presence in the healthcare space in India. It comprises of a broad and diverse range of players, including standalone clinics, private hospitals, diagnostic centres, pharmaceutical companies, biotechnology companies, and medical device manufacturers, all of which contribute substantially towards healthcare delivery and innovations. The private sector provides a substantial portion of healthcare services in India, particularly in urban areas. The private hospitals and clinics are more likely to offer advanced medical and diagnostic facilities specialized treatments compared to most public facilities.

The pharmaceutical industry in India is a major global player with the private sector contributing significantly to the development, production, and distribution of medicines, both in the domestic and regional markets and across the world, by private companies. The key private players deploy huge production units and cater not only to the domestic needs but also to exports to numerous countries. Drug development, coupled with biotechnological advances, has brought innovation in this sector, encouraging attention to common or rare diseases, promoting treatment options, and rendering medication easily available and cheaper.

The private sector has been on the forefront in ensuring the growth of medical devices and health technologies. Right from diagnostic equipment to minimally invasive surgical implements, the private sector invests heavily in such research and the work involved in producing quality medical devices.

In addition to the above aspects of healthcare service delivery, public-private partnerships are being increasingly utilized as a means to achieve delivery of healthcare and infrastructure. The partnerships allow private organizations to use their expertise, resources, and innovation in achieving the objectives of public health. For example, private firms may be called upon to participate in government led health interventions, such as vaccination campaigns or disease control programs, which helps intensify their reach and effectiveness.

Private organizations also often engage in policy advocacy to influence healthcare regulations and reforms. Industry associations and corporate bodies work together with the policy framers to fix regulatory standards and in matters impacting their industry interests. This presents an opportunity to weigh in considerations private sector's perspectives and needs in the broader health policy framework.

SUMMARY

The critical role of health governance in shaping and managing healthcare systems to ensure the delivery of quality and equitable health services cant be overstated. This section highlights how effective governance frameworks encompass policies, regulations, and accountability mechanisms that guide decision-making processes across all levels of the health sector. The importance of collaboration among diverse stakeholders, including governments, international organizations, private sector entities, civil society groups, healthcare providers, and the general public is also a critical aspect of health governance. Each stakeholder plays a unique role in influencing health policies, implementing programs, and ensuring that healthcare systems are responsive to community needs. It also explores how transparent, inclusive, and accountable governance structures are essential for addressing health disparities, optimizing resource allocation, and managing public health emergencies. The need for continuous stakeholder engagement to adapt to evolving health challenges and to achieve sustainable health also comes out clearly from the foregoing analysis.

QUESTIONS FOR PART III

Q.1 What are the primary objectives of public health policy in India?

Q.2 How has the evolution of public health policy in India addressed key health challenges over time?

Q.3 Discuss the role of prevention and health promotion in public health policy.

Q.4 What are the key social determinants of health in India, and how do they impact health outcomes?

Q.5 Outline the key components of the National Health Policy, 2017. How does it aim to achieve universal health coverage?

Q.6 Who are the key stakeholders in health governance in India, and what are their roles?

Q.7 How does collaboration between government, private sector, and non-governmental organizations (NGOs) enhance health governance in India?

PART IV

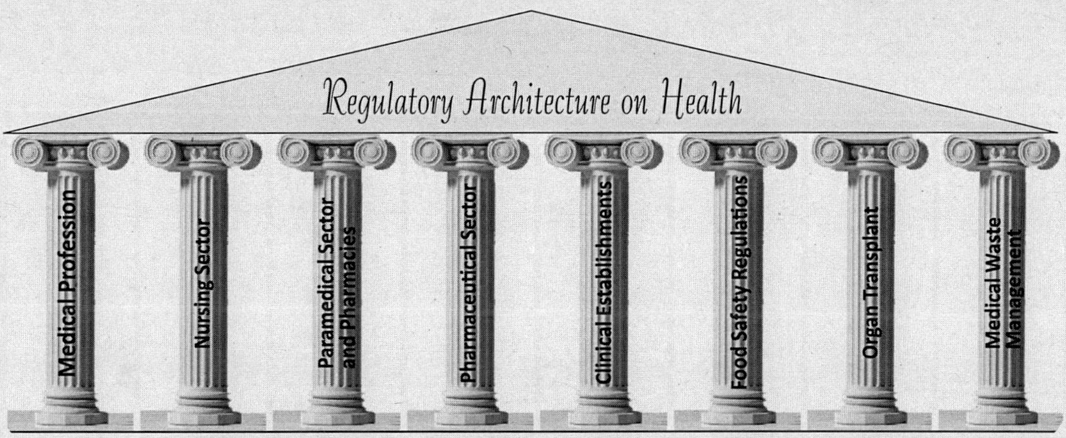

Regulatory Architecture on Health

CHAPTER

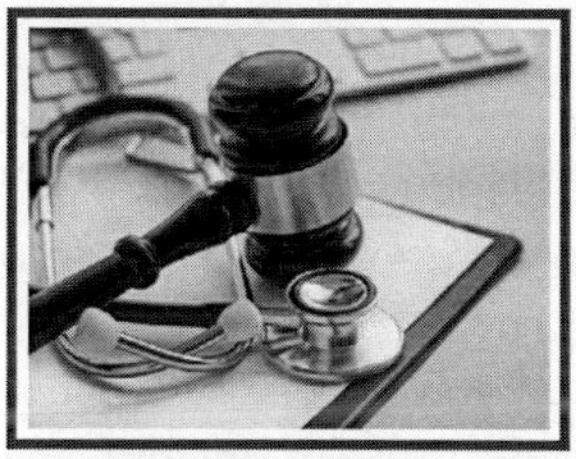

10 Regulation of the Medical Profession

INTRODUCTION

India's Healthcare landscape is vast and complex. A huge and diverse population in India poses enormous challenges in effectively channelizing healthcare delivery. Effective regulation is thus essential to establish, maintain, and enforce standards of medical education, practice, and ethics and to ensure that healthcare professionals are properly trained, licensed, and adhere to established practices and protocols.

Patient safety is accorded a high priority in healthcare, and regulation also plays a role in ensuring this. Regulation of medical profession also plays a major role in the prevention of malpractice and fraud. Ethical as well as legal standards established by regulatory authorities mandate legal requirements to be followed by practitioners so that fraudulent practices are avoided. Ethical practice is the cornerstone of medical professional practice, and regulation ensures that medical professionals conduct themselves in an ethical manner. Ethical guidelines cover aspects such as consent by patients, patient confidentiality, and truthfulness in reporting medical matters. The regulatory bodies provide guidelines and to the practitioners on ethical issues to help negotiate through a host of difficult situations and make decisions that ensure the interest of the patients is paramount. Proper regulation is meant to instil confidence in patients concerning the healthcare provider.

Regulation also ensures the continuous professional development of medical practitioners. Medical science is rapidly evolving which requires continuous education, training and skill development. The regulatory bodies often require the medical professionals to attend various professional development activities and programs. It is thus evident that a comprehensive regulatory framework is necessitated in the healthcare sector to effectively manage the various aspects of healthcare service delivery. However even more importantly a regulatory framework on healthcare also contributes in terms of providing a monitoring and oversight mechanisms to manage the many diverse and complex roles of the various professional stakeholders involved in healthcare. An overview of some of the important stakeholders in the health delivery ecosystem and their regulatory architecture can be discussed as below:

10.1 REGULATORY MECHANISMS FOR MEDICAL PROFESSIONALS

The **Medical Council of India (MCI)** constituted in 1933 was the first professional body to regulate medical professionals. For a considerable length of time, the Medical Commission of India (MCI) was the apex regulatory body in charge of medical education and standards of medical schools, evaluation of qualifications, and code of ethics among doctors. It was also entrusted with the mandate to promote professional self-regulation with necessary internal checks and balances. The MCI was given powers relating to standards of good medical practice, standardization and accreditation of medical education, registration and licensure of doctors, and concerns pertaining to doctors' fitness to practice. In 1956, the original MCI Act of 1933 was itself repealed and replaced by a new act. The MCI, in due course, faced a growing criticism for non-transparency, arbitrary decisions, questionable composition, prejudiced regulatory actions, corrupt practices, and lack of accountability, which finally resulted in its dissolution and replacement by a Board of Governors. However, with increased complexity in the healthcare ecosystem, there was also an increasing need for a more dynamic and transparent regulatory system better suited to meet emerging challenges and relative inefficiencies. Fast changing medical technologies and patient expectations also called for better accountability within the system.

To meet these emerging requirements, the **National Medical Commission (NMC)** was established through the National Medical Commission Act, 2019[1], replacing MCI. Establishment of NMC is a progressive step towards achieving a more structured and transparent system of medical regulation. The National Medical Commission was formed to overcome various deficiencies of MCI with an aim to create a more streamlined and transparent regulatory mechanism. The National Medical Commission Act, 2019 which established the National Medical Commission outlines its role in overseeing medical education and practice with a focus on enhancing transparency and efficiency. The regulatory functions of the NMC are thus varied and essential for improving the overall quality of medical practice. One of its key functions is to accredit medical colleges, which involves evaluating their curricula, faculty, and facilities to ensure they meet established standards with an aim to produce well-trained medical graduates who are equipped to handle the complexities of modern healthcare by setting and maintaining high educational standards

Ethical practices and patient safety are central to the NMC's regulatory framework. The comprehensive Code of Ethics formulated and enforced by the commission provides detailed guidelines on professional behaviour, including the safeguarding of patient confidentiality, ensuring informed consent, and maintaining professional conduct. This ethical framework is essential for building and maintaining trust between healthcare providers and patients. It emphasized on the commitment of the medical profession to deliver care with integrity, respect, and a focus on patient well-being. Moreover, the National Medical Commission, in conjunction with State Medical Councils, holds the authority to take disciplinary actions against practitioners who violate the established ethical standards. This is crucial for protecting patients from malpractice and ensuring that healthcare providers adhere to established ethical norms.

The structure and composition of the NMC are also pivotal aspects of the Act outlined in Sections 5–8 of the Act. The NMC is comprised of a chairperson, who is appointed by the

1. https://www.nmc.org.in/nmc-act/

central government, and ten members who are experts in fields such as medical education, public health, and clinical practice.

Another notable feature of the Act is its emphasis on decentralization through the autonomous boards. This decentralized approach allows for more focused and efficient oversight, aiming to streamline processes and enhance the responsiveness of the regulatory framework to emerging issues in medical education and practice (Sections 17 to 22). To facilitate specialized oversight, the Act provides for the formation of four autonomous boards within the NMC: the Medical Education and Standards Board, the Undergraduate Medical Education Board, the Postgraduate Medical Education Board, and the Ethics and Medical Registration Board. Each board has distinct responsibilities aimed at addressing specific aspects of medical education and professional conduct.

NMC has been vested with a broad range of powers and functions contained in Section 10 of the Act. These include regulation of medical education, setting standards for medical colleges, and overseeing the licensing and registration of medical practitioners. The NMC is also tasked with accrediting medical institutions, establishing educational standards for both undergraduate and postgraduate programs, and regulating medical practice, including the enforcement of ethical guidelines and handling of disciplinary actions against medical professionals.

The Act also places a strong emphasis on maintaining high ethical standards and professional conduct. The Ethics and Medical Registration Board is responsible for enforcing a comprehensive Code of Ethics that addresses critical issues such as patient confidentiality, informed consent, and overall professional behaviour (Sections 27). The Act also introduces the National Exit Test (NEXT). NEXT serves a dual purpose: it acts as a licensing exam for medical practice and an entrance exam for postgraduate medical education. NEXT is designed to ensure that medical graduates meet the required standards for practice and to streamline admissions to advanced training programs (Sections 14 and 15).

Furthermore, The NMC is also empowered to register medical professionals and maintain a national register of practitioners. This centralized register ensures that all practicing doctors meet the required standards and are accountable for their professional conduct (Section 31). The NMC and its boards have the authority to address issues of malpractice and impose disciplinary actions, including suspending or revoking licenses, thereby maintaining the integrity of medical practice.

The Act underscores the importance of transparency and accountability in the regulatory process. The NMC is required to operate in a transparent manner, with provisions for public access to information about medical institutions, standards, and regulatory decisions. This emphasis on transparency is intended to build trust in the regulatory framework and ensure that stakeholders can hold the NMC accountable for its actions.

The constitution of the NMC was thus a significant improvement upon its predecessor, the MCI, which was quintessentially a doctor-centric regulatory body. The creation of the NMC had been intended to ensure an upgrade in medical education and much greater transparency and health delivery. But despite the progress, there are concerns regarding its implementation and function. One of the concerns raised is that it represents a monopolization of power. Though the NMC was intended to ensure speed and efficiency in the regulatory process, there is criticism about the substantial control it has still retained over medical education and practice. This could potentially undermine the autonomy of state medical councils and local institutions limiting their ability to respond to regional needs and making necessary policy adaptations.

Other concerns involve the NMC and its autonomous boards in terms of representation and inclusivity. There are concerns that the structure of NMC may not adequately represent the diverse perspectives of the medical community. For example, there is a fear that boards will have insufficient represented by rural practitioners and representatives of the various specialties or streams of medicine, which could lead to decisions that do not fully address the needs of all stakeholders.

Equally contentious has been the recent introduction of a National Exit Test-NEXT-which is supposed to double as both a licensing examination and an entrance test for postgraduate courses in medicine. Questions have been raised on its feasibility, equity, and the implication this test may have on students from underprivileged groups. Critics are concerned that the test might exacerbate existing inequalities in medical education even more, especially for students who cannot afford prolonged preparation or hail from resource-challenged settings. In addition to the concerns raised above ensuring regulation within a large number of medical institutions and practitioners is a big challenge to the NMC. There is also the issue of enforcement of the code of ethics.

It can thus be concluded that even as the NMC marks a significant step forward to improve medical regulation in India, a number of challenges remain. Centralization, representation, implementation of the NEXT, regulatory efficiency, ethical standards, medical education, and transparency are some aspects which will be crucial considering the mandate of the NMC for betterment of quality in medical education and practice in the country.

SUMMARY

This chapter has examined the regulation of medical professionals in India, emphasizing the critical role of effective governance in ensuring high standards of professionalism, ethical conduct, and patient safety. It traces the evolution of medical regulation from the establishment of the Medical Council of India (MCI) in 1933 to its dissolution due to inefficiency, corruption, and lack of transparency. In response to these challenges, the National Medical Commission (NMC) was established through the National Medical Commission Act, 2019, marking a significant shift towards a more structured, transparent, and accountable regulatory framework. The NMC is tasked with overseeing medical education, accrediting institutions, enforcing ethical guidelines, and maintaining a national register of medical practitioners. Its decentralized structure, supported by four autonomous boards, enables specialized oversight of medical education and professional conduct. Notably, the introduction of the National Exit Test (NEXT) aims to standardize medical licensing and postgraduate admissions. However, concerns persist regarding the centralization of power, lack of representation of diverse medical voices, and the potential inequities posed by NEXT. While the NMC represents progress in regulating India's healthcare system, challenges related to inclusivity, ethical enforcement, and effective implementation must be addressed to fully realize its mandate of enhancing the quality and accountability of medical education and practice.

CHAPTER

11

Regulation of the Nursing Sector

INTRODUCTION

The regulation of the nursing sector is as important as that of the medical professionals. Nurses constitute a vital part of the overall healthcare system and their contributions range from providing direct care in hospitals to serving in community health centres. Nurses usually serves as an initial point of contact among patients, spend more time with them and play a very important role in monitoring and managing health conditions. Regulating the nursing sector efficiently can ensure that nurses who are an integral part of healthcare delivery ecosystem have the knowledge, skills, and competencies necessary for high-quality care provision to improve the outcomes of the patients and their safety.

Another important aspect of nursing regulation is standardization and consistency. It ensures that standards of practice and education are uniformly maintained across regions, thereby guaranteeing that nurses, regardless of their geographical location, adhere to the same professional and ethical codes of conduct. This uniformity ensures the maintenance of a high level of care, whereby wherever services are sought, the care provided shall be proper and competent. Equally important is professional competence. Just like medical practitioners, nurses have to study and learn continuously in order to keep themselves updated with the latest on medical science and technology. Therefore, regulatory bodies require continuing education and professional development to update themselves on current best practices and treatments. In this way, there is continuous improvement and the maintenance of competence in order that care be delivered effectively. Moreover, nurses are employed in multidisciplinary healthcare and work in teams in assisting doctors, often working with doctors, therapists, and others. Good teamwork requires that each member works to consistent standards and behaviour. Regulation means that nurses are well-trained and can make a valued contribution to such teams, raising coordination and standards of care overall. A well-regulated nursing sector also serves to ensure efficiency in the healthcare system. By ensuring proper training and regulation of the nursing profession, the healthcare system can operate in a seamless, straightforward manner where different levels of care are clearly defined with roles and responsibilities. Efficiency is a critical part in dealing with patient loads, minimizing accidents, and optimizing resource allocation in health facilities.

11.1 LEGISLATIVE FRAMEWORK FOR NURSING REGULATION IN INDIA

A systematic regulation of the nursing sector regulation in India started after the enactment of the Indian Nursing Council Act of 1947[1]. This act established the Indian Nursing Council (INC), an autonomous body under the Ministry of Health and Family Welfare responsible for the conduct of the nursing profession at the national level. The INC has been entrusted with the responsibility for framing educational and practice standards, accreditation of nursing schools, and licensing. The Act dictates that each nursing institution should conduct its operations strictly according to the standards laid down by the council for ensuring homogeneity of standards across the country. It also ensures that a proper legal framework is in place for addressing issues concerning nursing practice such as maintaining professional ethics amongst practitioners and ensuring their competency. Indian Nursing Council is the apex regulatory body entrusted with the duty of maintaining the standards of nursing education and profession in India. The INC lays down the curriculum for various nursing courses. It also examines the competency of nursing students by holding examination and issues licenses them if they meet the requisite standards. INC also has the task of ensuring that nursing practices are carried out in accordance with national and international standards. It also updates itself continuously regarding the latest advancements in the healthcare sector as well as nursing science. Apart from this, INC also aims at professional ethics and code of conduct among the nursing professionals so that they can deliver appropriate and safe services to the patients.

State Nursing Councils work under the aegis of the Indian Nursing Council and address specific issues that may arise in particular states. The state councils are responsible for the implementation of standards as laid down by the national council, INC, considering regional variation and needs. They carry out registration and licensure of nurses within their state boundaries, maintain specific state regulations, and monitor state-specific activities relating to the compliance of nursing institutions with national and state guidelines. State councils also look into disciplinary actions by investigating complaints filed against practitioners and ensuring their conduct is within prescribed ethical and professional standards. Nursing education in India has been regulated in a bid to ensure that the training provided in the country conforms to uniform national standards. It is meant to equip the candidate with subject knowledge and practical experience in handling a patient. Institutions offering nursing courses are regularly inspected by the Council to ensure they maintain requisite educational standards. It lays emphasis on developing multifunctional training with emphasis on both theoretical knowledge and practical skills. Moreover, the INC also periodically updates the curriculum by incorporating new medical advancements and changed healthcare practices. The professional conduct and code of ethics form the basis for regulating nursing practice in India. The Indian Nursing Council and the State Nursing Councils lay down codes of conduct that define clearly what must be expected of a registered nurse as a professional. These cover a broad perspective on the practice of nursing in general and include situations such as patient care, confidentiality, and cooperation with colleagues. The core of this approach to ethics is the need to ensure confidence and optimum standards of care. Breach of this code can lead to negligence or other forms of unethical behaviour that could lead to suspension or revocation of a license to practice nursing. Having

1. https://www.indiannursingcouncil.org/uploads/files/16141575032256.pdf

set rules such as this helps nurses conduct their business at the highest level of professionalism and integrity in their practice.

Continuing education and professional development are crucial for nursing professionals to stay abreast of changing times in healthcare services and nursing. The nurses are supposed to attend to workshops, seminars, and other learning activities to achieve ongoing learning. Continuous learning would help them get updated regarding skill adoption, new techniques, and latest research and developments that are going on in their respective field. Indeed, that is how continuing education was prescribed for license renewal, so the nurses will be competent enough to serve and treat their patients with expertise. The regulatory framework encourages a culture for lifelong learning that will enable the nursing workforce to grow and improve continuously.

Despite regulations being in place, challenges still prevailed in the nursing sector of India. These include non-uniform implementation of standards at state levels, shortage of trained faculty to impart education in nursing, and an urgent need to revise curricula to reflect advances in the healthcare field. Besides, more practical training and on-ground experience are required. With an attempt to overcome these issues, the ongoing reforms have been trying to adopt measures for better regulatory oversight, quality improvement of nursing education, and better implementation of standards. These reforms underline a more integrated and efficient regulatory environment that shall further enhance patient care and, finally, the nursing profession in India.

In view of the challenges outlined above, the Parliament passed the National Nursing and Midwifery Commission (NNMC) Act, 2023[2]. This is a significant and ambitious piece of legislation. The Act replaces the old Indian Nursing Council with a contemporary regulatory framework and brings about a major reform for the sector.

The major provisions of the provisions under the NNMC Act, 2023, are aimed at upgrading nursing education and practice standards, professional conduct, transparency and accountability in the profession. Salient features of the Act can be discussed as follows:

- **Establishing National and State Commissions:** The NNMC Act dictates the setting up of a National Nursing and Midwifery Commission and separate National boards as well as State-specific Nursing and Midwifery Commissions. These would ensure enforcement and maintenance of standards in education and service, supervise the professional conduct of, and a total, online and real-time registers of nurses and midwives.
- **Tenure and Accountability:** An important reform brought by the Act relates to the provision for fixed tenures for the members and the chairperson of the Commission. This will eliminate possibilities of reappointment, curb claims of vested interest, enhance transparency and accountability in the nursing education sector.
- **Uniform Admission Process and Competence:** This Act ensures that all institutions offering nursing education follow the same admission process bringing about uniformity and consistency. This Act also lays emphasis on acquisition of high levels of competence by nursing and midwifery professionals in ensuring they are able to offer quality health services.
- **Innovation and Partnership:** The NNMC Act fosters the introduction of best state-of-the-art and innovative practices for nursing education. The Commission will promote

2. https://www.indiacode.nic.in/bitstream/123456789/19796/1/a2023-26.pdf

partnership with industry stakeholders and other institutions into excellence, fostering research, and advancing the profession of nursing.

- **Focus on the Development of Soft Skills and Specialized Courses:** The Act also emphasizes the importance of developing soft skills among professional nurses and recognizes the value of specialized courses and certification programs. This has been done in an attempt to further enhance the expertise of nurses in specialized nursing domains, thus improving quality overall.
- **Global Mobility and Expertise:** The NNMC Act aims to enhance the global mobility and employability of Indian nurses by establishing a standardized and internationally recognized framework for their qualifications and professional credentials This will allow open the gateway of greater career opportunities in international healthcare systems and allows Indian nurses to compete more effectively with other professionals from all over the world. The Act supports the development of skills and expertise that respond to the demands of international health and help in the professional growth and global mobility of Indian nurses.
- **National Advisory Council and Coordination:** The Act also stipulates setting up a National Advisory Council that would have balanced representation from all the states and union territories. It would give advisory guidance in matters relating to nursing education, services, training, and research. In addition, the Act promotes joint consultations with relevant statutory bodies such as the National Medical Commission, the Pharmacy Council of India, the National Commission for Allied and Healthcare Professions, the National Commission of Indian System of Medicine, and the National Commission of Homeopathy. It aims to enhance teamwork and coordination within the healthcare sector.

Overall, the NNMC Act is a progressive piece of legislation. Among other things, it aims to regulate and develop the nursing profession in India by standardizing education and credentials to international benchmarks for improving the global mobility and employability of Indian nurses. However, its success depends much on its effective implementation. Some of the practical impediments include integrating the new professional standards across various diverse regions, which might face resistance from existing institutions. It will also require substantial investment in training and infrastructural support. The success of the Act will thus depend on the resolving implementation hurdles so that the ambitious objectives of the Act could be truly realized.

SUMMARY

The critical role of nursing regulation in strengthening India's healthcare system has been discussed in this chapter, highlighting how efficient governance ensures that nursing professionals possess the necessary knowledge, skills, and ethical standards to deliver high-quality patient care. It traces the evolution of nursing regulation from the Indian Nursing Council (INC), established under the Indian Nursing Council Act of 1947, to the recent enactment of the National Nursing and Midwifery Commission (NNMC) Act, 2023. The INC was responsible for setting educational standards, accrediting institutions, and enforcing professional ethics. However, challenges such as inconsistent implementation across states, faculty shortages, and outdated curricula hindered progress. To address these issues, the NNMC Act, 2023, introduced significant reforms, including the creation of National and State Commissions to oversee nursing education and professional conduct, fixed tenures for leadership to enhance accountability, a uniform admission process, and the promotion of innovative practices and partnerships. The Act also emphasizes soft skills development, specialized courses, and global recognition of Indian nursing qualifications to improve international employability. The establishment of a National Advisory Council facilitates collaboration with other healthcare regulatory bodies, promoting integrated healthcare delivery. NNMC Act presents a comprehensive framework for advancing nursing education and practice. Nevertheless, its success hinges on effective implementation, overcoming institutional resistance, and ensuring adequate resources to achieve its transformative goals.

CHAPTER

12 Regulation of the Paramedical Sector

INTRODUCTION

Paramedical professionals are a diverse group of healthcare workers who support doctors and nurses in providing patient care. These include Emergency Medical Technicians and paramedics, which attend to emergencies, radiology and laboratory technicians who perform the necessary diagnostic tests, physical and occupational therapists that would aid recovery and rehabilitation, speech-language pathologists that treat communication disorders, and respiratory therapists that handle breathing problems. Besides, medical assistants, phlebotomists, dietitians, and biomedical equipment technicians all help to provide an array of patient care services that contribute towards ensuring that the treatment and recovery processes are effective and smooth.

12.1 REGULATORY FRAMEWORK

Despite such skill intensive set of professional requirements and crucial role played by paramedical professionals, there was no central or uniform framework to effectively regulate the various aspects related to the paramedical professionals. In order to bridge this regulatory gap, the National Commission for Allied and Healthcare Professions Act, 2021[1] was brought by the Parliament. The Act establishes and provides for the regulation and maintenance of standards of education and service for allied and healthcare professionals. The provisions of the Act include carrying out assessments of institutions, maintaining a central register and state register, and establishing the system with the purpose to improve access, facilitate research and development, and absorb the new scientific advancement. The salient aspects of the Act may be discussed as follows:

1. National Commission for Allied and Healthcare Professions Act, 2021

- **Definition of Allied Health Professional:** The Act [Section 2(d)][2] defines an allied health professional as an associate, technician or technologist trained to assist in the diagnosis and treatment of a range of health conditions pertaining to diseases, illnesses, injuries, or impairments. Allied health professionals play an important role in the healthcare system, working in alignment with the doctors, nurses and patients. Their training prepares them to assist in diagnostics and treatments, which makes them extremely useful in clinical and rehabilitation settings. To be recognized as an allied health worker in this Act, individuals must take a diploma or degree that has a minimum of 2,000 hours of study, which is usually spread over two to four years. This requirement ensures that professionals are adequately prepared to handle the complexities of patient care, thus preparing a competent and skilled workforce. Emphasis on formal education and standardized training may lead to improved patient outcomes since trained professionals can effectively implement treatment protocols and work in close collaboration with medical staff.
- **Healthcare Professional:** A healthcare professional defined separately under Section 2(j)[3], also encompasses a wide range of professionals including scientists, therapists and others specialists engaged in various aspects of health service delivery. They practice in preventive, curative, rehabilitative, therapeutic, or promotional domains. This broad scope reflects the multifaceted nature of healthcare wherein a diverse expertise is needed to satisfy patients fully. A healthcare professional is required to obtain a degree requiring at least 3,600 hours of study to qualify under this Act spanning 3 to 6 years. This extensive training ensures that the professionals have a depth of knowledge to handle complex medical situations and can effectively undertake patient care. This is intended to create a more structured and efficient delivery of healthcare services leading to better clinical outcomes.
- **Allied and Healthcare Professions:** The Act also defines specific categories of allied and healthcare professions that are officially recognized. The Act enumerates various such fields, such as life sciences, trauma care, surgical technology, physiotherapy, and nutrition. Recognition under the Act provides a legal framework for identifying as well as establishing accountability with respect to such listed professions in the healthcare delivery sector as well as enables such professions to grow in tandem with changing healthcare requirements and emerging fields. This adaptability is very important in a rapidly changing medical landscape.

---

2. Section 2 (d) of the Act provides the following definition of Allied Health Professional "allied health professional" includes an associate, technician or technologist who is trained to perform any technical and practical task to support diagnosis and treatment of illness, disease, injury or impairment, and to support implementation of any healthcare treatment and referral plan recommended by a medical, nursing or any other healthcare professional, and who has obtained any qualification of diploma or degree under this Act, the duration of which shall not be less than two thousand hours spread over a period of two years to four years divided into specific semesters;
3. "healthcare professional" includes a scientist, therapist or other professional who studies, advises, researches, supervises or provides preventive, curative, rehabilitative, therapeutic or promotional health services and who has obtained any qualification of degree under this Act, the duration of which shall not be less than three thousand six hundred hours spread over a period of three years to six years divided into specific semesters;

- **National Commission for Allied and Healthcare Professions:** The Act establishes the National Commission for Allied and Healthcare Professions, which would play a pivotal role in governing this sector. The composition of the Commission includes a Chairperson, a Vice-Chairperson, members from different government Departments, a representative of the Directorate General of Health Services, and others. The diverse composition is intended to draw from a wide range of experiences and perspectives to facilitate better and considered decision making. The establishment of the Commission centralizes the regulatory framework with an aim to establish uniform standards throughout the allied and healthcare sectors. This central oversight is essential to ensure that the quality of education and practice is maintained. The Commission will set strategic direction for the development of the allied and healthcare professions as well as identify and fill gaps in training and practice, hence providing a robust and responsive healthcare workforce.

  The Commission has been entrusted with several key functions relating to allied and healthcare professionals. The Commission plays an important role in shaping the training landscape by developing policies and standards for education and practice, and would ensure that curricula remain relevant to provide adequate and skillsets to the trainees. The creation and maintenance of an online Central Register of registered professionals facilitates transparency and accountability, allowing stakeholders to verify credentials and ensuring that only qualified individuals practice..
- **Professional Councils:** The Commission has also been empowered under the Act to establish a Professional Council for all categories of professions in the allied and healthcare professions recognized by the Commission. The councils shall have a president as well as members drawn from various professions to ensure that diverse opinions and voices are adequately represented in the councils in the decision-making process. This representation can lead to more tailored policies and practices. The commission can also delegate certain functions to the Councils, which enable operational efficiency by allowing the Commission focus on general, strategic, issues, while the Councils deal with profession-specific issues. The Councils may also provide avenues for professional development through teamwork, networking, and continuous education among the practitioners.
- **State Councils:** The Act also mandates setting up State Allied and Healthcare by State governments within six months after the passage of the Act. State Allied and Healthcare Councils are to be constituted so that attention is paid to localized contexts and needs since the State Councils better positioned to understand the needs and professional exigencies of their respective regions and can respond better to the challenges of community health. Like the central commission, state councils shall also consist of professionals with wide ranging experience from different sectors to guide allied healthcare professionals and contribute to regulating their practice at local levels. State Councils will also be expected to enforce code of conduct and ethics, maintain state register of professionals as well as inspect institutions, to uphold standards and ensure accountability among healthcare personnel within their respective jurisdictions. The Act also provides that no person is allowed to practice as a qualified allied and healthcare practitioner other than those enrolled in a State Register or the National Register. Any person who contravenes this provision will be punished with a fine of ₹ 50,000.

- **Establishment of New Institutions:** Any new institution or modification of an existing one is only allowed upon prior permission of the State Council. Moreover, a new institution shall be able to start a new course, increase the admission capacity or admit new batches only after it has satisfied the requirements stipulated by the state council. In order to ensure quality educational and training standards, the Act further stipulates that any qualifications awarded by an institution which has not sought the necessary approvals shall not be recognized under the Act.

The National Commission for Allied and Healthcare Professions Act, 2021 is also undoubtedly a progressive piece of legislation. While the Act, 2021 aims to create a structured and regulated environment for allied health professionals, its implementation challenges reveal critical shortcomings. The implementation of the Act has been delayed even though a significant time has elapsed after its promulgation. Supreme Court has strongly pointed out the slow progress in the establishment of state councils[4]. With only 14 out of 36 states and union territories having constituted their respective councils, the effectiveness of the Act is compromised. The lack of operational councils further undermines the regulatory intent of the Act, raising questions about the commitment of both the central and state governments to advance allied health professions. This delay not only reflects bureaucratic inertia but also signals potential gaps in political will to prioritize healthcare reforms. To address the implementation challenges, it is essential to strengthen political and a sense of active commitment from the state as well as the central and state governments. Furthermore, clearer rules and guidelines must also be formulated to facilitate its implementation.

SUMMARY

Role of paramedical professionals is vital in India's healthcare system. Keeping this in mind the regulatory reforms introduced through the National Commission for Allied and Healthcare Professions (NCAHP) Act, 2021 have been introduced. The Act standardizes education and accountability for various healthcare workers, including technicians and therapists, by establishing central and state councils to regulate professional practices. However, slow implementation, with many states yet to form councils, has led to regulatory gaps. Stronger political commitment and better coordination are essential to fully realize the Act's goals and enhance healthcare service delivery.

4. https://www.hindustantimes.com/india-news/sc-sets-two-month-deadline-for-implementing-allied-healthcare-professions-act-2021-101723487167960.html

CHAPTER

13 Regulation of the Pharmaceutical Sector

INTRODUCTION

Regulatory supervision and quality monitoring of medicines and pharmaceutical products are essential to ensure public health and safety. Rigorous standards for production, manufacturing, and distribution are required to prevent substandard or counterfeit drugs from entering the market and thereby saves consumers from the harm such drugs can cause. Regulatory bodies can ensure that medicines are effective and safe by conducting rigorous reviews of clinical trial data and manufacturing practices. This ensures public confidence in healthcare systems by ensuring the efficacy and safety of approved products. Quality monitoring must, therefore, be a continuous process in the lifecycle of any product. Continuous monitoring of drug safety and efficacy after the launch of products into the market is basically done through post-marketing surveillance and pharmacovigilance. These systems can help identify adverse reactions and long-term effects, which cannot be observed in clinical trials. Quality control measures enable regulatory authorities to respond promptly to any safety issues.

India's pharmaceutical sector has grown to become one of the major players in the world market. As one of the fastest-growing science based and knowledge intensive sectors in the country Indian pharmaceutical industry not only caters to the domestic market but is also a leading global supplier of pharmaceutical products. Besides, the pharma industry also engages in high value activities like clinical trials, research and development, amongst others. Such diversifications and the resultant penetration of both developed and developing necessitates strict regulatory control to sustain quality and attracts significant investments and partnerships.

13.1 DRUGS AND COSMETIC ACT

Among the most important laws in India's pharmaceutical regulatory framework is the **Drugs and Cosmetic Act**[1]. The Act was first promulgated in 1940 and has undergone a number of subsequent amendments over the years. The Act aims to regulate the sales, imports, and distribution of drugs and cosmetics by establishing a strong system of licensing. Subsequent

1. https://www.indiacode.nic.in/bitstream/123456789/15278/1/drug_cosmeticsa1940-23.pdf

to the coming into force of the Act, the Drug and Cosmetics Rules, 1945 were formulated to categorize drugs into different schedules, and to make provisions for their sale, storage, and prescription.

13.1.1 Objectives of the Drugs and Cosmetics Act

- **Regulation of Drugs:** The Drugs and Cosmetics Act mandates that all drugs must undergo rigorous testing and evaluation to demonstrate their safety and efficacy before they are approved for use. This involves conducting pre-clinical and clinical trials to assess the impact of drugs on human health. The approval process established by the Act ensures that only safe and effective drugs reach the market, with thorough reviews by regulatory authorities. Additionally, post-market surveillance is crucial for monitoring drugs after approval, allowing for the identification of any adverse effects or long-term safety issues that may arise.
- **Quality Control:** To maintain high standards in drug production, the Act emphasizes the importance of quality control. This includes enforcing Good Manufacturing Practices (GMP) that require manufacturers to adhere to strict guidelines regarding production processes, equipment, and facility conditions. Batch testing is mandated to ensure that each batch of drugs produced meets predetermined specifications. Moreover, implementing measures to prevent contamination is vital to maintaining the integrity of drugs throughout the manufacturing process.
- **Cosmetic Safety:** The Act plays a crucial role in ensuring the safety of cosmetics by regulating their ingredients and usage. It prohibits harmful substances in cosmetic formulations, ensuring that only safe ingredients are utilized. The Act also mandates accurate and clear labelling, requiring products to disclose ingredients, usage instructions, and safety warnings. Furthermore, consumer education about safe cosmetic use and potential allergic reactions is emphasized, promoting informed choices.
- **Licensing:** A robust licensing framework is established under the Act to ensure that only qualified entities manufacture and sell drugs and cosmetics. Regulatory bodies are designated to issue licenses, and specific eligibility criteria are set for businesses seeking approval. This framework ensures that manufacturers and distributors are competent and compliant with safety standards. Regular audits and inspections further ensure ongoing adherence to licensing requirements, reinforcing accountability within the industry.
- **Prohibition of Misleading Information:** To protect consumers, the Act specifically addresses advertising practices related to drugs and cosmetics. It mandates that all promotional materials accurately reflect the efficacy and safety of products, preventing misleading claims. Regulatory authorities are empowered to scrutinize advertisements and take action against those that mislead consumers. By ensuring access to truthful information, the Act helps consumers make informed decisions about drug and cosmetic use, safeguarding their interests.
- **Monitoring and Compliance:** The Act empowers regulatory bodies to monitor compliance continuously. This includes market surveillance to ensure adherence to established standards and regulations. Enforcement actions are available against

manufacturers or distributors who violate the Act, including penalties, fines, and product recalls. Additionally, reporting systems for consumers and healthcare professionals are established to report adverse effects or safety concerns, promoting accountability and responsiveness.

- **Consumer Protection:** Consumer protection is a key priority of the Act, focusing on safeguarding public health. Thorough safety assessments of drugs and cosmetics are conducted to identify any potential health risks before products are marketed. Public awareness campaigns educate consumers about safe use and potential dangers associated with certain products. Moreover, the Act provides mechanisms for consumers to seek redress in cases of harm caused by unsafe products, reinforcing the commitment to consumer safety.
- **Harmonization with International Standards:** To promote global best practices, the Act focuses on harmonization with international standards. This involves engaging with global health organizations to align domestic regulations with international guidelines. Standardization ensures consistency with those of other countries, facilitating international trade and ensuring product quality. The Act is also adaptable, regularly updated to incorporate advancements in science and technology, thereby keeping pace with global standards and practices.

The Drugs and Cosmetics Act defines several important terms crucial for understanding its provisions. The Act clarifies what is a drug. According to the Act, A **Drug** encompasses various categories, including medicines for internal or external use on humans or animals, diagnostic and treatment substances, and components like empty gelatine capsules. It also covers devices used for diagnosing or treating diseases, as specified by the Central Government. A cosmetic, similarly defined, refers to any item intended for application on the human body for purposes such as cleansing, beautifying, or altering appearance, including components meant for such use. The Act also addresses misbranded drugs, which are considered misbranded if they lack proper labelling, are altered to conceal defects, or bear misleading statements on their packaging. Also, as per the Act, Ayurvedic, Siddha, or Unani drugs refers to medicines manufactured according to traditional formulae for diagnosis, treatment, or prevention in humans or animals. In contrast, patent or proprietary medicine refers to formulations from traditional systems that do not include parenteral drugs, as well as drugs prepared for administration in other systems not listed in the Indian Pharmacopoeia.

The Act also addresses adulteration in drugs. A drug is deemed **adulterated** if it contains decomposed substances, has been prepared or stored under unsanitary conditions, includes harmful ingredients, or is mixed with substances that diminish its quality. While the term manufacture is not explicitly defined, it generally includes processes related to making or altering drugs and cosmetics for sale, excluding retail compounding. Likewise, a spurious drug is identified if it is imported under a false name, resembles another drug in a misleading manner, or claims association with a non-existent producer. In terms of cosmetics, a misbranded cosmetic contains unapproved colours, lacks proper labelling, or features false statements. A spurious cosmetic is one that falsely claims a legitimate producer's identity or misleads consumers through its labelling. In many scenarios, a cosmetic may be considered misleading and illegal, for example when it is imported under the name of a different cosmetic, and when it purports to be or replaces another product so as to deceive consumers.

Moreover, a cosmetic is also held to be problematic if its container or label bears the name of another cosmetic, or if it otherwise purports to have been manufactured by some imaginary person or concern. In addition, if it declares that it is a product manufactured by a company that does not exist, then that also falls into false representation. All these provisions have been put in place to guard against deception and bring in the element of transparency into the drugs and cosmetics sector.

These definitions outlined in the Drugs and Cosmetics Act are crucial for establishing a clear regulatory framework within the pharmaceutical and cosmetics sectors. In clearly spelling out definitions for terms such as "drug," "cosmetic," and "misbranded drug," the Act creates a standardized language that facilitates consistent interpretation and enforcement of regulations. This clarity is essential for manufacturers, distributors, and healthcare professionals, as it helps ensure that all stakeholders understand their responsibilities and the requirements they must meet.

The definitions play a vital role in protecting public health and safety by preventing the circulation of substandard, adulterated, or spurious products in the market. This is particularly important in a diverse and complex marketplace where consumers rely on these products for their health and well-being. Effective regulation through well-defined terms not only builds consumer trust but also supports the ongoing development of high-quality pharmaceutical and cosmetic products, ultimately contributing to better health outcomes across the population.

The Act also establishes **The Drugs Technical Advisory Board (DTAB)** is a statutory body established by the Central Government under the provisions of the Drugs and Cosmetics Act. It is required to provide advice to both the Central and State Governments in regard to technical matters related to the Act. Further, the DTAB formulates guidelines in respect of various types of drug formulations as requested by the Central Government.

The board is constituted with 18 members which include ex-officio members, nominees, and elected representatives. It ensures that all facets of the pharmacy and medical profession are represented adequately. The Chairman of the DTAB is the Director General of Medical and Health Services, Government of India and its Member Secretary is the Drugs Controller General of India.

The establishment of DTAB exemplifies the need for expert and technical advice in the structure that governs the pharmaceutical field in India. By providing guidance on technical issues and laying down guidelines, the authority performs a critical function in ensuring that drugs and cosmetics are manufactured with safety, effectiveness, and quality. Since the association comprises different kinds of constituencies, it throws light upon the challenges and needs of the pharmaceutical and healthcare industry as well. Such heterogeneity guarantees even wiser decisions in constantly changing medical practices and technology. The total importance of DTAB lies in the fact that India's drug regulations cannot be left anything less than strong and responsive to public health requirement.

The Drugs Consultative Committee is an advisory committee constituted under Section 7 of the Drugs and Cosmetics Act. Its principal functions are to advise the central government, the states, as well as the Drugs Technical Advisory Board towards uniform implementation of the Act and associated rules. The committee consists of two nominees from the central government, one nominee from each of the state governments, and one nominee from the union territory administrations. Generally, a nominee who is the Director of Drug Control Administration or the Drug Controller of that particular state or union territory is appointed to this council.

The Act also establishes under Section 6, the Central Drug Laboratory headed by a director appointed by the central government. It performs a number of functions that include the analysis of drug and cosmetic samples sent by customs officials, courts and other departments. The laboratory also offers advisory services to government bodies while accepting samples for analysis from private parties for a fee. It also engages in research and development to improve drug analysis techniques.

To enforce the provisions of the Act, Drug inspectors are appointed under Section 3 (e) by both the state and central governments as important machinery for enforcing the provisions of the Drugs and Cosmetics Act. They are entrusted with the responsibility of ensuring compliance within their respective jurisdictions. Drug inspectors carry out regular inspections, sample collection for analysis, complaint investigations, and initiation of prosecutions in cases of violations. Other than the prosecution task, inspectors are empowered to detain imported packages on account of violation of the drug regulations.

13.1.2 The Drugs and Cosmetics Rules of 1945[2]

The Drugs and Cosmetics Rules of 1945 further supplement the Drugs and Cosmetics Act. These rules include provisions for categorizing drugs into schedules, as well as guidelines for storing, selling, displaying, and prescribing drugs within each schedule. In addition to the aforementioned rules, the New Drugs and Clinical Trial Rules were notified in 2019[3] to provide an enabling framework through which new drugs and clinical trials are approved. The New Drugs and Clinical Trial Rules (NDCT Rules), 2019 were established to streamline the approval process for new drugs and clinical trials while ensuring patient safety and ethical conduct. Key objectives include expediting access to innovative treatments, protecting trial participants through clear definitions of adverse events and compensation requirements, and promoting transparency and accountability in the regulatory framework.

These rules define a "new drug" broadly to include any drug not significantly used previously in India, modified drugs, fixed dose combinations and various innovative therapies including vaccines and stem cell products. The NDCT Rules govern every activity related to new drugs including investigational new drugs, clinical trials, bioequivalence studies, and bioavailability studies, besides stipulating Ethics Committees to oversee violations.

NDCT Rules also define "adverse events," which are all the adverse medical incidents occurring during treatment with investigational drugs. In such cases, the rules mandate that compensation must be provided to the trial subjects. The Drugs Controller General of India, who acts as a Central Licensing Authority, accords licenses and makes approvals based on these rules.

As per these rules, to conduct any clinical trials or related studies, the entity is required to form and register an Ethics Committee. In fact, these committees are going to play a very important role in the ethical conduct of a trial, as they will have to provide approval before proceeding with any studies. In case of serious adverse events, the committee is duty-bound to investigate and report to the Central Licensing Authority.

---

2. https://www.indiacode.nic.in/handle/123456789/1362/simple-search?query=The%20Drugs%20and%20Cosmetics%20Rules,%201945&searchradio=rules
3. https://cdsco.gov.in/opencms/opencms/en/Acts-and-rules/New-Drugs/

The NDCT Rules establish streamlined processes for conducting clinical trials. Applications for trial permissions shall be made using specific and detailed forms and supporting accompanying documents and fees. Significantly, the rules provide that applications for such drugs discovered or developed in India shall be disposed of within a period of thirty working days, and if no communication is received by the applicant within this period, the permission shall be held to be granted. Compensation for any clinical injury or death during a clinical trial has also been provided in related sections, providing a precise account of how such compensation shall be assessed. Lastly, under the rules, a manufacture or import of new drugs for clinical trials shall be subject to the Central Licensing Authority's permission; and such permissions are valid for three years.

13.2 CENTRAL DRUGS STANDARD CONTROL ORGANIZATION

The Central Drugs Standard Control Organisation (CDCSO) is the apex regulatory body in India under the Drugs and Cosmetics act. The main role of this body is to ensure that drugs, cosmetics, and medical devices sold in India are safe, effective, and of good quality. Working under the Director-General of Health Services in the Ministry of Health and Family Welfare, CDSCO performs the sensitive and gigantic task of protecting and promoting public health across the country. With a strong framework of six regional offices, four sub-offices, 13 port offices, and seven laboratories, CDSCO is well-equipped to do its regulatory responsibility effectively. The functions of CDSCO can be discussed below:

- **Drug Regulation:** CDSCO as the National Regulatory Authority in the country plays a significant role in overseeing the entire lifecycle of drugs. Its role involves approving new drugs, where thorough assessment is carried out to ensure that these new drugs pass all safety and efficacy standards set before their use in the markets. This includes reviewing clinical trials data and the manufacturing process. The CDSCO also regulates clinical research by setting guidelines and monitoring compliance to prevent malpractices to safeguard the rights of participants and to ensure informed consent. It also monitors drug quality standards which are in line with international standards, regulates the import of drugs, and coordinates with State Drug Control Agencies so that the enforcement of national policies is uniform.
- **Regulation of Medical Equipment:** The regulation of medical equipment is also among the critical roles assigned to CDSCO. This is an area which has gained more attention lately due to increased technological investment in the healthcare industry. The medical equipment production in India is approved by the Drug Controller General of India who heads the CDSCO. A license from the CDSCO is essential to manufacture and sell medical equipment so as to ensure a benchmark of safety as well as efficacy standards. Moreover, CDSCO must always monitor the market performance of the devices after their release ensuring that these products are always safe and effective for use by the public. CDSCO also plays a role in developing regulatory frameworks for emerging medical technologies, such as digital health solutions. It also collaborates with manufacturers to promote best practices in device development.
- **Regulation of Biological Products:** Regulation of biological products is another area where CDSCO plays an important role. Biologicals include vaccines, blood transfusion

products, antimicrobials, human cells and tissues etc. The organization has the task of ensuring that production, storage, distribution, and handling of these products are done strictly with high safety protocols. CDSCO also issues NOCs for biological products to be used in testing and clinical use. Advanced therapies, such as stem cell and gene therapies, are also licensed and scrutinized for high safety and efficacy by the organization.

From the above discussions it is evident that CDSCO has an extremely crucial role to play in India's drug regulatory landscape comparable to the role played by its counterparts such as the Food and Drug Administration (FDA) in the US and the European Medicines Agency. However, while the organization plays an equally sensitive role certain concerns have been raised with respect to its functioning. One of the major concerns is the inadequacy of this agency in terms of manpower and resources that would allow them to handle the drug evaluation and regulation well. For instance, the Parliamentary Standing Committee on Health and Family Welfare in its recent report[4] highlighting issues with CDSCO's operations, such as understaffing and insufficient resources. This report emphasized concerns about the drug approval process and conflicts of interest within the agency recommended higher budgets and more employees to efficiently run activities. Another requirement highlighted was greater transparency in the drug approval process. There must be explicit rules provided and a record of each evaluation and decision available to the public to increase the confidence of the people and encourage accountability by the agency.

Additionally, strengthening clinical trial requirements particularly emphasizing on the necessity for robust phase III trials would help ensure that medications are safe and effective for the Indian population, and actually take into account potential ethnic variations in drug responses.

Addressing conflicts of interest is another vital area for improvement. This can be done by establishing independent review panels for drug approvals. This can mitigate biases and prioritize public health over industry demands. Last but not the least investing in the training of regulatory staff is also a must. This would enable the organization to keep pace with global best practices and emerging medical technologies. This would enhance CDSCO's overall effectiveness.

13.3 THE DRUGS, MEDICAL DEVICES AND COSMETICS BILL, 2022[5]

The Union Ministry of Health and Family welfare has framed and introduced the Drugs, Medical Devices and Cosmetics Bill, 2023 to modernize and update the Drugs and Cosmetics Act of 1940. This legislation is intended to overhaul the regulatory framework governing imports, manufacture, distribution, and sale in India for the drugs, medical devices, and cosmetics space. Thus addresses a critical need to frame regulations that keep pace with the advancements in the medical technology sector. The bill aims to respond to the dynamic nature of medical products in the context of increased global emphasis on health and rapid technical change. The key features of the Bill can be discussed as follows:

4. https://prsindia.org/theprsblog/lapses-in-the-process-of-drug-approval-in-india?page=14&per-page=1
5. The Drugs, Medical Devices and Cosmetics Bill, 2022.

- **Medical Devices as a Separate Category:** The Drugs and Cosmetics Act, 1940 categorized medical devices as a subset of drugs subjecting them to the same regulations. However, the rapid technological development of medical devices and their distinctiveness requires them to be appropriately classified. The new Bill proposes a more comprehensive definition of medical devices. This includes all types of equipment and software employed in the diagnosis, treatment and disease management. Such devices include implants, disability assistance devices, life support systems among others. The Drugs, Medical Devices and Cosmetics Bill 2023 provides for a risk-based classification of medical devices. Devised are categorized in terms of the risks they pose (low, moderate, and high levels of risk) as per intended use, invasiveness, or possible effects on patients' safety. A regulatory framework based on the risk level allows for specific tailored requirements and greater scrutiny before such product enter the market. For high-risk products post-market surveillance needs to be of a significantly higher order, while moderate or low risk devices will go through an easier approval process.

  The Bill also proposes to establish a "**Medical Devices Technical Advisory Board**" which would be a consultative body to advise the government on technical facets of medical devices. The Board shall consist of members from different departments of government such as the Health Ministry, Department of Atomic Energy, Department of Science and Technology, Ministry of Electronics, Defence Research and Development Organization etc. In addition to this, experts in the fields of biomedical, biomaterial and polymer technologies will also be a part of this board. Medical Device Testing Centres, are also proposed to be established at central and state levels to ensure that these devices are safe to deploy and effective.
- **Emphasis on Alternative Systems of Medicines (AYUSH):** The Bill expands the AYUSH framework and also now incorporates Sowa-Rigpa and Homeopathy as well. It introduces two forms of drugs: "drugs" approved by authoritative pharmacopoeias and "innovative drugs" that are formulated from natural products that are not listed there. More traditional forms of medicine will be monitored by separate boards responsible for every category falling under the AYUSH umbrella. This would be supplemented by the establishment of the National Medicinal Plant Board along with a Scientific Research Board to foster inter-disciplinarity and to harmonize modern science with the development of new AYUSH medicines.
- **E-Pharmacies:** The Bill has provided for the setting up of regulations by the Central Government in view of the emerging need for regulation in the e-pharmacy industry so that drugs sold online are regulated. The bill duly forbids selling, stocking, or distributing any drugs online, without proper licenses and authorizations so that unregulated sale of online drugs is checked. Central Government will fix guidelines for all the licensing and regulatory processes involved, which thereby would enhance compliance burden upon e-pharmacies.
- **New Drugs and Clinical Trial:** Clinical trials relating to drugs are also governed by the New Drugs and Clinical Trials Rules, 2019; clinical investigations concerning medical devices are covered by the Medical Devices Rules, 2017. Neither, however, is part of the current Act. The present Bill attempts to bridge this gap in relation to both clinical trials and investigations. The bill provides that permission from the Central

Licensing Authority must be sought before any such trials or investigations take place. The bill further enunciates provisions for the medical management and compensation of the subjects who incidentally bear adverse effects during such studies.

SUMMARY

Overall, the Drugs, Medical Devices and Cosmetics Bill would be a reform-oriented bill which intends to redesign India's current drugs and cosmetics regulatory regime, which has not kept pace with the dynamic landscape of drug cosmetics and devices regulation. It fulfils the long-felt necessity of having a consolidated mechanism for modern health innovations in the country. Nevertheless, for its practical implementation to be successful when enacted the capacity of regulatory bodies to enforce new regulations effectively will need to be augmented. Moreover, adequate resources and trained personnel need to be allocated to regulatory bodies to ensure that the intended improvements materialize effectively. Without sufficient funding and training, these bodies may struggle to enforce new regulations, conduct thorough evaluations, and maintain effective oversight of the industry.

CHAPTER

14

Regulation of Clinical Establishments

INTRODUCTION

The hospitals and clinical establishments in India that had been for a long time remained largely unregulated. This has led to a number of problems in healthcare delivery. A major area of concern has been the lack of uniform standards across medical establishments due to the inconsistencies in the standards governing healthcare establishments. It has led to extreme inequalities in healthcare quality and proliferation of medical establishments with substandard, even non-existent infrastructural and medical facilities.

Patient safety has been another major issue. Due to a lack of regulatory oversight, many clinical establishments had been functioning in potentially unsafe conditions, unsanitary environment, ineffective sterilization of equipment, and often employing personnel who are not duly qualified. Lack of regulation also resulted in the exploitation of patients. Overcharging, unnecessary medical procedures, and low-quality medications for profit motives rather than concerns about the patient's well-being were rampant. Poor accountability characterized the system: there were few avenues for grievance redressal due to malpractice or negligence and even they were ineffective and time consuming. This created an atmosphere of impunity among some of the healthcare practitioners.

14.1 REGULATORY FRAMEWORK FOR CLINICAL ESTABLISHMENTS

The fragmentation of the regulatory framework further complicated effective oversight. Different states adhered to different regulations leading to confusion and inconsistencies on compliance.

All these problems forced the government to bring in an overall reform in the regulation of the healthcare facilities in the country. This led to the promulgation of the Clinical Establishments Act 2010[1]. This Act sought to address several critical gaps pertaining to the regulation of medical establishment.

Clinical Establishments (Registration and Regulation) Act, 2010 has a wide regulatory scope and covers a wide range of entities both in the government as well as in the private

1. http://www.clinicalestablishments.gov.in/

sectors. The definition of clinical establishments Section 2(c) includes hospitals, from large multi-specialty institutions to smaller facilities. Nursing homes offering inpatient care on a much smaller scale are also covered within its ambit. The definition also covers diagnostic centres which carry out all kind of laboratory tests and imaging services by maintaining standardized operations procedure. Additionally, outpatient services, day care centres, rehabilitation centres, which focus on the recovery process for the patient after illness or injury, maternity homes with maternal and child health services and blood banks also come under the purview of this Act.

The Act at its inception was made applicable to all union territories and four states (Arunachal Pradesh, Himachal Pradesh, Mizoram, and Sikkim) [Section 1(2)]. Other states were required to adopt the central law by passing a resolution in the state legislatures. Following the enactment of the Clinical Establishments (Registration and Regulation) Act, 2010 at the national level, several Indian states including, Tamil Nadu, Karnataka, Madhya Pradesh and Odisha have passed their own legislation to regulate clinical establishments within their jurisdictions.

The Act establishes a National Council of Clinical Establishments. The council will enact minimum medical care standards for clinical establishments, classify such establishments, and maintain a national, integrated register of clinical establishments. The 22-member council will be headed by the Director General of Health Services (DGHS) and its members will comprise of representatives of consumer groups as well as associations of Indian systems of medicine.

Before being allowed to admit patients every clinical establishment will need to register itself in compliance with certain norms. These norms provide for certain minimum standards of facilities and minimum qualification of personnel. The council may also prescribe different minimum standards pertinent to different categories of clinical establishments. This would reflect diversity in healthcare services offered from place to place within the country while ensuring that minimum standards are met.

The Act also provides that a National Register of clinical establishments that shall be compiled within two years of enactment of the law along with the first set of standards for clinical establishments. Additionally, every state and Union Territory will develop a State Council for Clinical Establishments, whose members will include key health officials and locally elected representatives from state medical, nursing, and pharmacy councils, plus local consumer groups or NGOs. This decentralized approach is intended to strengthen regulatory effectiveness at the local level. At the district level there will be a District Registering Authority for registering clinical establishments. The members will include the District Collector, the District Health Officer and three other qualified professionals as prescribed by the central government. The District Health Officer and Chief Medical Officer will be the registering authority for provisional registrations. The councils will also prepare state registers and dispose of appeals against registration decisions.

The Central Government shall specify standards for different categories of clinical establishments which will facilitate a gradation given to hospitals based on criteria such as capacity, infrastructure and facilities etc. The proposed Bill contemplates a scheme of provisional and permanent registration. Provisional registration is granted up to one year subject to compliance with the notified minimum standards. Permanent registration shall be valid for five years and every application for renewal of permanent registration shall be made six months prior to expiry. The clinical establishments seeking permanent registration shall furnish such documentary evidence, as it considers necessary, for evidence of compliance with the prescribed standards. The authority entrusted with registering an establishment may conduct an inspection or inquiry of clinical establishments through a multi-member inspection team for enforcing compliance. In case the clinical establishment fails to comply with the terms of registration, the authority may serve a show-cause notice or cancel the registration. In addition, if there are reasons or suspicions of unregistered operations, the authority shall be permitted to enter and search the premises after reasonable prior notice has been provided.

An analysis of the various provisions of the Act demonstrates that it attempts to provide a comprehensive regulatory framework which can have a positive effect in making healthcare establishments more accountable thereby strengthening patient rights in India. However, even though a significant time has elapsed since the enactment of this Act, a number if challenges have plagued its implementation. Although this Act intended to improve quality healthcare services, long delays in its uniform implementation raises concerns regarding the importance given to healthcare regulation. Since health is a state subject the implementation of this Act is contingent upon state governments passing enabling legislations in their respective jurisdictions. However, many state governments have not passed such legislations. There has also been a lot of resistance from the private healthcare sector which has been one of the biggest challenges for the implementation of the act. Many of the private providers feel it is an infringement upon their autonomy. The smaller scale establishments in particular are apprehensive that the costs incurred due to compliance requirements would threaten their financial viability either by compelling them to shut down or reducing the services given. This brings to fore a deeper issue on the balance between regulatory oversight and the operational independence of healthcare providers.

Procedural and implementation barriers also the plague the implementation of the Act. The registration process is often believed to be too bureaucratic and too complicated. This can be overwhelming and burdensome for smaller providers without enough resources to work through the requirements. Lastly, insufficient clarity on regulatory standards can create uncertainty, thereby being applied inconsistently This could undermine compliance as well as perpetuate an atmosphere of uncertainty within the healthcare sector.

Implementation challenges also present themselves due infrastructure constraints within regulatory agencies. Inadequate financial resources and personnel to monitor compliance have induced gaps in oversight. This can further lead to geographical and rural-urban imbalances in accessibility and quality thus worsening inequality within the healthcare system.

Furthermore, it has been pointed out that stakeholder engagement has remained weak while formulating and implementing the Act. The absence of input from health professionals has resulted in provisions that possibly do not reflect practical realities in clinical practice adding to the compliance burden. Similarly, lack of mechanisms for including patient feedback makes the policy further dispatch from their needs. Moreover, there are also concerns that overregulation and excessive control over clinical practices many stifles innovation and personalized care. The fear of punitive measures for non-compliance can result in a culture of fear rather than a culture of continuous improvement for patient care.

SUMMARY

Regulation of healthcare services is quintessential for better service delivery and the Clinical Establishments Act is a laudable initiative in this direction. Although the intent of the Act in enhancing and promoting the quality and safety of healthcare services is noble and ambitious, the Act faces challenges due to recalcitrance of the private sector as well as procedural hurdles. These impediments need to be addressed through a more constructive engagement with stakeholders, streamlined processes, and a focus on collaborative quality improvement. This would enable the Act to realize its objectives of providing a more functional framework for regulating healthcare establishments.

CHAPTER

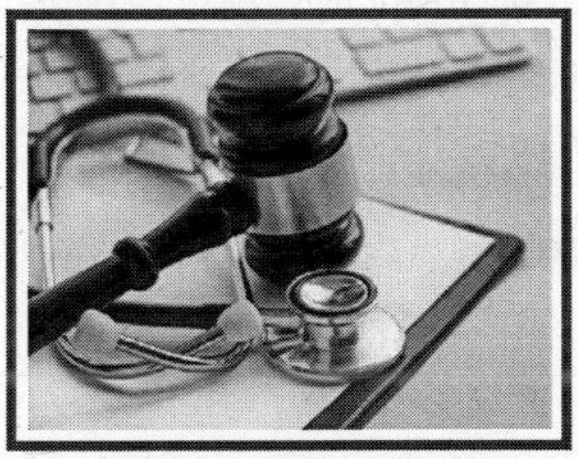

15 Food Safety Regulations in India

INTRODUCTION

Food safety is a very crucial aspect of public health as it directly influences the nutritional quality and safety of the food consumed by the population. Contaminated or improperly processed food can lead to a range of health issues, from mild gastrointestinal disturbances to severe illnesses and even fatalities. It therefore makes it imperative to ensure that food safety involves implementing measures at every stage of the food supply chain, from production to consumption to help mitigate risks associated with pathogens, chemicals, and allergens. A robust food safety system contributes to overall community health by preventing outbreaks, lowering healthcare burdens and costs, and enhancing food security. This in turn leads to a healthier society which can contribute to its development.

The rationale for food safety regulations centres on protecting public health and ensuring the safety of the food supply chain. Foodborne illnesses can lead to significant health issues, economic burdens, and loss of consumer trust. This in turn necessitates the establishment and enforcement of standards pertaining to food production, processing, and distribution. These regulations aim to minimize the risks of contamination and outbreaks. Additionally, effective food safety measures are also crucial for maintaining standardized and stable food manufacturing and marketing practices in compliance with international trade standards.

Public health objectives of food safety regulations focus on preventing foodborne diseases through rigorous monitoring, education, and enforcement. By implementing strict hygiene practices and safety standards, regulatory frameworks aim to reduce the incidence of food-related illnesses. Public awareness campaigns also play a vital role in informing consumers and food handlers about safe food practices. Furthermore, a collaborative regulatory approach that involves various sectors, such as agriculture, health, and environment can ensure a holistic response to food safety challenges, ultimately enhancing the overall health and well-being of the population.

15.1 THE FOOD SAFETY AND STANDARDS ACT (FSSA)

As far as India is concerned much like other health-related domains, regulatory architecture around food safety in India has historically been complex and fragmented. This complexity was the result of a patchwork of multiple laws and regulations, as well as the prevalence of regulatory enforcement at various levels, central, state, and local which often lead to overlaps and inconsistencies. The existing regulations separately focused on the quality of food and drugs; standards of additives, contaminants, colours, preservatives, and labelling, etc. In order to rationalize, consolidate and integrate all such laws into a single, modern food safety law, the Food Safety Standards Act was promulgated in 2006[1]. The Food Safety and Standards Act (FSSA), 2006 created an overarching legal and policy framework and attempted to provide a single-window approach to regulate all stakeholders involved in the manufacture, marketing, processing, handling, transportation, import, and sale of food. The promulgation of the Act had the effect of formally repealing a plethora of legacy food safety related enactments such as the Prevention of Food Adulteration Act (PFA) of 1954, the Fruit Products Order of 1955, the Meat Food Products Order of 1973, and other enactments related to edible oils, milk, food commodities, etc. The Act also created the Food Safety and Standards Authority of India (FSSAI) at the Centre and the office of the Commissioner of food safety in states. The Act covers the entire food processing chain, from primary production to distribution, retail, and catering. In sync with the mandate of the Act, the FSSAI undertakes the task of formulating regulations in respect of establishing food safety standards. It also frames guidelines for the accreditation of laboratories involved in food testing. FSSAI gives scientific advice and technical support to the Central Government, besides contributing to the development of international technical standards related to food. It also focuses on standards and quality control in food regulations, collecting and analysing data on food consumption, contamination, and emerging risks.

The Act also deals with contemporary challenges in the food sector. It contains provisions on Genetically Modified (GM) crops, functional foods, and international trade of food items. It confers the FSSAI enabling statutory powers to make regulations for establishing safety standards for food, guidelines for laboratory accreditation besides providing scientific and technical support to the Central Government. In addition, the FSSAI collects and collates data with respect to consumption, contamination, and emerging risks of food besides creating awareness about food safety and nutrition in India.

The Act comprises of 12 chapters delineating the regulatory framework for food safety in India. It begins with Preliminary definitions to elucidate the key terms which are necessary for understanding the legislation. The second chapter outlines the Food Safety and Standards Authority of India (FSSAI), which establishes the central body responsible for implementing the Act. General principles of food safety are listed in chapter three of the Act. They emphasize that there is a need for safe food handling practices. Chapter four outlines the specific prohibitions that are intended to ensure public health. The Act also incorporates provisions relating to import to ensure that food entering the country is regulated in Chapter 5.

Moreover, the Act mandates special responsibilities as to food safety it outlines inter alia responsibilities of the food business operator, manufacturers, packers, wholesalers, distributors and seller. Mechanisms for enforcement are enshrined in Chapter 7. Chapter 8 provides guidelines for the analysis of food, including the roles of laboratories, sampling and public analysts. Offences and penalties and adjudication mechanisms are laid out in Chapters 9 and 10.

1. https://indiacode.nic.in/bitstream/123456789/7800/1/200634_food_safety_and_standards_act,_2006.pdf

The remaining two chapters deal with finance, accounts, audits, and reports as well as certain miscellaneous provisions to support the core regulatory framework.

15.1.1 Definitions under the Act

The Act defines key terms to ensure clarity and consistency in its provisions and to eliminate ambiguity, supporting effective implementation and compliance with food safety standards. Clear definitions also guide regulatory bodies and industry participants in fulfilling their roles and responsibilities. Some of the key definitions in the Act have been listed below[2]:

- **Adulterant:** Any material which is or could be employed for making the food unsafe or sub-standard or misbranded or containing extraneous matter.
- **Contaminant:** Any substance, whether or not added to food, which is presented in such food as a result of the production (including operations carried out in crop husbandry, animal husbandry or veterinary medicine), manufacture, processing, preparation, treatment, packing, packaging, transport or holding of such food or as a result of environmental contamination and does not include insect fragments, rodent hair and other extraneous matter
- **Food:** Any substance, whether processed, partially processed or unprocessed, which is intended for human consumption and includes primary food to the extent defined in the Act, genetically modified or engineered food or food containing such ingredients, infant food, packaged drinking water, alcoholic drink, chewing gum, and any substance, including water used in the food during its manufacture, preparation or treatment but does not include any animal feed, live animals unless they are prepared or processed for placing on the market for human consumption, plants, prior to harvesting, drugs and medicinal products, cosmetics, narcotic or psychotropic substances.
- **Food Additive:** Any substance not normally consumed as a food by itself or used as a typical ingredient of the food, whether or not it has nutritive value, the intentional addition of which to food for a technological (including organoleptic) purpose in the manufacture, processing, preparation, treatment, packaging, transport or holding of such food results, or may be reasonably expected to result (directly or indirectly), in it or its by-products becoming a component of or otherwise affecting the characteristics of such food but does not include contaminants or substances added to food for maintaining or improving nutritional qualities.
- **Processing Aid:** Any substance or material, not including apparatus or utensils, and not consumed as a food ingredient by itself, used in the processing of raw materials, foods or its ingredients to fulfil a certain technological purpose during treatment or processing and which may result in the non-intentional but unavoidable presence of residues or derivatives in the final product. Advertisement means any audio or visual publicity, representation or pronouncement made by means of any light, sound, smoke, gas, print, electronic media, internet or website and includes through any notice, circular, label, wrapper, invoice or other documents; Food business means any undertaking, whether for profit or not and whether public or private, carrying out

2. Source, The Food Safety Act.

any of the activities related to any stage of manufacture, processing, packing, storage, transportation, distribution of food, import and includes food services, catering services, sale of food or food ingredients; Food business operator in relation to food business means a person by whom the business is carried on or owned and is responsible for ensuring the compliances of this Act, rules and regulations made there under.

- **Advertisement:** Any audio or visual publicity, representation or pronouncement made by means of any light, sound, smoke, gas, print, electronic media, internet or website and includes through any notice, circular, label, wrapper, invoice or other documents.
- **Food Business:** Any undertaking, whether for profit or not and whether public or private, carrying out any of the activities related to any stage of manufacture, processing, packing, storage, transportation, distribution of food, import and includes food services, catering services, sale of food or food ingredients.
- **Food Business Operator:** In relation to food business means a person by whom the business is carried on or owned and is responsible for ensuring the compliances of this Act, rules and regulations made there under.

15.1.2 Salient Features of the Act

In the light of these definitions some salient provisions of the Act can now be discussed as follows:

- **Establishment of Authorities:** The Food Safety and Standards Act, 2006 (FSSA), establishes the Food Safety and Standards Authority of India (FSSAI). This authority is responsible for ensuring that food safety and standards are set and maintained nationwide. FSSAI plays a central role in proper implementation of the Act. It comprises of a chairperson and 22 members. These members are elected by the Central Government which appoints a selection committee, representing diverse expertise in fields such as public health, agriculture, and consumer rights for this purpose. FSSAI's headquarter is located in Delhi.

  Additionally, the authority also has regional offices in different regions of the country. Besides the FSSAI, the Act provides that there shall be a Central Advisory Committee to promote consultation between FSSAI and enforcing agencies at the central level and state levels. Section 16 of the Act provides for the constitution of scientific panels consisting of independent experts who provide scientific advice and assessments on matters related to food safety, including contaminants and additives. In addition to this, the respective state governments also appoint Commissioners of Food Safety in every state. Such commissioners are in charge of food safety at the local level and may further delegate officers at the district level to comply with the food safety standards thus, forming a multi-tiered structure of food safety regulations.
- **Licensing and Registration:** Section 31 of the food safety Act mandates that no person shall run a food business without obtaining a license. This provision is to ensure that every business dealing with food items strictly adheres to all measures of safety and quality in foodstuffs. Every applicant seeking a license to operate the food businesses is required submit a written request to the designated officers who is vested with the authority to consider the application on merits and either allow or decline the

applications submitted. In case of rejection of an application the reasons for rejection should be clearly cited and documented in the interest of transparency. The provision aims to protect public health and safety by ensuring that only such businesses that comply with the required eligibility criteria are allowed to operate.

The Act also provides for certain exceptions with respect to the licensing requirement for small food operators, such as petty manufacturers, hawkers, and temporary stall holders. Small operators have been exempted from the requirement to obtain a license, but they are still obliged to register with the concerned authority to ensure accountability and traceability. This dual system of licensing and registration is to ensure that even the smallest food business conform to a minimum safety level, while bureaucratic hurdles to low-risk operators are reduced. The Commissioner of Food Safety has the power to hear appeals against license rejections, which provides a grievance redressal mechanism for operators who feel that they are wrongfully denied a chance to operate.

- **General Principles of Food Safety:** Section 18 provides the general principles that should guide the food safety measures. These principles reflect a concern for safeguarding human life and health consumer interests on another hand. The Act wants to ensure that there are always risk management actions that are taken towards potential hazards along the food supply chain. These aim to create a safety and accountability culture both in food business operators and regulatory agencies so that food safety is maintained during all phases of production and distribution. It further contains provisions on specific regulations of food products which provide information about the application of food additives, contaminants, and labelling in Chapter IV. For example, additions have to be within tolerable limits; no food product shall contain hazardous residues of pesticides or veterinary drugs, and certain provisions refer to food packaging and labelling to protect the consumer from misleading information. Unfair trade practices and misleading advertising are ruled out specifically, thus adding more layers of protection towards the consumer. This holistic approach to food safety reflects the commitment of the Act towards maintaining high standards for the quality of food and public health.
- **Food Analysis:** Under the FSSA, the Food authority is responsible for notifying food laboratories as well as research institutions which are accredited for the purposes of analysing food samples. This is necessary because it ensures that food products meet the safety and quality standards established by the Act. Such tests are conducted by food analysts which are appointed by the Commissioner of Food Safety for determining whether such food commodities are in accordance with regulatory requirements and do not pose any risk to consumers. The accreditation of laboratories is to harmonize standardized procedures of testing and to ensure integrity of the testing process. This provision, therefore, enables proper inspection and sampling of food articles available in the market with a view to regular monitoring of food safety. Besides, it also helps identify any food safety risks and ensures prompt removal and recall of unsafe products from the market. Such an analysis also helps in taking sound decisions regarding enforcement action. This increases confidence among citizens and customers regarding food safety.

- **Offences and Penalties:** Section 48 of the FSSA elaborates on various offenses related to food safety and gives provision for penalties in case of such offenses. The section lays down offences, liabilities and penalties for offences such as like selling food which is injurious to health, manufacturing sub-standard products, or misleading advertisements. For instance, penalties for failure to meet food quality parameters can be as high as five lakh rupees. Similarly, misbranding and misleading advertisements attract larger fines of up to ten lakh rupees. Besides monetary punishment, the Act also prescribes imprisonment for severe offenses such as the preparation of unsafe food articles. The Act empowers the enforcement officers, including the Food Safety Officers, to confiscate unsafe food articles from any place or premises. It also penalizes the persons who prevent these officers from the performance of their duties. Last but not the least, the Act has provisions relating to repeat offenders wherein severer punishment is meted out to subsequent offenders.

15.1.3 Challenges and Limitations

The FSSAI Act has significantly contributed to the improvement of food safety in India through the establishment of a comprehensive regulatory framework that sets stringent standards for food quality and safety. The Act has consolidated various food safety laws into a single legislative framework, thereby making better oversight and enforcement possible so that food businesses are guided accordingly. This has resulted in enhanced monitoring of food production processes, labelling, and hygiene practices and, above all, consumer confidence.

Nevertheless, its implementation still leaves scope for improvements. One major limitation has been enforcement-related disparities between states. Urban areas have better infrastructure and resources to fulfil and bring about food safety standards, while rural areas tend to lag behind in terms of monitoring and enforcement. Lack of resources and trained personnel as well as funds needed to monitor food production properly leads to variability in food safety practices, with unsafe food being marketed and consumed. This variance negates the purposes the Act was meant to meet.

The other challenge comes in the form of fluctuating food production and consumption trends. With the growth of e-commerce and online food delivery services, new risks are emerging owing to the modern forms of supply chains which the traditional regulatory mechanisms are not as effective in handling. Also owing to the rapid technological advancements in food production, storage and distribution there is also a need for the regulatory framework around food safety evolves with time otherwise this will leave regulatory gaps in consumer protection since the newly introduced food products and methods of delivery may not covered under the previous standards for safety.

Furthermore, public awareness about food safety standards is a serious concern. The FSSAI has launched several campaigns educating consumers about their rights and the importance of food safety. However, many people particularly in rural and backward areas still lack proper knowledge regarding the standards that govern food safety. This gap in consumer awareness leads to complacency in scrutinizing food products or report violations. Public education initiatives should be enhanced to empower consumers to make informed choices and advocate for their own safety.

Lastly, compliance among small food businesses has also proved to be a persistent issue. Small vendors and producers in local areas often do not have the means or wherewithal to support the strict guidelines prescribed by the FSSAI. Even though exemptions are provided and regulations simplified, the process can still overwhelm smaller businesses. Moreover, due to a lack of institutional support they can end up compromising food safety creating problems more systemically. Addressing these challenges shall require a multipronged approach which would combine better training and increased funding with more public engagement to create a comprehensive food safety ecosystem within India.

SUMMARY

This chapter examines the framework of food safety regulations in India, primarily governed by the Food Safety and Standards Act, 2006. The Act established the Food Safety and Standards Authority of India (FSSAI) to oversee the manufacture, storage, distribution, sale, and import of food products, ensuring they meet safety and quality standards. It consolidates various food-related laws to create a unified system focused on consumer health protection. The FSSAI enforces regulations through licensing, inspections, and compliance checks, while also promoting awareness about food safety. Despite significant progress, challenges like enforcement gaps, unregulated street food sectors, and adulteration persist, requiring stronger implementation, stricter monitoring, and greater public awareness to ensure safer food practices across the country.

CHAPTER

16 Organ Transplant Laws in India

INTRODUCTION

Organ Transplant is a medical procedure where an organ or any tissue which is healthy can be surgically removed from an individual (donor) and surgically implanted within another individual whose organ has failed or not working properly. This procedure involves a living donors and partial donation of organ, for example the kidney or the liver lobe as well as deceased donors from whom organs are retrieved after death. The Organ transplantation aims to restore normal functioning among the recipients thereby improving the quality of life among the recipients. However, transplant is a complex medical procedure which requires a careful matching of the donor and the recipient and also post-transplant medical management is provided to prevent the rejection of the transplanted organ.

Organ transplantation is one of the most remarkable achievements in medical science and provides hope to patients who are at the end stage organ failure. However worldwide including in India, alongside the development of transplant technologies and growing number of successful transplants, unethical medical practices also began to raise their head, especially commercialization and consequent organ trafficking and trade. This necessitated the need for a proper and stringent legal and regulatory framework to keep unethical and commercial practices in check.

16.1 TRANSPLANTATION OF HUMAN ORGANS AND TISSUES ACT (THOA)

The culmination of the endeavour to create a legal framework for organ transplant was the enactment of the Transplantation of Human Organs and Tissues Act (THOA) in 1994[1] as a landmark legislation. THOA provided a comprehensive structure and established legal standards and protocols to protect donors and recipients in human organ transplantation procedures. The Act was subsequently amended in 2011 and subsequent organ transplant rules were amended in 2014. The Act prohibits any form of commercial trade in human organs. It criminalizes

1. Transplantation of Human Organs and Tissues Act (THOA) in 1994

the buying and selling of organs, aiming to prevent exploitation and trafficking The major provisions of the Act can be discussed as follows:

- **Brain Death:** THOA introduced the concept of brain death Section 2(d) into Indian medical and legal practice. The Act defines brain death as follows:

  "brain-stem death" means the stage at which all functions of the brain-stem have permanently and irreversibly ceased".

  This condition is fundamentally different from other states of diminished consciousness, such as coma or persistent vegetative state, where some brain activity may still be observed. The distinction is critical because it informs both medical and ethical considerations in the context of organ donation. The THOA is very specific and clear in its definition of brain death and calls for standardized, thorough evaluation by a board of qualified medical professionals to establish brain death. Such an evaluation must be, necessarily, in accordance with set protocols to confirm the total lack of activity of the brain before the death determination may be made.

  Legal recognition of brain death has considerable implications for the practice of organ transplantation. This act permits the ethical procurement of organs from patients, who, though still being kept on life support, have been declared brain dead. This increases the possibility of donor availability and can give hope to many in need of life-saving transplants. In addition, the act mandates that the consent be informed, whether it is obtained from the patient when he or she is still alive or obtained after brain death from the relatives of the patient. This ensures that the dignity of the deceased and his rights are maintained while, at the same time, ensuring that families are properly informed and involved in making decisions regarding organ donation.
- **Appropriate Authorities:** The Transplantation of Human Organs Act provides for the appointment of appropriate authority at both the central and state levels. Section 13 describes the role of the Appropriate Authority in relation to organ transplantation and tissue banking within Union territories and states. The Central Government is entrusted with the appointment of officers as Appropriate Authorities for Union territories. Likewise State Governments can establish such authorities within their jurisdictions. Such authorities are vested with powers such as to grant, review and renew the registration of hospitals and on tissue banks as well cancelling or suspending the registrations in case of regulatory violations. They are also responsible for enforcing prescribed standards for hospitals and tissue banks involved in organ and tissue management, investigating complaints regarding breaches of the Act, and conducting periodic inspections to ensure compliance with quality standards and proper follow-up care for transplant recipients. Sections 13A and 13B further elaborate on the establishment and role of Advisory Committees and Appropriate Authorities regarding the transplantation of human organs and tissue. Section 13A mandates that the Central and State Governments establish Advisory Committees for two years to enable the Appropriate Authorities to perform their duties.

  These committees should have a diverse membership, including an administrative expert, medical specialists, social workers, legal professionals, NGO representatives, and a transplantation specialist to ensure a multidisciplinary approach to oversight of transplantation practices. It is so designed to be able to provide wide-ranging advice from the administrative, medical, social, legal, and ethical perspective, which would make the Appropriate Authority more effective.

Section 13B has provided the Appropriate Authority with wide powers comparable to a civil court under the Code of Civil Procedure, 1908. These powers include the power to summon persons with such information, discovery of documents, issuing search warrant for suspected illegal activities concerning the removal or transplantation of the organ, and any other power as may be prescribed. This statutory power positions the Appropriate Authority in an active position of ensuring compliance with the Act, as well as conducting thorough investigations into potential violations. The sections speak to a strong governance mechanism that ensures accountability, maintains ethical expectations, and guards the rights of individuals involved in organ and tissue transplantation.

- **Classification of Donors:** The Transplantation of Human Organs Act classifies living organ donors into two categories: near-related and non-related donors. The near-related donors are the immediate family members, including parents, siblings, spouses, grandparents and grandchildren who are preferred for organ donation due to their high genetic affinity to the recipient. The Act and the corresponding rules specify stringent screening and authorization protocols to maintain ethics and integrity in organ donation and to ensure that organ donation is driven by love, affection and altruism and not by influence or coercion. The procedure is even more formal for living non-related donors. Such donors need to be authorized by the Authorization Committee in accordance with Section 9 of the Act. This committee verifies the donor's reasons for donation to make sure the donation was given without coercion and no exchange of money was involved.
- **Deceased Donors** form another major category under THOA. The Act allows retrieval of organs from brain dead patients and people who had undergone cardiac arrest. This, under Section 3 of the Act, opens up the donor pool significantly for potential donors. This provision aims to address the critical shortage of organs available as opposed to patients waiting for transplants.
- **Swap Donations:** Brought about in 2014 rules swap donations provide a viable solution to the blood-type incompatibility challenges involved in organ transplantation. For instance, if Family 1 has a donor having the type A+ blood and the recipient of type B+, but Family 2 has a donor having B+ and the recipient A+, then the two can swap. This diversifies donor availability and increases the probabilities of successful transplants. One important aspect of swap donation is that the transplants should be done simultaneously. This eliminates the need to avoid donor reneging, which occurs in a situation where one donor withdraws having allowed the other party to prepare for surgery. Since both transplants will take place simultaneously, it safeguards all parties' interests while minimizing recipient risks both emotionally and medically.
- **Restrictions on Removal and Transplantation of Human Organs:** The Transplantation of Human Organs Act outlines the specific restrictions on the removal and transplantation of human organs and tissues. Section 9 provides that human organs

or tissues shall not be removed for transplantation except under circumstances where the donor is a near relative of the recipient. Furthermore, if either the donor or recipient is a foreign national, then prior authorization from the Authorization Committee will be required. Besides these, the Act also protects vulnerable populations. For instance, the Act prohibits organ removal from minors before their death without adhering to prescribed regulations and also stipulates a complete prohibition of organ removal from persons suffering from mental disability before their death. If the donor has consented to the removal of his organs after his death, such organs can be transplanted to any recipient in need provided proper consent protocols are followed.

Furthermore, if the organ donor wishes to donate to someone who is not a near relative, the Authorization Committee's approval is mandatory. The Act also permits "swap donations," where the compatible donors and recipients can swap organs within a controlled framework.

- **Eligibility/Registration Requirements:** Chapter V of the Transplantation of Human Organs Act, THOA identifies the need that any institution or tissue bank undertaking a removal, storage, and transplantation of human organs/tissues must be registered. Section 14(1) states that no hospital, including human organ retrieval centres can commence such activities without prior registration. Under this Act hospitals which are already functioning need to be registered within a period of sixty days of the commencement of the Act and cease their operations after three months thereof unless they are registered or their applications are pending. The registration shall be made by making an application in such form, accompanied by the fees, if any, prescribed thereon under Section 14(2).

  For registration, hospitals must demonstrate that they possess the necessary specialized services, qualified personnel, and equipment as stipulated in Section 14(3). Furthermore, Section 14(4) calls for the appointment of a transplant coordinator with specified qualifications, which indicates that the process of transplantation requires qualified personnel. Tissue banks are also required to be similarly registered under Section 14A which covers their registration requirements and conditions for operation. According to Section 15(1), subject to satisfactory inquiry and compliances, the registration certificate is granted by Appropriate Authority to the hospitals or the tissue bank. The application is liable for rejection if it does not meet the conditions specified upon specifying the specific reasons for rejection.

  The rejecting order should also contain written reasons for the same. According to Section 15(3), renewal period of the registration certificates has been dealt with. Section 16 talks about suspension as well as cancellation of registration. An order under Section 20 will include the issue of notice by the Appropriate Authority on hospitals or tissue banks showing cause why their registration shall not be cancelled and such registration may be suspended or cancelled in case there is any confirmed breach of the Act or rules which could be done after an adequate hearing, and all such actions will be necessary to uphold accountability and other necessary ethical standards required while adopting organ transplantation practices. The Authority may suspend a registration based on urgent public interest cases without notice as well, noted on the provisions above.

- **Penal Provisions for Commercial Dealings in Human Organs:** Section 19 of the Human Organs Act provides for penalties for anyone involved in commercial transactions related to human organs. It prohibits activities such as making or receiving any payment for the supply of human organs, soliciting any person to supply or to offer to human organs and supply of human organs monetary considerations. Likewise managing organizations involved in such activities and publication of advertisements inviting or encouraging commercial organ supply, aiding preparation of false documents for misrepresenting the nature of organ donation etc are also considered offences under the Act. Violators face imprisonment of five years or above, with an additional punishment in form of fine to be not less than twenty lakh and may extend to one crore. Similarly, Section 19A covers illegal dealings in human tissues, dealing with analogous matters such as offering or receiving payment for human tissue, seeking to procure a source for pay, and guiding entities engaged in that act. Section 19A further prohibits dissemination of advertisements which solicit remuneration for human tissue, or attempting to conceal or falsify the donor-recipient relationship. Offenders are liable to imprisonment that may extend from one to three years along with fines ranging between five lakhs and twenty-five lakh rupees.

  Section 20 relates to punishment for contraventions of any other provisions of the Act or associated rules and conditions of registration. Persons found violating these can be imprisoned for up to five years and fined up to twenty lakh rupees.

16.2 OBSTACLES IN ORGAN TRANSPLANTATION

Although there exists a strong legal structure formulated by the THOA, several challenges continue to limit the efficiency of organ transplantation in India. The greatest need of the moment is for highly specialized Intensive Care Units that would carry out the task of diagnosing brain death. Such institutions are even more scarce in the rural areas. This geographical imbalance is a bottleneck towards the discovery of potential organ donors. Further challenges arise due to complexities and difficulties in getting informed consent from relatives. This often makes the task difficult for medical professionals, who are unable to even approach the grieving families over organ donation. Consequently, many opportunities for organ retrieval are missed. Such situations can jeopardize the organs meant for transplantation. These issues need to be addressed with a multi-faceted approach through upgradation of healthcare infrastructure, targeted training of healthcare professionals in handling the communication regarding organ donation sensitively, and awareness among people regarding the need for organ donation. Improvement in these areas would not only facilitate the process of organ transplantation but also help build a more conducive environment for the potential donor and their families.

Moreover, the current situation about organ transplantation in India remains largely under the domain of the private sector of healthcare, for the simple reason that the former possesses better resources and facilities necessary for the performance of complicated transplant surgeries. However, such an emphasis on the private sector results in inequities in the service delivered to low-income patients: these patients are faced with such huge financial burdens that may deter them from availing these medical treatments. Therefore, the organ transplantation system is more prone to favour the affluent, raising grave ethical issues regarding the commodification of human life and exploitation of vulnerable groups. Inequitable access to life-saving treatments urgently calls for systemic reform so that organ transplantation is not just a privilege of the elite but it is available to all.

Such inequities must be addressed through reforms that enforce a more inclusive organ transplantation framework. The first step in doing this is public awareness regarding organ donation, since most people may not understand the full significance and impact of their contribution. Campaigns endorsing altruistic donation practices may help shift societal attitudes towards a more generous and compassionate perspective on organ donation. There is also the need to provide state funding or subsidy that is aimed at promoting low-income patients who require transplantation. This may ensure that the financial barriers do not undermine access to this crucial lifesaving medical care and can thus be used to create a more just healthcare system.

In conclusion, while organ transplantation forms one of the most notable achievements in modern medicine, the current reality of the system in India exposes several critical gaps that require attention on an urgent basis. The existing framework often favours those who can afford the high costs associated with private healthcare and leaves more economically and socially vulnerable patients at a severe disadvantage. Thus, an improved organ transplantation system to reap its true value needs to be based on inclusivity and equitableness and by becoming accessible in its proper sense. This can be achieved only by adopting a holistic approach involving infrastructure alongside promoting a culture associated with altruism, compassion and justice.

SUMMARY

The legal framework governing organ transplants in India is primarily guided by the Transplantation of Human Organs and Tissues Act, 1994, and its amendments. The Act aims to regulate and ensure ethical practices in organ donation and transplantation, preventing trafficking and exploitation. It establishes clear guidelines for the donation, removal, storage, and transplantation of human organs, while also setting up authorization committees to oversee ethical issues such as consent and donor eligibility. Despite these provisions, challenges like organ shortages, illegal trade, and inadequate awareness persist, highlighting the need for stricter enforcement, public education, and reforms to enhance the transparency and accessibility of organ transplant services in India.

CHAPTER 17

Medical Waste Management

INTRODUCTION

Medical waste refers to the hazardous byproducts generated by healthcare activities, including hospitals, laboratories, and clinics. This waste ranges from infectious materials and used sharps to chemical substances and pharmaceutical residues, all of which can pose serious threats to public health and the environment if not managed properly. Effective medical waste management involves implementing safe and sustainable practices for segregation, treatment, and disposal to minimize risks of disease transmission, environmental contamination, and harm to living organisms. With proper protocols, medical waste management can play a vital role in supporting public health and environmental preservation.

17.1 MEDICAL WASTE

Medical waste is generated as a byproduct of healthcare practice and can be potentially hazardous to both health and the environment. Medical waste is usually grouped into two major categories, general and hazardous. General medical waste is in the nature refuse similar to household waste, and hence it can be treated like municipal waste. However, between 10% to 25% of the waste generated is hazardous in nature, which includes materials potentially infectious, toxic, or radioactive in nature. The hazardous waste is further categorized into five main groups based on the nature of risk they possess:

- **Sharps Waste:** This group includes items that can cause potential injury, such as needles, scalpels, and broken glass.
- **Infectious Waste:** This refers to body parts, tissues, or waste containing blood, secretions, and other fluids with infectious agents, and thus indicates a potential contamination risk.
- **Pharmaceutical and Chemical Waste:** Contains old drugs, cytotoxic chemicals, heavy metals such as mercury, chemical residues that are toxic or carcinogenic or flammable.
- **Pressurized Containers:** Contains gas cylinders, aerosol cans, that have explosive tendencies.

- **Radioactive Waste:** Radioactive wastes, which can be produced due to nuclear medicine or some kinds of laboratory practice due to the risk of radiation exposure.

All these categories are sensitive and thus require proper disposal and treatment to avoid causing injury to human beings and the environment. There are numerous health hazards associated with medical waste particularly medical waste in the hazardous category. This includes trauma from sharps, infections, chemical hazards from pharmaceuticals, heavy metals, and chemical waste. Additionally fires or explosions can also be caused due to improper disposal of waste that contains flammable or pressurized materials. Radioactive waste also poses significant dangers because poses aggravated risks of radiation exposure.

Exposure to medical waste can be through injury (cuts or punctures), direct contact with skin or mucous membranes, inhalation of toxic fumes, or ingestion of contaminants, all of which can lead to severe health consequences, including infections, poisoning, and long-term chronic illnesses.

Medical waste is also a vector for the spread of dangerous microorganisms, including bacteria and viruses. Many of these pathogens survive under certain conditions in the environment, especially warm and humid climates.

It is therefore clear that the risk of disease spread would greatly be increased as a result of inappropriate handling and disposal of medical waste, in both the healthcare establishments and in the surrounding neighbourhoods. Also, improper processing and disposal of hazardous medical wastes can lead significant risk of environmental pollution. For instance, improper burning (incineration) of medical equipment made from plastic or other PVC plastic material releases other dangerous elements, such as dioxins, furans, and hydrochloric acid. These pollutants, other than affecting air quality, cause acid rain and have the long-term results of weakening the human immune system, reproductive problems, and cancer. In some instances, in the course of metals like mercury and lead incineration, these harmful substances find entry into the environment and add to the problem of pollution.

Moreover, haphazard disposal or the dumping of uncontrolled medical wastes is also a very severe environmental risk that affects soil and water. Improper burial of hazardous waste can lead to the release of toxins in the ground, affecting the local ecosystems and potentially entering the food chain. The same is true for discharging raw sewage from healthcare facilities, especially untreated pharmaceutical and chemical waste, into waterways, contaminating water sources, and thereby contributing to the spread of antibiotic-resistant bacteria. This affects not only the environment but also has a public health risk as it enables the spread of resistant pathogens.

It brings to fore the imperative of establishing strong international and national regulatory frameworks to mitigate and control the human and environmental risks associated with hazardous waste of medical origin ensure its proper safety management. Various international conventions, such as Basel and Stockholm Conventions for example, guide and control and safe disposal measures for hazardous waste.

The Basel Convention emphasizes that hazardous waste should be minimized in production and also controls its trans-boundary movement unless the receiving country can ensure adequate infrastructure for disposal. Similarly, the Stockholm Convention mainly aims to reduce persistent organic pollutants such as dioxins and furans which may be released from the medical waste during its incineration. Certain principles of environmental law, such as "polluter pays" also entails that the producer of waste is liable for its safe disposal, hence holding him liable. International agreements and national legislation aim to guide healthcare facilities in managing their medical waste in an environmentally sound and legally compliant way.

Medical waste management must be arranged properly with accurate segregation and proper methods of disposal. The hospital and health centres must develop and implement stringent protocols regarding the effective management of waste, classification, safe handling and treatment of the waste through autoclaving, incineration, or chemical disinfection, and proper disposal. However, their implementation is challenging, particularly in low-resource settings where there is a lack of infrastructural support, equipment, and trained personnel. In addition, hazardous medical waste is often disposed of incorrectly due to ignorance of the set regulations or failure to adhere to them; this again poses a grave threat to public health as well as the environment.

Besides the technical challenges, there also is a need for public education and training on the part of healthcare institutions. All medical personnel and waste handlers should be educated on the hazards associated with medical hazardous waste and management procedures. Additionally, regulatory authorities should enforce compliance while providing effective oversight and monitoring of all the medical waste management systems to ensure they are operating at their optimum best. This practice calls for active coexistence between the private and public sectors to enhance a better and safer health service without jeopardizing public safety with unsustainable waste disposal measures as healthcare waste is increasingly alarming around the world.

However, while international conventions and protocols serve as enablers, the risks attached to harmful medical waste would, of course, definitely require strong national legislations, regulatory mechanisms and guidelines to ensure proper waste management, safe handling, transportation, treating and ultimate disposal. Such robust regulatory framework are required so that healthcare institutions follow standardized protocols in dealing with medical waste. The potential serious health and environmental impacts associated with poor handling of medical wastes mean that tight controls have to be imposed over every aspect of waste management, from generation and segregation up to treatment and disposal. Such frameworks would not only be critical to control the risks of public health hazards but also to ensure accountability from health service providers. Without a stringent system of checks and balancing, medical waste can rapidly become a major source of widespread harm for individuals as well as for ecosystems.

17.2 EVOLUTION OF MEDICAL WASTE MANAGEMENT RULES IN INDIA

In India, the Biomedical Waste Management Rules were drafted in recognition of the grave dangers posed by medical and biomedical waste and the consequent need for their proper handling and disposal. The rules mandate hospitals and healthcare units to segregate and dispose waste according to established protocols specified in the rules. India also adheres to and operates in tandem with the international standards evolved through the Basel Convention and the Stockholm Convention to adequately meet the global challenge of hazardous medical waste while also protecting the health of its people and the environment.

Indian medical waste management has changed a lot in the decades, with increasing awareness of environmental hazards and public health risks. The first formal attempt to regulate medical waste management in India was made in 1998, when the Ministry of Environment and Forests (MoEF) introduced the **Biomedical Waste (Management and Handling) Rules[1] in exercise of the powers conferred by Sections 6, 8 and 25 of the Environment (Protection) Act, 1986**. This laid down guidelines for healthcare facilities regarding segregation, handling, and proper disposal of biomedical waste. The rules were again amended in 2000, 2003, and 2011 in order to incorporate the rising challenges of new technologies in waste treatment, growth in the health sector, and awareness regarding waste minimization. The Biomedical Waste Management Rules, 2016, came into effect in 2016 to replace the older 1998 guidelines with stricter compliance requirements and an emphasis on segregation of waste at source, increased surveillance, and deterrents against non-compliance. The Biomedical Waste Management Rules, 2016 is the most recent and updated version of rules that further amended in the year 2018.

In the light of the above discussion, the salient features of the Indian Biomedical Waste Management Rules (BMWM) can now be examined as follows:

- **Scope and Applicability:** The waste management rules cover a wide ambit. All healthcare facilities, including hospitals, clinics, research labs, blood banks, and even institutes of animal research, have to comply with the Biomedical Waste Management Rules, 2016. The rules cover any establishment that generates biomedical waste, such as human anatomical waste, blood, discarded medicines, syringes, and other medical items, irrespective of whether the healthcare facility is private or public. Section 2 of the rules defines terms such as "biomedical waste" and stipulates the scope and application of the rules.
- **Duties of the Occupier and the Operator:** Section 4 and 5 respectively delineate duties of the occupier (a person having administrative control over the institution and the premises generating biomedical waste) and the operator (means a person who owns or controls a Common Biomedical Waste Treatment Facility (CBMWTF).

The occupier's duties for biomedical waste management focus on ensuring safe, environmentally responsible handling of waste. The handling and disposal without proper authorization with some form of on-site pre-treatment for spills as in laboratory samples, and blood bags, among others. They must provide secure, ventilated storage for segregated waste, prevent unauthorized handling or spillage, and ensure proper on-site pre-treatment (e.g., disinfection or sterilization) of specific types of waste like laboratory samples and blood bags. Occupiers are required to gradually discard chlorinated plastic products, and segregate liquid chemical waste with proper treatment before disposal. They must also provide training and immunization for all staff dealing with biomedical wastes, maintain a biomedical waste management register, report fire or blast incidents of injuries or deaths to the competent authorities. Moreover, the occupiers must follow the local waste disposal rules and upload the online records of biomedical waste management.

For the operators of common biomedical waste treatment facilities, the following obligations shall exist as per the rules. Operators are required to ensure safe transport, treatment,

1. https://dhr.gov.in/sites/default/files/Biomedical_Waste_Management_Rules_2016.pdf

and disposal of waste in consonance with the prescribed rules and environmental standards. Additionally, they are also required to ensure proper bar coding and tracking for the handling of waste, with record of collection at appropriate times. Operators must provide continuous training and medical check-up for their employees, use Personal Protective Equipment (PPE), record all activities of the waste treatment processes, report accidents, maintain logs for equipment use, and manage treated waste by ensuring recyclables are given to authorized recyclers.

- **Source Segregation:** Source segregation at the point of generation of waste is one of the features of the 2016 rules. Section 5 mandates that biomedical waste must be segregated into the categories specified under Schedule I of the rules. This will mean that any waste is categorized accordingly to nature; whether it's infectious or hazardous, hence handled within the right procedure in disposal procedures. Hospitals will have particular coloured bins on different categorizations of the waste.
- **Handling and Storage of Biomedical Waste:** Section 8 provides for Segregation, packaging, transportation and storage of biomedical waste. Biomedical waste shall be segregated at the point of generation as per guidelines in Schedule I, before its storage, transportation, treatment, and disposal. The wastes shall be put in a container or bag with such labels as are specified in Schedule IV. The rules mandates that the occupier and common biomedical waste treatment facility shall be equipped with barcodes and Global Positioning System (GPS) tracking within one year. For transport purposes, the vehicles used shall meet the labelling and notification provisions under Schedule IV and any special conditions as may be stipulated by the State Pollution Control Board or Pollution Control Committee or the Motor Vehicles Act 1988. The rules also provided that certain biomedical wastes classified should not be stored for more than 48 hours. These comprise un-treated human anatomical wastes, animal anatomical wastes, soiled wastes, and bio-technology wastes. If storage for more than 48 hours is unavoidable, the occupier must ensure that the waste shall not pose a risk to human health or the environment and must notify the prescribed authority with reason. In addition, biomedical and clinical laboratory wastes are required to be pre-treated by sterilization and disinfection before packaging and dispatch for the common biomedical waste treatment facility. Furthermore, biomedical waste has to be collected in proper color-coded containers that have been labelled following standardization and codification of all categories of biomedical wastes for preventing contamination or accidental exposure. Storage facilities in the healthcare institutes shall be securely designed and must provide all the precautionary measures to avoid cross-contamination. Storage periods have a specified limitation as does disposal or treatment as stated in the defined period.
- **Biomedical Waste Disposal and Treatment**: As stipulated in Section 7, the treatment and disposal of biomedical waste shall be effected through suitable treatment methods posing minimum risks to health and the environment. Incineration, autoclaving, microwave treatment, or deep burial are the waste treatment and disposal methods under the said rules, depending upon the type of biomedical waste involved as well as for ensuring minimal release of pollutants in air or water.
- **Monitoring and Compliance:** The 2016 rules brought into effect an entire mechanism of monitoring. It clearly requires each and every hospital and other related healthcare

facilities to establish a biomedical waste management committee for effective rule compliance. The committee will ensure that biomedical wastes are segregated, stored, treated, and disposed of. The monitoring and enforcing authority of the regulations would lie with the Central Pollution Control Board and the State Pollution Control Boards.

Biomedical Waste Management Rules therefore attempts to provide a comprehensive policy on handling, segregation, transportation, and disposal of biomedical waste with regard to both public health and environmental issues. Mandatory segregations at the point of generation, labelling, and use of modern technologies such as barcodes and GPS can go a long way in traceability and responsibility with which the biomedical waste could be handled.

However, even though procedures to be followed are quite clear, success in implementation boils down to effective mechanisms in place for monitoring as well as enforcement. The compliance with various state pollution control boards along with the Motor Vehicles Act is a welcome development however it may place additional compliance burden on smaller healthcare facilities and waste management operators, specifically in regions with limited infrastructure. This may result in inconsistent adherence especially in under-resourced areas, and might require more financial and technical support towards the uniformity that could be required across the country.

Further, although while the rules encourage technological advancements like GPS tracking, the actual implementation of such systems may face logistical challenges, especially in rural or remote areas or other isolated locations. Stronger oversight, combined with audits, and more importantly, investment in the infrastructure, would be necessary to ensure that these provisions enhance public health and environmental protection from the adverse impacts of biomedical waste.

SUMMARY

This chapter has delved into the important yet often neglected issue of medical waste management in India. It focuses on the legal frameworks, challenges, and best practices for handling healthcare waste. The chapter has examined the Biomedical Waste Management Rules, 2016, which regulate the segregation, storage, transportation, and disposal of medical waste to minimize environmental and public health risks. It highlights the importance of proper waste segregation at healthcare facilities, training staff, and the role of authorized disposal agencies in ensuring compliance with regulations. Despite progress, challenges such as lack of awareness, inadequate infrastructure, and improper disposal practices continue to hinder effective management, emphasizing the need for stronger enforcement and awareness campaigns to safeguard public health and the environment.

QUESTIONS FOR PART IV

Q.1 What are the key regulatory bodies for the medical profession in India, and what roles do they play?

Q.2 Discuss the ethical standards and professional conduct guidelines for medical practitioners as outlined by regulatory authorities.

Q.3 How are paramedical professions regulated in India, and why is standardization important in this sector?

Q.4 What are the key provisions under the Pharmacy Act, 1948, regarding the regulation of pharmacies in India?

Q.5 What is the role of the Drugs and Cosmetics Act, 1940, in ensuring the safety and efficacy of drugs in India?

Q.6 Discuss the approval and monitoring process for new drugs in India.

Q.7 What are the responsibilities of the Food Safety and Standards Authority of India (FSSAI) in ensuring food safety?

Q.8 Discuss the key features of the Transplantation of Human Organs and Tissues Act, 1994, and its role in preventing illegal organ trade.

Q.9 What are the main guidelines for biomedical waste management under the Biomedical Waste Management Rules, 2016?

Q.10 Why is the proper management and disposal of biomedical waste critical for public health and environmental safety?

PART V

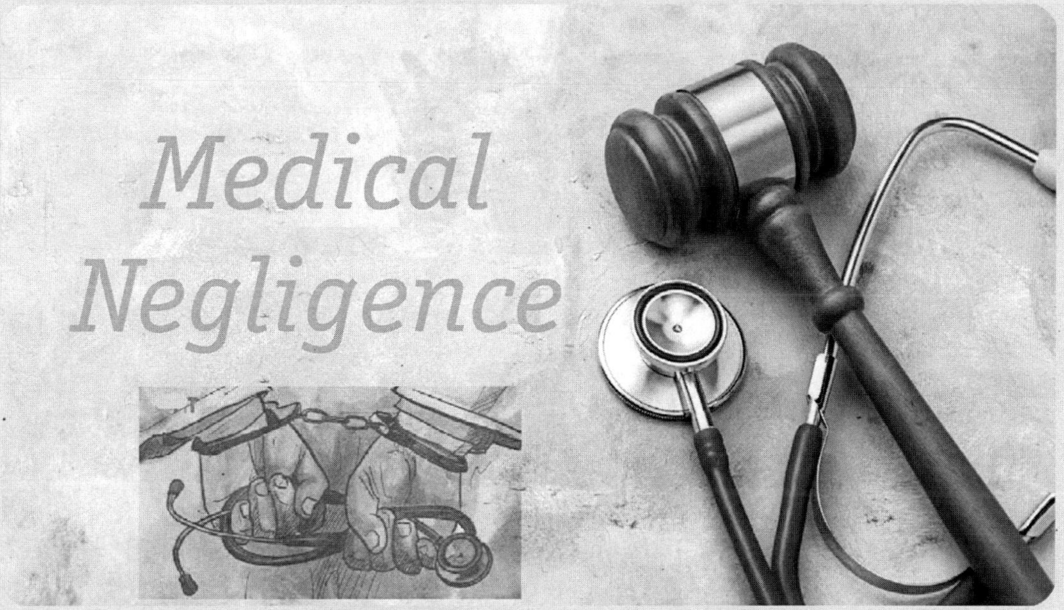

Medical Negligence

CHAPTER

18

Concept of Negligence

INTRODUCTION

Conventionally the medicine has been a highly revered profession. Doctors were treated with a lot of respect as custodians of life and health. The patient's trust and respect for the physician were based on the presumption that the physician would act with professionalism and care in the best interest of his patients. However, the practice of medicine has changed overtime, particularly during the late twentieth and early twenty-first century, the relationship between the patient and doctor changed immensely. With rising commercialization of health services, the medical services started being perceived more as a transaction. This kind of commodification contributed to rampant medical malpractice and negligence. The fiduciary and paternalistic relationship between doctor and patient started eroding as patients became more informed of their rights while medical service providers began to be increasingly brought under scrutiny and held accountable for their actions and professional conduct. As a consequence medical negligence started emerging as important area of medical jurisprudence as well as legal practice

18.1 DEFINING MEDICAL NEGLIGENCE

It is difficult to precisely define medical is challenging. This is because determining medical negligence involves assessment of the dynamic interactions between professional standards, clinical judgment, and individual circumstances. Negligence depends on the particulars involved based upon the specific duties and expectations of many different areas of practice and the particular legal and ethical standards that apply. A health provider will be vicariously liable for negligence if they fail to uphold the accepted standard of care. However, this standard may vary depending on the type of treatment applied, the condition of the patient, and the resources at their disposal. This therefore may make it difficult to create a definition of negligence that could apply universally across all the contexts.

Besides, medicine itself is not an exact science and is entirely predicated upon incomplete information, personal experience, and circumstances of every patient. This introduces into the process an element of judgment and discretion that can never be really quantified, especially when an adverse result has occurred despite best efforts of the provider. Thus, these systems rely on expert evidence as well as case-by-case assessment to determine negligence; thereby making the line between acceptable medical practice and negligence a matter of interpretation rather than a clear rule.

Nevertheless, in this modern setting, patient protection has become one of the foremost issues and in the legal landscape mirror there is a growing understanding that patients' rights cannot be ignored, and hence determining liability and accountability in the field of medicine is necessary to curb medical malpractices and consequent violations of patient rights. It is thus important to at least have a broad-based understanding of what constitutes medical negligence so that appropriate levels of accountability can be fixed.

Medical negligence refers to any act or omission by healthcare professionals, such as doctors, nurses, as well as hospital and clinic staff who do not meet the established and expected standard of medical care. This substandard care results in harm, injury, or exacerbation of the condition of the patient either directly because of improper treatment or indirectly through failure in diagnosis, delay in treatment, or inappropriate communication. Medical negligence can occur in many forms such as giving wrong medication, surgical mistakes, misdiagnosis, failure to monitor patient progress or failure to inform patients of certain risks. Such negligence not only undermines the trust between patients and care providers but can also have adverse consequences for the patient which are severe or even irreversible. Most legal claims for medical negligence often seek to hold healthcare providers accountable and ensure that patients receive the care they deserve.

18.2 INGREDIENTS OF MEDICAL NEGLIGENCE

In order to file a medical negligence claim, certain elements need to be present and proved to impute liability on the accused. This kind of liability can be civil, that is compensatory liability in case there are civil claims against the patient and with criminal liability if the act of negligence is found serious enough to punish. Usually, medical negligence is determined within the "Four D's framework":

- Duty
- Dereliction or Breach of that duty
- Direct Causation
- Damage.

These four elements can be analysed as follows:

Duty and Standard of Care

Duty of care is one of the essential principles in medical negligence cases. A healthcare professional owes a duty of care to his patient in regard to providing competent and reasonable care according to the accepted standard of the medical profession. Duty arises as soon as a patient approaches a health professional for medical advice, treatment, or care either through a direct doctor-patient relationship or indirectly where the healthcare provider accepts responsibility for the patient's welfare. In simple words, the duty of care connotes that a health provider must act in such a manner that protects the health and safety of his patient. For this purpose, he uses his knowledge, skill, and judgment that aligns with medical standards and practices. The duty goes beyond just performing the correct procedure or prescribing the right medication. It also includes a responsibility to provide information, obtain informed consent, maintain patient confidentiality, and take into consideration the overall welfare of patients. In medical negligence cases, the duty of care is usually easily established, since the relationship of a patient to a healthcare provider is inherently one of responsibility. However, there are a few conditions that help define when this duty exists.

- **Existence of a Relationship:** The element of duty of care usually is determined by an acknowledged relationship between a patient and a healthcare professional. Such a relationship may occur in any healthcare environment, where the patient goes to see a general practitioner, is in a hospital, or is receiving treatment from a specialist. The law describes such a relationship as a "physician-patient" relationship.
- **Professional Responsibility:** A healthcare provider has a professional duty to his or her patient based on the role and the expertise. The more qualified the healthcare provider is, the greater the duty he or she owes to the patient. For instance, a surgeon has a duty to act in accordance with the accepted surgical practices while a general practitioner may have a bigger responsibility ensuring that general healthcare is provided competently.
- **Competence and Skill:** The healthcare provider should have the proper training, qualifications, and experience in order to deliver care of the expected standard. This is not merely performing the job but doing it so as to run the risks to a minimum level with the maximum benefit possible to the patient. The healthcare professional must pay attention to the needs of the patient in a way that encompasses all aspects of the person's medical condition and history in order to carry out an accurate diagnosis, appropriate prescription for treatment, and observing the progression of the patient during the course of care.
- **Informed Consent:** Consent is an important aspect of duty of care. The patient needs to be adequately informed about the risks, benefits, and alternatives to the treatments or procedures recommended and his consent should only then be obtained. A healthcare provider must secure permission from the patient before engaging in any serious treatment. If there is no informed consent or if improper information is given, then there has been a breach of duty of care.
- **Confidentiality:** Duty of care includes confidentiality as well. A healthcare professional is legally and ethically bound to keep the privacy of information of the patients. These breaks into confidentiality do not only damage the patient but could also be a legal complaint for the professional.
- **Prevention of Harm:** The primary goal of the duty of care is to prevent harm. It means that healthcare professionals should take all reasonable precautions and make medical decisions with the best possible knowledge of the requirements of medicine to prevent risks and acts for the good of the patient. If provider actions cause harm or injury and it can be determined that harm was preventable, then a duty of care could have been breached.

Donoghue v. *Stevenson* (1932)[1] was a landmark cases of tort law which concluded that a manufacturer owes a duty of care to consumers even in the absence of a contractual relationship thereby forming the very first principle of duty of care. It is not a medical case but it laid the preliminary foundation for future medical negligence cases because it established that professionals have a duty to protect their clients or end users of service from harm. Same jurisprudence can also be applied to medical negligence as it can be established that a doctor owes the same duty to care to each patient according to the general duty of care premise of negligence.

Likewise, the *Caparo* v. *Dickman*[2] case is one of the leading English cases that sets general principles of duty of care in English law. The case helps in understanding the nature of a duty of care to be delivered upon health professionals in medical practice. The court in this case developed a three-fold test for determining the existence of a duty of care in negligence. These are:

- *Proximity:* That the defendant, at all times, has a close or direct relationship with the plaintiff, in that his actions or omission directly affects the plaintiff.
- *Foreseeability:* The consequences of what happens must be reasonably foreseeable.
- *Fair, Just, and Reasonable:* The obligation of care due from the defendant in this case needs to be fair, just, and reasonable.

In medical negligence, the principles are applicable similarly. For instance, a doctor owes a duty of care to his patient; it is reasonably foreseeable that failure to diagnose leads to harm, and justice will not be done if the result of that harm was caused through the doctor's own negligence.

Bolam v. *Friern Hospital Management Committee (1957)*[3], a very important case on the standard of duty which the medical man must observe towards his patient. It established the "Bolam test" which holds that, if a doctor has acted in accordance with practice accepted as proper by a responsible body of medical opinion, he cannot be held negligent. The case revealed that the standard in medical negligence cases is determined by the opinion of the medical community, not that of a layperson, and that it could thus determine how duty of care was evaluated in the medical field.

Standard of Care: The standard of care in medical practice is "the level of care, skill, and attention" a healthcare provider gives in the treatment of a patient. This standard is determined considering the skills, experience, and qualifications of the healthcare provider in relation to the treatment being provided. The medical professional should act as any other competent professional in the same field would do, taking into consideration the medical guidelines, peer-reviewed practices, and evolving research. The courts look to see whether the healthcare provider's actions are within what is appropriate as evaluated by a responsible and skilled practitioner in similar circumstances.

1. *Donoghue* v. *Stevenson* (1932)
2. *Caparo Industries Plc* v. *Dickman* [1990] 2 A.C. 605
3. https://www.healthcareethicsandlaw.co.uk/negligence-1/bolam-v-friern-hospital-management-committee-1957-bolam-test

In the case of *Maynard* v. *West Midlands Regional Health Authority (1984)*, the question of medical negligence regarding the standard of care was taken before the court. This was the case where a surgeon conducted an operation to remove a gallstone; however, a complication arose that led to the patient's death. The technique adopted by the surgeon came under scrutiny, and the court relied on the Bolam test to determine whether the procedure had been carried out in accordance with accepted medical practices. Thus, it held that provided the body of medical opinion was for the surgeon's approach, there was no finding of negligence. It reinforced the principle that a medical man is not vicariously liable or strictly liable for mistakes in accordance with accepted practices, however obstinate other experts might be.

Dereliction or Breach of Duty

Breach of duty involves an obligation to meet the standards required in that medical profession. In other words, the existence of a breach of duty is where the healthcare provider failed to deliver the standard level of care contemplated in his specialty through negligence or intent. The breach in medical negligence could be manifested in a misdiagnosis, medication errors, surgical mistakes, or failure to inform the patient of risks involved. Once it has been established that there was a breach, the plaintiff must prove that this deviation and not anything else caused the harm. In *Reeves* v. *The Commissioner of Police for the Metropolis (2000)*[4], facts relating to a breach of duty were considered involving a patient treated in custody. This case deals with the duties of medical practitioners regarding observance of the safety of detainees. A patient, suffering from mental illness, resorted to suicide while under inadequate medical care. The court held that the negligence of healthcare providers for not following a standard led to direct harm arising from such violations. It, therefore, underscores the duty of care by healthcare providers to vulnerable persons even beyond traditional hospitals.

In the leading case on the doctrine of informed consent, *Chester* v. *Afshar (2004)*[5], the issue was whether there was a breach of the surgeon's duty in not telling the patient of the risks involved in conducting the procedure. The court said that the risks were not communicated to the patient, and that with this lack of informed consent, he owed a duty to the patient which was thereby breached. Even though risks were very low, the court held that failure to disclose the information was deemed to result in breach of duty of care, which affirms the notion of having medical professionals provide clear and explicit information about risk factors of treatment with the patient.

Direct Causation

Direct causation in medical negligence refers to a clear link between a substandard action or omission of a healthcare professional and injury or harm sustained by the patient. To establish direct causation the plaintiff must ascertain that the failure of the healthcare provider to meet the standard of care directly led to the patient's injury or deterioration of health. This means that but for the careless act or omission of the doctor, the medical condition would have not worsened, nor would harm have resulted. For example, if a doctor failed to make an appropriate diagnosis

4. https://publications.parliament.uk/pa/ld199899/ldjudgmt/jd990715/reeves01.htm
5. https://publications.parliament.uk/pa/ld200304/ldjudgmt/jd041014/cheste-1.htm

of a severe disease that consequently worsened the patient's condition because treatment was delayed, that could be directly connected to the subsequent harm caused. In the same way, if a surgical team made a mistake during the procedure that resulted in an infection or injury, the direct causation would be the mistake during the procedure. Merely showing that harm occurred is insufficient; there must be evidence of direct and proximate cause for the harmful acts or omissions in demonstrating negligence. Direct causation is an essential component of proving medical malpractice and often can be established through expert testimony showing the relationship between a provider's acts or omissions and the patient's result.

Damage

Harm or damage in medical negligence means injury or loss sustained by the patient caused by a healthcare professional's negligent act or omission. To recover damages, harm must meet two key criteria: it must be shown to be causally connected with the act, and it must be of a type that the law recognizes as compensable.

Causal connection, the first requirement implies that there must be a direct and proximate connection between the act/omission and the resultant harm. The complainant must demonstrate that the provider's breach of duty precipitated or caused the harm suffered by him. This could be by showing that **"but for"** the provider's negligence the injury may not have occurred. This is also known as the but for test in medical negligence. Whether physical, psychological, or economic in nature, the patient must show that the provider's actions or failure to act were the proximate cause of his injury. For example, in the situation where a surgical error complicates things or in misdiagnosis, causing delay treatment, the patient must establish that the harm suffered was a foreseeable consequence of the provider's failure to meet the required standard of care. *Barnett* v. *Chelsea & Kensington Hospital Management Committee*[6], demonstrates the principle of direct causation. In this case the patient died after consuming poison which the hospital failed to diagnose in time. The court held that the doctor's failure to diagnose did was not the direct cause of death since the poisoning would have been fatal in any case. This case clearly demonstrates the vital significance of proving causation. If the harm would have occurred regardless of the provider's negligence, then no damages can be awarded.

The second requirement is that the damage must be recognized by law as compensable. Not all injuries or losses can be compensated in a negligence claim. The law distinguishes between tangible losses, which include medical costs and lost wages, and intangible losses, which are pain, suffering, and emotional distress. While the injury of the body, generally is compensable, the law often restrains compensation for non-economic harm, like psychological distress unless it is demonstrated to be clearly linked to a glaring act of negligence.

18.3 THE BOLAM AND BOLITHO TESTS IN MEDICAL NEGLIGENCE

The Bolam and Bolitho tests are two of the seminal principles in medical negligence law used to determine whether there has been a breach of duty of care in any specific situation by a healthcare professional. These tests are closely related to the main ingredients of medical

6. [1969] 1 QB 428

negligence: duty of care, breach of duty, causation, and harm; they also reflect the growth of the law in how cases of medical negligence are considered.

The Bolam Test (1957)

The Bolam test originated in the case of *Bolam* v. *Friern Hospital Management Committee*[7]. This is one of the landmark cases that profoundly impacted the medical negligence law. In this case the patient had been undergoing Electro Convulsive Therapy (ECT) for mental illness. During the procedure, she fractured her hip because she was allegedly improperly restrained by the medical staff to administer the treatment. He argued that the hospital staff were negligent in failing to properly inform him of the risks involved and that the use of physical restraints was not an appropriate method for the treatment.

In this case, the court ruled that medical professionals are not held to be negligent if he acts in a way that is supported by a responsible body of medical opinion, even if the other practitioners would have acted otherwise. The court said that the standard of care is whatever the medical profession determines to be reasonable and that so long as the doctor's conduct accords with accepted medical practice, the latter cannot be held liable for negligence. The Bolam test lays down that the breach of duty is judged by what would be considered adequate at the time within the medical profession and not what the man in the street would regard as reasonable.

The Bolam test is connected with the elements of duty of care and breach of duty of medical negligence. There is a duty of a doctor to exercise reasonable care and skill towards his patient. The breach will occur only if the doctor fails to act in accordance with the accepted practices of a responsible body of medical opinion. Thus, the Bolam test resulted in a more deferent approach towards medical professionals, who are de facto accorded deference by the superior expert opinions of those within the medical profession.

The Bolitho Test (1997)

Conversely, the Bolitho test, emanating from case *Bolitho* v. *City and Hackney Health Authority*[8], represents a shift towards increased judicial examination of medical views. In this case a young child, who, after experiencing difficulty in breathing was not attended to even when the nurse requested the presence of the doctor. The child died from respiratory failure. The doctors argued that they would not have done anything differently even if they had attended to the patient. This was also supported by medical opinion from other doctors in the field.

The court ruled, however, that it was insufficient for the doctors to rely on a medical opinion which supported their actions. Lord Browne-Wilkinson, in delivering judgment, held that although the Bolam test remained applicable, the medical opinion had to be reasonable and logical and relevant considerations also needed to be taken into account. The court in this case held that the doctors in question had failed in their duty because the medical opinion supporting their actions was not logically sound. In the Bolitho case, it was laid down that courts could review the reasonableness of the medical judgment and are not bound to accept it merely because it comes from a body of medical experts.

---

7. [1957] 1 WLR 582
8. [1997] 3 WLR 1151

Hence while the Bolam test had been the standard of determining medical negligence, the Bolitho test heralded a new approach to the assessment of medical negligence in courts. This transition reflects a shift from how the breach of duty regarding medical negligence is ascertained. Under this new test, although medical practices are still factored in, the opinions of medical professionals must be rational and bases on sound medical reasoning. In Bolitho, the court held that mere reliance on the opinion of peers is not enough where that opinion does not make coherent or logical sense. In other words, the Bolitho test introduced a critical judicial oversight of the professional judgment in medical decisions by maintaining a balance between professional judgment and legal scrutiny.

The Bolitho now enabled the courts to question the logic and rationale behind the decisions made by those in the profession, even when these fall within a responsible body of medical opinion.

The Bolam and Bolitho tests thus addresses the key ingredients of medical negligence—duty of care, breach of duty, causation, and harm. The first duty owed by the healthcare provider is the duty to exercise reasonable care when treating a patient. Both tests affirm this duty but come at it in different ways. In Bolam, emphasis was placed on whether the doctor's conduct was consistent with accepted medical practices whereas, Bolitho puts a more considerable weight on if those practices were reasonable and sensibly sound. As regards the breach of duty, the Bolam test stipulates that a medical professional would be absolved if they showed their conduct was supported by a responsible body of medical opinion. However, while the Bolitho test introduced a stricter standard, as it says the medical opinion must not only be widely accepted but also reasonable and rational. This change consequently means that courts can no longer accept medical practices which are theoretically supported by the medical community but are illogical or unreasonable in their application. Both tests address causation in that if a breach of duty leads to harm, the patient can seek compensation. On the other hand, the Bolitho case entails reasonableness of the breach, which, in turn, affects causation. Causation can be disallowed in case the medical opinion or practice was unreasonable, leading to harm.

The transition from the Bolam test to the Bolitho test reflects an evolution of the assessment of medical negligence in English law. Under the Bolam test, if medical professionals found support for their actions from a responsible body of medical opinion, they would be able to avoid liability. The Bolitho test deems necessary the judgment of the reasonableness and logic behind the medical opinion by the courts. It ensures medical practices are not only widely accepted but coherent and rational, hence better protecting patients from harmful effects of illogical or outdated medical practices. Consequently, the Bolitho test introduces a more critical judicial review into the medical decision-making process while still respecting professional expertise.

SUMMARY

Medical negligence, occurs when healthcare professionals fail to provide the standard of care expected in their field, resulting in harm or injury to patients. The legal basis for medical negligence focuses on the duty of care, breach of that duty, causation, and resulting damages. The section highlights key cases and legal principles that establish negligence in medical practice, as well as the challenges in proving such claims. It discusses the role of informed consent, medical standards, and the evolving nature of medical practice in determining liability. Finally, the importance of maintaining ethical standards and the potential consequences for healthcare professionals found guilty of negligence, including legal actions and reputational damage have been discussed.

In addition to defining medical negligence, the chapter also examines the various factors that contribute to it, such as misdiagnosis, surgical errors, medication mistakes, and failure to obtain informed consent. It highlights the critical role of expert testimony in establishing whether a healthcare professional's actions deviated from accepted medical practices. It further discusses the different legal frameworks governing medical negligence in India, including the role of consumer protection laws, medical boards, and civil and criminal courts. In this analysis the need for a balance between accountability and the challenges of medical practice has been highlighted while suggesting reforms to improve the system for both patients and medical professionals.

CHAPTER

19

Liability in Medical Negligence

INTRODUCTION

The laws related to medical negligence provide many avenues for liability and redressal. Medical negligence can give rise to tortious, criminal, disciplinary, consumer, vicarious, and contractual liabilities. These liability mechanisms determine the nature of legal remedies to be provided to as well as appropriate compensation for injury caused by negligence in medical practices. Such different forms of liability can now be discussed as follows.

19.1 REMEDY UNDER THE LAW OF TORT

The law of torts has its foundation in the English common law principle of *ubi jus ibi remedium* (where there is a right, there is a remedy). It is based on the principles of "justice, equity, and good conscience", which helps address wrongs for which statutory remedies are not available or are insufficient. Tortious claims enable the victims of negligence to plead for redress and compensation Under the law of torts to establish negligence against the healthcare provider, it has to be proved that the healthcare provider failed to provide care as expected from a reasonable healthcare provider in the profession. Law of torts presumes the competency of registered medical practitioners unless proven otherwise. Hence even if a doctor's treatment causes harm, the assumption is that the treatment followed accepted medical practices, unless evidence shows otherwise. A medical practitioner is not expected to be infallible; they are only required to perform their duties in accordance with accepted standards. This approach acknowledges that medical practice is not an exact science and that outcomes cannot always be predicted. Therefore, to charge a healthcare professional for negligence, it must be shown that the doctor failed to perform his duties consistent with what is expected from a reasonably competent medical practitioner.

This test is applied retrospectively, examining the facts of the incident in question. A law that aims to deter negligent conduct acknowledges the fact that medical procedures carry inherent risks. The courts have repeatedly made rulings regarding whether or not doctors should not be held liable for merely permitting an outcome to go wrong unless their actions were clearly negligent. In *Hatcher* v. *Black*[1], Lord Denning observed that medical treatment carries some degree of risk never occasioned by accidents on the road or in factories. It should never be the case that a doctor is held liable just because things have gone wrong unless it can be demonstrated that he has acted below the standard expected of a skilled medical professional. Equally, Lord Denning in the case of *Roe* v. *The Ministry of Health*[2] pointed out the dangers in medical developments and warned against allowing hindsight to condemn earlier decisions. He noted that doctors learn from experience and that the results cannot be anticipated all the time.

In any tort claim therefore, the plaintiff must show that loss or damage ensued from the defendant's actions. In medical negligence claims this means proving in what precise manner the doctor's negligence caused the type of injury or harm alleged. If the plaintiff can prove negligence, but cannot demonstrate that any actual damage ensued, the claim will not be sustained. Consequently, damage is an essential ingredient of the cause of action in medical negligence claims, and in the absence of proof of harm, the claim cannot be sustained.

Causation is another substantive principle in Medical Negligence. In a tort claim for negligence, it is not enough for the plaintiff to show that they suffered damage. In fact, aside from proving that there was actual harm, the injured party must also show that the negligent act or omission of the defendant was indeed the cause of the damage. In case no causation was established by the plaintiff, the claim will still fail despite damage being proved. In contract law, a plaintiff who proves a breach of contract may be entitled to nominal damages, but substantial damages will only be awarded if the plaintiff can establish a causal connection between the breach and the loss suffered. This is equally critical in negligence claims, where establishing causation is a significant hurdle.

In some situations, courts modify the rigid application of causation when causation becomes difficult to establish due to scientific uncertainty. The House of Lords in *Bonnington Castings Ltd* v. *Wardlaw*[3] ruled that the claimant did not need to prove that the defendant's breach of duty was the sole cause of the damage. Instead, it was enough to demonstrate that the defendant's actions had a material contribution to the damage. In this case, the claimant contracted pneumoconiosis or lung disease from inhaling dust at work, part of which was caused by the employer's negligence in maintaining dust extraction equipment. Although it was conceded that no evidence was available regarding the percentage of injurious versus non-injurious dust, the court inferred that the negligence had contributed to the injury, and thus the employer was held fully liable.

Similarly in *McGhee* v. *National Coal Board*[4] also, the House of Lords re-emphasized the principle of material contribution to the risk. In this case, the claimant contracted dermatitis with brick dust at work. The court held that the employer's breach of this duty materially increased the risk of the claimant developing dermatitis. This principle has been adapted in many cases, including medical negligence

Non-disclosure is another important element in proving negligence. A negligence is established if the complainant can prove that, had he been given proper warning about the

1. *Hatcher* v. *Black, The Times*, 1954.
2. *Roe* v. *Minister of Health* | [1954] 2 All ER 131
3. https://e-lawresources.co.uk/Bonnington-Castings-Ltd-v-Wardlaw.php
4. [1972] 3 All E.R. 1008

dangers associated with a treatment, he would have declined to undergo the treatment. For instance, in *Thake* v. *Maurice (1986)*[5], the court held the defendant liable for failing to inform the wife of the plaintiff that she could get pregnant despite her husband getting a vasectomy. The court found that if she had been alerted, she would have made the necessary interventions to avoid conception.

Remoteness and Foreseeability is also a crucial element in proving negligence. Medical negligence cases cannot be established by just proof of a duty of care, breach of that duty, and loss or injury recognized by law. Apart from such elements, it is essential to prove that the loss had to be foreseen within reasonable consideration at the time the duty was breached. If the loss arising from the breach is sufficiently remote and not one which a reasonable man could see happening, the defendant will be found not to owe a duty for the injury or the harm.

A classic case illustrating the use of the concepts of remoteness and foreseeability is the case *R* v. *Croydon Health Authority*[6]. In this instance, a qualified nurse visited the defendants for a medical evaluation in preparation to take up work with the latter. On examination, her X-rays were reviewed by the radiologist who communicated that she would not be able to conceive. However, the plaintiff was subsequently pregnant and claimed damages on the basis of the inconvenience caused by pregnancy bearing the cost of raising the child. The court held that the claimant's domestic circumstances were beyond the scope of the radiologist's duty of care, and therefore, the loss was not reasonably foreseeable within the context of the radiologist's duties .

As evident in the foregoing analysis, tortious liability arising out of medical negligence is a complex interaction of legal principles and practical healthcare realities. A patient who has been harmed by a healthcare provider's negligence might institute proceedings for compensation in the civil courts under the law of torts. The fundamental elements that must be proven include the duty of care, breach of that duty, causation, and resultant damage. Although theoretically robust, tort law still faces many challenges. The burden of proof is clearly on the plaintiff since medical negligence claims require convincing and cogent evidence, including expert medical testimony. Procedural and litigation costs may deter patients from filing claims. Justice is also delayed by the slowness of the judicial process, extending the sufferings of a patient.

While the tort law framework holds healthcare providers accountable, it has a practical limitation. Alternative mechanisms such as consumer protection forums provide a more accessible and expedient means of redressal. Again, the scope of these forums is limited again, as far as free services rendered by governmental hospitals are concerned.

19.2 INDIVIDUAL AND INSTITUTIONAL LIABILITY IN MEDICAL NEGLIGENCE

Medical negligence can involve cases where doctors or healthcare institutions fail to give the quality of care that is expected from them, which causes damage to patients. In such cases liability can be attributed to both individual healthcare professionals as well as the institutions with which they are associated. Individual liability is referred to as the responsibility of doctors,

5. *Thake* v. *Maurice* (1986)
6. 1978 Lloyd's Rep Med. 44 CA

nurses, and other members of the medical profession for their direct actions or omissions that cause injury to patients. Conversely institutional or corporate liability refers to the liability of hospitals or health organizations towards negligence brought about by poor administration, inadequate staff, and failure to maintain good medical facilities. Both the types of liability are very significant in upholding the rights of patients and maintaining high levels of care among health providers.

- **Individual Liability of Medical Practitioners:** Individual liability of medical practitioners involves cases where injury or damage is done to a patient by the medical practitioner with regard to the negligent conduct. A doctor owes a duty of reasonable care while diagnosing and treating patients. It would thus hold a medical practitioner liable for medical negligence when they fail to meet such a duty, either due to errors in judgment or misdiagnosis and improper treatment. Such liability extends both to physical harm and to psychological damage. If a patient dies as a consequence of negligence by a medical practitioner, the practitioner may be liable for damages payable to the family of the deceased. Even executors, administrators, heirs, or representatives of a deceased medical practitioner may be liable for any wrongful acts committed by the doctor during his lifetime. Liability of the individual doctor is essential in ensuring that the patient has recourse when any such wrongdoing takes place
- **Institutional or Corporate Liability:** Hospitals or healthcare institutions can also be held liable for medical negligence. Such liability can be categorized into two forms: primary (or direct) liability and vicarious liability. Primary liability of hospitals refers to circumstances where the institution itself is liable for the harm caused to the patients, usually by administrative or operational fault. In *Hillyer* v. *Governors of St. Bartholomew's Hospital*, the court held that hospitals are not liable for the actions of surgeons or anaesthetists, as they are independent professionals rather than employees. However, the hospital does have a primary duty to exercise due care in selecting qualified staff and ensuring that appropriate facilities are available for patient care. The decision in this case was influenced by the historical application of the "control test" for employer-employee relationships, which excluded those not under direct supervision, such as independent contractors. This case underscores that a hospital's primary responsibility is to ensure that competent professionals are employed and that the institution is adequately equipped to provide patient care.

Vicarious liability is defined as the liability of a hospital to its patients on account of the negligence of doctors, nurses, and other medical personnel of the hospital. In *Gold* v. *Essex County Council*, the court held the hospital liable for the negligence of its radiographer and nurses and extended the primary liability of hospitals beyond just doctors to all staff members who are directly employed by the hospital. The key case of *Cassidy* v. *Ministry of Health* further clarified that a hospital could be held vicariously liable for the negligence of its permanent staff, including doctors. This principle was extended in the case of *Roe* v. *Ministry of Health*, where the court ruled that the hospitals are vicariously liable for all the employees' negligence including visiting doctors irrespective of their employment status. This marked a trend of extending the shift towards a more expansive view of vicarious liability, holding the hospital responsible for all the personnel provided they are acting within the scope of their employment.

19.3 LIABILITY OF DOCTORS AND HOSPITALS IN LAW OF CONTRACT

Medical malpractice is, primarily governed by tort law but there can be also be contractual action especially in the private health sector. As soon as a patient enters into treatment agreement with a private doctor or a hospital, a contract is created; this places a duty of care to provide medical services with reasonable skill and competence. Breach of such a contract can lead to action for damages on the principle of contract law. However, proving negligence in the context of the contract is more tenuous because the patient has to demonstrate that the service was provided for consideration and that the professional did not perform their duties according to the agreement.

The legal framework in many jurisdictions does not support the idea that a doctor guarantees a particular medical result, only that they will exercise reasonable care in the treatment provided. Remedies are sought both under tort and contract law in cases of medical malpractice. Tort law usually allows for greater compensation, but often damages can be sought owing to breach of contract where the healthcare provider has failed to live up to an agreed obligation. Most common remedy for medical negligence is compensation for injury, such as medical costs, lost income, and pain and suffering. In the contractual sense, a patient may seek a remedy for the doctor or hospital's failure to provide the service with the standard amount of care or expertise. However, the difficulty in proving a breach of contract in medical cases limits its applicability compared to tort law, where a wider scope of negligent actions can be addressed. In contract cases, the burden is on the patient to prove the failure of service as agreed, which can be a complex process.

19.4 ACCOUNTABILITY OF HEALTHCARE PROVIDERS AND THE CONSUMER PROTECTION ACT, 1986

The Consumer Protection Act (CPA)[7], provides a framework for addressing consumer disputes through a three-tier redressal system at the national, state, and district levels. This system aims to offer a quick, inexpensive, and efficient mechanism for resolving complaints related to defective goods, deficient services, unfair trade practices, restrictive trade practices, and excessive pricing. These forums are structured as follows:

- **District Forum:** Deals with complaints where the value of goods or services, along with compensation, does not exceed ₹ 20 lakhs.
- **State Commission:** Handles cases where the value of goods or services and compensation range from ₹ 20 lakhs to ₹ 100 lakhs.
- **National Commission:** Has jurisdiction over complaints where the value exceeds ₹ 1 Crore.

The Act also mandates the payment of nominal fees for filing complaints, which was introduced to reduce the filing of frivolous or inflated claims that occurred when no fee was required. In addition, an appeal must be accompanied by a deposit, and the decision-making process is time-bound, with disputes typically resolved within 3 to 5 months depending on the

7. https://ncdrc.nic.in/bare_acts/CPA2019.pdf

complexity of the case. In cases of medical negligence, the applicability of the Act depends on the determination of certain issues.

The first issue is whether a patient qualifies as a "Consumer" Under the Consumer Protection Act (CPA)[8]. As established by the CPA, a "consumer" is any person who avails a service for consideration, or for commercial purposes. It means that whenever a patient pays for medical services, that patient is usually a consumer and therefore protected under the Act. However, in cases of free services provided, like in government hospitals or charitable medical facilities, complications arise. Such being the scenario, it has been clarified that patients availing free medical services do not fall within the definition of 'consumer' under the CPA because no consideration is exchanged. Such an exclusion has been criticized as it may leave patients without remedies available through consumer forums where they suffer due to medical negligence in such settings.

Another contentious issue is whether medical services should be classified as "services" under the CPA, considering the nature of the relationship between the doctor and the patient. A key distinction made in several cases is between a "contract of service" and a "contract for service." A contract of service typically involves a master-servant relationship, where the employer can direct how the work is to be performed, and the employee is bound to obey those directions. In contrast, a contract for service pertains to professional or technical services where the provider is not under the direct control of the client in terms of how the work is done.

The National Commission in the case of *M/s. Cosmopolitan Hospitals and Another* v. *Vasantha P. Nair*[9] rejected the argument that medical services are personal services. It noted that while a doctor's service might be termed personal in a loose sense, it involves professional or technical skills that do not fall under a traditional employer-employee relationship. Hence, medical services provided for consideration, whether by private or public practitioners, should be considered "services" under the CPA.

Another issue to consider is whether medical negligence amounts to deficiency in service. Medical negligence is a failure by a medical provider to supply, in a specific case, the standard of care expected in the medical profession or it results in harm or injury to the patient. According to the CPA, a "deficiency in service" means a lapse or failure in the quality, quantity, or manner of the service rendered. The key question here is whether medical negligence, like errors in diagnosis, treatment, or surgery, amounts to deficiency in service. In many court rulings it has now been established that if a medical practitioner or hospital fails to meet the expected standards of care and causes harm to the patient, it would amount to deficiency in service, and the patient can claim compensation in the consumer forums. It has enabled patients to hold medical practitioners liable for negligence with the right to seek redress against any other service provider under the CPA.

A critical concern in medical negligence cases is also the extent to which liability can be attributed to a medical practitioner under the Consumer Protection Act. The CPA provides for the right of patients to present grievances against any medical practitioner or healthcare service provider for medical negligence, if such services were rendered for a consideration. However, the scope of liability remains a matter of intense debate.

8. See, *Ibid.* Section 2 (7).
9. (1992) CPJ 302 (NC)

Medical profession is governed by standards and codes issued by different professional councils such as the Medical Council of India, which sometimes creates a complex relationship between professional obligations and legal liability. While the CPA accords patients the right to redress over service deficiencies, medical practitioners generally claim that their professional judgment cannot be subjected to consumer law standards of judgment, especially when such judgments involve exercising discretion or complicated, subtle medical judgments.

However, judicial pronouncements have clarified that medical negligence falls under the CPA by holding healthcare providers liable over injury caused by substandard care, irrespective of their professional standing. The court also made a clarification that the absolute liability of medical professionals in the CPA is upon proof of negligence or deficiency in service. Such liability ensures that the healthcare system assumes responsibility and prevents negligence on the part of medical professionals while advocating the rights of patients to have quality care.

To fall under the definition of 'consumer' in the CPA, an individual must have availed services for a consideration. While the term "consideration" is not explicitly defined in the Act, it serves as a critical criterion in determining whether a patient is a consumer. The patient must have hired the service, received it, and paid or promised to pay for it.

19.4.1 Medical Services and the Consumer Protection Act, 1986: Legal Interpretations and Jurisprudence

The application of the Consumer Protection Act (CPA) to medical services, particularly in government hospitals, has been a topic of significant legal debate. Initially various courts and consumer for a had different views on whether the patient can be classified a consumer under the CPA. In the case of *Dr. A.S. Chandra* v. *Union of India*[10], the court held that individuals receiving medical services for a fee in private hospitals or nursing homes are consumers. However, in *Dr. Subramanian* v. *Kumaraswamy*[11], the Madras High Court ruled that services rendered by a doctor or hospital, whether diagnostic or treatment-based, could not be classified as consumer services under the Act.

Various State Commissions across India, including those in Delhi, Karnataka, Rajasthan, Punjab, Haryana, Kerala, Maharashtra, and Tamil Nadu, have observed that patients who avail themselves of medical treatment in government hospitals are not considered 'consumers' under the CPA. The primary reasoning is that the medical facilities in government hospitals are not regarded as services hired for consideration. Since these services are typically provided free of charge or funded by public taxes, patients in such institutions are not viewed as consumers within the framework of the CPA.

On the other hand, the State Commission of Odisha held a differing view, asserting that services rendered by doctors in government hospitals, even if free of charge, could be scrutinized by the Consumer Forum. The rationale was that doctors in government hospitals are compensated for their services, making the services subject to consumer protection laws.

10. *Dr. A.S. Chandra* v. *Union of India*
11. [1996]86COMPCAS747(MAD)

However, this view was overturned by the National Commission in the **Consumer Unity and Trust Society** case[12], which upheld that patients receiving free treatment in government hospitals are not considered consumers, as no direct consideration (payment) is involved. Such questions were settled in Indian *Medical Association* v. *V.P. Shanta (1996)*[13] wherein the Supreme Court after through deliberation laid down the following propositions concerning the applicability of the CPA to medical practitioners. After deliberation, the Supreme Court laid down the following propositions concerning the applicability of the CPA to medical practitioners:

- **Service for Consideration:** Services rendered by a medical practitioner, except where services are provided free of charge or under a contract of personal service, would be considered as "service" within the meaning of Section 2(1)(o) of the CPA. This includes services such as consultation, diagnosis, and treatment.
- **Professional Law cannot Exclude CPA:** It cannot be said that the fact that medical practitioners are subjected to professional regulations, such as the Medical Council of India or State Medical Councils, excludes their services from the ambit the CPA. Disciplinary control of the medical councils does not exclude the scope of medical services from the scope of consumer protection.
- A "contract of personal service" and a "contract for personal service" are terms which are commonly confused but must be kept distinct from each other. In the absence of a master-servant relationship between a patient and a medical practitioner, the services rendered by a medical practitioner are regarded as "services rendered under a contract for personal service." Such services are not excluded from the definition of "service" in Section 2(1)(o) of the CPA.
- The term "contract of personal service" should not be restricted to domestic servants or employment contracts. It may also extend to the employment of a medical officer rendering services to the employer. Services that a medical officer renders as an employee are beyond the scope of the CPA as such services are not regarded as "services" for Section 2(1)(o).
- **Free Service Rendered by Medical Practitioners:** When a medical practitioner undertakes services gratuitously, especially when those services are provided to all patients in a hospital or nursing home, such services are not "services" under the CPA. A nominal fee charged for registration purposes at a hospital does not alter this position.
- **Free Service at Non-Government Hospitals:** If all patients were provided free of cost services by a non-government hospital or nursing home, which does not collect any charges from them, then such services are excluded from the CPA. A registration charge, however is not considered here for determining the status of the services.
- **Service for Charge at Non-Government Hospitals:** If a non-government hospital or nursing home requires payment for services rendered, then those services are "services" under the CPA because they are rendered for a fee.
- **Free Service and Paid Service at Non-Government Hospitals:** In those instances where a non-government hospital provides free services to those who cannot afford to

12. Ref: *Indian Medical Association* v. *V.P. Shanta* 9NR 1996 SC 550
13. *Indian Medical Association* v. *V.P. Shanta* 9NR 1996 SC 550.

pay for the services provided and chargeable services to other persons, such services would be construed under the definition of "service" under the CPA, Notwithstanding the fact that some of the patients are receiving free services, as the Act covers all persons receiving the services in such circumstances.

- **Free Service at Government Hospitals:** Services provided at a government hospital or health centre without any payment to any patient irrespective of the patient's financial status cannot be considered as "services" under the CPA. Even if a small fee is collected for registration, the situation does not change.
- **Free Service and Paid Service at Government Hospitals:** Where government hospitals offer some services on a paid basis, others free of charge, then such services shall fall within the purview of the CPA, as defined in Section 2(1)(o) of the Act irrespective of the fact that the service is rendered free of charge to persons who do not pay for such service. Both paid and free services are defined as "services" under the Act, and a recipient of either is defined as a "consumer."

From this discussion the current position of the applicability of the Consumer Protection Act in medical negligence is established. In summary, there are three types of medical practitioners and hospitals depending on the charging practices: (1) those that provide free services to all; (2) those that charge all patients for services; and (3) those that charge most patients but provide free services to those who cannot pay. On the first two categories, there is no major problem in terms of applicability to the relevant Act. For instance, free clinics and doctors operated by hospitals do not come within the definitions of "providing service" in the Act, whereas those charging everybody will necessarily come within it. The third category poses a slightly complicated situation especially for patients in a government or charitable hospital, or even in a private hospital providing free services. If in such medical establishments a patient is harmed due to negligence, they would be unable to bring a complaint under the Act. This aspect has been criticized since this suggests that when services are provided as charity, there may be no accountability for negligence under the Consumer Protection Act (CPA) of 1986. As a result, millions of people who cannot afford expensive treatment could be left vulnerable to negligence, as they would not have legal recourse if they receive free or subsidized care.

19.5 MEDICAL NEGLIGENCE AND PROFESSIONAL BODIES

Professional bodies such as the Medical Dental, Nursing and Pharmacy Councils along with their state councils also regulate the professional conduct of their members which includes medical negligence. These professional bodies are responsible for ensuring that only qualified professionals are allowed to practice and that they uphold strict ethical and professional standards. Professional bodies like the Medical Council of India (MCI), the Dental Council of India (DCI), Nursing Councils, and the Pharmacy Councils—along with their state councils play an important role in the regulation of professional conduct in India. These councils are charged with ensuring that practitioners conform to guidelines or standards of practice as well as legal obligations that protect public health and the professions' integrity in medicine, dentistry, nursing, and pharmacy. They supervise the professional conduct of members and have authority to act, for instance, against negligence, since those who do not meet these standards shall be held accountable.

The role of these councils, therefore, is primarily aimed at ensuring that practitioners in the medical, dental, nursing, and pharmacy professions are indeed adequately qualified and maintain a high level of competence in their practice. This is primarily achieved through the setting up of rigorous qualification requirements for registration and accreditation, thereby allowing only those who meet the educational and professional standards to practice. Along with this, they also formulate and enforce codes of ethics and conduct, to which practitioners are expected to adhere. These codes of conduct are crucial in maintaining professionalism in the healthcare system and ensuring patients are treated with respect, dignity, and care.

Medical negligence is also a form of professional misconduct that can be investigated by these councils. Allegations against medical professionals are investigated by the MCI and State Medical Councils. If a medical professional is found guilty of negligence, these councils have the authority to take disciplinary action. This can include temporary suspension, permanent debarment, or other penalties, depending on the severity of the offence.

When allegations of medical, dental, nursing, or pharmaceutical negligence arise, the professional bodies are expected to carry out a thorough investigation into the matter. The process generally begins with a complaint lodged by a patient or a concerned party. Upon receiving a complaint, the councils can set up an investigation committee. The investigation often comprises reviewing the patient's records, consulting medical experts, and taking testimony from other professionals. More serious allegations, however, may lead to formal hearing level, in which the complainant will present his or her evidence and be responded to by the practitioner.

Disciplinary action may then be taken by the professional council if the investigation confirms that the practitioner has breached ethical requirements or acted negligently. This may take the form of issuing a warning or suspending the person from practicing; or it may result in permanent debarment from the register of professionals. In extreme cases, the practitioner may be permanently excluded from their profession.

Besides these specific councils to the medical, dental, nursing, and pharmacy professions other institutional mechanisms may also provide avenues for redress. For example, the National Commission for Human Rights may step in. This gives an added layer of protection and supervision of patients, especially in cases where their rights are violated.

19.6 CRIMINAL LIABILITY IN MEDICAL NEGLIGENCE

Medical negligence is to be treated as a criminal liability if the medical professional's actions cause harm, injury, or death and negligence is so severe and incriminating that it warrants criminal charges. Under the "Indian Penal Code" medical negligence can lead to criminal liability under provisions.

Section 304A (Causing death by negligence): If the negligence of a medical practitioner leads to the death of a patient, action can be taken under Section 304A, which deals with causing death by negligent acts. This section gives punishment for death through gross negligence.

Section 337: Causing hurt by act endangering life or personal safety of others. This section applies when any such medical professional's negligent acts cause hurt. It deals with causing hurt by endangering the life or personal safety of another. Charges can be brought upon the negligence resultant with harm to the patient.

Section 338: Causing grievous hurt by act endangering life or personal safety of others: Criminal liability can be established if the negligence results in grievous injury or hurt under Section 338, which pertains to causing grievous hurt through negligent conduct.

Criminal liability in medical negligence will be established if it can be proven that the professional has acted with gross negligence or recklessness so as to endanger the patient, failing the standard of a reasonable professional with similar knowledge and skill under similar circumstances. Negligence has to be of such a degree that amounts to a serious breach of duty, rather than errors of judgment or minor lapses.

The liability of criminal action in medical negligence cases is relatively infrequent and very hard to prove. Courts require clear evidence of extreme carelessness or intentional harm, while minor mistakes or lapses in judgment typically do not meet the threshold for criminal negligence. Moreover, the prosecution must prove that the action taken by the medical professional directly caused the harm or injury to the patient, which complicates the case for criminal liability.

19.6.1 *"Res Ipsa loquitur"* in Medical Negligence

Res ipsa loquitur is a Latin phrase meaning "the thing speaks for itself." In the context of medical negligence, it refers to situations where the negligence is so apparent that it does not require detailed explanation or evidence to prove that a breach of duty occurred. Essentially, *Res ipsa loquitur* allows the court to infer negligence based on the nature of the incident itself, without needing to demonstrate exactly how the negligence occurred or what specific act led to the injury.

Medical negligence and its use of *res ipsa loquitur* are applied when the following conditions are met:

- The injury is of a kind which does not, in ordinary circumstances, occur without negligence: The injury must be such that, in the ordinary course of events, would not have occurred but for negligence by somebody. Illustration: Normally, a surgical instrument left in a patient's body after an operation would come within this guideline since such an occurrence would not be anticipated, but for negligence.
- The defendant (medical practitioner) was in control of the circumstances: A medical practitioner or healthcare provider ought to have been in control of the circumstances that led to the injury. For instance, a surgeon has the duty to ensure that a patient leaves the operating room without having any foreign objects within his body.
- No contributory negligence from the patient or third parties: The injury should not be caused by any action or omission, whether on the part of the patient or any third party. In other words, the medical professional's actions are the cause and reason for the injury happening.

When *res ipsa loquitur* is applied the burden of proof shifts to the respondent, the healthcare provider to explain why such injury occurred and that it was not due to negligence. This can help the plaintiff to establish the case since the facts are so clear that the mere occurrence of injury can be enough to raise a presumption of negligence. For instance, in medical malpractice, the presence of a surgical instrument or sponge left inside a patient's body with surgical complications constitutes an example of *res ipsa loquitur* . This is because it is implausible for this event to happen in the absence of negligence, considering the extent of care due to be exercised. Additionally, in wrongful-site surgery examples, such as operating on wrong organ or limb, may fall under *res ipsa loquitur* because such mistakes arise mostly from negligence.

However, *res ipsa loquitur* is not always relevant to medical negligence cases. It is most effective when the cause of injury is apparent and does not necessarily need expert testimony to prove, but in complex cases where the application of specialized knowledge establishes negligence or causation, it is often still necessary for expert testimony. Its application also varies with the circumstances and jurisdiction.

Moreover, the Indian Penal Code also exempts medical professionals under criminal law. Such exemptions acknowledge the fact that the medical professionals are supposed to act with good intention and for the benefit of the patient. For example, Section 88 (Act not intended to cause death, done by consent in good faith for a person's benefit) exempts acts done in good faith, without the intent to cause death, when performed for the person's benefit with their consent. It acknowledges that medical procedures often involve risks, and consent is an important factor in determining criminal liability. Section 92 also permits an exception relating to acts done in good faith for the benefit of the person when he or she does not give consent and some unintended harm is caused. The exception here applies only when it is perceived that the medical act was necessary for the well-being of the person. Section 93 saves from criminal liability for certain communications made by a medical professional in good faith.

These exceptions thus point to the fact that medical professionals are held to have a different standard and level compared to other professionals. Though they may be subject to criminal liability when they are grossly negligent, the law does appreciate that medical professionals act for the benefit of the patients, though risks or harm may result from the action. Hence they should not be unduly punished for acts done in good faith unless gross negligence can be established.

In *Dr. Laxman Balkrishna Joshi* v. *Dr. Trimbark Babu Godbole*[14], the Supreme Court was asked to assess the question of medical negligence following allegations against Dr. Trimbark Babu Godbole. The complainant claimed that the doctor had failed to exercise the necessary degree of care in diagnosing and treating his condition, resulting in significant harm. The case revolved around whether the doctor had fulfilled his duty of care in the medical treatment provided. Dr. Joshi's argument was that the doctor had neither properly diagnosed his ailment nor administered the correct treatment, leading to avoidable complications and loss. The Court had to decide if this failure constituted negligence, as the complainant argued the doctor had not met the medical standards expected.

The Court further clarified that the medical profession owed a duty of care to the patient, including taking reasonable care in deciding whether or not to accept a case, choosing the right form of treatment, and in administering the treatment. Any departure from the standard accepted practices of the medical profession would be considered negligence. The court explained the concept of medical negligence and described active, criminal, gross, and collateral negligence. Each of these manifestations illustrates failure to deliver the necessary care in standards. The

14. AIR 1969 SC 128

court held that the doctor's action or inactions which resulted in harm are liable to be subjected to claims to compensation.

This case illustrated how very wide is the ambit of medical negligence and again restated the fact that doctors are lawfully obliged to provide specified standards of care in each phase of the treatment. Any deviation from those standards by incorrect diagnosis, by improper treatment, or in the way a procedure is handled can make a medical practitioner liable at law. It was thereby established that such breach of duty owed to a patient could trigger an action in damages, hence much needed clarity on legal obligations owed by medical professionals. It served as a critical reminder of the legal risks involved when doctors do not adhere to the expected standards of medical care.

A.S. Mittal v. *State of U.P*[15]: In this case, allegations of medical negligence were levelled against a doctor through a public interest litigation for failing to take appropriate precautions while performing operations during an eye camp. Many patients suffered irreversible damage to eyes during the procedure. The petitioners submitted that had the doctor followed normal medical procedures, their condition would not have worsened. The issue before the Court was whether the doctor had departed from the professional standards of medical care expected in such a case and, if so, whether such a departure could amount to negligence.

The Court reiterated that medical negligence occurs when a doctor fails to meet the standard of care expected from a reasonable practitioner. The judgment emphasized that doctors are obligated to exercise the level of care and expertise that is reasonably expected from a professional in a similar situation. In this case, the Court focused on the doctor's failure to take due precautions treatment, which had a direct impact on the patient's worsening condition. This would bring into question whether such a failure could be classed as negligence under the circumstances of diagnosis and the treatment provided. The Court also indicated that negligence might be active, in other words overt failure to deliver appropriate care or collateral failure, which refers to the inability to prevent harm while giving treatment.

The decision reiterated the legal right of patients to expect competent care from medical professionals and how any deviation from the standard of care, particularly that results in harm, should attract compensation for the patient. The judgment further stressed that medical professionals should exercise judgment and skills in accordance with accepted medical standards and that they could be liable for negligence if they failed to do so. This case therefore reinforced the need for medical professionals to act with caution and precision in diagnosing and treating patients to avoid the risk of legal repercussions.

In *Poonam Verma* v. *Ashwin Patel*[16], the Supreme Court considered the case of a homeopathic doctor practicing allopathic medicine without the proper qualifications that caused harm to the patient. The complainant had consulted a homeopathic practitioner, for treatment but later suffered complications because the doctor provided allopathic treatment for which he lacked the necessary medical qualifications. The core issue in the case was whether Patel's conduct amounted to medical negligence because he was practicing medicine outside his scope without adequate training or qualification in allopathic medicine.

The Court held that practicing medicine without necessary qualifications is, by its very nature, negligent and illegal. It found that Patel's conduct fell under the principle of "negligence

15. AIR 1989 SC 1570
16. (1996) 4 SCC 322

per se," whereby no further evidence of negligence was required. The Court underscored the fact that medical practitioners have to work within the confines of their qualifications, and working outside these boundaries would place patients in harm's way. In this particular case, the doctor, by giving allopathic treatment outside the confines of his qualification, directly violated the canons of medical ethics as well as legal provisions. The Court clarified that failing to respect professional boundaries in the practice of medicine would be considered negligent per se and punishable by law.

This ruling had significant implications for the medical community, reinforcing that practitioners must operate strictly within their licensed field. It also highlighted the risks associated with unqualified individuals offering treatments outside their expertise. By emphasizing that practicing beyond one's qualifications is inherently negligent, the case served as a deterrent to unqualified individuals attempting to provide medical care, while also protecting patients from potential harm caused by such actions. The judgment highlighted the relevance of qualifications and professional boundaries within the healthcare system.

In *Samira Kohli* v. *Dr. Prabha Manchanda*[17], the Supreme Court had held that unauthorized surgery without active and informed consent of the patient amounts to medical negligence. In this case the appellant had agreed only for a minimally invasive investigation procedure called laparoscopy. However, the doctor proceeded with a much-complicated surgical procedure while the patient was under anaesthesia by obtaining consent from the mother even when there was no emergency. The issue in this case hence was to determine if the absence of informed consent for such an invasive surgical procedure was a negligence on part of the doctor.

The Court reiterated that such an action is a breach of medical ethics as well as a gross breach of the duty of obtaining consent because informed consent is a foremost principle of medical practice. Doctors are obligated towards ensuring that patients are fully aware of the implications, benefits, and risks before embarking on treatment, particularly while carrying out a major procedure.

This ruling strengthened the principle of respecting patients' autonomy in medical choice decisions and the legal compulsions of informed consent in any procedure. The ruling pointed out that medical practitioners must ensure patients understand the nature of the procedure and consent to it willingly. It also established a precedent in addressing the issues of unauthorized surgeries and emphasized that even if the patient is temporarily incapacitated, proper consent must be obtained or deferred until the patient can make an informed decision which is an important constituent of the duty of care.

In *State of Haryana* v. *Smt. Santra*[18] the Supreme Court addressed the issue of defective medical procedures when a sterilization operation performed by the government hospital failed, resulting in an unintended pregnancy. The sterilization process was aimed at being an ever-lasting mode of birth control but was erroneously performed thereby damaging the fallopian tubes of the patient. The patient approached the district forum against the failure of the process of sterilization under the Consumer Protection Act as the method adopted for sterilization had not been performed appropriately.

The Court found that the sterilization procedure was performed negligently. Medical negligence was determined here by failure to properly perform the procedure, which ultimately

17. (2008) CPJ 56 (SC)
18. (2000) CPJ 53 (SC)

led to an unintended pregnancy, clearly violating the medical professionals' duty of care. It indicated that for procedures like sterilization that have long-lasting effects on the patients, the care providers have a responsibility of ensuring such practices are properly done without error, because an error might have long-term adverse consequences on the patients.

In the case of *Spring Meadows Hospital and Anr.* v. *Harjol Ahluwalia*[19], it was held that a child permanently incapacitated by the mistake of the nurse is entitled to damages. A nurse had, in this case, by mistake, administered an adult dose of medication to a child, causing significant harm to the patient. The High Court also granted an amount of INR 5 lakhs to the parents on account of emotional distress, besides an amount of INR 12 lakhs on account of medical expenses of the child. The court underscored the fact that the direct cause of injury had been the negligence of such unqualified persons as the nurse involved,.

This judgment emphasizes that all doctors and supporting staff should be well-trained and experienced as hospitals can be held accountable for the acts of their employees. The principle of vicarious liability was emphasized in the judgment. It was held by the court that institutions shall be held accountable for negligence or medical and paramedical staff under "respondeat superior doctrine," where employers are made accountable for the acts of their employees conducted within the ambit of employment.

The case also reminds one of the larger legal obligations that healthcare institutions have to ensure a safe environment for their patients. Hospitals are obliged to ensure rigorous staff training, adherence to protocols, and appropriate supervision. These steps assist in avoiding mistakes and protecting against the dangers that come with irresponsible or unqualified staff. Failing to meet these standards can have serious legal and financial consequences for the hospital.

Jacob Mathew v. *State of Punjab (2005)*[20], the Supreme Court held a different view of medical negligence. In this case, a patient died due to a lack of oxygen supply in the hospital. The son of the patient claimed that the doctors were negligent and therefore had committed criminal charges under Section 304A of the IPC. The Court, however, made a distinction between civil and criminal negligence. The Court held that the hospital could be liable for civil negligence but not the doctors unless they showed gross negligence. Further, the Court held that for criminal liability in medical negligence, negligence has to be on a higher standard, namely reckless or gross rashness.

The ruling declared only that gross negligence could expose the doctors to criminal liability. Thus, it increases protection for doctors against criminal prosecution and further limits the number of medical negligence cases that are actually well-grounded on mere allegations but really require actual proof with a support credible medical opinion. It issued guidelines for the prosecution of doctors in negligence cases, like getting an independent medical opinion before criminal charges and arrests must only be made if it's necessary for further investigation.

The case set some precedents in medical negligence law protecting doctors from arbitrary arrest so that criminal charges are not bestowed frivolously. It also sets down a value of the importance of Bolam test, that has defined itself as whether a medical person acts as a fellow competent doctor would have done in other like cases. This judgment forms the backbone for important reference for patients' rights balance by an interest of India healthcare professionally

19. (1998) CPJ 110 (NC)
20. AIR 2005 SUPREME COURT 3180

However, despite established jurisprudence and judicial precedents, challenges persist. Delays in legal proceedings, inconsistent judicial interpretations, and the burden of proof on complainants have a negative effect on the ability of the system to redress medical grievances effectively. In addition to legal standards, ethical considerations such as compassion, patient welfare and beneficence should also be accorded due priority.

SUMMARY

Liability in medical negligence is a critical aspect of healthcare law, addressing the legal responsibility of healthcare providers when their actions or omissions result in harm to patients. This chapter examines both civil and criminal liabilities, highlighting how negligence claims are typically pursued through civil courts for compensation, while serious cases may lead to criminal prosecution for gross negligence or malpractice and examines the key components of establishing negligence, including the duty of care owed to patients, breach of that duty, and causation of harm. It also emphasizes the role of consent and the challenges faced in proving negligence, given the specialized nature of medical practice and the need for expert testimony. In addition, the chapter outlines the evolution of medical negligence laws in India, focusing on the growing importance of patient rights and the efforts to ensure greater accountability and safety in healthcare through regulatory frameworks. The analysis of case laws make it evident that the legal landscape of medical negligence in India is shaped by the need to balance patient rights, professional accountability, and ethical standards. Moreover, patient autonomy, institutional responsibility, informed consent, vicarious liability etc. are all significant aspects to be considered in cases of negligence and while fixing accountability.

QUESTIONS FOR PART V

Q.1 What is the legal definition of negligence, and how does it apply to medical practice?

Q.2 Discuss the essential elements required to establish negligence in a medical context.

Q.3 How does the "reasonable standard of care" principle determine whether a medical professional has been negligent?

Q.4 Under what circumstances can medical negligence result in criminal liability?

Q.5 How is medical negligence addressed under tort law, and what remedies are available to victims?

Q.6 Explain the role of the Consumer Protection Act in addressing grievances related to medical negligence.

PART VI

Global Health Governance

CHAPTER 20

Global Health and Human Rights Instruments

INTRODUCTION

Global Health Governance is a term used to describe systems, institutions, and policies that manage and address transnational health issues. A very broad set of actors participates in global health governance, including international organizations, national governments, NGOs, and other stakeholders. These actors collaborate on health challenges such as pandemics, health inequalities, and access to health resources. Global Health Governance is necessary to enable international cooperation in the mitigation of common health risks and in ensuring that health solutions are available and equitable.

Global Health Governance is important for several reasons. It is necessary to control transnational health risks. Many communicable diseases and health challenges such as COVID-19, malaria, and antimicrobial resistance have no borders. They need international cooperation to prevent their spread and to manage outbreaks. Regulatory mechanisms to address such challenges allow coordinated responses, mobilization of resources, and sharing of information between jurisdictions. This also aims to secure health equity for countries, especially resource-poor countries to enable them to access necessary health services, medicines, and technologies.

Governing health at a global scale also supplements the national efforts and enhances health security through disease detection, prevention, and response systems. This preparedness is very vital to mitigating health emergencies, such as pandemics, and ensuring that countries are equipped to handle future health crises. In addition, Global Health Governance also plays a significant role in health diplomacy and international policy coordination. It offers countries the opportunity to harmonize health policies at the national level with global health goals. Global health initiatives also aim to address persistent global health challenges such as non-communicable diseases, and look for long-term solutions by making efforts to strengthen healthcare systems generally.

Global health governance is premised upon the idea of recognizing health as a global public good, a concept that highlights the shared responsibility for improving health outcomes. Health as a global public good is non-excludable, which means the benefits of improved health extend beyond individual nations and are available to all. For instance, if one country vaccinates its population, it would contribute to the global reduction of disease transmission, benefitting other countries as well. It is non-rivalrous which implies that advances in global health do not reduce its value to anyone else. A healthier population globally leads to mutual advantages for all countries in decreasing the burden of disease around the world and in promoting general well-being.

Global health is also a form of global public good as it is connected with greater development objectives. A healthy population is more productive and has better educational outcomes. It also helps to improve economic stability. By viewing health as a public good, the global community acknowledges that investments in health systems, disease prevention, and medical research have far-reaching benefits, promoting long-term social and economic development worldwide. Health as a human right also reinforces this perspective, emphasizing that everyone, regardless of nationality or socio-economic status, should have access to basic health services. This common vision has further strengthened the point of global cooperation and regulatory frameworks to make sure that health is everyone's imperative, everywhere.

Global Health Governance addresses the multi-faceted nature in which health problems affect cross-border interactions. An understanding of health as a global common good, then improvement demands a collective and joint efforts. Nations must work together to create sustainable and equitable health systems and to manage the risks affecting all of humanity. It will be possible to cultivate peace, stability, and prosperity for future generations only when the world invests in health as a common good.

Another idea that underlies the understanding of health as a global public good is the recognition of health as an international human right to ensure that everyone, irrespective of his or her nationality, social status, or financial resources, has access to the essential healthcare services. Health is one of the basic human needs and is a critical factor for the ability of a person to live a satisfied life. Without access to healthcare, people are at risk of suffering from preventable diseases, injuries, and conditions that can limit their potential and overall quality of life. The international community can eliminate these disparities by recognizing health as a fundamental human right to create a world where all people have equal opportunities for the highest attainable standard of health.

One of the most important reasons why there is a need for the international right to health is that it would help maintain equity and social justice. In many parts of the world, vulnerable groups, women, children, minorities, and the poor, find it difficult to access the healthcare services they need, mainly due to discrimination and inequality and lack of a proper healthcare infrastructure. This is a global right to health that forms the legal framework for the guarantee of accessibility of the services of healthcare to every citizen, more so to those who are marginalized and who should not have to depend on their locality or social background to determine their chances. The right to health contributes to developing global health security. Transboundary health challenges require concerted effort of all nations so that pandemics, antibiotic resistance, and emerging infectious diseases could be addressed globally. A fundamental right to health guarantees a coordinated approach in preventing health threats between countries. An international right to health promotes resource and knowledge sharing and good practices towards a coordinated response to health crises. This collaboration is a key aspect in protecting individuals' health and preventing disease spread across borders.

A second significant reason why this international right to health is necessary is that it contributes towards economic stability and development. A healthy population is highly productive and capable of supporting the economy. Poor health often leads to absenteeism, disability, and death before the expected age. All these can negatively affect national development. The recognition of the right to health by countries encourages investment in health systems that are not only beneficial to individuals but to society at large. Healthy populations are better able to access education, work, and participate in social and economic activities, thus supporting sustainable development and reducing poverty.

Finally, the global right to health is important as it addresses emerging challenges such as Non-Communicable Diseases, mental health issues, and environmental health problems. The nature of health risks, is changing. Climatic change, urbanization, and lifestyle change are putting more people in danger of becoming diabetic, contracting cardiovascular disease, and getting mental disorder. Upholding the right to health compels governments to create policies and programs responsive to these emerging threats.

20.1 HEALTH AS HUMAN RIGHT

Right to the highest attainable standard of health[1] is one among the most fundamental human rights recognized under the international human rights law which seeks to provide a broad, inclusive and integrated framework and serves as an international structure for the protection and promotion of global health. Several international covenants express this right as the most significant contributor of human dignity and quality of life.

Universal recognition of the right to health in international human rights instruments imposes a duty on states to ensure that their populations have access to the resources and services needed to achieve the highest standard of health possible. It is not only a matter of the right to exist but the right to be protected in conditions that preserve, promote, and allow for well-being itself, including medical attention and safe environments, clean water and diet, education, and capacity for physical and mental performance. Health is considered an aspect of human dignity and consequently an obligation of governments under legal, policy, and program measures.

International human rights law, from instruments like the Universal Declaration of Human Rights (UDHR) to the International Covenant on Economic, Social, and Cultural Rights (ICESCR), affirms the right to health as a cardinal element of social justice. Such universal acknowledgment appears to suggest that health is not only a privilege but a right due to everyone regardless of their nationality, economic class, or social status. It puts obligations on the states to actively remove impediments to healthcare and enhance the quality of health services, besides dealing with some of the broader social determinants of health like poverty, inequality, and discrimination.

Many international instruments aim to achieve the "highest attainable standard" of health which signifies that every state is expected to do its best to secure the best possible health outcomes for its population in consonance with its own peculiar social, economic, and political

1. See, Art 12 ICESCR, *Available at*; thttps://www.ohchr.org/en/instruments-mechanisms/instruments/international-covenant-economic-social-and-cultural-rights

conditions. It acknowledges the fact that different countries will have different resources, and it allows for the fact that an ideal standard of health might be an ideal long-term goal. Nevertheless, the States are still expected to ensure that citizens receive the best care, treatment, and conditions for health without discrimination.

An important aspect of the right to health is the recognition of equal importance of mental and physical health. Traditionally, in most countries, mental health has been considered secondary to or not as important as one's physical health. Indeed, the international health rights framework distinctly requires protection of mental as well as physical health-a sign of more holistic views of health. This is a critical development within human rights law because it emphasizes that well-being is not just the absence of physical illness only but also mental and emotional health. The right to the highest attainable standard of health imposes specific obligations on states. Governments must take steps towards progressively realizing this right using available resources to provide access to healthcare and health-promoting services for all people. The responsibility encompasses a number of dimensions such as:

1. **Availability of Health Services:** States should ensure that all have adequate health services available, including medical facilities, medicines, and skilled health professionals.
2. **Accessibility:** Health services should not be discriminated against and should be accessible to anyone, including physical accessibility or transport, financial accessibility or affordable, and non-discriminatory access to care no matter the race, gender, or socio-economic position.
3. **Quality of Health Services:** The health services delivered need to be of adequate quality, meaning they are appropriate scientifically and medically as well as culturally.
4. **Non-Discrimination:** The right to health is to be equally enjoyed by all citizens without any discrimination of race, gender, age, or disability and on any status.
5. **Accountability and Transparency:** States are expected to ensure that the health system is transparent, accountable, and responsive to the people's needs, which includes ensuring mechanisms for violations of the right to health.

Health-related human rights encompass a broad range of essential and interconnected rights that guarantee individuals a healthy and dignified living. These rights are enshrined in various human rights conventions. Some of the most important rights include the right to an attainable standard of physical and mental health, equitable access to healthcare, and an adequate standard of living. All these rights target not only physical parameters of health but also its broader social, economic, and environmental determinants.

Right to the highest attainable standard of physical and mental health not only include access to health services but also protection for their mental health and reproductive rights. This right acknowledges the interrelationships that exist between physical, mental, and reproductive health to ensure that individuals have access to all-inclusive healthcare services that promote overall wellness. It places greater value on health services that value the rights of health for an individual and communities in regard to sexual and reproductive health which is often neglected.

The right to equal access to healthcare and health-related services underlines that health services must be accessible for all people irrespective of any extraneous considerations such as race, class or gender etc. This principle of non-discrimination in healthcare means that everyone should be able to obtain necessary medical care without barriers. This includes equal access to medical treatment, preventive care, health education, and other health-related services, ensuring that marginalized or vulnerable groups are not excluded from the benefits of health systems. Discriminatory practices that hinder access, such as racial or gender biases, must be addressed to fulfil this right.

The right to an adequate standard of living, which includes access to adequate food, housing, safe drinking water, and sanitation, is essential for health. Good health cannot be achieved in the absence of these basic necessities. Adequate nutrition, clean water, safe sanitation, and proper housing are foundational to preventing diseases, promoting physical and mental well-being, and ensuring individuals live in safe environments. The governments are duty-bound to make the resources available to everyone to ensure that people use these resources for survival, let alone to thrive in the society.

Moreover, many human rights treaties also aim to ensure a safe and healthy workplace as well as environmental health. The right to work in a safe and healthy environment guarantees that individuals work in environments that do not pose a threat to their health. This may include special rights for pregnant women such as protections against hazardous conditions at work and guarantees against exposure to hazardous working conditions. Safe and healthy environments constitute a basic right, further underlined by the influence of the environment on health, requiring clean air, safe food, and safety from pollution. These rights, then, point towards a broad understanding of health beyond only healthcare services, stressing instead the need for a whole approach to keeping public health.

Lastly, education and access to information provide the right to enable the individual to make informed decisions regarding their health. These include education on reproductive health, family planning, among other critical health issues. In addition, it underlines the need to ensure children grow up in an environment that is conducive to physical and mental development. All of these rights further reflect the importance of non-discrimination and the right to a life free from violence and oppression, such as female genital mutilation, pre-natal gender selection, and female infanticide. In sum, all these rights create a comprehensive framework to ensure that people not only survive but thrive in healthy, equitable conditions.

20.2 AN OVERVIEW OF THE SALIENT HEALTH-RELATED PROVISIONS IN INTERNATIONAL HUMAN RIGHTS INSTRUMENTS

As discussed above provisions related to health are enshrined in some of the most important global human rights treaties and conventions. They can be discussed as follows:

The Universal Declaration of Human Rights (UDHR): Article 25[2] of UDHR underlines the fundamental human right to an adequate standard of living. This includes the basic essentials of life such as food, clothes, shelter, medical healthcare, and social services. It also recognizes the right of people to social security in the event of unemployment, sickness disability and also in case of widowhood or old age etc. This article reflects a wider

2. See, Article 25 UDHR
https://www.un.org/en/about-us/universal-declaration-of-human-rights

understanding of human dignity; that a person cannot continue to live without access to basic necessities and social security.

Further, Article 25 explicitly stresses the protection of the most vulnerable members of society, mothers and children. It demands special care and support for motherhood and childhood, considering that the health and well-being of the different groups demand unique consideration. It also emphasizes on the principle of non-discrimination since it is recognizes that children born out of wedlock must receive equal social protection that children of married parents receive. These provisions reflect a broader global commitment to equality especially protecting the rights of the most vulnerable.

- **The International Covenant on Civil and Political Rights, 1966 (ICCPR)**[3], also spells out specific human rights related to health. Article 6[4] of the covenant states that "Every human being has the inherent right to life," and this right must be protected by law. It further provides that no one shall be arbitrarily deprived of his life. All conditions necessary to make life meaningful, including health services by the state parties, are comprised in the right to life. Article 7[5] of the ICCPR points out that "No one shall be subjected to torture or to cruel, inhumane or degrading treatment or punishment." This article specifically highlights that no one should be submitted to medical or scientific experimentation without their free and informed consent. Provisions under Articles 6 and 7 of the ICCPR highlight fundamental relationship between health and human rights. In fact, the very existence the right to life contained within Article 6, implies living conditions that adequately ensure an individual's physical and mental well-being. Access to essential health services is seen as a very important ingredient of this right. Moreover, Article 7 safeguards individuals from inhumane treatment, medical or scientific experimentation without informed consent. This provision thus aims to protect bodily integrity and dignity. Together, these articles affirm that health is not only mere survival but also about enhancing the quality of life, ensuring that individuals are protected from harm and exploitation, with their fundamental rights upheld by the law.
- **International Covenant on Economic, Social and Cultural Rights (ICESCR)**[6]: The International Covenant on Economic, Social, and Cultural Rights (ICESCR) 1966 establishes a range of human rights that are directly linked to the protection of public health. Notable provisions in the covenant are Article 7 which speaks about just and humane working conditions which allow everyone to have a healthy working environment[7]. This is a critical provision, because many spend a considerable amount of time at workplace. Hence ensuring that the workplace is safe and working environment is non-hazardous for human health is therefore fundamental to the right to health.

---

3. https://www.ohchr.org/en/instruments-mechanisms/instruments/international-covenant-civil-and-political-rights
4. See, Article 6 ICCPR.
5. See, Article 7 ICCPR
6. https://www.ohchr.org/en/instruments-mechanisms/instruments/international-covenant-economic-social-and-cultural-rights
7. See, Article 7 ICESCR

Article 11[8] of the Covenant also recognizes the right to an adequate standard of living as being necessary for access to services such as healthcare. This article underlines that a standard of living for any individual is inherently associated with overall well-being. This relates to health services, nutrition, and basic conditions of life. Living standards are integral to the health of one's body as well as mind; therefore, the provision under discussion is essentially a critical component in implementing the right to health.

The most directly relevant provision for health in the ICESCR is Article 12[9], which guarantees the enjoyment of the highest attainable standard of physical and mental health. This article lays down specific steps for its realization, such as reducing infant mortality, promoting child health, improving environmental and industrial hygiene, and preventing and controlling diseases. It also emphasizes guaranteeing access to medical services in the event of illness. Such a comprehensive approach is critical for the development of a global structure to address health challenges and promote well-being among people. Over the years, the Covenant has influenced a myriad of human rights conventions targeting rights of specific groups. Over time, such efforts have further enhanced recognition of health as a fundamental human right. The ICESCR serves as a significant international framework in protecting the right to health through its various articles, which not only focus on conditions at work and living standards but also establish a broad, proactive approach to healthcare access and disease prevention. By ensuring that both individuals and governments prioritize health in their policies, the Covenant lays the foundation for global health equity and social justice.

- **The Convention on the Elimination of All Forms of Discrimination against Women**[10], which was adopted in 1979 specifically deals with women's human rights. This was effected an with aim to eradicate discrimination based on gender in all aspects of life. Article 10[11] of the Convention requires states to give educational information to women concerning aspects necessary for the health and well-being of families, including family planning advice. This calls for women to be empowered with information that can help them make appropriate decisions in matters of health and family relationship.

  Article 12 of CEDAW [12]is devoted specifically to the right of women to health. The article obligates state parties to take appropriate measures to eliminate discrimination against women in healthcare services, thereby providing women equal access to medical care relative to men. This includes family planning services as well as comprehensive care during pregnancy, childbirth, and post-natal periods. Article emphasizes free services when needed as well as adequate nutrition for the women during pregnancy and lactation, thus acknowledging a very critical role of healthcare for ensuring maternal health and promoting gender equality in healthcare access.

---

8. See, Article 11 ICESCR
9. See, Article 12 ICESCR
10. https://www.ohchr.org/en/instruments-mechanisms/instruments/convention-elimination-all-forms-discrimination-against-women
11. See Article 10 (h), The Convention on the Elimination of All Forms of Discrimination against Women.
12. See Article 12, The Convention on the Elimination of All Forms of Discrimination against Women.

Article 14[13] extends the above provisions for women living in rural areas by putting emphasis on eliminating discrimination based on geography. It calls for ensuring that rural women have equal access to health services, information, and counselling for family planning. Furthermore, the article ensures that women in rural areas can benefit from improved living conditions. These include access to adequate housing, sanitation, water supply, transport, and communication. This reflects a holistic approach towards women's rights inasmuch as the realization of gender equality in health and living standards is concerned. The CEDAW Convention is one of the major international attempts aimed at the interface between gender, health, and development. Its provisions go beyond the recognition of women's rights to healthcare and family planning, but also emphasizes equal access to essential services, particularly for women in rural areas who are marginalized. CEDAW obligates states to ensure that access to health services, education, and improved living conditions be provided in order to dismantle the barriers that prevent women from enjoying their full human rights.

- **The Convention on the Rights of the Child of 1989**[14] outlined several provisions that protect and safeguard children's health and security. Article 24[15] requires that states provide facilities to overcome illness and rehabilitation for each child to be able to reach the highest attainable level of health. For this purpose, the states must undertake several steps: reduce infant and child mortality, provide necessary medical care with emphasis on primary healthcare, combat diseases and malnutrition, and provide access to nutritious food and clean water. The convention also lays stress on pre-natal and postnatal care for mothers and education of parents and children on health practices like breastfeeding, hygiene, and accident prevention.

  Besides health, the CRC has brought to the fore prevention of harm caused by external dangers. Article 33[16] addresses the protection of children from illicit use of narcotic drugs and psychotropic substances. States are obliged to take measures to prevent children from engaging in the illicit manufacture and distribution of drugs in compliance with international drug control treaties. Article 34[17] addresses the issue of sexual exploitation and abuse. The Convention therefore promises to safeguard children from any kind of sexual exploitation and sees that proper measures are established for protecting children against such hurts. The convention also calls for designing preventive healthcare strategies and educating parents to enable them to understand what is bad for the health of children. ensuring the health, rights, and well-being of children.

20.3 CHALLENGES AND BARRIERS IN REALISATION OF HEALTH AS A HUMAN RIGHT

Although well recognized in international human rights law, the right to the highest attainable standard of health remains difficult to achieve, particularly for low-income countries. The right

13. See Article 14, The Convention on the Elimination of All Forms of Discrimination against Women
14. https://www.ohchr.org/en/instruments-mechanisms/instruments/convention-rights-child
15. See, Article 24 CRC
16. See, Article 33 CRC
17. See, Article 33 CRC

is often undermined by scarce resources, political instability, lack of proper health infrastructure, and social inequality. Global health inequalities and underfunding of health systems in the poorer regions remain a further obstacle in an effort to improve health conditions globally. Other global challenges such as pandemics, for example, COVID-19, climate change, and even migration also present obstacles in achieving universal availability of healthcare to all without discrimination especially among vulnerable individuals such as refugees, marginalized communities, and indigenous people. This is another area where international cooperation and solidarity can play a crucial role in redressing health inequality and making the right to health a reality.

In conclusion, the right to the highest attainable standard of health, as proclaimed in international human rights law, indicates a deep commitment to the advancement of the health and welfare of all people obligating states to adopt proactive and concerted actions aimed at ensuring access to quality healthcare. It simultaneously confronts the social, economic, and environmental factors affecting health outcomes. A fuller achievement of this right however would call for national commitment along with international collaboration to counteract inequalities, promote mental health, and ensure that every individual, irrespective of the situation they are in, is able to achieve the highest possible standard of health.

SUMMARY

The right to health is enshrined as a fundamental human right in various international human rights instruments, reflecting the global recognition of health as essential to human dignity and well-being. This discusses various international treaties and declarations that guarantee the right to health, such as the Universal Declaration of Human Rights and the International Covenant on Economic, Social and Cultural Rights and other specific conventions focusing on vulnerable groups such as women and children. These instruments define the right to health, not merely as access to healthcare, but as the provision of conditions that enable individuals to lead healthy lives, including adequate living conditions, clean water, sanitation, and education. The need to address challenges in the enforcement of these rights, understanding disparities in access to healthcare across different nations and the need for stronger international cooperation and accountability to ensure that the right to health is universally realized also clearly comes out from the analysis.

CHAPTER

21 Institutional Mechanisms for Global Public Health and Disease Prevention

INTRODUCTION

As discussed in the preceding chapter, health is one of the universally accepted fundamental human rights, which was also enshrined in some of the most important international instruments such as the Universal Declaration of Human Rights in 1948 and the International Covenant on Economic, Social and Cultural Rights in 1966. The declarations clearly reflect a global commitment to providing healthcare for all across borders. This ideal, however is not yet realized in a world characterized by stark disparities in health outcomes. This raises questions about whether the current framework is sufficient or whether more institutional machinery is required to promote global public health equity.

This realization that only enshrining these ideals in human rights instruments is not enough unless strong, globally coordinated institutional mechanisms are put in place to translate these aspirations into actionable objectives on the ground. Moreover, while public health is primarily the responsibility of countries, an increasing number international and global health concerns such as pandemics, climate change, HIV and health inequities in general need collective action.

The Charter of the United Nations specifically outlines the promotion of human rights as a core purpose of the organization and places particular emphasis on the interdependence between international peace and security and the realization of fundamental rights. International human rights treaties further describe in detail the role of United Nations bodies and specialized agencies in the practical implementation of these rights. This framework is based upon cooperation between States and various multilateral institutions. For example, agencies, like the World Bank, the International Monetary Fund (IMF), and many specialized bodies such as the United Nations Children's Fund or UNICEF, the Joint United Nations Programme on HIV/AIDS known as UNAIDS, the United Nations Population Fund or UNFPA engage States to help meet national human rights obligations on all fronts, including health. For example, UNICEF campaigns focus on children and take up issues of malnutrition as well as access to education and care. UNAIDS addresses the stigma factors as well as increasing the range of accessibility to anti-retroviral treatment at all infected HIV/AIDS populations. UNFPA on the other hand engages with issues of reproductive health. Each of these institutions and their specific activities are geared towards keeping human rights principles at the core of health policies or programs.

While various international organizations and agencies play critical roles in addressing specific aspects of global health, the World Health Organization (WHO) stands as the apex coordinating agency for global health governance. Established in 1948 as a special agency of the United Nations, who's mandate is to direct and coordinate international health activities, set health standards, provide technical assistance, and serve as the global body for monitoring health trends. Its responsibilities span the full spectrum of health concerns from disease prevention and health promotion to ensuring equitable access to healthcare services. The World Health Organization is an international agency whose primary goal is to help countries around the world tackle common challenges in the field of health. Since its very foundation, it has functioned at the intersection point of health and human rights as mandated by its constitution, which states that "the enjoyment of the highest attainable standard of health is one of the fundamental rights of every human being." It fights against communicable diseases, responds to health crises, works to strengthen global health systems, and address social determinants of health. In setting international health standards, providing technical assistance to its member countries, and encouraging cooperation throughout the world, WHO has placed itself at the core of international health leadership. The WHO's unique global mandate is grounded in the notion that health is a fundamental human right, as stated in its Constitution. This provision emphasizes on the organization's role in advancing global public health by guiding states in the development of national health policies that align with international standard.

21.1 WHO STRUCTURE AND FUNCTIONS

The World Health Organization (WHO) is the world's apex international body for global health governance, being the lead agency coordinating international health efforts and shaping health policy at the global level. It is a specialized agency of the United Nations (UN) and hence WHO is entrusted with the task of guiding global health initiatives, set agenda for health policy, offer technical assistance to countries, and ensure the development of effective global health strategies. Consequently, the governance structure of WHO is designed to reflect its complex mandate, allowing for the coordination of diverse health priorities while maintaining its global leadership in public health. The structure has been discussed in detail below.

21.1.1 World Health Assembly (WHA)

World Health Assembly or WHA is the World Health Organization's supreme governing body. Its role is legislative in character. The WHA consists of representatives from all the 194 Member States. The assembly meets each year to deliberate and reach decisions on matters related to global health. It determines priorities for the organization as well as deliberates over and decides policies, and guidelines for steering WHO by providing it with a framework of strategic direction. The functions of the WHA are crucial for that the WHO remains responsive to global challenges in health but at the same time aligns its goals with the needs of its Member States.

The most important responsibilities of the WHA include approval of the biennial budget and work plan for the WHO, making decisions on the adoption of international health regulations, and providing the organization with the political mandate to implement global health strategies. It also serves as a platform where health ministers and senior officials meet to address critical health issues, including preparedness for pandemics, Universal Health Coverage, antimicrobial resistance, and global response to emerging diseases. Through its resolutions, the WHA shapes global health policy to ensure that WHO acts in line with the world's top health concerns.

21.1.2 The Executive Board

The Executive Board is composed of 34 technically qualified members elected for a three-year term by the World Health Assembly. As the name suggests the Board's primary function is to implement the decisions and policies made by the World Health Assembly. It also advises the WHO Secretariat on its activities. The Executive Board convenes two meetings during the year for the purposes of discussing and reviewing progress of WHO's work. It also provides guidance on public health priorities, develops recommendations for future WHO strategies and assess the overall performance of the organization.

The Board closely collaborates with the Director-General of WHO to support the operational mandates of the WHO which comprises of managing day to day activities and providing policy review for health matters besides advising the organization about the financial and technical programs. The Executive Board acts as a bridge between the policy decisions taken at the highest levels of the WHA and the secretariat to carry out such decisions of the WHO to ensure global health objectives efficiently and effectively. Its role is vital in translating WHO's strategic directions into actionable initiatives across the world.

21.1.3 The Secretariat

It is the operational arm of the WHO. It puts into practice its policies and programmes. The Secretariat, led by the Director-General, is appointed by the WHA, and it is responsible for ensuring that the organization functions smoothly and delivers on its mandate. The Director-General is the highest-ranking official in WHO and oversees its activities, coordinates its response to health emergencies, and represents the organization at global health forums. The Secretariat runs the activities through technical programs and regional offices, providing the requisite support to member States and international partners.

Among the most important responsibilities of the Secretariat is to provide technical assistance to countries. This involves helping Member States to strengthen their health systems and manage disease outbreaks effectively. Besides the secretariat is also responsible for conducting research, collecting data and monitoring global health trends. The secretariat is also responsible for sharing information through mechanisms such as the Global Health Observatory. The secretariat is also responsible for coordinating emergency responses, such as during pandemics and other disasters, and guiding countries in the development of national health strategies compatible with international standards.

21.1.4 Regional Offices

WHO operates through six regional offices, each of which is covering a specific geographic area and plays a crucial role in regional health governance. These offices are located at different parts of the world and tailor WHO's global strategies to address region-specific health issues. The six regional offices are:

- African Region (AFRO)
- The Americas (PAHO)
- South-East Asia (SEARO)
- Europe (EURO)
- Eastern Mediterranean (EMRO)
- Western Pacific (WPRO)

Each regional office is led by a Regional Director who is responsible for the implementation of health programs and policy initiatives specific to that region. The role of these offices is to act as intermediaries between the global policies set by the WHO's headquarters and the unique health needs of each region. By adapting WHO's global health strategies to local contexts, regional offices enhance the effectiveness of the WHO's programs, ensuring that health initiatives are both relevant and practical at the local level.

For example, in the African region, WHO's office focuses on diseases like malaria, HIV/AIDS, and the health systems challenges faced by many low-resource countries. In contrast, the European office works closely with high-income countries on issues such as antimicrobial resistance and universal health coverage (UHC). The regional offices allow WHO to respond flexibly to the diverse health challenges faced by different parts of the world, ensuring that solutions are contextually appropriate and regionally specific.

21.1.5 Country Offices

WHO maintains a presence in over 150 countries through its Country Offices, which play a critical role in the implementation of WHO's health programs at the national level. These offices work closely with governments and local stakeholders to develop and implement national health policies, provide technical assistance, and build the capacity of national health systems. Country offices are directly involved in tailoring WHO's global strategies to meet the specific needs of each country.

These offices assist with the development of national health programs, help manage health emergencies, and provide support for health system strengthening. They are also instrumental in facilitating international cooperation, especially during health crises, by coordinating with local partners and organizations to address health challenges. The WHO Country Offices are crucial for ensuring that global health standards are adhered to at the national level and that countries receive the guidance and support they need to tackle both routine health issues and emergencies. In addition to health system support, Country Offices play an important role in monitoring and evaluation, ensuring that health programs are implemented effectively and that progress towards achieving global health goals is assessed.

21.2 WHO FUNCTIONS

WHO undertakes a wide range of functions which range from formulating policies, conducting research, emergency responses, and building capacities. WHO spearheads global health initiatives across the world which impact people's health and well-being across the world.

- **International Health Standards Setting:** The most important role the WHO has is developing and enhancing international health standards. Such standards contribute to making sure that practices and policies of global health are aligned and evidence-informed. WHO is an international body that establishes requirements in matters related to several health concerns, such as disease prevention, treatment protocols, and surveillance on public health, sanitary, food safety, as well as immunization guidelines.

  International Health Regulations (IHR) are an example of such binding international treaties, guiding the countries towards the prevention of the spread of diseases at borders. It makes sure that all countries are in a position to detect, assess, report, and respond in an integrated way. Through these standards, WHO ensures that health practices everywhere are of the same standards and of high quality because, in a globalized world, diseases and health threats do not respect national borders.
- **Health Policy and Advocacy:** WHO's role in health policy is at the heart of its mission to improve health globally. The organization sets the global health agenda by identifying emerging health threats, formulating responses to those threats, and advocating for health policies that place equity and access to care above all else. The organization plays a key role in advocating for universal health coverage, which aims to ensure that all individuals, regardless of their income or background, have access to essential health services.

  WHO also provides leadership in global health-related campaigns, such as tobacco control, vaccination, malaria prevention, and HIV/AIDS. These advocacy campaigns not only create attention to crucial health matters but also mobilize resources for governments and international partners together with political commitment. By means of advocacy, WHO makes certain that health is on the foremost agenda internationally and health matters should be addressed holistically or globally.
- **Monitor and Evaluate Health Trends:** It has a fundamental role of observing and providing reports on health trends on the global scene. That involves data on disease outbreak, health systems, and several other health critical indicators. There is a repository at the WHO Global Health Observatory site that can help to obtain global health statistics: an answer to the many questions being asked, about life expectancy, mortality, burden of diseases, and other such determinants like access to services. This data collection will enable WHO to review emerging health threats and monitor its progress towards health goals internationally, which include SDGs. The same will provide member states with policy-based guidance because proof of health evidence is hereby presented. WHO health surveillance remains the cornerstone of spotting outbreaks, learning health-related patterns, and guiding policies in international health.
- **Providing Technical Assistance and Capacity Building:** WHO provides technical assistance to nations to enhance their health system, improve disease surveillance, and implement national health policies. This technical assistance takes the form of training for healthcare workers, the provision of diagnostic tools, expertise in disease management, and advice in health policy development. For example, the Health Systems Strengthening (HSS) program of WHO is aimed at ensuring that countries, especially Low and Middle Income Countries (LMIC), are better positioned to respond to public health emergencies and provide essential health services to their populations.In addition,

WHO assists a country in developing its capacity to respond to public health issues by providing emergency medical resources, developing emergency preparedness plans, and facilitating cooperation between countries during health emergencies. The efforts of WHO in building capacities are very important for giving national governments and local health organizations the ability to produce better health outcomes and respond to local health issues.

- **Response to Health Emergencies:** The most prominent function of WHO is in emergency response. The organization coordinates efforts worldwide to respond to health emergencies such as pandemics, epidemics, and natural disasters. WHO's Emergency Response Framework outlines the protocols for rapidly mobilizing resources, technical expertise, and logistical support during health crises. For example, when the Ebola epidemic erupted in West Africa, WHO took the lead in the global response by offering coordination in medical teams and training in the timely provision of the most essential medical equipment. Likewise, during the COVID-19 outbreak, WHO supplied crucial guidance on infection control and prevention, engaged in research on vaccine development, and provided equal access to vaccines by means of the COVAX facility. It therefore shows the strategic position that WHO holds in coordinating international efforts and offering technical expertise on global health emergencies.

21.3 WHO OPERATIONAL ISSUES AND CHALLENGES

As discussed above WHO acts as the most prominent actor in global health governance at the international levels and plays a pivotal role in coordinating international efforts to address and mitigate existing and potential health challenges. However, the organization faces several issues and challenges. These challenges impact the effective functioning of the WHO and impede and inhibit adequate responses to contentious health issues. Some such issues can be discussed in the following paragraphs.

One of the most pressing challenges before the World Health Organization is its dependence on voluntary contributions from its member states and other external donors. This can lead to inconsistency in funding and influence from powerful contributors and specific agenda of certain influential donors can vitiate fair and equitable initiatives. Furthermore, because of the overbearing bureaucratic and governance structures of the organization the decision-making process is delayed which impedes actions on the ground. For instance, decision-making by consensus by member states could limit it in response during an emergency. Emerging health threats like emerging diseases, antimicrobial resistance, and climate change-driven health impacts further stretch WHO's capacity to address multiple crises simultaneously

The second is the over-reliance of WHO on member states for political decision making, since it has limited authority and cannot enforce policies or implement programs directly without the cooperation of national governments. This usually undermines global health goals. Geopolitical pressures further complicate the functioning of WHO since it functions in a dynamic political context with conflicting national interests. This can put severe limitations on its capability to act impartially and can consequently undermine its credibility. Such coordination issues are even more aggravated during health emergencies because WHO needs to engage with various stakeholders including national governments, NGOs and civil society organizations, who may have different priorities and capacities, leading to fragmented responses.

The shortage of health practitioners presents another pressing challenge; according to WHO, by the year 2030, nearly 18 million additional health workers are needed in low-and middle-income countries. WHO, therefore, advocates better investment for education, training, and well-remunerated work with fair wages for health professions.

Improving sanitation and hygiene at health facilities is also another challenge that WHO is confronted with Inadequate Water, Sanitation and Hygiene (WASH) services raise infection levels and compromise the quality of care. WHO is supporting 35 low- and middle-income countries to improve WASH conditions, ensuring a safer and healthier environment for all. These efforts will allow WHO to develop resilient health systems that can meet the various health challenges across the globe effectively. However, resource constraints and lack manpower often limits its ability to make effective interventions.

Because of such challenges and issues, global health inequities still persist in the access to healthcare, vaccines, and prevention of diseases particularly in resource-poor settings. In fact, the COVID-19 brought to light most of these challenges. WHO was also criticized for its delayed and inconsistent response to the pandemic, including delayed declarations of public health emergency, lack of transparency, and ineffectual early warning systems for the outbreaks of Ebola and COVID-19.

The above discussion has brought to light the contributions of WHO for global health governance as well the challenges face as well as its structural and operational weaknesses. To improve its effectiveness, the WHO needs to work towards increasing its financial autonomy. One of the ways can be diversifying its funding mechanisms while maintaining transparency. Also streamlining decision-making processes and taking steps towards enhancing its operational autonomy especially during crises would accelerate responses. This would require binding commitments from member states and robust accountability frameworks. Investments in its human resources, health infrastructure and provisioning of allied services are also essential, alongside leveraging technology and real-time data for better health outcomes. Also strengthening coordination with regional offices, NGOs, and multilateral agencies would address recurring issues of disjointed and piecemeal responses to health issues. Finally, building public trust through strategic communication and shielding WHO operations from geopolitical pressures would also go a long way in enhancing its credibility and operational efficiency.

21.4 OTHER INSTITUTIONAL MECHANISMS FOR GLOBAL HEALTH

In addition to the World Health Organization, many other agencies and other actors too play a crucial role in international health governance often in close collaboration with WHO and sometimes also independently. A brief discussion on their functioning can be undertaken below:

United Nations Agencies

The United Nations has a network of agencies that focus on different dimensions of global health. Most of them target specific populations or challenges. For example, United Nations Children's Fund (UNICEF) plays a pivotal role in securing the health and well-being of children.

Some of its measures include immunization drives, nutrition programs, and maternal care. The agency also acts during emergencies that include pandemics and conflicts where the health of vulnerable children is impacted.

Similarly, UNAIDS, the Joint United Nations Programme on HIV/AIDS is also another very important mechanism which coordinates efforts for combating the HIV/AIDS epidemic globally. It helps in scaling up prevention and treatment programs across countries through policy reforms, raising public awareness, and mobilizing resources. It also addresses social and structural barriers that fuel the epidemic, including stigma and discrimination.

Similar to this, the Food and Agriculture Organization also indirectly addresses health in relation to food insecurity and malnutrition which pose enormous challenges pertaining to health worldwide. FAO also contributes towards prevention of prevention of zoonotic diseases related to animal-human transmission which are increasingly on the rise and one of the primary causes of pandemics.

These UN agencies collectively provide a multidimensional approach to global health through direct interventions coupled with structural improvements for sustainability.

Global Health Partnerships and Alliances

Global health partnerships and alliances are also crucial for the mobilization of resources, building cooperation, and achievement of health goals and targets. An excellent example of such partnerships is the Global Fund to Fight AIDS, Tuberculosis, and Malaria, which is highly effective in channelling financial resources into low- and middle-income countries in the fight against these diseases. The Global Fund has made a significant impact in reducing mortality rates through prevention, treatment, and health system strengthening.

Likewise, Gavi the Vaccine Alliance, also focuses on enhancing access to vaccines in the low-income populations. This organization addresses any financial or logistical barriers inhibiting immunization. It provides essential vaccines and ensures access to underserved populations. Gavi played a very prominent role in the COVID-19 pandemic by coordinating global vaccine distribution through initiatives like COVAX. Coalition for Epidemic Preparedness Innovations (CEPI) complements Gavi by funding research and development for vaccines on emerging infectious diseases. Such alliances demonstrate the importance of collaboration for addressing complex health problems as well as for the actualization of sustainable development.

International Financial Institutions

International financial institutions play a very important role in global health through providing much-needed finances to enhance health systems and respond to crises. The World Bank, for example, helps countries create sustainable healthcare infrastructure and finances public health programs. It works towards preventing diseases, preparing for pandemics, and increasing access to healthcare in developing countries. Most investments in health are complemented with technical assistance to ensure that financial support translates into practical interventions. The International Monetary Fund (IMF) too provides financial packages during health emergencies. Thus, during the COVID-19 pandemic, it enabled emergency financing to stabilize the economy and continued providing funds for public services including health.

Regional development banks, such as the African Development Bank and Asian Development Bank, also provide financing for health initiatives.

Regional Health Organizations

Regional health organizations also supplement the work of international organizations such as the WHO is facing up to health challenges in their specific regions. Pan American Health Organization (PAHO) for example addresses health improvement in the Americas. Being WHO's regional office, PAHO initiates region-specific programs, which may include control of tropical diseases and intervention against diseases. It also helps respond to such natural disasters as hurricanes or outbreak diseases. Another important regional organization is Africa Union's Africa Centre for Disease Control and Prevention, popularly known as the (Africa CDC), formed for ameliorating health capacities in Africa for the preventing and responding to diseases and epidemics within that region. Africa CDC has special focus on surveillance as well as on preparedness and research.

In Europe, the European Centre for Disease Control supports the EU member countries in responding to public health threats in Europe. The ECDC provides scientific advice, surveillance of disease outbreaks, and collaboration among countries. Regional health organizations in this way ensure that health efforts are tailored to address local contexts, making their efforts more effective and sustainable.

Non-Governmental Organizations (NGOs) and Foundations

Non-governmental organizations and foundations, alongside governments and intergovernmental action also complement global efforts in health. An example includes Médecins Sans Frontières, or Doctors Without Borders which offers emergency medical relief in conflict-affected war zones, epidemic-ridden zones, and disaster-prone zones operating in the most challenging settings in the world. Other influential foundations include the Bill & Melinda Gates Foundation that invests in medical innovation, vaccine development, and disease eradication activities among other things. The efforts of such organizations complement conventional national and international mechanisms by bringing alternate sources of funding and research etc and also facilitating public-private collaborations. In addition to all of these roles, NGOs and foundations contribute a lot to advocacy and mobilization of community work. They include examples such as Oxfam and CARE International for addressing issues that impact the social determinants of health like poverty and inequalities. Their involvement is not only direct by providing services but also involves indirect interventions by advocating system level changes that create more opportunities for improvement.

Research and Surveillance Networks

The importance of research and surveillance networks to monitor global health trends for evidence-based interventions is also very significant in global health contexts. One such example is the Centre for Disease Control and Prevention (CDC) of the United States. CDC is a global leader in disease surveillance, research, and outbreak response. This organization also offers technical expertise, training, and resources through its international programs to the countries facing health crises.

The other key mechanism is the Global Outbreak Alert and Response Network (GOARN), an international mechanism coordinating international resources for epidemic response. The mechanism is based on a collaborative approach involving governments, NGOs, and academic institutions to work on health emergencies. It pools the necessary expertise and resources for immediate response and ensures the timely minimization of impacts to public health. The Institute for Health Metrics and Evaluation (IHME) provides some of the most critical data required in global health policymaking. Through comprehensive analyses and forecasts, IHME has helped governments and organizations in prioritizing interventions and resource allocation. These research and surveillance networks form the backbone of global health, providing information and tools to address both emerging and current challenges.

21.5 INTERNATIONAL LEGAL MECHANISMS ON PANDEMICS AND INFECTIOUS DISEASE CONTROL

Pandemics and infectious diseases have increasingly become a growing global concern, posing significant threats to public health, economic stability, and social well-being. The rapid spread of diseases across borders, driven by globalization, urbanization, and climate change, spells out in unequivocal terms the need for robust international cooperation and legal frameworks to manage these crises effectively. International legal mechanisms provide the foundation for coordinated responses by establishing guidelines for disease surveillance, information sharing, and emergency preparedness. These frameworks are essential for ensuring that countries work together to detect, prevent, and control the spread of infectious diseases while upholding global health security and protecting human rights. Some of the existing as well as proposed international mechanisms in pandemic disease contexts can be discussed as follows.

21.5.1 Current Legal Instruments for Pandemic and Infectious Diseases

International Health Regulations (IHR, 2005)

The International Health Regulations (IHR) were designed to prevent the spread of diseases internationally while respecting the sovereignty of nations. They emphasize the importance of information-sharing, early detection, and swift responses to potential health threats. When an outbreak is classified as a Public Health Emergency of International Concern (PHEIC), the IHR obligates member countries to notify the WHO, provide data, and implement measures that can contain the spread of disease. The regulations also define the responsibilities of countries in terms of surveillance, monitoring, and response. The IHR's key advantage is its universal applicability, binding all 196 member countries, which helps to promote a global response to infectious disease outbreaks. However, the IHR has been criticized for lacking robust enforcement mechanisms. While the regulations provide guidelines for countries on how to handle health emergencies, they do not mandate a strict course of action. This limitation has resulted in some countries being slow to act or even failing to report outbreaks in time. Furthermore, the IHR's voluntary compliance model has sometimes undermined its ability to address the global health threats that emerge in an interconnected world. The lack of punitive measures for countries that delay or obstruct reporting undermines the capacity of the WHO to effectively coordinate a global response.

Another challenge with the IHR is its dependence on the political will of countries to implement recommendations. The IHR provides the WHO with the authority to suggest interventions such as quarantine or travel restrictions, but it does not give the organization the ability to enforce these recommendations. This issue was particularly evident during the early stages of the COVID-19 pandemic, where some countries delayed lockdowns and border closures despite early warnings from the WHO. Reforming the IHR to grant the WHO more powers of enforcement and surveillance could enhance the global community's ability to mitigate pandemics in real-time.

Global Outbreak Alert and Response Network (GOARN)

The Global Outbreak Alert and Response Network (GOARN) is a key element of the WHO's emergency response capabilities. This network involves partners from various organizations, including the WHO, non-governmental organizations (NGOs), and governments, who collaborate to provide real-time assistance during health emergencies. GOARN enables the rapid deployment of experts, resources, and technology to countries experiencing outbreaks, helping them control the spread of infectious diseases. The network's ability to mobilize a diverse set of partners has been vital in responding to various global health crises, including the 2014-2016 Ebola outbreak in West Africa and the COVID-19 pandemic. One of the strengths of GOARN is its capacity to draw on a wide array of expertise. The network brings together epidemiologists, virologists, public health experts, and logistics specialists who work on the ground to provide technical support and coordinate interventions. In addition to providing expertise, GOARN can facilitate the rapid distribution of vaccines and other medical supplies, which can be crucial in halting the spread of infectious diseases in their early stages. This global collaboration enables a more cohesive and efficient response, with countries working together to share data, monitor trends, and implement control measures.

However, the limitations of GOARN lie in its dependence on voluntary partnerships and international goodwill. Although the network has proven effective in many instances, it can face challenges in terms of resource allocation and political coordination. Countries in need of support may be hesitant to accept outside assistance due to sovereignty concerns, or they may be unable to provide the necessary infrastructure for external teams to operate effectively. As global health risks continue to rise, strengthening GOARN's operational capacity, increasing funding, and formalizing its structure could help ensure that it remains a crucial resource for pandemic response in the future.

International Convention on Biological Diversity (CBD)

The Convention on Biological Diversity (CBD) is an international treaty that focuses on the conservation of biodiversity, the sustainable use of natural resources, and the equitable sharing of benefits derived from genetic resources. While not explicitly designed for pandemic prevention, the CBD plays an indirect but vital role in reducing the risk of zoonotic diseases, which are diseases that are transmitted from animals to humans. The CBD encourages the sustainable management of ecosystems, which helps to mitigate the risk of zoonotic outbreaks by maintaining healthy wildlife habitats and reducing the encroachment of human activities into fragile ecosystems. The CBD also emphasizes the importance of protecting biodiversity in the context of global health. Focusing on ecosystem health, the CBD aims to reduce the conditions that allow pathogens to jump from animals to humans, which has been a significant cause of recent pandemics. For example, deforestation, the illegal wildlife trade, and habitat destruction can increase the likelihood of zoonotic diseases emerging and spreading to human populations. Through its commitment to biodiversity conservation, the CBD helps to address the root causes of many emerging infectious diseases and contributes to global pandemic prevention efforts.

Nevertheless, the CBD faces challenges in integrating health considerations into its framework. While it highlights the links between biodiversity and public health, the convention does not have specific legal mechanisms for addressing pandemics directly. Greater integration between public health and biodiversity policies could enhance the global response to infectious diseases. Besides, the CBD's focus on biodiversity protection is often overshadowed by short-term economic and development goals, making it difficult to prioritize public health risks such as pandemics in its agenda. Strengthening the role of the CBD in pandemic preparedness could ensure that conservation efforts are more directly aligned with global health objectives.

Trade-related Aspects of Intellectual Property Rights (TRIPS)

The TRIPS agreement under the WTO governs the intellectual property rights (IPR) of member states, setting minimum standards for patent protection, copyrights, and trademarks. In the context of pandemics, the TRIPS agreement plays a critical role in determining how the intellectual property associated with essential medicines and vaccines is managed. The agreement allows patent holders to control the production and distribution of new drugs and vaccines, which can lead to high prices and limited access in low- and middle-income countries. During the COVID-19 pandemic, the issue of intellectual property rights became a major point of debate. Countries and international organizations called for the temporary waiver of certain intellectual property protections under the TRIPS agreement, to enable broader access to life-saving treatments and vaccines. The TRIPS waiver proposal aimed to allow countries to produce generic versions of COVID-19 vaccines and treatments, thereby reducing costs and increasing the availability of these products. While some progress was made, the debate highlighted the tension between intellectual property protections and the need for equitable access to healthcare resources during a global health crisis. Although the TRIPS agreement has provisions for compulsory licensing, which permits countries to bypass patent protections in certain situations, the process remains cumbersome and politically sensitive. Some argue that the TRIPS framework must be reformed to ensure that public health considerations are prioritized over commercial interests, particularly in the face of pandemics. Strengthening international cooperation on intellectual property rights and creating mechanisms to ensure the equitable distribution of medical technologies could improve global responses to future health emergencies.

Pandemic Influenza Preparedness Framework

Another important international instrument of global health governance is the Pandemic Influenza Preparedness (PIP) Framework[1]. Established by the World Health Organization

1. *Pandemic influenza preparedness (PIP) framework. World Health Organization.* Available at: https://www.who.int/initiatives/pandemic-influenza-preparedness-framework

(WHO), PIP aims to serve as a pivotal instrument in global health governance, with an objective to bolster worldwide readiness and response capabilities against influenza pandemics. PIP was adopted during the 64th World Health Assembly in May 2011. It is currently the only international mechanism for pathogen centric Access and Benefit Sharing (ABS). It acknowledges the sovereign rights of nations over their biological resources while aiming to establish a fair, transparent, and equitable system. Central to this framework is the exchange of pandemic influenza virus samples by WHO Member States with the Global Influenza Surveillance and Response System (GISRS), a global network of WHO-affiliated laboratories[2]. This exchange mechanism is pivotal for global health solidarity as it aims to ensure that countries can collectively monitor and respond to influenza pandemics. Sharing virus samples through GISRS, nations enable countries to contribute to global surveillance efforts, enhancing early detection and response capabilities worldwide. This collaborative approach is essential in addressing the transboundary nature of infectious diseases, highlighting the principle that effective pandemic preparedness requires coordinated international cooperation.

The PIP Framework emphasizes the equitable distribution of benefits derived from shared virus samples. Pharmaceutical companies and vaccine manufacturers, receiving these samples under binding Standard Material Transfer Agreements (SMTAs), commit to sharing benefits such as vaccines and therapeutics with WHO. This commitment ensures that medical countermeasures developed from shared viruses are made available to all countries, regardless of their economic status or capacity to produce vaccines independently.

21.5.2 Proposed International Legal Mechanisms

While the international arrangements on pandemics and international disease prevention and control have provided a structural framework, they have not proven to be adequate and fully effective in controlling pandemic outbreaks. This is mainly because of a lack of strong enforceability mechanisms which has led to inconsistent compliance on part of countries with respect to aspects such as timely reporting, capacity building, equitable distribution of resources etc. To alleviate such difficulties certain reforms are being actively discussed to strengthen the infectious disease control arrangements. One of the most significant reforms being mulled over is the formulation of a binding international treaty on pandemics. The salient aspects of the treaty have been discussed in the following paragraphs.

The global pandemic treaty is being envisaged to be a formalized international agreement designed to coordinate responses to pandemics. The proposed treaty would create binding legal commitments for countries to enhance their pandemic preparedness, share information transparently, and take collective actions to mitigate the spread of infectious diseases. The treaty would address the systemic gaps exposed by the COVID-19 pandemic, such as uneven vaccine access, the delay in global responses, and the failure to ensure equitable health interventions in the Global South. It would include provisions for sharing virus samples, facilitating cross-border medical aid, and enhancing the capacity of international organizations like the WHO to enforce compliance.

2. *Global Influenza Surveillance and Response System (GISRS), World Health Organization*. Available at: https://www.who.int/initiatives/global-influenza-surveillance-and-response-system (Accessed: 16 June 2024).

One of the proposed treaty's key components would involve strengthening the capacity of the WHO to take decisive action during pandemics. This could include providing the WHO with greater authority to coordinate international health measures, including mandating certain public health interventions, such as quarantine or travel restrictions. A global pandemic treaty would also focus on financing mechanisms to ensure that all countries, particularly low-income nations, can access critical health resources like vaccines, diagnostics, and treatments.

The treaty would also have provisions for creating global surveillance systems and increasing transparency in the early reporting of outbreaks. Setting clear standards for data sharing, the treaty would ensure that the international community can respond rapidly to emerging health threats. The implementation of a pandemic treaty, however, would require the full commitment of international stakeholders and the political will to enforce the rules and commitments established. Countries with strong health systems might resist the treaty's mandatory measures, making negotiations complex and challenging.

Another widely debated aspect in the context of developing a treaty is ensuring that the human rights of individuals are protected during pandemic responses. This includes safeguarding the rights to privacy, ensuring equitable access to healthcare, and protecting vulnerable populations from discrimination or exclusion during crisis management.

To achieve all this strengthening the WHO's legal authority would be critical in the context of a treaty to ensure a more coordinated and effective response to future pandemics. Proposals include granting the WHO the power to enforce binding measures, such as issuing directives on international travel, imposing quarantine protocols, and coordinating the global distribution of medical supplies. This would address the current weakness in the International Health Regulations where the WHO can recommend but cannot effectively compel countries to act. Expanding the WHO's enforcement capacity would be crucial for ensuring that global health standards are met during health emergencies, preventing delays and fragmented responses that can worsen the spread of infectious diseases. Moreover, the WHO could be empowered to play a greater role in crisis management, including organizing the global distribution of vaccines, setting standards for diagnostics, and overseeing the equitable allocation of resources. This expanded authority could make the WHO a more central player in global pandemic management.

The creation of international legal frameworks to ensure universal access to vaccines and treatments during pandemics is another critical proposal. This could involve new agreements that mandate the sharing of intellectual property related to pandemic treatments and vaccines and ensure that these technologies are affordable and accessible worldwide, especially in low-income countries. Another provision being discussed is to create global surveillance systems that can monitor infectious diseases in real-time. These systems would improve early detection, allowing for rapid responses to potential pandemics before they spread globally. With such a system in place, countries would be legally required to share real-time epidemiological data, genomic sequencing data, and other critical health information to prevent outbreaks from turning into pandemics.

Establishing a global health fund is also a critical issue being discussed. It could ensure continuous funding for pandemic preparedness, response, and equitable vaccine distribution is a proposed mechanism. This would help mitigate the financial challenges countries face during public health emergencies and allow for a more coordinated global response to infectious diseases.

In addition to formulating a pandemic treaty there have been calls to revise the IHR 2005 to include stronger enforcement mechanisms. For instance, countries could be required to implement specific public health measures (e.g., travel restrictions, quarantine protocols) in response to WHO recommendations. This would make the IHR more robust and effective in addressing future pandemics.

On the basis of the above discussion it is apt to say that while international legal mechanisms for pandemics and infectious diseases have provided a working mechanism, gaps remain in global preparedness, response, and equity. Strengthening existing frameworks like the IHR, creating a global pandemic treaty, and improving surveillance, data sharing, and resource access will be crucial in building a more resilient and equitable global health system. A reform of the existing system is thus need of the hour. Addressing these legal and ethical challenges will be essential to managing future pandemics and preventing infectious diseases from wreaking havoc on global populations.

SUMMARY

This chapter has emphasizes the critical role of institutional mechanisms in promoting global health equity and addressing transnational health challenges. The discussion has brought out the pivotal significance of international human rights frameworks, such as the Universal Declaration of Human Rights and the International Covenant on Economic, Social, and Cultural Rights, etc. in recognizing health as a fundamental human right. Such instruments and multilateral agreements, though aspirational, require robust institutional systems for practical implementation. To his end organizations such as WHO and its partners have been established and they have contributed to the cause of global health significantly by promoting health as a public good, by trying to ensure equity, and collective action against shared challenges like pandemics, antimicrobial resistance, and various health inequities.

Collaboration among other actors, which includes the UN agencies, global partnerships, and regional organizations and partnerships such as Gavi, CEPI, and global financial institutions , regional bodies and NGOs ensure more specific interventions suited to the practical needs and exigencies of specific regions. Such mechanism needs to work cohesively to address systemic inequities and prepare for future challenges by making use of their strengths in closing gaps in health access and outcomes, especially in resource-poor settings. All of these efforts must work towards maintaining the principle of health as a universal right, fostering global solidarity and resilience in health governance.

CHAPTER

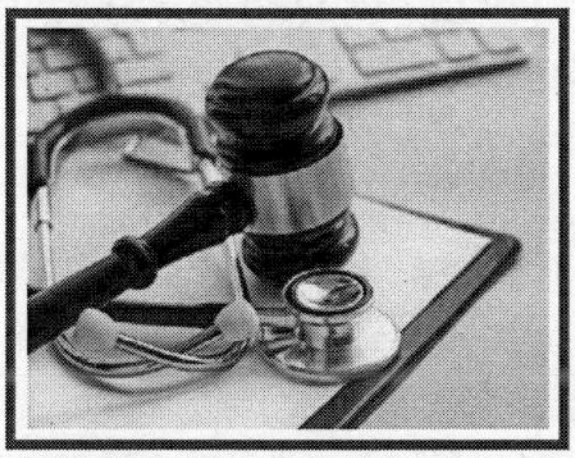

22

Intellectual Property Rights and Health

INTRODUCTION

The rights-duty relational paradigm seldom takes a more starkly dichotomous form than it does in any policy debate around Intellectual Property Rights and Human Right to health. While the former essentially revolves around proprietary concerns of private interests, individual or institutional, the latter is pivoted on universalistic and transcendental human rights principles of access to healthcare and embedded distributive justice priorities.

Conventionally Intellectual Property Rights (IPR) and Human Rights (HR) have both been independent fields of study in their own right and have witnessed tremendous growth and proliferation in recent times. Intellectual Property Protection has played a significant role in bringing about positive changes in a great number of diverse areas ranging from socio-cultural to science and technology.

However, they have also raised important questions about the widening technology gap between the rich and the poor people as well as between developing and developed nations, over protection of intellectual property leading to monopolistic pricing, issues of access and affordability. Health sector is one area where protection of intellectual property rights and protection of human rights to health have come face to face with each other and posed difficulties of striking the right balance.

22.1 IPR AND HUMAN RIGHTS: PARALLEL UNIVERSES

Human rights and IPR for a long time existed and operated as two parallel universes without cutting into each other. The reason for it was that the common elements necessary for establishing a correlation between them were not recognized or even conceptualized.

Another reason has been that the conflicting nature and character of these two domains between the two was traditionally given more emphasis than an exploration of the possibilities of finding commonalities between the two. The public sphere that is the state and as well as non-state actors pin their hopes on Human Rights while IPR is traditionally geared towards according profit centric rights which was conceived as a mechanism to promote Innovation and enterprise.

Therefore, the conflict between human rights and IPR can also be looked at as a conflict between public rights and the private rights and in so far as the stakeholders are concerned Sate and Civil society become advocates of a human centric approach whereas private organizations and entrepreneurs' dwell upon protection of IPRs.

These reasons therefore to a large extent precluded the mention of intellectual property rights in the human rights discourse. The intellectual property discourse also reciprocated the same sentiments and therefore references to human rights do not appear in the major intellectual property treaties such as the Paris and Berne Conventions. These treaties do refer to the protections granted to authors and inventors as "rights" but this notion of rights has a distinct economic and instrumental benefits or profit centric overtone[1].

In essence therefore the mutually exclusive existence of the two domains can be explained by the fact that both bodies of law were preoccupied with issues that concerned them directly and were therefore more important, and they were not perceived as either complimenting each other nor helping each other grow.

As a result of factors enunciated above, intellectual property and Human rights existed in silos for a considerable length of time despite the fact that the 1948 Universal Declaration of Human Rights itself recognizes the *authors' moral and material interests" in their "scientific, literary or artistic production[s]"* as an essential fundamental liberty[2].

The neat compartmentalization discussed above however in due course showed signs of a breach. This was in a way a natural consequence of the expansion both human rights as well as the intellectual property regimes. While the human rights evolved from being circumscribed within a limited arena of first generation civil and political rights to gradually expanding and covering within their scope a whole range of second and third generation rights such as those related to economic, social and cultural rights that included within their ambit a plethora of rights such as healthcare, cultural heritage, healthy environment, natural resources to name a few.

The right to health consequently emerged as one of the most important areas of this extended new human rights discourse and was included in some of the important international human rights instruments which accorded a high priority to the right to health and incorporated them in their texts.

One of the earliest attempts to define health can be traced to the preamble of the 1946 World Health Organization (WHO) Constitution which defines health broadly as follows[3]:

[Health is] a state of complete physical, mental and social well-being and not merely the absence of disease or infirmity. "The Constitution defines the right to health as "the enjoyment of the highest attainable standard of health.

This definition of health and the subsequent elaboration of the right to health has been widely acknowledged as the pioneering attempt to envisage health as a fundamental and inalienable human right. It also enumerates some principles of this right as healthy child development; equitable dissemination of medical knowledge and its benefits; and government-provided social measures to ensure adequate health.

1. Laurence R. Helfer, "Human Rights and Intellectual Property: Conflict or Coexistence?", *available at*: https://scholarship.law.umn.edu/cgi/viewcontent.cgi?article=1399&context=mjlst.
2. Article 27(2) UDHR, *Available at*: http://www.un.org/en/udhrbook/pdf/udhr_booklet_en_web.pdf
3. *Available at*: http://apps.who.int/gb/bd/PDF/bd47/EN/constitution-en.pdf

This definition of health and the subsequent elaboration of the right to health has been widely acknowledged as the pioneering attempt to envisage health as a fundamental and inalienable human right. It also enumerates some principles of this right as healthy child development; equitable dissemination of medical knowledge and its benefits; and government-provided social measures to ensure adequate health.

Frank P. Grad commenting on the preamble of the WHO says that the preamble analyses the obligation of the states to contribute to the health of their citizens, this Grad argue is not an imported obligation but is intrinsic to the fundamental right of every human being and observes:[4]

From the fundamental right to health of every human being, the Preamble moves to the health of all peoples, observing that this is fundamental to their attainment of peace and security, and depends on the fullest cooperation of individuals and states. The connection between health, peace and security is self-evident when diseases coupled with poverty and other social ills destabilize governments and societies. The Preamble notes that the achievement of any state in the promotion and protection of health is of value to all.

Similarly, the International Covenant on Economic, Social and Cultural Rights also recognizes this right as an important constituent of human right. Article 12 of the covenant exhorts the states to take steps to ensure the fullest availability of these rights. The Article states[5]

The States Parties to the present Covenant recognize the right of everyone to the enjoyment of the highest attainable standard of physical and mental health. The steps to be taken by the States Parties to the present Covenant to achieve the full realization of this right shall include those necessary for:

- *The reduction of the stillbirth-rate and of infant mortality and for the healthy development of the child;*
- *The improvement of all aspects of environmental and industrial hygiene;*
- *The prevention, treatment and control of epidemic, endemic, occupational and other diseases;*
- *The creation of conditions which would assure to all medical service and medical attention in the event of sickness.*

Apart from these two instruments mentioned above right to health is also mentioned in a number of other instruments such as the United Nations Committee on Economic, Social and Cultural Rights released General Comment No. 14[6] as well as in the Convention on Elimination of All Forms of Discrimination Against Women (CEDAW)[7] which also echoes the same sentiments in so far as it advocates protection of women from gender discrimination when it comes to receiving health services particularly with respect to reproductive and sexual rights.

Both General Comments and CEDAW therefore serve as torchbearers of the global distributive aspects of human rights by advocating the expansion of healthcare to hitherto

4. Frank P. Grad: The Preamble of the Constitution of the World Health Organisation Available at: https://scielosp.org/pdf/bwho/v80n12/8012a13.pdf.
5. *Available at*: https://www.ohchr.org/en/professionalinterest/pages/cescr.aspx
6. *Available at*: https://www.refworld.org/pdfid/4538838d0.pdf (last visited April 1, 2020).
7. *Available at*: https://www.un.org/womenwatch/daw/cedaw/text/econvention.htm (last visited April 1, 2020).

marginalized sections of the global society and especially for women belonging to poorer sections of the societies and inhabiting poorer or under developed geographies and therefore face a double discrimination by virtue of their gender and marginalization.

While the human rights discourse as clear from the above was giving an increasing prominence to health, the Intellectual Property domain with respect to health and healthcare was also expanding and new innovations and technological developments ensured that societies had better access to healthcare, better living conditions and better resources at their disposal.

However, they also brought in the questions of access and affordability and therefore consciously and unconsciously created a divide based on economic affluence, social and cultural dominance and political power among others. In geopolitical terms they also resulted in creation of a divide between the developed world on the one hand and the developing world on the other. Innovators also were guilty many a time of utilizing the natural resources of the latter as well as indigenous know how of the primitive societies without passing the benefits to them and thereby directly impinging on their human rights.

The gradual but definite proliferation of the two legal domains engendered overlaps and therefore had the effect of a breaching of boundaries between the two. This also led to the establishment of an interface and interaction between them.

It was the human rights community that first took notice of intellectual property law as laws which encroached upon their territory. "*Two events caused intellectual property to be placed on the agenda for human rights lawmaking. The first was an emphasis on the neglected rights of indigenous peoples. The second was the consequence of linking of intellectual property and trade through the TRIPS agreement which sought to strengthen the IPR regime often at the expense of human right considerations*"[8].

Audrey Chapman[9] talking about a human rights perspective in Intellectual Property and access to the benefits of science puts it quite succinctly.

Commercialization has introduced market considerations into the conduct of science and changed its public character

... Commercialization has also changed intellectual property from a means to provide incentives to researchers and inventors to a mechanism to encourage investment and protect the resources of investors.

The IPR-HR interaction is deliberated upon and discussed at various fora that are associated with governing or administering intellectual property and human rights regimes such as the World Intellectual Property Organization (WIPO), the U.N. Commission on Human Rights and the Sub-Commission on the Promotion and Protection of Human Rights, the World Trade Organization (WTO), the World Health Organization (WHO) to name a few. If an analysis is sought to be done regarding the subject matter of legal debates in these for a, two distinct conceptual paradigms regarding the human rights-intellectual property interaction shall emerge.

The first of these paradigms looks at human rights and intellectual property rights as being inherently contradictory and even at cross roads to each other. This kind of framework regards IPR and HR duality as a zero-sum game which implies that a strong IP regime essentially implies a weak HR protection regime and vice versa. This also acts under the presumption that

8. *Supra* note 6.
9. https://www.wipo.int/edocs/mdocs/tk/en/wipo_unhchr_ip_pnl_98/wipo_unhchr_ip_pnl_98_5.pdf

these two are structurally inconsistent with each other and that. Intellectual property protection does not only undermine but is also incompatible with the entire gamut of human rights and responsibilities allied to it, especially in the area of economic, social, and cultural rights. A case in point is a resolution by the Office of the High Commissioner for Human Rights which recognizes the existence of such a conflict[10].

.... Noting further that actual or potential conflicts exist between the implementation of the TRIPS Agreement and the realization of economic, social and cultural rights in relation to, inter alia, impediments to the transfer of technology to developing countries....

The identification of these contradictions however also provides an impetus to the efforts to resolve the conflict and to harmonize the two regimes in a way that they become mutually complimentary.

The alternative paradigm of the human rights and intellectual property binary relationship endorses the viewpoint that both areas of law can find a common ground. Private monopoly rights and consequent incentives that authors and inventors deserve on account of their creativity coexist with the genuine requirements of the public to gain access to these innovations as a matter of right and not just charity. This school of thought therefore looks at striking a balance between these two legal domains, however to strike this balance is not as simple as it sounds.

This is best reflected in an ECOSOC report which refers to Article 15 of the International Covenant on Economic, Social and Cultural Rights (ICESCR) as well as Article 27 of the Universal Declaration on Human Rights both of which essentially deal with the obligation of the State to 'respect, protect and fulfil people cultural rights and at the same time recognize the need to harmonize both public and private interests in intellectual property.

The report states[11]

"The starting point for a human rights analysis of TRIPS Agreement is Article 15 of the International Covenant on Economic, Social and Cultural Rights (ICESCR) and the similarly worded Article 27 of the Universal Declaration on Human Rights (the Universal Declaration) Article 15 of the Covenant obliges States parties to respect, protect and fulfil people's cultural rights. The article identifies a need to balance the protection of both public and private interests in intellectual property. On the one hand, Article 15 recognizes the right of everyone to take part in cultural life and to enjoy the benefits of scientific progress and its applications. On the other hand, the same article recognizes the right of everyone to benefit from the protection of the moral and material interests resulting from any scientific, literary or artistic production of which he or she is the author (emphasis added). Taking these two aspects of Article 15 together, ICESCR could be said to bind States to design IP systems that strike a balance between promoting general public interests in accessing new knowledge as easily as possible and in protecting the interests of authors and inventors in such knowledge....

Consequently, there is a degree of compatibility between Article 15 and traditional IP systems. However, the question essentially is where to strike the right balance (emphasis added)."

10. Audrey Chapman, "A Human Rights Perspective on Intellectual Property Scientific Progress, and Access to The Benefits Of Science" *available at*:https://www.wipo.int/edocs/mdocs/tk/en/wipo_unhchr_ip_pnl_98/wipo_unhchr_ip_pnl_98_5.pdf 10 See, e.g., Intellectual Property Rights and Human Rights, Res. 2000/7.
11. *Available at*: https://documents-dds-ny.un.org/doc/UNDOC/GEN/G01/143/45/PDF/G0114345.pdf?OpenElement

22.2 INTELLECTUAL PROPERTY AND RIGHT TO HEALTH DEPENDENCIES AND DIVERGENCES

Right to health has been considered as one of the most important human right in a number of international instruments. The constitution of the World Health Organization recognizes the right to health as follows[12]:

The enjoyment of the highest attainable standard of health is one of the fundamental rights of every human being without distinction of race, religion, political belief, economic or social condition.

Article 25 of the Universal Declaration of Human Rights (UDHR) states[13]:

Everyone has the right to a standard of living for the health and well-being of himself and of his family, including food, clothing, housing and medical care and necessary social services, and the right to security in the event of unemployment, sickness, disability, widowhood, old age or other lack of livelihood in circumstances beyond his control.

More recently addressing the International Coordinating Committee of National Institutions of Human Rights, Mary Robinson, the then UN High Commissioner for Human Rights observed[14]

National Human Rights Institutions have the full range of human rights in the remit... An area which we have not touched on, and which I would like to mention here for further consideration is the right to health...

By virtue of its primal position among human rights it has also been recognized by the Constitution of India under the directive principle of state policy. Article 47 for example enjoins the state to raise the level of nutrition and standard of living and to improve public health.

Apart from international instruments and constitutional texts, the judiciary has also played a stellar role in establishing the Right to Health as among the most significant fundamental rights by bringing it within the ambit of Article 21 through judicial interpretation.

For example, in *Vincent Panikurlangara* v. *Union of India*, it was observed[15]:

.... Maintenance and improvement of public health have to rank high as these are indispensable to the very physical existence of the community and on the betterment of these depends the building of the society which the Constitution envisages. Attending to public health, in our opinion is, therefore of high priority—perhaps one at the top

in *State of Punjab* v. *Ram Lubhaya Bagga* the Supreme Court reiterated its stand the government and public authorities have a duty to focus on public health and observed as follows[16]:

This Court has time and again emphasized to the Government and other authorities for focusing and giving priority to the health of its citizen, which not only makes one's life

12. *Available at*: https://www.who.int/about/mission/en
13. *Available at*: https://www.un.org/en/universal-declaration-human-rights/index.html (last visited March 3, 2018)
14. *Available at*: http://shodhganga.inflibnet.ac.in/bitstream/10603/128256/19/13_chapter%206.pdf (last visited March 03, 2020)
15. (1987) 2 SCC 165, para 16
16. (1998) 4 SCC 117, para 6.

meaningful, improves one's efficiency, but in turn gives optimum output. Further to secure protection of one's life is one of the foremost obligations of the State. It is not merely a right enshrined under Article 21 but an obligation cast on the State to provide this both under Article 21 and under Article 47 of the Constitution. The obligation includes improvement of public health as its primary duty.

These cases are only illustrative and similar observations have been made by the Supreme Court in a number of other decisions. From the above discussion it is amply clear that right to health is firmly and undisputedly established as one of the most fundamental of human rights and sanctified not just in global instruments but also in the domestic jurisprudence including India.

However apart from the distinct human right facet health and health sector is also a potent market for a variety of entities ranging from healthcare service providers to pharmaceutical and allied sectors and therefore this is also an arena of innovation, discoveries and therefore a strong playground for Intellectual Property actors. It is therefore not surprising that in the health sector domain the questions of human rights versus intellectual property assume a significance unmatched by any other area.

22.3 TRIPS AND THE RIGHT TO HEALTH CONTOURS OF A SYNERGY

The Agreement on Trade related aspects of Intellectual Property (TRIPS)[17] was adopted in 1994 with an aim to strengthen the IPR regime. The adoption of TRIPS at the same time gave rise to acrimonious debates about their potential and often negative impact on Human Rights.

It is also important to understand that TRIPS is not just limited to the medical field but covers all areas concerning intellectual property, however its effect on the healthcare and on health as a right is arguably the most profound since it directly relates to issues of accessibility and affordability in countries of the developing world.

TRIPS obligated the countries to make suitable changes to their respective legislations in order to bring about a certain uniformity in the IPR protection regime. WTO members were obligated to implement TRIPS provisions within specified timeframes This impacted the developing and underdeveloped countries the most because of the highly technological nature of patents etc. and therefore brought to fore the faceoff between the developed and the developing world on the question of granting patents particularly in those areas of technologies that directly impact human life on a mass scale, health-related technologies being the most important.

The Sub-Commission on the promotion and protection of human rights recognized this dichotomy and remarked as follows[18]:

"Since the implementation of the TRIPS agreement does not adequately reflect the fundamental nature and indivisibility of all human rights, including the right of everyone to enjoy the benefits of scientific progress and its applications, the right to health, the right to

17. https://www.wto.org/english/tratop_e/trips_e/intel2_e.htm
18. Intellectual property rights and human rights, Sub-Commission on Human Rights resolution 2000/7. *Available at*: https://www.aaas.org/sites/default/files/SRHRL/PDF/IHRDArticle15/E-CN_4-SUB_2-RES-2000-7_Eng.pdf

food, and the rights to self-determination, there are apparent conflicts between human rights law, on the other."

India is an example of how TRIPS jeopardized the abilities of the developing nations to protect public health. India was obligated to make suitable legislations to conform to the TRIPS agreement by 2005 and it therefore passed the Patent Amendment Act in 2005 to fulfil its obligations. Prior to this act, India allowed for the manufacture of generic versions of many drugs. After TRIPS agreement came into force India had to implement a globally harmonized product patent regime in the pharmaceutical sector. This however had far reaching implication for access and availability to medicines in India. Patents enforce monopoly rights and tend to increase prices and consequently restrict availability and affordability.

The problem between TRIPS and Human Rights does not only relate to access to medicines alone, it also extends to traditional knowledge and technology transfer. Traditional communities use their traditional knowledge to make medicines. Sometimes giant pharmaceutical companies commercialize this knowledge without even paying royalty or acknowledging the source. Developing countries have serious concerns about protecting traditional knowledge owned by the traditional communities in their countries. Furthermore, one of the main purposes of TRIPS is to facilitate transfer of technology to foster development in developing and least developed countries. However, multinational companies are not always willing to co-operate. Developing countries have voiced their concerns against the effects of IP system on health, traditional knowledge and technology.

The above analysis of the Indian context gives a fair idea of the problems faced by the developing world since they have the same impact on all such countries.

This conflict was nevertheless identified largely due to the strong reservations places by the developing and the least developed countries and attempts were made to resolved inconsistencies while remaining within the core parameters of the agreement. A few representative provisions in this regard are worth mentioning[19].

Article 7 of the TRIPS agreement seeks to balance the rights of producers and users in a manner conducive to `social and economic welfare. Article 8 (1) specifically mentions that members may formulate their domestic policies and adopt measures necessary to protect among other things public health and nutrition. Article 27 (2) and (3) also provide a leeway to members to exclude certain subject matters from patentability certain inventions for protecting human life and health as well as certain diagnostic, therapeutic and surgical methods for the treatment of humans or animals. In addition, other articles also provide for aspects such as public non-commercial use during emergencies (Art 31), technical cooperation (Art 40, 67) etc[20].

These TRIPS provisions mentioned above even though significant, however remained splinter provisions spread across various articles and were open to multiple interpretations which were sought to be used by the patent holders particularly by the big Multinational enterprises in their favour and to the detriment of consumers and end users. To address these ambiguities and bring about certainly in interpretation the WTO members in 2001 adopted a

19. For details see AGREEMENT ON TRADE-RELATED ASPECTS OF INTELLECTUAL PROPERTY RIGHTS, particularly Articles 1,3,4,5,6 7,8, 27, 30,31,39,40,41,67,73. *Available at*: http://www.tripsagreement.net/trips_files/documents/TRIPS_E.pdf
20. See, https://www.wto.org/english/tratop_e/trips_e/intel2_e.htm for an elaboration of these articles.

special Declaration at the WTO Ministerial Conference in Doha to allay ambiguities between the need for governments to apply the principles of public health and the terms of the Agreement on Trade-related Aspects of Intellectual Property Rights (TRIPS).

The Doha declaration on TRIPS Agreement and Public Health also attempted to address the enormity of the public health concerns afflicting the developing and LCD countries of the world and called for a wider consensus to remedy these problems. Paragraphs 4,5 and 6 are particularly significant in this respect. Paragraph 4 of the declaration states[21]:

"*We agree that the TRIPS Agreement does not and should not prevent members from taking measures to protect public health. Accordingly, while reiterating our commitment to the TRIPS Agreement, we affirm that the Agreement can and should be interpreted and implemented in a manner supportive of WTO members' right to protect public health and, in particular, to promote access to medicines for all. In this connection, we reaffirm the right of WTO members to use, to the full, the provisions in the TRIPS Agreement, which provide flexibility for this purpose*".

Doha declaration was therefore one of the most significant attempts to harmonize the contradictions between intellectual property and human rights ecosystems. The ministerial conference acknowledged that intellectual property protection is indeed important to encourage innovation and development of medicine and health-related technologies however at the same time issues such as the high prices of medicines, non-transfer of technology made both access and affordability extremely difficult for poorer countries and poorer populations. Special provisions therefore were sought to be incorporated for poorer economies including transfer of technologies from developed to least developed countries particularly those who lacked manufacturing capacities.

The conference therefore made certain adaptations to mitigate the challenges brought about by the TRIPS regime. It provided for certain options to the national governments to address public health needs which is also termed as flexibilities that are mentioned in paragraph 5 of the declaration[22].

22.4 FLEXIBILITIES: INCORPORATION OF A HUMAN RIGHTS ELEMENT INTO IPR

Flexibilities can be construed as special or limited exceptions to the otherwise stringent IPR protection mechanisms granted to the rights holder under TRIPS and have a distinct human rights aspect to them. The only condition is that they should not hinder normal exploitation of the patent or unreasonably prejudice the legitimate interest of the right holder.

Developing countries can use these flexibilities to mitigate problems particularly in the healthcare domain like access to medicines, checking high prices, and ensuring availability.

21. *Available at*: https://www.wto.org/english/thewto_e/minist_e/min01_e/mindecl_trips_e.

22. Article 5 recognizes these flexibilities and states "Accordingly and in the light of paragraph 4 above, while maintaining our commitments in the TRIPS Agreement, we recognize that these flexibilities include". The paragraph subsequently lists compulsory licensing, emergency and public health crises such as HIV/ AIDS, tuberculosis, malaria as well as national exhaustion as flexibilities to circumvent IPR wherever required without diluting its basic principles.

These flexibilities have been incorporated in paragraphs 4,5 and 6 of the Declaration and provide for compulsory licensing, national emergencies and exhaustion with an aim to introduce certain flexibility as per country specific requirements

Article 66.1 of the TRIPS agreement[23] also refers to flexibilities and provides the rationale as follows:

"In view of the special needs and requirements of least-developed country Members, their economic, financial and administrative constraints, and their need for flexibility to create a viable technological base, such Members shall not be required to apply the provisions of this Agreement, other than Articles 3, 4 and 5...... The Council for TRIPS shall, upon duly motivated request by a least-developed country member, accord extensions of this period."

There are many flexibilities envisaged throughout the TRIPS agreement but some of the most important ones particularly in the context of the human right to health are as follows:

1. **Compulsory Licensing:** A compulsory license is issued by a government authority or a court to make certain use of a patented invention without the consent of the patent holder. This mechanism is generally present. in most patent laws, is recognized as a permissible option or flexibility under the TRIPS Agreement, and has been used by a number of WTO members in the pharmaceutical field. Compulsory licensing is subject to the following considerations[24].

   - authorization of such use must be considered on its individual merits
   - scope and duration of such use without the patent holder's authorization must be limited to the authorized purposes.
   - authorization of such use must be predominantly for the supply of the domestic market of the Member authorizing such use.
   - adequate remuneration must be paid to the patent holder, based on the economic value of the license
   - decisions relating to the authorization of, and remuneration for such use, must be subject to judicial or other independent review in the Member authorizing such use.

However, TRIPS rules originally restricted compulsory licenses to serve mainly the domestic market (Article 31f)[25] and it was therefore of little use to countries which did not have sufficient manufacturing infrastructure domestically.

The DOHA Ministerial conference and the subsequent declaration on the TRIPS agreement and Public Health recognized that Members with insufficient or no manufacturing capacities in the pharmaceutical sector could find it difficult to make use of the compulsory licensing flexibility and instructed the TRIPS Council to find an expeditious solution to this problem

23. *Available at*: https://www.wto.org/english/docs_e/legal_e/27-trips.pdf
24. Flexibilities In the Trips Agreement and its Impact on National Intellectual Property Policy. *Available at*: http://www.belipo.bz/wp-content/uploads/2011/12/TRIPS-FLEXIBILITIES.pdf
25. Article 31(f) stipulates that generic drug produced under compulsory licensing "must be authorised predominantly for the supply of the domestic market of the Member authorising such use". Doha Declaration, Paragraph 6: WTO members with insufficient or no manufacturing capacities in the pharmaceutical sector could face difficulties in making effective use of compulsory licensing under TRIPS.

and to report to the General Council before the end of 2002. This came to be known as the 'Paragraph 6 issue[26]' because it was contained in the paragraph 6 of the declaration.

Pursuant to this an amendment to the TRIPS agreement added a new Article 31 bis (1)[27] which introduced a compulsory license for exports which provided for the export of a pharmaceutical product to developing or least developed countries to meet their public health requirements when they lack domestic infrastructure to manufacture the said drugs subject to certain conditions.

Another flexibility in the form of parallel imports was therefore envisaged.

Exhaustion and Parallel Imports: Exhaustion or the first sale doctrine postulates that once a good is sold to another party with the authorization of the IP owner, the IP right is exhausted with respect to that good and subsequent transactions like sale, renting, lending can't be controlled by the first or original right holder. Three kinds of exhaustion principles have been envisages depending on the scope and geographical extent of their applicability namely national, regional and international. The wider the exhaustion the more advantageous it is for the consumers and the user country. Therefore, the developing and least developed countries advocate international exhaustion while the developed or producer countries are votaries of a narrower national exhaustion principle. Parallel imports are directly linked to the principle of exhaustion and involves the import and resale in a country without the consent of the right holder, of a protected product which was put on the market of the exporting country by the right holder or in another legitimate manner. Along with the doctrines of exhaustion of rights, parallel importation allows protected goods to be imported at a cheaper price from a foreign market.

In the context of healthcare, it is of huge benefit to countries which have insufficient or no manufacturing capacities in the pharmaceutical sector. One of the best specimens of the effective use of such flexibilities has been in the case of HIV/AIDS where anti-retroviral medication has transformed HIV/AIDS into a clinically manageable condition. However, for a long time despite the proven efficacy of anti-retroviral treatment donors as well as international organizations often choose to focus on prevention, at the expense of treating the disease owing to a very high cost of such treatment

The proven success of anti-retroviral medications in prolonging life expectancy and increasing productivity was to a large extent nullified due to issues of accessibility and had a detrimental impact on the political, social, and economic systems of countries ravaged by the pandemic. The culprit was stringent intellectual property rights regime which acted as a major impediment to increased access to affordable anti-retroviral drugs.

Certain countries like India however have brought in the public health angle and given primacy to human rights aspect by adopting a relaxed regime by condoning and even encouraging generic manufacturers and parallel imports which has ensured availability of these drugs at a significantly lower prices and increases access to anti-retroviral treatment. Cipla for

26. Para 6 of the Declaration on the TRIPS agreement and public health states: We recognize that WTO members with insufficient or no manufacturing capacities in the pharmaceutical sector could face difficulties in making effective use of compulsory licensing under the TRIPS Agreement. We instruct the Council for TRIPS to find an expeditious solution to this problem and to report to the General Council before the end of 2002.
27. See, Article 31 bis (1) TRIPS agreement.

example sold generic drugs which were far cheaper than the upscale patented versions and literally transformed the fight against AIDS.

Poorer countries of Asia and Africa also indirectly benefited through parallel imports. Indian example has shown that instead of poverty, the true impediment to access is unaffordability. The MNCs were arguing that poverty and ineffective administration of healthcare services are the real obstacles.

These flexibilities however have been naturally resented by the rights holders with include pharmaceutical companies who argue that such policy spaces actually work as disincentives to innovation and infusion of funds for further research and development. There has also been an attempt to secure patents by series of incremental inventions as well as by blocking manufacturers of generic drugs by dragging them to courts. The judiciary world over including India therefore has become a participant to this IPR-HR debate and through landmark decisions added new dimensions to the debate.

22.5 NOVARTIS JUDGEMENT: THE GAME CHANGER

The Novartis judgement[28] is an example of how judiciary in India has looked at this often-dichotomous relationship and given primacy to human rights when pressing questions of human right to health is involved. This judgement in particular sought to promote public good and accessibility while discouraging negativities such greenwashing, monopolistic pricing and innovation with.

The issue was concerning the patent application of in 1997 by Novartis, a Switzerland based company manufactured a drug Gilvec and got it patented in several jurisdictions including US. Novartis applied for patent in India which was taken up for consideration in 2005 when India became party to TRIPS. It was denied by the patent office relying on Section 3(d) of Patent Act 2005 stating that the drug does not demonstrate any known therapeutic efficacy[29].

Novartis filed a writ petition in Madras High Court challenging the refusal by the patent office and also Section 3(d) of the Patents Act on the ground that it was not in conformity with TRIPS agreement and that it was also violative of Article 14. of the Indian constitution. The petitions were refused on jurisdictional grounds but mainly also on the ground that Section 3(d) is not arbitrary since the its purpose was to ensure affordable access to life saving drugs to people.

The case then came to the Supreme Court as a Special Leave Petition. The Supreme Court also refused patent and among other things held that the purpose of the said section was to prevent evergreening of patents and also reiterated that objective of the said Act was to ensure affordable access to life saving drugs to people which was also the constitutional objective.

On the issue of novelty and inventive step also the Court held applied the test of therapeutic efficacy which needs to be clearly proved. The Court however decided that the drug Novartis seeks to patent is the modification of a known drug and it did not differ significantly as far as properties enhancing efficacy are concerned.

---

28. *Novartis AG* v. *Union of India*, (2013) 6 SCC 1.
29. See, Patents Act 2005, *Available at*: https://ipindia.gov.in/writereaddata/Portal/IPOAct/1_69_1_patent_2005.pdf

The Supreme Court also held that the true intention to enact Section 3(d) was to prevent the concept of evergreening and thus if the invention does not fulfil the test of Section 3(d), it cannot be granted a patent. The court further specified that this case should not be interpreted to mean that Section 3(d) bars all incremental inventions. It is with regard to the field of medicine especially in cases of life-saving drugs, great care and caution needs to be taken so as to protect the right to life of the masses. Patent was therefore refused with respect to this product

This judgement therefore came as a huge relief because it accorded prime consideration to public policy and public health issues, discouraged efforts to "evergreen" patents and enabled Indian companies to continue producing generic version of drugs to ensure affordable access.

The judgement garnered widespread support from international organizations and advocacy groups like Médecins Sans Frontières, WHO, etc. who welcomed the decision against evergreening of pharmaceutical patents and for keeping human rights considerations while rendering the decisions.

SUMMARY

Right to health, its non-discriminatory and affordable access has been embedded and prominently highlighted in numerous human rights instruments something which has played a significant role in forcing a rethink about their reconciliation with the essentially private nature of rights bestowed by Intellectual property. In the domain of healthcare there has been some success, however there remains a pressing need to do more for giving the human rights including the right to health by evolving a stricter patentability regime by allowing only genuine innovations and filtering out frivolous ones.

Many experts are also of the view that strict patent requirement instead of a relaxed requirement of incremental invention would actually encourage innovation as the pharmaceutical companies would have to invest more in R&D to come up with new cures rather than rearrange and repackage known compounds and to keep patenting them forever. This is particularly useful for countries like India given the extent of poverty and lack of availability of affordable medicines in the country.

However, this alone is not sufficient and the redistributive processes will also need to be strengthened in order to reduce gaps of all kinds geographical, economical, educational, age and gender in availability and affordability of healthcare to all. This can be achieved only with the essential recognition that IP rights are in the ultimate analysis themselves human rights. This will enable a cohesive and mutually beneficial integration of the legal norms that surround the two regimes and further harmonize the IPR-HR interface.

QUESTIONS FOR PART VI

Q.1 Which key international human rights instruments recognize the right to health, and how is it defined?

Q.2 Discuss the obligations of states under international law to ensure the right to health for their citizens.

Q.3 How do international human rights frameworks address health inequities and access to care globally?

Q.4 What are the roles of global institutions such as the WHO, UNICEF, and World Bank in promoting health and preventing disease?

Q.5 How do international health partnerships contribute to addressing global health crises, such as pandemics?

Q.6 Analyse the challenges faced by global health institutions in achieving their objectives.

Q.7 How do intellectual property rights (IPR) impact access to essential medicines and healthcare technologies?

Q.8 Discuss the role of TRIPS (Trade-related Aspects of Intellectual Property Rights) in balancing innovation incentives with public health needs.

PART VII

Contemporary Issues in Public Health

CHAPTER

23 Gender and Health

INTRODUCTION

The dynamics between **gender and health** is a very important area of study and research, which reveals how biological, social, and cultural dimensions shape health outcomes and access to care. Gender is not only a biological construct but also a social determinant of health that profoundly influences individuals' experiences within healthcare systems and their vulnerability to specific health conditions. Such experiences are compounded by systemic inequities which create and sustain significant health disparities across populations. Women as a category often have to confront disproportionate hindrances in accessing reproductive healthcare. Women also have to face stigma and structural barriers that hinder equitable treatment to them in comparison to men.

Deeply entrenched social norms perpetuate these vicious cycles of inequality. This is further aggravated by differential allocation of health resources and implicit biases in healthcare systems on account of gender. Also, historically women have not been sufficiently represented in clinical trials. This has created gaps in understanding how various conditions and treatments affect them. This chapter shall examine some of the most significant health issues facing the women and what role law and policy play in mitigating such challenges.

23.1 REPRODUCTIVE AND MATERNAL HEALTH

Maternal health remains a cornerstone of women's healthcare and reflects a nation's overall health system performance. In India, maternal mortality rates (MMR) have declined over recent decades, yet significant disparities persist between rural and urban areas and between states and regions. As of 2023, India's MMR stands at 97 per 100,000 live births, with certain states exceeding this national average[1]. The factors that have a role to play in this include inadequate healthcare infrastructure, shortage of skilled birth attendants, and limited access to emergency obstetric care, especially in rural and tribal regions.

1. https://pib.gov.in/PressReleaseIframePage.aspx?PRID=1879912

It is indeed paradoxical that the most common causes of maternal mortality in India stem out of those factors that can be easily prevented such as postpartum haemorrhage, eclampsia, and sepsis. Just to take one example postpartum haemorrhage causes over 25% of maternal deaths globally and its incidence is particularly severe in resource-poor setting. These examples point to the need for securing timely medical intervention in both ante and postnatal care. With this view in mind in our country programs, such as the Janani Suraksha Yojana (JSY)[2] have been envisaged to reduce maternal deaths by promoting institutional deliveries. India's National Health Mission (NHM) has also introduced several initiatives to address maternal mortality, including the Janani Shishu Suraksha Karyakram (JSSK)[3], which provides free maternal healthcare services.

However, while these schemes are ambitious, they themselves often suffer from interregional variations and disparities in effectiveness and implementation. Moreover, despite these measures, socio-cultural barriers such as early marriage and teenage pregnancies exacerbate the risks. Early marriage is a direct cause of adolescent pregnancies. Such pregnancies experience higher incidences of maternal mortality owing to underdeveloped physiology and lack of access to antenatal care. Additionally, another critical area where urgent policy intervention is called for relates to the provision of emergency obstetric care. In India, an extremely small proportion of health facilities are able to cater to the requirements of providing such services. Another such health issue is Anaemia associated with pregnancy conditions affecting more women during the reproductive or the childbearing years. Iron deficiency, which leads to anaemia, increases the chances of preterm delivery and major postpartum complications. Programs such as the Anaemia Mukt Bharat Campaign aim to address the problem by providing iron-folic acid supplements and fortified staple foods. However, its success depends on continuous implementation and community awareness.

These are pressing issues that would be overcome if suitable investment is made in the healthcare sector at all fronts. This would include boosting health infrastructure, training health professionals and the establishment of well networked systems for hospital referrals. Legal frameworks such as the Maternity Benefit Act, 1961[4] , have also attempted to provide essential protections for working women during pregnancy. The subsequent amendments carried out in 2017 have extended maternity leave to 26 weeks. This is a progressive step towards safeguarding maternal health. However, these benefits are largely limited to women in formal employment, leaving a vast majority of informal sector workers without legal protections or remedies.

In addition, the maternal health programs in India are also aligned with Sustainable Development Goals, specifically, SDG 3, which aspires that global maternal mortality reduce to less than 70 per 100,000 live births by 2030[5] . It requires the improvement of public health systems and sanitation while addressing social determinants of health that affect women disproportionately. Moreover, maternal health policies also need to adopt an intersectional approach incorporating caste, class, and geographical disparity. It is necessary since such exclusionary disparities systematically impact marginalized women groups facing resulting in very high levels of maternal mortality.

2. The Janani Suraksha Yojana (JSY)
3. https://www.nhm.gov.in/index1.php?lang=1&level=3&sublinkid=842&lid=308
4. https://www.indiacode.nic.in/bitstream/123456789/17115/1/maternity_benefit.pdf
5. https://globalgoals.org/goals/3-good-health-and-well-being/

Reproductive health is a fundamental component of women's overall well-being, encompassing physical, mental, and social aspects. One of the central challenges in reproductive healthcare is access to contraception. India faces a significant unmet need for contraception, particularly among rural and adolescent women. According to the National Family Health Survey (NFHS-5), approximately 9.4% of married women aged 15-49 in India have unmet contraceptive needs[6]. This gap leads to unintended pregnancies and unsafe abortions, undermining women's health and autonomy. While government initiatives like the Antara[7] program for injectable contraceptives and the provision of free condoms and oral contraceptives aim to bridge this gap, implementation challenges persist. Rural health centres often face shortages of contraceptive supplies, and frontline workers lack adequate training to counsel women about contraceptive options. Cultural resistance to contraception, particularly in patriarchal societies, further limits uptake, as women often lack agency in family planning decisions.

To overcome such practical difficulties, it is essential to sensitize society at large about the health and also the overall benefits of spacing in childbirth and also family planning. Comprehensive sexuality education (CSE) in schools can also go a long way in reproductive health outcomes. In India, the introduction of sexuality education in schools has been met with stiff resistance from conservative groups who perceive it as an affront to the traditional Indian value systems. However well-designed CSE programs play a very important role in awareness generation and can have a direct role in improving reproductive health outcomes, reducing adolescent pregnancies and checking the transmission of sexually transmitted infections (STIs). Such initiatives also have the effect of empowering young women with knowledge about their reproductive health and related rights which is a critical step towards achieving gender equality in healthcare.

Reproductive tract infections (RTIs) and Sexually Transmitted Infections (STIs) are other significant concerns in India. Poor menstrual hygiene, lack of access to clean sanitation facilities, and limited awareness contribute to high rates of RTIs among Indian women. It is estimated that over 70% of Indian women of reproductive age suffer from RTIs at some point in their lives. These infections often go undiagnosed and untreated, leading to severe complications such as pelvic inflammatory disease and infertility. Government schemes like the Rashtriya Kishor Swasthya Karyakram (RKSK)[8] focus on addressing adolescent health issues, including menstrual hygiene and RTIs. However, social taboos surrounding menstruation often prevent women and girls from seeking medical care for issues related to menstruation. Efforts to break these taboos through public awareness campaigns and access to affordable menstrual hygiene products, such as the government's free sanitary pad distribution schemes, are thus crucial. Violence against women, sexual violence and marital rape, also impacts reproductive health. Survivors of sexual violence often suffer from unwanted pregnancies, STIs, and psychological trauma. India's healthcare system must integrate survivor-centric care into its reproductive health services, offering counselling, emergency contraception, and safe abortion services. Strengthening the implementation of laws like the Protection of Women from Domestic Violence Act, 2005, is critical to addressing these issues.

6. https://mohfw.gov.in/sites/default/files/NFHS-5_Phase-II_0.pdf
7. https://pib.gov.in/newsite/PrintRelease.aspx?relid=170537
8. https://hfw.delhi.gov.in/fw/adolescent-health-rashtriya-kishor-swasthya-karyakram

23.2 ABORTION AND WOMEN'S HEALTH

Abortion is one of the most important healthcare services for women and directly determines their physical, mental, and social condition. In India, it is legalized under the Medical Termination of Pregnancy (MTP) Act, 1971[9], which allows abortion up to 20 weeks of gestation. According to the 2021 amendment, the act can be extended to 24 weeks in specific cases. Even in such a progressive framework, unsafe abortions account for the greatest cause of maternal morbidity and mortality, especially in rural settings where health facilities are not available. Unsafe abortion has become one of the key issues in India's public health scenario. The studies estimate that 45% of all abortions are unsafe; most are performed either in unregulated settings or by untrained providers. Due to stigma, ignorance about legal rights to abortion, and unsafe services unavailable, women have to often take recourse to the unsafe methods. This usually results in complications in the form of haemorrhage, infections, and perforation of the uterus and can cause illness and can even prove to be fatal.

The Medical Termination of Pregnancy Act has been successively amended in India to enhance access and ensure women's security. The 2021 amendment raised the gestational limit for abortion to 24 weeks for rape survivors and victims of incest and in cases of foetal anomaly. It also opens up the right to abortion for unmarried women under the same conditions as in the case of married women. However, despite such legal measures, logistical barriers and societal resistance generally pose hindrances in accessing these services. Abortion stigma is also a challenge that particularly effects developing societies particularly in India. A woman who decides to opt for abortion often faces judgment and discrimination by within families. This results in avoidance and delays and subsequent complications may arise. One of the means to alleviate such issues is widespread awareness campaigns geared towards normalizing abortion and projecting is as a healthcare service and to fight against entrenched cultural taboo.

Financial and geographical barriers further limit access to safe abortion care. Many rural health centres lack trained staff and proper infrastructure to carry out abortions, and most women have to travel far to access the urban facilities. High cost of abortion services in private clinics dissuades low-income women and pushes them towards unsafe alternatives. In this context government initiatives through programs like Comprehensive Abortion Care (CAC)[10] become significant in training service providers and strengthening public healthcare infrastructure to bridge the gaps. Another crucial element that services offering abortion often lack, is post-abortion care. A woman who experiences complications associated with an unsafe abortion or a miscarriage must be rapidly attended to by medical providers. This needs to be ensured through the availability of post-abortion care services such as management for sepsis and counselling against recurrent future unsafe abortions. Addressing this component can prove to be an important contributor to the reduction of maternal mortality.

On the social front abortion is very closely linked to gender-based violence. Many women who seek abortion have experienced or are survivors of rape and domestic violence. For such women having access to safe and confidential abortion services becomes a just and autonomous

9. https://www.indiacode.nic.in/bitstream/123456789/1593/1/A1971-34.pdf
10. https://nhm.gov.in/New_Updates_2018/NHM_Components/RMNCHA/MH/Guidelines/CAC_Training_and_Service_Delivery_Guideline.pdf

right. The policies also need to be able to integrate support systems such as counselling and legal aid aimed at the special needs for survivors. Another challenge that teenagers have to encounter in accessing abortion services due to the laws of parental consent and stigma related to teenage pregnancies. The Protection of Children from Sexual Offences (POCSO) Act has a provision for reporting of pregnancies in minors, which deters young girls from seeking abortions on time. Balancing mandatory reporting with the need for confidentiality for adolescent health remains a major policy challenge which needs to be carefully considered and calibrated. Additionally, India's abortion policies must also address the needs of marginalized groups, including Dalit, Adivasi, and transgender individuals. These communities face systemic discrimination that limits their access to healthcare, including abortion services. Ensuring inclusivity in abortion care requires targeted outreach programs, policy reforms, and efforts to combat biases within the healthcare system.

23.3 SURROGACY AND WOMEN'S HEALTH

Surrogacy involves an assisted reproductive process whereby a woman known as a surrogate mother carries a baby for another individual or a couple, referred to as the intended parents. Traditional and gestational surrogacy are the two forms of surrogacy. The surrogate uses her own egg in traditional surrogacy and thus is related to the child. In gestational surrogacy the surrogate carries an embryo created with the sperm and eggs of the parents, but she is not related to the child in any way. Surrogacy is governed by complex legal and ethical frameworks that vary widely across countries.

Aside from the medical and legal aspects, surrogacy also has a complex and contentious social and economic dimension which raises deeper concerns about women's health and rights. Most women who opt to be surrogates belong to poor communities and undertake surrogacy work for economic gain. But such financial incentives often result in exploitation, as agents and clinics are known to take advantage of their circumstances. Most contracts that are signed favour commissioning parents leaving surrogates with little or no options in the event of falling out or other unfavourable circumstances.

Attention also needs to be paid towards the health and well-being of these children born through surrogacies. There are more pre-term babies delivered and more babies of low birth weight in surrogacy situations as a result of multiple births or perhaps lack of adequate pre-natal care of the surrogate. In addition, the citizenship status of these children tends to be unclear, especially in the surrogacy cases in which foreigners may be involved as intending parents. While surrogacy presents a medical alternative to resolve the problem of childless parents by enabling them to have biological children, it also raises issues which include health concerns, exploitation and the rights of surrogate mothers. From a legal and financial standpoint, surrogacy has been classified under two categories—altruistic and commercial surrogacies. Altruistic surrogacy is often undertaken by a close relative or a friend. It is often driven by compassion and emotional support and financial gain is not the motive. In this kind of arrangement surrogate is entitled to the reimbursement of the medical expenses incurred in carrying the pregnancy. Commercial surrogacy on the other hand involves monetary transactions or rewards over and above the medical expenses. Commercial surrogacy became legal in India in 2002 which then made India the epicentre of surrogacy worldwide. However, the move witnessed rampant abuse of commercial surrogacy arrangements. Commercial surrogacy was thus banned and currently the law allows only altruistic surrogacy. The surrogacy landscape of India is currently governed by the Surrogacy Regulation Act of 2021[11]. In particular, the Act bans commercial surrogacy in India while allowing only altruistic surrogacy, which means that the surrogate mother cannot be compensated monetarily for her services. Additionally, there are provisions in the Act that are intended to address the ethical, moral and legal concerns around surrogacy practice. In India, the Surrogacy (Regulation) Act, 2021 establishes the legal framework of surrogacy practices in the country. Section III mandates that surrogacy should be restricted only for altruistic purposes. Clause 4(ii)(b) of the Act only permits medical necessity-based surrogacy for intending couples which needs to be certified by the authorities. Surrogate mothers, per Clause 4(iii)(b), must fulfil specific eligibility criteria, including marital status, age, and prior parenthood, to ensure their well-being and prevent exploitation. The law recognizes surrogate mothers' right to grant or withhold consent (Section 6) and incorporates measures to prevent forced or excessive surrogate motherhood (Section 4(iii)(b)).

In order to safeguard the interests of surrogate children, Section 7 prohibits abandonment of surrogate children for any reason whatsoever including congenital abnormalities in order to grant them full rights and entitlements. Section 8 expressly declares that all surrogate children will be recognized as biological children of the intending parents and consequently are free to enjoy all the legal privileges which accrue to such a child. They also deal with the number of embryos to be implanted (Section 9) and termination of pregnancy without permission (Section 10) in order to protect the health and dignity of surrogate mother and unborn children.

The legal provisions under Section VII have been incorporated to create a strong deterrent against the breach of law. Section 38 criminalizes commercial surrogacy, sex determination and exploitation for which a maximum term of imprisonment of 10 years and a substantial fine up to Rupees 10 Lakhs can be imposed. Sections 39 and 40 also provide for additional penalties for contravention of provisions of Act and for not following altruistic surrogacy.

Overall while the legal regulation of surrogacy in India provides measures for protecting women against exploitation, there is also a deep concern that not allowing commercial surrogacy, the economics of surrogacy will be pushed underground making it even more unsafe thereby encouraging the evil that the Surrogacy Act aims to curb. Moreover, the fact that surrogacy is limited to non–commercial reasons also significantly decrease the pool of surrogates and makes it even more difficult for potential intending parents desirous of having a child of their own.

Also, as is the case with many women related issues, the cultural perception of even surrogacy in India is determined by the cultural and religious factors. For instance, there is a general moral judgment against women who agree to carry fetus of other couples. Tackling such social issues requires a community-based challenge where the public is educated on the scientific and humanitarian aspects of surrogacy and the need to develop respect for surrogate mothers.

In conclusion, it can be said that while surrogacy as an assistive reproductive process addresses issues posed by infertility it also brings many ethical and many sociological dilemmas for women who chose to be surrogates. It is important to find a solution that will provide

11. https://www.indiacode.nic.in/bitstream/123456789/17046/1/A2021-47.pdf

the health and rights protection of women who are in the role of surrogate maternity while balancing the rights and aspirations of childless parents.

23.4 SEX DETERMINATION AND FEMALE FOETICIDE

Sex determination and female foeticide are critical issues in India which have a direct impact on women's health and well-being. This practice is deeply rooted in cultural and patriarchal bias that demonstrates a distinct preference for male children. Determining the sex of a foetus and consequent female foeticides have dire consequences at a demographic level. This has led to a skewed male to female ratio which causes a demographic imbalance in terms of gender imbalance which has harmful consequences for the society at large in in the long term. The preference for male children stems from socio-economic factors. Male children are looked upon as economic assets who provide financial support to parents in old age. On the contrary daughters are regarded as liabilities. This is also due to the prevalence of dowry and related practices still prevalent in our society. Such lopsided cultural practices have not only encouraged but perpetuated the vicious cycle of gender discrimination. This has further fuelled the demand for sex determination tests. Such tests ae often conducted clandestinely despite legal restrictions.

These malpractices still continue even after the enactment of the Pre-Conception and Pre-Natal Diagnostic Techniques (PCPNDT) Act, 1994[12], which bans pre-natal sex-selection and abortions. The PCPNDT Act criminalizes conducting sex determination and also the making use of the results obtained for sex selective abortion. It requires ultrasound clinics to be thoroughly regulated with thorough documentation and record keeping. However, enforcement continues to be a problem, especially in the more rural areas where they may not have the capacity as local officials or simply because of the pull of society.

To reiterate female foeticide has severe demographic and social consequences. The 2011 Census of India has shown an alarming child sex ratio of 919 girls for every 1000 boys[13]. This data clearly indicates that sex ratio has declined over decades. Skewed sex ratios result in various long-term societal issues. This includes a shortage of women for matrimonial alliances, increased human trafficking, and the commodification of women in certain regions. Aside from the social implications, the healthcare implications of sex-selective abortions are also profound. Women undergo such procedures often face severe complications owing to unregulated practices carried out by inadequately trained professionals and often at ill equipped clinics. A lack of post-abortion care is also often evident due to the absence of regulation. Additionally, the psychological toll on women who are often coerced into terminating female foetuses by family members is also a crucial mental health issue which has not been given adequate weightage in public health discourse.

The Beti Bachao Beti Padhao campaign is targeted at the root causes of sex-selective practices. It aims to educate the general public on the worth and significance of girl children, to bring them up in a healthy manner and educate them at par with boys. The campaign has

12. https://www.indiacode.nic.in/bitstream/123456789/8399/1/pre-conception-pre-natal-diagnostic-techniques-act-1994.pdf
13. https://censusindia.gov.in/nada/index.php/catalog/42610/download/46272/Census%20of%20India%20 2011-Child%20Sex%20Ratio.pdf

been successful in raising awareness, but the implementation has been criticized for not being focused on ground-level enforcement and ignoring systemic gender biases. There is thus a need to strengthen the PCPNDT Act. This needs to be done by increasing penalties for violators, enhancing surveillance mechanisms, and training healthcare professionals to avoid social pressures. In addition to this, interventions at the community level, such as engaging local leaders and influencers to question prevalent patriarchal norms, are of utmost importance in changing public mindset. Education with young people is the pivotal way in which to address the issue. Furthermore, discussions about gender equality and making people understand the adverse consequences of sex selection can break the cycle of discrimination against women. Such topics must also be incorporated in their school and university curricula to inculcate a culture of respect and equality. The emergence of new technologies in the health sector poses new challenges to regulate sex determination. Technologies are now available that can detect the foetal sex at early stages in pregnancy and are increasingly misused in the Indian subcontinent. Emerging technologies must be proactively regulated by policymakers before their misuse for sex-selective practices. India needs to eliminate female foeticide and sex determination for a balanced and equitable society. These practices are not only legal or medical problems but socio-cultural issues. They must be tackled through advocacy and change in cultural perception, education as well as strict enforcement.

23.5 MENTAL HEALTH CHALLENGES IN WOMEN

Mental health is a vital but often overlooked dimension of overall health and in many ways it is even more true for women. Women are more prone to suffering from a mental health conditions like anxiety, depression and post-traumatic stress disorder (PTSD). This can arise from a variety of gender specific reasons including problems faced by women in reproductive health, societal bias, gender-based violence and also often a lack of economic independence. Women's mental healthcare in India is also rendered more complicated by stigma, poor resource allocation and absence of gender-specific approaches to healthcare. Depression is one of the most common mental health issues faced by women. WHO suggests that women are twice as much likely to experience depression as men. The factors that lead to depression are linked to hormonal changes during menstruation, pregnancy, or menopause. Among the varied forms of depression in Indian women, postpartum depression is the most common yet it is often underdiagnosed. Many women thus suffer in silence, lacking the support or resources to seek help.

Domestic abuse and gender-based violence also takes a direct toll on women's health and well-being. The long-term effect of sexual abuse can have irreversible effects such as anxiety, PTSD, and at worst suicidal tendencies in women . Almost every other Indian woman who experiences domestic violence also goes through trauma which in most cases leads to mental issues. The Protection of Women from Domestic Violence Act, 2005[14] aims to protect women and children against violence, and offers assistance to the victims and their families. However, in this case also inconsistent adherence in practice leaves many gaps and adequate and

14. https://www.indiacode.nic.in/bitstream/123456789/15436/1/protection_of_women_from_domestic_violence_ac%2C_2005.pdf

commensurate remedies remain out of reach of many women who have to bear the implications including adverse health consequences. Reproductive health issues such as infertility and miscarriage, also affect mental health among females. Infertility and associated social stigma in India trigger negative emotions in the form of stress, shame, guilt, and social withdrawal. This is also often further aggravated by attempts to become pregnant through fertility treatment or surrogacy. Moreover, miscarriages, which can be equally devastating and emotionally draining, something which is not often addressed, leaving women without support while going through such an extremely trying time. Other social determinants including poverty, lack of education, and unemployment, disproportionately affect the mental health of women in India. Women from marginalized communities, such as Dalit and Adivasi women, face compounded disadvantages, with limited access to mental healthcare and higher exposure to stress inducing factors like discrimination and economic insecurity.

Moreover, cultural stigma surrounding mental health also prevents many women from seeking treatment. Mental illness is often viewed as a personal failing leading to delayed diagnosis and treatment. Women are particularly vulnerable to societal judgment, with conditions like depression or anxiety dismissed as "normal" responses to their roles as caregivers. Addressing this stigma requires community-based awareness campaigns and education initiatives. India's mental healthcare system faces significant resource constraints, with just 0.05 psychiatrists per 100,000 people. The Mental Healthcare Act, 2017[15], represents a step forward by recognizing mental health as a basic human right and emphasizing patient-centric care. However, the implementation of this law remains uneven, particularly in rural areas where mental health services are scarce. Gender-sensitive training for mental health professionals is essential to ensure that women's specific needs in terms of mental health are addressed.

Among the extreme manifestations of mental health, suicide is a growing concern among Indian women, particularly younger women. The National Crime Records Bureau (NCRB) reports that over 45,000 women died by suicide in 2021, with family problems, marriage-related issues, and mental illness cited as common reasons. Programs like the National Mental Health Programme (NMHP)[16] must be expanded to include targeted interventions for at-risk groups, including adolescents and survivors of domestic violence.

Adolescent girls face unique mental health challenges, including pressure to conform to societal expectations, body image issues, and early exposure to marriage or motherhood. The Rashtriya Kishor Swasthya Karyakram (RKSK) seeks to address adolescent health, including mental health, but its reach is limited. Schools and colleges must play a more proactive role in providing mental health education and counselling services to support young women. Addressing women's mental health in India therefore would require a multifaceted approach that combines policy interventions, community engagement, and gender-sensitive healthcare. Efforts must focus on breaking stigma, expanding access to mental health services, and integrating mental healthcare into existing public health programs. By prioritizing mental health, India can improve not only women's well-being but also the health and prosperity of the entire society.

15. https://www.indiacode.nic.in/bitstream/123456789/2249/1/A2017-10.pdf
16. https://nhm.gov.in/index1.php?lang=1&level=2&sublinkid=1043&lid=359

23.6 GENDER-BASED VIOLENCE AND ITS HEALTH CONSEQUENCES

The health of women is negatively affected by gender-based violence at several levels which includes physical, psychological and social dimensions. Gender violence takes many forms such as domestic violence, sexual violence, trafficking, and various harmful practices like honour killing or acid attacks. Such acts affect the civil and political rights of women and have a tremendous cost social as well as economic. Domestic violence is one of the most common forms violence against gender in India. According to the National Family Health Survey-5, nearly one out of three women within the 15–49 age bracket has experienced physical or sexual violence. The effects on women's health are deep and long lasting, ranging from physical injuries to chronic conditions like hypertension and gastrointestinal disorders. Survivors also have to face psychological trauma that can manifest in depression, anxiety or post-traumatic stress disorder. Sexual violence, which also includes rape also continues to be a serious challenge. According to National Crime Records Bureau, in the year 2021 the number of reported cases of rape stood around 31,000 although actual data may be considerably higher due to significant underreporting. Survivors of the sexual violence also end up facing a lot of stigma and social isolation making them reluctant to even go for seeking legal or medical help. In India, The Criminal Law (Amendment) Act, of 2013[17] enhanced the punishment for offenses of a sexual nature against women and made it obligatory for the survivor of the offense to be provided with medical treatment. However, there are still many challenges when it comes to actual implementation. Trafficking of women for purposes of servitude or for sexual exploitation is yet another major concern. Women and girls belonging to the under privileged sections suffer disproportionately and this is because the traffickers capitalized on their social and economic disadvantage. The social and physical violence and poor mental health experienced by women who had been trafficked is further exacerbated by the absence of medical attention and legal aid. To alleviate some of these challenges there is a need to design rehabilitation programs that provide holistic support, including medical care, counselling, and vocational training..

In many regions of the world, societies continue to subject women and girls to marry during their childhood and other such harmful traditional customs undermine the right to health of women and girls. In spite of laws such as the Prohibition of Child Marriage Act, 2006[18], that outlaws this practice, India has the highest number of child marriages. Child marriages not only lower the age at which women begin to bear children but also place them at elevated risk of maternal mortality. The underlying drivers of child marriages such as poverty, lack of education and social norms have to be dealt with in any interventions aimed at curbing child marriages.

Acid attacks are one of the most heinous forms of violence in India. Survivors usually require specialized medical treatment and psychological counselling to rebuild their lives. Severe penalties have been imposed for acid attacks under Indian laws such as Section 326A of the Indian Penal Code[19] and some other legal provisions. However stricter monitoring of acid sales and better support systems for survivors are needed to curb the menace.

---

17. https://www.india.gov.in/criminal-law-amendment-act-2013
18. https://www.indiacode.nic.in/bitstream/123456789/15943/1/the_prohibition_of_child_marriage_act%2C_2006.pdf
19. https://www.indiacode.nic.in/show-data?abv=null&statehandle=null&actid=AC_CEN_5_23_00037_186045_1523266765688&orderno=365&orgactid=AC_CEN_5_23_00037_186045_1523266765688

Economic privation, including deprivation of financial resources and control over earnings, is an often-overlooked form of violence. Women subjected to such violence are usually financially dependent on an abusive partner which makes them more vulnerable to violence limits their chances of escaping the abusive relationship. Financial empowerment and self-reliance programs, better educational and vocational training and legal reforms that guarantee property and inheritance rights of women can be useful measures to help curtail this kind of aggression.

The role of law enforcement in addressing gender violence is critical but fraught with challenges. Survivors often encounter dismissive attitudes, delays in filing cases, and inadequate investigation. Gender-sensitive training for police officers and fast-track courts for gender violence cases are essential to improving the justice delivery system. Programs like women help desks in police stations aim to create a more supportive environment for survivors. In addition to legal reforms and enforcement, community-based interventions are vital for preventing such violence and supporting survivors. Engaging local leaders, forming women's support groups, and raising awareness about the health and legal consequences of gender violence can drive cultural change. Educational initiatives targeting men and boys are equally important to challenge patriarchal norms and promote gender equality.

SUMMARY

This chapter has undertaken a detailed analysis of the dynamics between gender and health and has pointed out significant gendered inequalities in reproductive as well as non-reproductive contexts. It has analysed the societal and historical determinants such as cultural practices, economic factors, and stereotypes that create and sustain disadvantage and discrimination thus limiting the access of women to equitable health services. Maternal health, reproductive rights, and sexual violence, and the extent to which such structural disadvantage shapes the health of women has also been analysed in the chapter. Such inequities impede not only individual health but also negatively impact the broader population health agenda. Therefore, gender focused strategies have to be put into place to solve the equity issues. The socio-cultural determinants related to education, economic development, and societal norms also require urgent attention in contemporary societies to ensure health systems are inclusive. Dominant practices that perpetuate the social mores of the majority need to be challenged and altered. Actively pursuing these policy changes, community involvement and targeted action can lead to more just and lasting health outcomes for women.

CHAPTER

24 Health and Gender Diversity

INTRODUCTION

Gender identity represents the very core of an individual's concept of self and his or her relationship with the world. For transgender persons, whose gender identity is divergent from the sex assigned at birth, living within societal, legal, and healthcare systems can be particularly burdensome. This category includes very different identities, such as trans men, trans women, non-binary individuals, and many others who identify beyond the male-female binary. Recognition and affirmation of gender identity stand at the root of supporting the dignity and rights of transgender people. Unfortunately, widespread stigma, discrimination, and systemic obstacles influence the access of transgender people to healthcare, as well as their experiences with healthcare systems.

These disparities arise from failures of health systems to meet the specific needs of transgender people. Many trans individuals face prejudices from healthcare providers, a lack of understanding about gender-affirming care, and systemic exclusion of coverage for essential treatments by insurance providers are only some of the issues which are unaddressed. Most transgender persons require gender-affirming healthcare, such as hormone therapy and surgeries, to match their physical characteristics with their gender identity. However, access to these services is very often denied to them because of costs involved, imitated availability of services, and societal stigma. Apart from this, transgender persons face more significant incidents of mental health problems, like depression and anxiety, in addition to the experiences of denial, discrimination, and violence.

The superimposition of transgender identities and other dimensions of diversity such as race, socio-economic status, and disability magnifies health disparities. Members of marginalized communities often face more complex barriers to care which include geographic inaccessibility, cultural insensitivity, and systemic discrimination. Such issues require a multi-faceted response that includes legal reforms, training of service providers and community empowerment. Inclusive healthcare systems and societal acceptance are the only ways to ensure true health equity and uphold the rights and dignity of transgender people. Transgender persons face layered vulnerabilities compounded by the perception about their identity and their generally weaker socio-economic position. This has the cumulative impact of exacerbating their health risks. The layering of vulnerabilities signifies that health risks for transgender persons are all the more amplified. The prevalence of HIV/AIDS is significantly higher among transgenders as compared to general population. Sexual exploitation and forced participation in sex work often due to the lack of other suitable employment opportunities exacerbate risks to HIV and STI infections among transgender.

The systemic discrimination also mars access to healthcare. Transgender individuals often experience maltreatment, denial of services and harassment in the clinical setting. Lack of transgender specific and trained healthcare providers further alienates the population from essential care. Substance abuse and alcohol addiction has also been widely reported among transgenders. These are mainly coping mechanisms to deal with trauma and social rejection but further increase susceptibility to health complications. Mental health is another crucial aspect that remains even more invisible in case of transgenders. Because of transphobia, violence, and social exclusion mental health. These issues are often rarely dealt with in public health programs. In a real sense, lack of critical support systems results for TG persons. Social stigma is also encountered by in-community dynamics where HIV-positive TG persons are discriminated even more. This discourages disclosure, testing, and adherence to anti-retroviral therapy (ART), sustaining poor health outcomes.

24.1 VIOLENCE AGAINST TRANSGENDER INDIVIDUALS

Transgender individuals face systemic violence that permeates both private and public spheres. Such violence is often a direct expression or result of social biases against their trans identity or expression. Violence within their own families is rampant. This includes threats of exposing the individual's gender identity, coercing them into conform to traditional roles, including forced marriages. Beyond domestic spaces too, trans individuals encounter extreme forms of public violence. This is because of negative stereotypes that depict gender diversity as unnatural or pathological. This has often been used as an argument to dehumanize trans individuals and justify acts of brutality. Often even state actors, including police and prison officials have been found to be complicit in these abuses.

Incarceration within prisons and detention centres for example poses immense challenges for physical and mental health and well-being of individuals bearing transgender identity. Placement in prison cells is usually done without any regard to gender variations and is based on assigned gender at birth. This makes transgenders susceptible to violence and sexual abuse. To add to their plight many transgender inmates are deprived of essential healthcare that they may require owing to their special circumstances. This may include no provisions or arrangements for hormone therapies or other necessary and specific medical treatments. Support networks and shelters specifically for transgender individuals can provide immediate relief and long-term support to those escaping abusive environments. A holistic approach involving legal, social, and healthcare interventions is necessary to tackle the multifaceted nature of violence against transgender people.

Violence against trans individuals gets even more aggravated in cases where they belong to marginalized groups based on race, ethnicity, or socio-economic status. Another issue arises out of the failure at a global scale to collect consistent data pertaining to violence against transgender community. Lack of requisite information is another barrier to effective intervention or to undertake any advocacy efforts. Without robust statistics the scale of the problem remains unknown and unassessed. Governments and non-governmental organizations hence must commission studies and projects for systematic data collection on issues of violence against transgenders. This will facilitate evidence-based policymaking. Not only this such data can also serve to counter misinformation and raise awareness about the unique challenges faced by the transgender community.

24.2 GENERAL AND GENDER-AFFIRMING HEALTH SERVICES FOR THE GENDER DIVERSE PEOPLE

Healthcare access is a fundamental right, yet the well-being of transgender individuals is hindered by systemic barriers at every turn. Routine healthcare services are often not envisaged with transgender patients' special needs in mind. Most of the healthcare providers do not have the information or the sensitivity to provide such care which leads to misdiagnosing, denial of treatment, or outright discrimination.

Many transgender people require gender affirming treatments such as hormone therapy and surgeries so that their physical attributes align with their gender identity. For examples treatments like facial feminization surgery, genital reconstruction, and mastectomy make a strong positive impact towards psychological well-being and social integration. However, for most people among the transgender community such medical interventions are out of reach because the costs involved. There is also a general misconceived perception that gender-affirming treatments are cosmetic instead of a medical necessity. Thus, there is a complete absence of state led schemes or programs in this area. Insurance providers also usually exclude coverage from gender affirmation procedures and other gender confirming treatments. This implies that if at all such treatments are only provided through private healthcare systems that are prohibitively expensive. This economic hindrance leads some individuals to turn towards unsafe alternatives, including unregulated hormone treatments or very hazardous surgical practices, posing severe risks to their health. The differences in disparities require comprehensive reforms in healthcare policies to afford equal competent care to transgender people.

Lack of sensitization and training among the healthcare professionals aggravates these issues. Many health practitioners at all levels are not prepared to address the specific needs of transgender patients. This leads to inappropriate or inadequate care. This ranges from failures in maintaining confidentiality about a patient's transgender status, which may result in additional stigma or even violence. The establishment of robust training programs for medical professionals can foster inclusivity and competence within the healthcare sector.

Healthcare professionals must also address the psychosocial impact of transition something which requires specific training and sensitization. Transgender people can benefit from counselling that is especially designed for them and which is geared towards supporting them during and after their process of transition. In addition to medical interventions, it is also necessary to counteract the stigmatizing effects of society with appropriate mental health support to enable holistic care. Public education campaigns focused on the need for gender-affirming treatments will change societal views and push policymakers to prioritize funding and inclusivity within healthcare.

Gender-affirming healthcare must also not be limited to transitions in the physical attributes. Voice therapy, hair removal treatments, and facial surgeries are also very critical components for many transgender people in order to establish congruence with their gender identity. These aspects are not often discussed but are very important for the enhancement of quality of life and for the decrease in the risk of discrimination in their daily interactions. An inclusive and supportive healthcare environment may be developed through an approach that involves both the medical and psychological levels of gender affirmation.

Another significant concern pertains to the lack of credible and adequate research on the long-term effects of gender-affirming treatments. Even though there is ample evidence for their efficacy in reducing gender dysphoria and improving mental health, much remains to be understood regarding their impact on a larger scale covering all aspects of health. Funding medical research dedicated solely on transgender health can lead to better informed medical practices and alleviate the long-term health risks due to inadequately researched therapies and interventions.

Lastly, cultural competency is also equally essential in healthcare delivery. Providers need to be well versed with not only the procedures that are medically relevant but also the social and cultural aspects of the transgender patients they cater to. The conceptualization of gender differs vastly among transgender individuals, and being cognizant of such factors can help in better relations with the patient and also facilitate better care. Stakeholder consultation and inclusion of transgender voices in the training modules can prove to be very useful for developing empathy and fostering a sense of understanding.

24.3 HIV AND AIDS AMONG TRANSGENDER POPULATIONS

While stigma and discrimination are rampant against patients of HIV, the intersection of violence with stigma and exclusion through various systemic mechanisms significantly heightens the vulnerability of transgender subjects afflicted with HIV. Trans women engaged in sex-work are much more vulnerable since systemic and structural risks such as poverty and social marginalization for such women leave little option but to engage in such high-risk behaviour. This is compounded by limited access to prevention and treatment services, often driven by discrimination within healthcare systems.

Transgenders are far less likely to approach hospitals in cases of HIV because of the fears of mistreatment or a breach of confidentiality. Consequently, trans individuals continue to be underserved by existing HIV prevention programs. The lack of targeted interventions and inadequate data on the prevalence of HIV among transgender populations further complicates this crisis. There is thus a pressing need for mainstream, inclusive public health approaches that include transgender-specific needs. Widespread education and training for healthcare providers, along with increased funding for prevention programs is the need of the hour.

The absence of targeted interventions, coupled with insufficient data on HIV prevalence among transgender populations, further hampers efforts to address this crisis.

There is an urgent need for inclusive public health strategies that prioritize transgender-specific needs. These should include widespread education and training for healthcare providers, increased funding for prevention programs, and efforts to reduce stigma within healthcare settings. Such measures would empower transgender individuals to access vital services without fear of prejudice or discrimination.

Effectively addressing HIV prevalence among transgenders, will require striking the root cause that stems from social and economic inequalities and his heavily loaded against transgenders that is making them particularly vulnerable. Support to transgenders in education and employment and providing them with legal safeguards can reduce such vulnerability. Such efforts require active collaboration between government and civil society organizations and can reduce vulnerabilities leading to healthy as well as safe environments for transgenders as a community. Community-led initiatives can be a critical component of HIV prevention. Transgender advocacy groups and peer networks will provide culturally competent education and support tailored to the community's specific needs. Such programs have proved to be successful in building trust and improving access to healthcare services. It brings to fore the need for a greater collaboration between the public sector, non-profit organizations and community itself in order to develop an effective and sustainable HIV intervention program.

The need for inclusive sex education is also very important in this context. Gender-sensitive pedagogical approaches and curricula need to be developed to incorporate the specificities related to the transgender contexts. This would allow transgender persons to be informed of safe practices and help curb the risk of HIV infection. Such education should also target wider societal attitudes which is a must for challenging the stigma that facilitates exclusion as well as vulnerability. Any multi-pronged strategy that includes education, changing policies, and working with communities and organizations will be able to address the problem of HIV in transgender populations effectively.

There is a need to broaden access to preventive medications such as pre-exposure and post-exposure prophylaxis for transpeople at high risk of HIV exposure. These measures are known to work but are usually out of reach for disadvantaged populations. Incorporating and subsidizing these drugs into local health initiatives can help lower the number of virus transmissions. Everything is mostly related to advocacy promoting these measures and therapies free from the associated stigma.

24.4 ANALYSIS OF THE TRANSGENDER PROTECTION ACT IN INDIA

In India, the Transgender Persons (Protection of Rights) Act, 2019[1], was enacted to address discrimination and ensure the rights of transgender individuals. The Act is a holistic legal framework meant to safeguard the rights and dignity of transgender persons in India. The Act formally recognizes transgender individuals and prohibits discrimination in education, employment, healthcare, and public spaces. Some of the general provisions of the Act as well as its healthcare-related provisions can be discussed as follows:

Applicable nationwide, the Act defines a transgender person under Section 2(k) as one whose gender identity does not align with his or her sex assigned at birth. This includes a broad spectrum of people who are gender diverse such as trans-men, trans-women, intersex persons. In addition to this it also includes people who possess distinct socio-cultural identities

1. https://www.indiacode.nic.in/bitstream/123456789/13091/1/a2019-40.pdf

such as hijras. In this context, Section 4 ensures that every transgender person has the right to self-perceived gender identity, a progressive recognition of individual autonomy.

Under Section 3, the Act prohibits discrimination against transgender persons across different fields. It ensures equal access to education, employment, healthcare, housing, and access to public goods and services. Further, Section 12 also declares their right to stay with their families, disallowing forceful removal or eviction. For transgender persons who cannot stay with their families, rehabilitation facilities have been incorporated, which implies that the government would ensure safe dwelling.

One of the important features of the Act is the recognition of gender identity through a formal certification process. Section 5 provides for the application of a certificate of identity by transgender persons to the District Magistrate, which would legally establish their transgender status. Section 7 allows for the updating of the certificate in case of gender-affirming surgeries so that their gender identity can be officially recognized.

The government's responsibilities under the Act are outlined in Section 8, which mandates the formulation of welfare measures to promote the inclusion of transgender individuals in education, employment, and cultural activities. Healthcare provisions are detailed in Section 15, which obligates governments to ensure access to gender-affirming surgeries, hormonal therapies, counselling services, and insurance schemes. It also underscores the importance of training health professionals on transgender-specific health issues, filling a critical gap in healthcare delivery.

Employment protections are codified under Sections 9 and 11, which bar workplace discrimination and require establishments to designate complaint officers for grievances. Section 13 requires educational institutions to make learning environments more inclusive without stigma or bias. Overall, these provisions seek to empower transgender individuals and place them in the mainstream of society.

Section 16 establishes the National Council for Transgender Persons, which will be responsible for overseeing the enforcement of the Act, providing policy advice, and redressing grievances. Section 17 lists the functions of the council as reviewing policies and recommending improvements and promoting community engagement. This institutional framework is directed towards holding people accountable while providing a voice for transgender persons.

Section 18 is a list of offenses and punishments. It includes, for example, compelling the transgender person into bonded labour, denial of access to public spaces, and physical, sexual, or emotional abuse. Punishments range from six months to two years imprisonment with fines attached to them. These provisions point to the commitment towards protecting the safety and dignity of transgender persons.

The Transgender Persons (Protection of Rights) Act, 2019 represents a positive legal development for the transgender community which has long been on the receiving end of a legal vacuum in so far as the protection of their rights are concerned , the Act has also been criticized for some of its provisions. One of the major drawbacks pointed out is the mandate of obtaining the identity certificate to be issued by a District Magistrate under Sections 5 and 6. This provision is considered to be an infringement on the right to self-identification by many. This process imposes an unnecessary bureaucratic burden on transgender persons and has been construed as gatekeeping over their identities.

Another critique against the Act is that the punishments that are prescribed in Section 18, such as imprisonment up to two years for discrimination or abuse, are insufficient to deal with the severity of crimes such as physical assault or sexual violence against transgender persons.

A third criticism is that the Act does not have strong healthcare provisions. Section 15 states that there is a need for gender-affirming healthcare but does not provide for public funding and also does not clearly indicate the implementation mechanisms. Due to prohibitively higher cost, many transgender persons cannot afford necessary medical treatments. The Act does not succeed in addressing the systemic exclusion and bias experienced by transgender persons in housing, education, and employment. More to that, there is a lack of concrete measures aimed at including transgender persons in social security schemes and economic empowerment programs.

To bridge the gaps in the current legal framework certain reforms can be suggested. First, the provision of Section 15 about healthcare services should be suitably extended to incorporate public funding for gender-affirming treatments including surgeries and hormone therapy. Healthcare providers should also be trained and sensitized for competent and non-discriminatory care to transgender patients with empathy and inclusivity. Such measures must be accompanied by grievance redressal mechanisms that would concretely translate into tangible safeguards for the transgender individual.

Another crucial reform would be to simplify the process of gender identification is that the need for a certification from the District Magistrates should be substituted with a self-declaration model. This would be a positive move to empower transgenders to assert their identity without having to navigate bureaucratic hurdles. Campaigns should also be initiated in order to combat societal stigma by educating the public regarding the rights and contributions of transgender persons. Such campaigns will also make the social environment even more inclusive and reduce instances of prejudice, thereby acting as a good foundation for an effective Act.

Incorporating these reforms can enable the Act to develop into a more comprehensive and effective tool for advancing equality. By making sure that transgender persons are able to have access to healthcare, legal protections, and social support, the rights of these individuals would be asserted while furthering the larger objective of making society more inclusive and equitable for everyone

Efforts must also focus on empowering transgender communities to participate actively in policymaking and implementation. Representation within decision-making bodies can ensure that laws and policies reflect the lived experiences and needs of the community. Partnerships with civil society organizations can further amplify these voices, creating a robust framework for advocacy and reform.

A critical area for improvement lies in addressing rural-urban disparities. Transgender individuals in rural areas often face compounded barriers due to a lack of resources and heightened stigma. Tailored programs that address these regional disparities can make the Act more inclusive and impactful. The integration of local transgender leaders in implementing welfare measures can also enhance trust and participation, ensuring that the benefits of the Act reach all segments of the community.

SUMMARY

The intersection of transgender identity and access to healthcare that presents complex and multifaceted challenge riddled with systemic discrimination and disparities. This is a combination of societal and institutional barriers that contribute to a systematic denial of transgender individuals' basic right to preserve and enhance their physical and mental well-being. These issues are required to be looked at in greater detail so as to unravel the profound implications such inequities have on the health outcomes of transgender populations.

These challenges are also exacerbated by the persistent existence of discrimination within the health sector, where transgender persons are often exposed to untrained practitioners, stigmatization, and even denial of treatment. Systemic discrimination in healthcare is just a manifestation of the wider societal prejudices which have the impact of crating multiple barriers such as access to other medical gender-affirming intervention treatments, hormone replacement and reassignment surgery etc.

Addressing these disparities would entail educational and policy reforms that would include training medical and other healthcare professionals to be sensitive about transgenders and their specific healthcare expectations and needs. Equitable access to important health services is also very much dependent on securing public funding for gender-affirming medical procedures. An understanding that transgender people may require specific health responses, which will not only include medical intervention but also mental health support in dealing with the unique problems they face.

Mental health service plays a significant role in dealing with the psychological trauma arising from societal stigma and discrimination. The lack of adequate numbers of mental health providers who have knowledge and empathy towards trans experiences can worsen feelings of isolation. Healthcare systems must also recognize the interrelation between their mental and physical health so that they can create safety environments that are not just safe but also affirming, which will help clients pursue comprehensive care without facing the spectre of discrimination. Turning to the Indian context although the Transgender Persons (Protection of Rights) Act, 2019, is a welcome legislative intervention for according recognition to gender identity and rights it has failed to live up to the expectations it generated. The lack of support to transgender specific treatments such as gender-affirming treatments and the intrusive nature of the gender identity certification process for instance are only some of the issues that require more examination and a legislative course correction.

CHAPTER

25

Euthanasia and Living Wills Ethical, Legal, Medical and Social Perspectives

INTRODUCTION

Euthanasia and living wills represent two critical aspects of end-of-life care. Both these concepts pertain to an individual's right to take a decision to regulate conditions which govern their lives and death. These two concepts thus open up complex debates which are very closely connected with intertwined issues of on personal freedom, choice and agency as well as medical ethics and the responsibilities of society and the state. Euthanasia involves a considered act of commission with the intent of putting an end to life to relieve unbearable suffering. Living wills provide an opportunity to individuals to document their preferences and issue advance directives to govern the manner in which their medical treatment should proceed in scenarios where they can no longer communicate their decisions.

Discussions on the complex issues surrounding these concepts have been necessitated owing to the advancements in medical technology. Modern medical tools and procedures can potentially prolong life even in terminal cases. Medical advancements, such as life-support systems and resuscitation techniques, have blurred the line between preserving life and prolonging suffering. This has created ethical and legal dilemmas for patients, families, and healthcare providers alike. Discussions about euthanasia and living wills are not just abstract philosophical debates but also deeply practical matters impacting hospitals, patient rights, and healthcare policies.

A wide range of factors cultural, religious, or even socio-political deeply affect views and perception on such practices. The Indian scenario makes it even more complicated with family dynamics and spirituality intervening in such medical decision-making processes. Judicial decisions in India have been attempting to balance individual autonomy against the socio-cultural aspects making the Indian scenario rather complex.

25.1 UNDERSTANDING EUTHANASIA

The word "euthanasia" derives its origin from the Greek words "eu," which means good, and "thanatos," which means death. Euthanasia is a voluntary act of taking one's life to relieve unbearable pain and suffering. Ancient in its origins, it has recently gained importance because of medical technology advancements and human rights movements. Euthanasia is also a highly controversial practice that varies from as per the prevailing cultural perceptions .

Euthanasia radically challenges the social and medical understanding of life and death from the bottom up. With modern advances in medicine, the controversy shifted to issues of ethics and the law. Euthanasia is complicated by ethical questions involving autonomy and suffering. Autonomy relates to the individual's decision-making power regarding his life, including the right to end it. Those opposed would argue that the sanctity of life takes precedence over personal choice. Such dilemmas are made more poignant by improvements in pain control and palliative care which aim to eliminate pain rather than death.

The concept of a "good death," which underpins euthanasia, varies across cultures. In societies where personal autonomy generally determines an individual decision making. However, in most collectivistic societies including India, families play a paramount role in matters regarding the end-of-life care thus influencing the acceptance as well as the application of euthanasia. Such cultural variations greatly impact the law and policy frameworks across jurisdictions. Technological and medical advancements add more twists and turns to the debate regarding euthanasia. Supportive care, for example, artificially nourishing a patient with food and fluid can sustain life but to the detriment of what that patient or family members desire. Therefore, clear policies are necessary in dealing with ethics and the law about such a sensitive topic, hence the need for elaboration on the various kinds of euthanasia.

25.1.1 Types of Euthanasia

Voluntary Euthanasia

In voluntary euthanasia, a person gives an explicit consent to end his life, usually for terminal illness or unbearable pain. This form of euthanasia is pivoted around the human right to life and its extension to the freedom to choose a dignified death in cases of incurable or unbearable suffering. It focuses on autonomy and the ability to decide death over being in suffering for a protracted time. Advocates say that it gives people autonomy and dignity in death. But critics argue that depression, external coercion, or misinformation could affect this decision. So, such decisions should be protected against abuses by psychiatric evaluations to affirm that the consent is genuine.

Voluntary euthanasia, in this sense, also highlights a moral and legal dilemma since most countries prohibit it while others, like Belgium and the Netherlands, provide recognition under very strict regulations. Most require several medical opinions, waiting periods, and sometimes even psychological assessment before imposing any regulations. This stands as a sentinel for a very cautious approach in striking the balance between autonomy and protection. It thus seeks to create euthanasia as the last resort where other options fail.

Debates surrounding voluntary euthanasia also involve its impact on healthcare providers. Physicians often face moral dilemmas, balancing their duty to alleviate suffering with the Hippocratic Oath's directive of non-malfeasance or to "do no harm." The psychological toll on doctors performing euthanasia can be profound, necessitating emotional support and ethical guidance. This aspect emphasises on the interconnectedness of medical, ethical, and legal considerations.

Voluntary euthanasia's societal implication extends beyond individual cases. Critics holding the opposing view hold that it devalues society's respect for life, especially for the vulnerable populations. Supporters instead point that it can enhance compassion by prioritizing dignity and alleviate suffering. The need to strike a balance individual or personal ethics and collective and social ethics remains at the root of the euthanasia debate.

Non-voluntary Euthanasia

Non-voluntary euthanasia comes into the picture when individuals cannot make a decision regarding the choice of ending the life process due to serious diseases such as persistent vegetative states or severe brain injuries. Non-voluntary euthanasia brings to fore crucial questions regarding the sanctity of surrogate decisions, authority of health professionals as well as the resolution of such disputes by the judicial system. Often, it places families with extremely difficult choices with regard to maintaining quality life and considerations that are not only ethically correct but also emotionally turbulent.

Medical progress has brought alongside the dilemmas pertaining to non-voluntary euthanasia situations. Today such technological interventions are available that can support bodily functions even for a lifetime make patients exist in states of minimal or no consciousness. This challenges the traditional understanding of life and death, compelling societies to redefine the ethical and legal norms.

Surrogate decision making is at the centre of non-voluntary euthanasia. Surrogate decision making implies that typically, family members, close relatives or legal guardians, will need to decide on withholding or continuing life-extending treatments for individuals who are unable to do so for themselves. In order to take concrete actions to implement such decisions, matters such as advance wishes of patients, cultural beliefs, and medical prognoses tend to come into play. Such decisions become even more complex since because medical ethics stress on beneficence which signifies that decisions are to be taken in the best interests of the patients. But best interests can sometimes be extremely subjective to judge and decide on.

Legal frameworks governing non-voluntary euthanasia vary widely across jurisdictions. Some countries, like the Netherlands, permit the practice under strict conditions, including medical review boards and family consent. Others prohibit it entirely, reflecting societal discomfort with delegating life-and-death decisions. These divergent approaches underscore the need for global dialogue to establish consistent and humane practices.

Non-voluntary euthanasia also raises resource allocation concerns. Extending life for an unusually long time when the prospect of a good outcome obviously does not exist can create too much pressure on healthcare. It diverts resources that could be utilized on those with a better prognosis. Advocates argue that euthanasia may be one mechanism for relieving this burden. However, opponents warn against weighing life-and-death decisions on economic grounds is problematic.

Consent is the ethical bedrock of medical practice, and involuntary euthanasia is often looked upon as violating this sacrosanct principle and eroding the foundational ethos of medicine. These concerns have prompted stringent legal prohibitions worldwide.

25.1.2 Methods of Euthanasia

Modes of administering Euthanasia are the ways in which Euthanasia can be administered based in the nature of action or omission adopted to bring about death. Two modes of Euthanasia are broadly identified.

Active Euthanasia

Active euthanasia involves intentional actions aimed at extinguishing life, such as drugs that may result in death. It is very controversial because it completely defies traditional medical ethics and social understanding of life and death. Its supporters maintain that active euthanasia provides a merciful alternative to unbearable pain. It resonates with the principles of autonomy and mercy. Its opponents on the other hand caution on the possible abuse of this method and also mistrust towards health professionals.

The legal frameworks regarding active euthanasia are very different from each other. Countries like Belgium and the Netherlands allow it under strict circumstances which include patient consent, terminal illness, and independent review by a doctor. All these precautions ensure that the act of active euthanasia is done with much care and does not disturb the rights of the individuals and social concerns. However, most countries criminalize the act of active euthanasia, which reflects cultural and ethical resistance to the idea.

The medical community faces significant challenges in implementing active euthanasia. Physicians must navigate complex ethical dilemmas, balancing their duty to alleviate suffering with the Hippocratic Oath's principle to "do no harm." Training healthcare providers in ethical decision-making and emotional resilience is essential for addressing these challenges. Institutions must also establish clear protocols to guide practitioners in navigating legal and ethical complexities.

Passive Euthanasia

Passive euthanasia involves withholding or withdrawing life-sustaining treatments, such as ventilators or feeding tubes, allowing nature to take its course. Generally, this method is considered less controversial than active euthanasia since the former is often regarded as allowing death rather than causing it. Proponents argue that passive euthanasia respects the natural dying process, in which compassion and dignity inform decision making. Critics warn against the ambiguity in defining and enforcing passive euthanasia. In many clinical contexts, the line between active and passive euthanasia may become rather blurred. Turning off a patient's ventilator, for example, may technically be characterized as passive euthanasia but it may seem to be an act of commission to those involved in it. These subtleties highlight the importance of establishing clear legal and medical regulations in end-of-life care. The role played by the healthcare providers is very crucial in passive euthanasia. Physicians face complex ethical and emotional dilemmas when trying to strike a balance between their duty to preserve life and relieving suffering. Training the health professionals in compassionate communication and ethical decision-making helps in this regard. Also, there is a need for creating an accountability culture in ensuring that passive euthanasia practices are in alignment with ethical and legal standards.

25.2 LIVING WILLS

A living will or an Advance Medical Directive is a legal document through which an individual expresses their preferences regarding medical care in case they are unable to actively communicate their wishes at a certain stage in life. The directive becomes critical in situations of serious illness, incapacitation, or unconsciousness and guides the healthcare provider and family members as to how significant decisions of treatments can be made. By specifying their desires ahead of time, individuals make sure that their autonomy is respected, even when they are unable to subsequently participate in decision-making. A living will often contains directions concerning whether or not to commence or discontinue life-extending interventions such as a ventilator or dialysis, balancing the desire for life against the potential suffering of such interventions. Ordinarily, it addresses preferences regarding pain management, the manner of utilizing palliative sedation, targeting comfort and dignity. Also, people can specify whether they want to accept or refuse artificial nutrition and hydration, especially when they are in irreversible vegetative states. This helps ensure that care matches their beliefs about natural death. Preferences for organ donation are also important, as they let people agree to or refuse donation after death. These directives, taken together, guarantee that the end-of-life care provided respects the autonomy of the individual, thus reducing uncertainty for both families and healthcare providers.

A living will is a form of advance declaration and directive, which, before potential health problems set in, is written and prepared. A living will, therefore, assists healthcare professionals in implementing the person's choice on medical intervention as determined through the living will itself. This also fosters informed consent, which is an essential principle of medical ethics since one can make the decision about his body even before the time such an event may occur.

Many jurisdictions recognize such advance directives as long as they are made in specified formats and with safeguards. The document is intended to clearly describe the medical interventions to be carried out and thus minimizes all potential ambiguities for healthcare providers and relatives over what form of care to administer for a patient. Such documents can prove to be instrumental in protecting the rights of citizens in the healthcare delivery sector; however, their use often requires supportive legal and institutional structures.

Living wills also have an ethical purpose in that they eliminate the moral dilemmas that the families and healthcare professionals encounter. If there is a clear documentation of one's wishes, the emotional burden on family members would be less, as they may otherwise end up writhing with guilt or indecision. For medical professionals, living wills bring legal and moral certainty that the care being provided is indeed respectful of the patient's dignity and is in consonance with the expressed desire of the patient. Living wills thus bridges the gap between the advancement of medicine and individual freedom.

Living wills emerged as a response to the growing complexity of medical technologies capable of prolonging life. While these advancements have saved countless lives, they have also created ethical dilemmas where life is sustained without quality or dignity. Living wills bridge this gap by enabling individuals to proactively decide how they wish to be treated, alleviating the burden on families and medical professionals tasked with making these decisions in real-time.

Much like Euthanasia, the ethical foundations of living wills are rooted in the principles of autonomy and informed consent. By articulating preferences in advance, individuals assert their right to make decisions about their bodies and medical care. However, the practical implementation of living wills is fraught with challenges, including issues of interpretation, accessibility, and adherence by healthcare providers. Clear guidelines and legal recognition are crucial for ensuring that living wills are respected in practice.

25.3 KEY ASPECTS OF LIVING WILLS

Ethical Foundations

Living wills, then, are based in the ethical principles of autonomy, dignity, and informed consent. These are important to end-of-life care because autonomy means that patients maintain a sense of control over their medical decisions, even when they can no longer speak for themselves; it reflects their values, beliefs, and preferences and, in doing so, helps to preserve dignity and avoid treatments that are either too intrusive or futile. Living wills express, then, a broader commitment on the part of society to respect personal choice and avoid unnecessary suffering. There is also an important ethical rationale for living wills since they reduce the burden of the emotional and ethical consideration put on families and caregivers. In the absence of any advance directives, there is agonizing decision-making dilemma family members have to face; whether to pull or withhold life-sustaining treatments. A living wills serve to clarify the decisions involved and ensures that they agree with the wishes of the patient rather than external pressures or assumption.

Critics of the living will highlight the difficulties posed by such wills. They for example point out that it is difficult to predict future medical ailments and consequent requirements of providing care which can vary as per circumstances such as age, state of mental capacity or consciousness. Hence a simple document cannot possibly account for a number of complex possibilities. Ethical questions regarding potential societal or familial persuasion against an individual's determination also arise in the realm of living wills. Such challenges can be overcome with adequate controls in place, such as signing in the presence of witnesses, updating the document regularly, and professional counselling during preparation of the will.

Legal Recognition

The legal recognition of living wills varies across jurisdictions and reflects the differences in social attitudes and legal traditions. In countries with an advanced framework for end-of-life care, such as the United States, Canada, and some European nations, living wills are valid and enforceable. Generally, these jurisdictions have enacted detailed legislation on the formation, registration, and execution of living wills that gives people confidence that their wishes will be respected.

In India, the Supreme Court's landmark judgment in the case of Common Cause in 2018 brought much-needed legal clarity to the status of living wills. Recognizing the right to die with dignity under Article 21 of the Constitution, the court affirmed that living wills are an essential component of this right. It settled the guidelines for drafting and implementing living wills. The judgment laid down a principle that the safeguards against misuse should be strict enough, such as attestation by witnesses and medical boards.

However, despite this recognition, challenges remain in translating legal provisions into practical realities. The concept is still at a nascent stage except in a few countries. Because of this detailed legislation and guidelines governing living wills are currently absent in most jurisdictions including India. This has led to inconsistencies in their acceptance and implementation across healthcare institutions. Moreover, public awareness of living wills remains low. This limits their wider adoption and impact. Also, legal debates surrounding living wills often focus on issues of enforceability and interpretation. In some cases, healthcare providers or family members may challenge the validity of a living will, citing ambiguities or changing circumstances. These issues must be addressed through targeted legislation and awareness campaigns. Legal systems must balance the need for flexibility with the importance of upholding individual autonomy, ensuring that living wills are neither rigidly binding nor easily disregarded.

Emerging technologies like digital registries and electronic health records can facilitate increased legal and also physical accessibility of the living wills. These facilities will allow proper recording, storage and retrieval of wills. These systems must prioritize security and privacy, ensuring that sensitive information is protected while remaining easily retrievable during medical emergencies. Countries like the Netherlands and Australia have successfully implemented such systems, providing valuable models for other nations.

Adopting such technologies can reduce administrative bottlenecks and healthcare providers can benefit from the easy and prompt availability of documented patients' preferences or decisions. Such enabling technologies must be incorporated in the legal frameworks pertaining to living wills.

Living wills should also not just be easy to access but should also be easy to understand; moreover, healthcare and legal systems both need to be more accommodating with respect to this right. Making people aware of the choice to draw a living will and also familiarizing them with what the living will entails.

Healthcare providers are central to the effective implementation of living wills. Physicians, nurses, and hospital administrators must be trained to respect and act on patients' documented preferences, even when these conflict with conventional treatment protocols. This requires institutional policies that prioritize patient autonomy while ensuring compliance with legal and ethical standards. Regular workshops and ethical training sessions can help bridge the gap between theoretical principles and clinical practice.

It is also important to understand that interpreting and implementing living wills in complex medical scenarios can be challenging. For instance, a living will may specify a refusal of life support but lack clarity on whether this applies to temporary interventions, such as ventilators during acute illnesses. To address such ambiguities, healthcare providers must engage in open dialogues with families and legal representatives, guided by ethical principles and clinical expertise. Regularly updating living wills can also help address potential uncertainties.

Finally, living wills intersect with broader societal debates about aging and elder care. As populations age and chronic illnesses become more prevalent, living wills offer a framework for addressing the complexities of end-of-life care in a way that respects individual dignity and societal values. Living wills can help navigate the ethical and practical challenges of aging with compassion and foresight.

25.4 LEGAL AND CONSTITUTIONAL STATUS OF EUTHANASIA AND LIVING WILLS IN INDIA

Euthanasia, or the practice of ending a terminally ill patient's life to relieve suffering, has long been a contentious issue in India and the issue of living wills also assumes significance in this context since it finds a lot of common grounds with euthanasia. These issues give rise to complicated questions of morals, laws, and constitutional provisions, especially concerning the ambit of the fundamental rights provided by Article 21 of the Indian Constitution, which also includes a right to health, the right to livelihood, a right to live with dignity, a right to shelter, and the right to privacy.

Euthanasia has been one of the most contentious issues in India for long. It raises complex moral, legal, and constitutional questions, particularly concerning the scope of the fundamental rights guaranteed under Article 21 of the Indian Constitution, which reads: *"No person shall be deprived of his life or personal liberty except according to the procedure established by law*[1]. This right has been expansively interpreted to include a number of fundamental rights within the ambit of "personal liberty." These include the right to health, the right to a livelihood, the right to live with dignity, the right to shelter, and the right to privacy. The Supreme Court of India has consistently interpreted "life" under Article 21 in a broad and inclusive manner, emphasizing its integral connection with human dignity. The understanding of life within the framework of the Constitution extends beyond mere existence to include a life of quality, dignity, and personal autonomy.

The relationship between life and dignity under Article 21 has been underscored in landmark judgments. In *K.S. Puttaswamy* v. *Union of India*[2], the Supreme Court emphasized that human dignity is indispensable to the right to life and liberty. Furthermore, the Court has acknowledged that the right to live with dignity encompasses the notion of a dignified death for individuals suffering from terminal illnesses with no hope of recovery. While the "right to life" does not extend to a "right to die," the "right to live with dignity" implicitly includes the "right to die with dignity." This nuanced distinction forms the basis for India's evolving legal and ethical stance on euthanasia.

The right to autonomy and self-determination in medical decisions is also protected under Article 21, allowing individuals to decide the extent to which they consent to medical treatments. This autonomy extends to end-of-life decisions, ensuring that individuals retain control over deeply personal choices, including the decision to forgo life-sustaining measures when quality of life diminishes. The right to privacy, also encompassed under Article 21, reinforces the principle that decisions regarding life and death fall within the private domain of an individual, free from external interference.

1. https://indiankanoon.org/doc/1199182/
2. AIR 2017 SC 4161

Judicial interpretation of the right to life and its interplay with the right to die has been the subject of several significant cases. In *State of Maharashtra* v. *Maruty Sripati Dubal*[3], the Bombay High Court ruled that the right to life includes the right to die and declared Section 309 of the Indian Penal Code (IPC) unconstitutional. Similarly, in *P. Rathinam* v. *Union of India*[4], the Supreme Court observed that the right to life also implies the right not to live a life imposed against one's will, leading to a declaration that Section 309 IPC, which criminalizes attempted suicide, was unconstitutional.

This position was reconsidered in *Gian Kaur* v. *State of Punjab*[5], where the Constitution Bench upheld the constitutionality of Section 309 IPC. The Court clarified that the "right to life" does not include the "right to die" but does encompass the right to a dignified life, even until natural death. The Court distinguished between active euthanasia, which involves an overt act to end life, and passive euthanasia, which entails withholding life-prolonging measures. While active euthanasia was deemed unlawful, the Court left open the possibility of considering passive euthanasia in specific circumstances involving terminally ill patients in a persistent vegetative state (PVS).

In *Aruna Ramchandra Shanbaug* v. *Union of India*[6], the Supreme Court addressed the issue of euthanasia directly. The petitioner, a nurse in Mumbai, had been in a persistent vegetative state for 38 years following a brutal assault. A plea was filed seeking passive euthanasia to end her suffering. The Court, after detailed deliberation, legalized passive euthanasia under stringent conditions, requiring approval from a High Court and adherence to specific guidelines. While the Court did not equate the right to die with the right to life under Article 21, it allowed for passive euthanasia in cases where the patient's condition was irreversible and there was no hope of recovery.

The legal discourse on euthanasia gained further clarity with the *Common Cause* v. *Union of India*[7] case, where a five-judge Constitution Bench declared the "right to die with dignity" a fundamental right under Article 21. The Court upheld the legality of passive euthanasia and recognized the validity of Advance Directives or Living Wills, allowing individuals to specify their preferences for medical treatment in terminal conditions. The judgment emphasized the importance of self-determination and autonomy in end-of-life decisions while providing detailed guidelines for implementing Advance Directives, including the involvement of medical boards and judicial oversight.

The guidelines laid down in Common Cause were subsequently modified in 2023 following a Miscellaneous Application by the Indian Society of Critical Care Medicine[8]. The Supreme Court simplified the procedure for executing Living Wills and Advance Directives, addressing practical challenges that rendered the earlier framework complex and unenforceable. The revised guidelines reduced procedural barriers, clarified the roles of medical boards and judiciary, and streamlined the process to uphold the sacrosanct right to dignity and autonomy in end-of-life care.

3. 1987(1)BOMCR499
4. 1994 AIR 1844
5. 1996 AIR 946
6. India AIR 2011 SC 1290
7. AIR 2018 SUPREME COURT 1665
8. Writ Petition (Civil) No. 215 of 2005

Despite these legal developments, the debate on euthanasia in India remains unresolved. Critics argue that the practice risks misuse, coercion, and ethical dilemmas, particularly in a country with socio-economic disparities and inadequate healthcare safeguards. Supporters, however, emphasize the need to respect individual autonomy and alleviate suffering, advocating for robust legal frameworks to prevent abuse while enabling dignified death for terminally ill patients.

SUMMARY

The chapter has undertaken a discussion on the sensitive and multifaceted topics of euthanasia and living wills, shedding light on the moral, legal, and emotional dilemmas they present. It carefully distinguishes between active euthanasia, where deliberate actions are taken to end a life, and passive euthanasia, which involves withholding or withdrawing life-sustaining treatments. The discussion further delves into the ongoing ethical debates surrounding an individual's right to choose a dignified death versus the value society places on preserving life. The significance of living wills which are legal instruments that empower individuals to specify their medical treatment preferences should they become unable to communicate their wishes has also been discussed in the chapter. This proactive approach to end-of-life care not only upholds personal autonomy but also eases the emotional burden on families and guides healthcare providers in honouring patient choices. Overall it can be said that both euthanasia and living wills are complex issues that present themselves at the intersection between legal considerations, ethical perspectives, and human experiences and addressing them within any legal framework shall require a delicate balance of all these aspects given their profound impact on individuals and society at large.

CHAPTER

26 Clinical Trials, Ethics and Human Rights

INTRODUCTION

Clinical trial is a systematic research investigation aimed at developing new tests and treatments by evaluating their effects on human health. Clinical trials evaluate the impact of medical interventions, such as investigational drugs, vaccines, medical devices, surgical and radiological procedures, behavioural treatments, preventive measures, or biological products on humans. These medical interventions are tested on human subjects so that the necessary clearances for marketing and use among populations can be obtained. Clinical trials are carefully conducted to address the specific needs of key stakeholders, including patients, medical practitioners, and the sponsor commissioning the study. The procedure for the trial undergoes rigorous review, and it can only commence after receiving the necessary approvals. The clinical trial essentially involves systematically studying pharmaceutical products, whether on patients or healthy volunteers. Its purpose is to investigate, substantiate or confirm the clinical and pharmacological characteristics of the product, including its pharmacodynamics (how the drug works in the body), pharmacokinetics (how the body processes the drug), and any contraindications and adverse outcomes. The ultimate objective of the products is to assess whether they are safe and effective for public use as food products[1].

26.1 PHASES OF CLINICAL TRIALS

Clinical research is a structured and systematic process that includes several distinct phases. Each phase provides unique data on drugs for their safety, effectiveness, and pharmacological nature. It ensures that any product under trial is rigorously scrutinized before it is made accessible to the general public for mass consumption. Generally, the following sequence is followed:

- **Pre-clinical Research:** Before a drug is administered to humans, substantial pre-clinical research is done to establish the basic safety profile. The laboratory experiments

1. https://cdsco.gov.in/opencms/resources/UploadCDSCOWeb/2018/UploadImmunization/Clinical.pdf

are conducted mostly by in vitro (test tube) methods and in vivo (animal) models for the assessment of the toxicity, pharmacokinetics, and pharmacodynamics of the investigational product. This phase is regulated by following Good Laboratory Practices (GLP)[2] which are a set of guidelines and standard operating procedures that ensure that the data obtained is reliable, accurate and ethically obtained. Pre-clinical studies identify any potential side effects, therapeutic thresholds, and safe dosage ranges. The outcome of pre-clinical research is of paramount importance for getting approval from the regulatory authority to enter human trials and is submitted as part of an Investigational New Drug (IND) application to the concerned authority, such as the Central Drugs Standard Control Organization (CDSCO) in India.

- **Phase I:** Phase I trials represent the first stage of testing of a new drug on human beings and are carried out in a small group of 20–100 healthy volunteers or, in some cases, patients who suffer from the condition being targeted. The aim is basically to assess the drug's safety and tolerability. This leads the researchers to determine optimal dosages while studying pharmacokinetics, which is how the body absorbs, distributes, metabolizes, and excretes the drug, and pharmacodynamics, which is how the drug affects the body. This phase is often divided into distinct sub-phases, each designed to gather specific data. The Single Ascending Dose (SAD) sub-phase involves administering progressively higher doses of the drug to different volunteer groups, identifying the maximum tolerated dose. The Multiple Ascending Dose (MAD) sub-phase follows, where participants receive repeated doses to study cumulative effects and longer-term safety. Additionally, Food Effect Studies are conducted to evaluate how food consumption influences the drug's absorption and overall bioavailability. Phase I trials are not primarily focused on establishing the drug's therapeutic efficacy. Their major objective is to identify potential adverse effects, toxicity thresholds, and safe dosage limits. Nevertheless, the findings from this phase are critical since they provide a basis for subsequent trials with larger and more diverse populations. This is a phase where preliminary risk analysis is conducted which paves the way for a drug's further development.
- **Phase 2: Therapeutic Exploration:** Phase 2 trials involve a smaller number of 100–300 patients who are afflicted with the target condition and are designed to evaluate the therapeutic efficacy and safety of the drug. This phase is crucial to determine whether the drug results in the desired clinical effects and for determining optimal dosing regimens. Phase II trials are often randomized, double-blind, placebo controlled to minimize bias and to provide robust efficacy data. Patients are usually divided into groups for the administration of the investigational drug, an existing treatment, or a placebo. The effects are compared to determine the relative effectiveness of the drug. Phase II studies monitor side effects and safety data of short-term follow-up. Exploratory studies conducted on diverse subpopulations in Phase II explain variability in drug response. Data from Phase II aid in defining parameters for a large-scale study, like Phase 3.

2. See, https://www.regdesk.co/cdsco-guidance-on-good-clinical-practices-overview/

- **Phase 3: Therapeutic Confirmation:** Phase III trials are conducted at a large scale and usually involve thousands of participants. They are conducted in multiple centres and multiple times in several countries. It is meant to demonstrate the drug's efficacy and safety in a larger population over a more extended period. In such trials, the investigational drug is compared with known treatments or placebos, making them superior, equivalent, or non-inferior in comparison. Data collected comprehensively include effectiveness, side effects, and long-term safety of the drug. This phase also includes study of drug interactions, the dosing schedule, as well as its effects within specific subgroups, which may include children, pregnant women, or elderly patients. This phase utilizes methodologies like randomization, blinding, and stratification to ensure statistical robustness. Data from this stage forms the basis of any New Drug Application (NDA) or Marketing Authorization Application (MAA), which is submitted to regulating bodies. Marketing approval strictly requires a successful Phase 3 trial.
- **Phase 4: Post-marketing Surveillance:** Phase 4 trials are also referred to as post-marketing surveillance studies, which are conducted after the drug has been approved by regulatory authorities and is on the market and in public use. The main aim is to observe the performance of the drug in the real-life setting and detect rare or later adverse effects that were not present during earlier phases. This phase is where observations are noted via registries and the continued randomized controlled trials with respect to whether the drug actually works for different sorts of patients. Data from off-label use as well as its interaction, if possible, as far as the efficacy of improvement in quality of life. Phase IV studies are very important for pharmacovigilance, such that the benefits of the drug are greater than its risks throughout its lifecycle. Regulatory authorities may require more trials or impose restrictions depending on the findings from the Phase IV studies.

26.2 INTERNATIONAL LEGAL FRAMEWORK ON CLINICAL TRIALS

A number of international frameworks, protocols and guidelines seek to protect the rights of persons being subjected to clinical trials.

The Nuremberg Code of 1947[3] came in response to the Nazi atrocities in the medical experiments they conducted on humans during World War II. This laid the basis for modern ethics in human research as it established that no human experiment can be performed without the voluntary informed consent of the practitioner.

After the declaration of the Nuremberg Code, the World Medical Association formulated the **Declaration of Helsinki in 1964**[4]. Surrogate consent became a landmark development of this code which implied that legal representatives were entrusted with providing consent on behalf of individuals whose decision-making capacity is impaired. This change thus made it possible to include vulnerable groups such as people with mental disabilities to be research participants without compromising on ethics.

3. The Nuremberg Code of 1947. https://media.tghn.org/medialibrary/2011/04/BMJ_No_7070_Volume_313_The_Nuremberg_Code.pdf
4. https://www.wma.net/policies-post/wma-declaration-of-helsinki/

The **Council for International Organizations of Medical Sciences (CIOMS)**[5] guideline first appeared in 1993 and have subsequently been revised. These are yet another landmark in the development of guidelines for clinical trials. These guidelines highlight aspects such as cultural sensitivity, equitable distribution of research benefits, and protection of vulnerable subjects. CIOMS strongly addresses the ethical issues in low- and middle-income countries, while disparities in healthcare access also create power imbalances between sponsors and participants. The guidelines emphasize on the principle of distributive justice, which remains absolutely essential to ensure that research outcomes benefit all segments of society, particularly among the underprivileged.

In 1996, the **International Conference on Harmonization of Technical Requirements for Registration of Pharmaceuticals for Human Use (ICH)** released its Good Clinical Practice (GCP) Consolidated Guidelines[6]. These guidelines established globally accepted standards for the design, conduct, and documentation of clinical trials. By integrating scientific rigor with ethical considerations, the GCP guidelines ensured that clinical research is conducted with transparency and accountability. They also stressed the need for informed consent, data integrity, and the independent review of research protocols by ethics committees. However, implementing these standards uniformly across diverse regulatory environments remains a challenge, particularly in countries with limited resources or regulatory infrastructure.

The **Universal Declaration on Bioethics and Human Rights**[7], adopted by UNESCO, brought a holistic perspective to the ethical discourse in clinical research. It emphasized the interconnectedness of ethical principles, human rights, and cultural diversity and providing a universal framework to guide biomedical research. This declaration underscored the importance of respecting the autonomy and dignity of participants while promoting equitable access to the benefits of scientific progress. It also highlighted the role of community engagement in clinical research, recognizing the value of local knowledge and participation in ethical decision-making.

The International Declaration on Human Gene Data (2003)[8] also adopted by UNESCO acknowledges human gene data as a groundbreaking discovery that could revolutionize the healthcare sector, improve diagnoses, and help develop a new era of personalized medicine. Nevertheless, the declaration also draws attention to the ethical, legal, and social implications of genetic research and the related concerns over discrimination and stigmatization and misuse of genetic information. The declaration calls for transparency in collecting, storing, and making use of human gene data, handling such data in integrity and respect for autonomy of the individual. It focuses on seeking informed consent, protecting confidentiality, and promoting equal access to the fruits of genetic research. Further, it advocates international cooperation without disrespecting cultural differences and local norms so that science benefits humanity and not harm human principles.

These international guidelines are an evolving commitment to a balance the pursuit of scientific progress and moral imperatives. Each of these has helped progressively strengthening the rights of participants in clinical research. Nevertheless, in practice, several issues persist

5. https://cioms.ch/wp-content/uploads/2017/01/WEB-CIOMS-EthicalGuidelines.pdf
6. https://database.ich.org/sites/default/files/E6_R2_Addendum.pdf
7. https://www.unesco.org/en/ethics-science-technology/bioethics-and-human-rights
8. https://www.unesco.org/en/ethics-science-technology/human-genetic-data

in practical implementation, especially in addressing power relations, unawareness among the participants, cultural sensitivities, and resource disparities. Continuous effort in adapting and harmonizing these guidelines must be made to ensure that clinical research serves the interests of humanity without undermining individual dignity and rights

26.3 THE EVOLUTION AND FRAMEWORK OF CLINICAL TRIAL REGULATION IN INDIA

The clinical trials form the backbone of new drugs, therapies, and interventions in medicine. It creates the knowledge that the products under research, testing, and being approved are thoroughly screened regarding their safety, efficacy, and quality before entering the market. In a country like India, with its vast population, genetic diversity, and very high disease burden, not only do clinical trials provide opportunities to address unique health issues but also significantly contribute towards global medical research. At the same time, it does bring complex ethical, legal, and procedural issues for the conduct of clinical trials that call for a robust regulatory architecture.

Over the last few decades, the clinical trial ecosystem in India has witnessed a sea changed. From a largely unregulated environment during the mid-20th century, it has evolved to become a structured and globally aligned framework. This change is the combined outcome of legislative measures, international agreements, and judicial interventions. Currently, the Indian clinical trial framework is governed by a comprehensive framework comprising of Clinical Trial Rules of 2019 (CT Rules), CDSCO-GCP guidelines, and ICMR guidelines for biomedical and health research involving human participants, published in 2017.

26.4 HISTORICAL BACKGROUND AND EARLY REGULATION

The initial legislative efforts towards clinical trial regulation in India back to the Drugs and Cosmetics Act, 1940[9], and the Drugs and Cosmetic Rules, 1945[10] which dealt with the importation, manufacture, distribution, and sale of drugs in India. Clinical research remained unregulated, and pharmaceutical companies conducted trials without standardized protocols or accountability mechanisms. Schedule Y was introduced to the Drugs Rules in 1988 as the first attempt by India to regulate clinical trials. It required Phase III clinical trials for registration and marketing approval of new drugs, which primarily catered to the generic drug industry. This was a step forward, but it did not have provisions for participant protection, ethical oversight, or compensation mechanisms. Schedule Y was amended in 2005, introducing a comprehensive four-phase clinical trial scheme. This amendment also legalized the Guidelines on Good Clinical Practice (CDSCO-GCP), 2001, and aligned India's regulatory standards with international practices.

Despite advancements, ethical oversight and participant protection remained significant concerns. Deficient review procedures by ethics committees and the absence of a clear

9. https://www.indiacode.nic.in/bitstream/123456789/15278/1/drug_cosmeticsa1940-23.pdf
10. https://rajswasthya.nic.in/Rules/drug%20and%20cosnetic%20ruls.pdf

compensation mechanism for trial-related injuries or deaths led to public outcry and judicial intervention. To address these shortcomings, a series of amendments were introduced in 2005[11] and 2013 under the Drugs and Cosmetics Rules[12]. These rules aimed at a better and more robust control of the clinical trial processes. Some select and relevant rules are mentioned below:

1. **Rule 122 DAA (2005)** defines clinical trial as a systematic study conducted on human participants to gather data about a new drug. The goal is to discover or confirm the drug's clinical effects, pharmacological properties (including how the drug interacts with the body and how the body processes it), and any adverse effects. The primary objective is to assess the drug's safety and effectiveness.
2. **Rule 122 DA (2005)** Clinical trials for new drugs, whether for clinical research or experimentation by any institution, can only be conducted with written permission from the Licensing Authority, as specified under Rule 21(b). This ensures that all trials comply with the required legal and ethical standards.
3. **Rule 122 DAB (2013)** mandated free medical management for participants in case of trial-related injuries, for as long as required. It also established compensation mechanisms for injuries or deaths directly attributable to clinical trials, empowering the Licensing Authority to calculate and enforce compensation amounts.
4. **Rule 122 DAC (2013)** introduced stringent prerequisites for granting trial permissions, ensuring adequate safeguards for participant welfare. It also allowed the Licensing Authority to impose additional conditions for individual trials, enabling case-specific regulatory oversight.
5. **Rule 122 DD (2013)** required mandatory registration of ethics committees with the Licensing Authority and detailed their roles in reviewing and approving trial protocols. This ensured that ethics committees adhered to standardized practices and were held accountable for their decisions.

26.5 CLINICAL TRIAL RULES, 2019[13] (CT RULES)

The Clinical Trial Rules, 2019, were developed to introduce a comprehensive framework for conducting clinical trials in India, doing away with the gaps and complexities of previous regulations. These rules regulate all aspects of clinical trials, from approvals to participant safety also including functions of the ethics committee and reporting mechanisms. One of the most significant provisions concerns mandatory registration and functioning of ethics committees. Which comprises of medical, legal, and social representatives. This committee reviews and approves all trial protocols before they are conducted. Under the CT Rules, such committees are required to be registered with the Central Licensing Authority. This reduces the likelihood of unethical practices and promotes ethical standards for all clinical trials in India.

The CT Rules have streamlined the approval process with defined timelines to facilitate prompt decision making. The time taken from submission of an application to its approval is

11. https://ibkp.dbtindia.gov.in/DBT_Content_Test/CMS/Guidelines/20181115121749531_Schedule_Y.pdf
12. https://www.manupatra.com/manufeed/contents/PDF/634969625902580076.pdf
13. https://cdsco.gov.in/opencms/resources/UploadCDSCOWeb/2022/new_DC_rules/NEW%20DRUGS%20ANDctrS%20RULE,%202019.pdf

required to be 90 days for a new drug developed abroad and 30 days for the drugs developed in India. This mechanism incentivizes local research and at the same time ensures stringent oversight for foreign pharmaceutical companies. The CT Rules also contain waivers for certain classes of drugs such as drugs that have already been approved in other countries, under the conditions that guarantee safety and efficacy in the Indian context. Such provisions balance regulatory stringency with the need to encourage innovation and expeditiously bring new drugs and therapeutics to patients.

The CT Rules accorded primary importance to participant safety, with robust mechanisms for tackling injuries or deaths resulting from a trial. Medical care is mandated and offered to affected participants for as long as necessary ensuring that the cost of trial-related consequences shall fall on the sponsors involved. In cases of death or permanent disability, adequate compensation is made to families as calculated by age of participant, income, etc. These measures are accompanied by mandatory reporting of serious adverse events (SAE) to the ethics committee, licensing authority, and sponsor within 24 hours.

26.6 GOOD CLINICAL PRACTICE (GCP) GUIDELINES[14]

The GCP Guidelines were issued in 2001 by CDSCO and provide clear instructions for the ethical and scientific conduct of clinical trials. The guidelines highlight the fact that informed consent is one of the key requirements of any clinical trial. This means that the participants will be agreeing to take part in the trial, after being well-informed about the risks, benefits and procedures associated with the trial. This implies that information should be given in a language that the participant understands, addressing literacy barriers, and ensuring that sufficient time is taken to reflect on the decision to participate in the trial. In addition, guidelines require consent forms to be reviewed and approved by ethics committees for clarity and adequacy. High priority to informed consent enables the GCP guidelines to protect autonomy of the participants and also prevent exploitation, especially from vulnerable populations.

Scientific rigor is another cornerstone of the GCP guidelines, which mandate that all clinical trials follow a pre-approved protocol. The protocol serves as a blueprint for the trial, detailing its objectives, methodology, data collection procedures, and statistical analyses. Any deviation from the protocol must be documented and justified. Investigators are also required to maintain comprehensive records of participant data, adverse events, and trial outcomes. These requirements ensure that trials produce reliable and reproducible results, contributing to the credibility of clinical research in India.

The GCP guidelines assign specific responsibilities to sponsors and investigators to ensure participant safety and data integrity. Sponsors are responsible for ensuring that trials are adequately funded, ethical approvals are obtained, and monitoring mechanisms are in place. They must also provide adequate training to investigators and site personnel. Investigators, on the other hand, are tasked with maintaining detailed medical records, monitoring participant well-being, and promptly reporting any adverse events.

---

14. https://cdsco.gov.in/opencms/opencms/system/modules/CDSCO.WEB/elements/download_file_division.jsp?num_id=MTE5NTI=

26.7 GOOD LABORATORY PRACTICES (GLP)

The Good Clinical Practices framework is an important part of India's clinical trial ecosystem, as envisioned by the Clinical Trial Rules of 2019. Adopted in India from the framework originally developed by the Organization for Economic Co-operation and Development, GLP provides quality benchmarking for nonclinical safety testing so as to facilitate accuracy, reliability and integrity in trials. In India, GLP is governed by the National Good Laboratory Practice Compliance Monitoring Authority (NGCMA)[15] under the Department of Science and Technology.

GLP ensures that in vitro studies conducted in pre-clinical conditions like the toxicological and pharmacological properties of investigational products are done under uniform and reproducible conditions. This is important since laboratory-based experiments and animal tests also form a part of the drug development procedure to validate the safety profile of the drug before testing on a human being. Although these guidelines are not binding they are largely adhered to because of their practical utility. The GLP protocols makes it possible for good-quality data to be developed from the studies. This ensures that the data satisfies all the rigorous requirements for review at regulatory institutions such as the Central Drugs Standard Control Organization. Mandating GLP compliance for pre-clinical studies, the CT rules uphold the validity and credibility of safety data used in clinical trial applications.

Compliance with GLP principles is demonstrated by laboratories applying for GLP-Compliance Certification from the NGCMA. Although not a legal requirement, this kind of certification is considered more or less a de facto requirement for laboratories seeking approvals. It indicates that the laboratory complies with the international standards of quality and reliability in research. The certification is valid for three years, during which NGCMA conducts annual inspections to ensure continued compliance with GLP standards. This surveillance ensures that laboratories maintain consistent quality throughout their certification period.

India's adoption of GLP aligns its pre-clinical research ecosystem with international benchmarks, and helps build greater trust in data generated by Indian laboratories. Following the globally accepted OECD guidelines, Indian laboratories can prepare safety data which is accepted and recognized by international regulatory authorities. Not only does this facilitate cross-border collaborations in clinical research but also enhances India's credibility as a destination for pharmaceutical development. For multinational companies, doing GLP compliant studies in India offers an advantage of satisfying both domestic as well as global regulatory expectations.

GLP compliance also has a significant role in encouraging ethical research practices. Since the data from pre-clinical safety studies will be accurate and reliable, there is less chance that the wrong research reaches human clinical trials, thereby protecting participants from unnecessary risks. Additionally, structured protocols and quality controls under GLP help increase the transparency and accountability of research practices that build confidence among stakeholders in the clinical trial ecosystem.

15. National Good Laboratory Practice Compliance Monitoring Authority (NGCMA) https://dst.gov.in/ngcma

26.8 ICMR GUIDELINES FOR BIOMEDICAL AND HEALTH RESEARCH, 2017

In addition to aforementioned regulations and guidelines, the ICMR Guidelines for Biomedical and Health Research Involving Human Participants, 2017[16], provide a comprehensive ethical framework for conducting clinical and health research in India. These guidelines are built on four foundational principles: autonomy, beneficence, non-maleficence, and justice. Autonomy is emphasized through stringent informed consent requirements, ensuring that participants fully understand the purpose, risks, and potential benefits of the research before agreeing to participate. Special provisions are included for vulnerable populations, such as children, the elderly, and those with diminished decision-making capacities, mandating additional safeguards to protect their rights and welfare.

A distinguishing feature of the ICMR guidelines is that it encourages community engagement, highly relevant in India's socio-cultural context. The ICMR guidelines promote involvement of local communities in the planning and conduct of studies. This enables integration of culturally sensitive approaches to recruitment and the design of a trial, ensuring that community engagement contributes to the enhancement of the ethical acceptability of the research, results in better participant enrolment and ensures that local health priorities are addressed by the research. In fact, the ICMR guidelines highlight data protection and confidentiality because of the ever increasing need to protect information about the participants involved, especially with the increase in digital health records. Wherever possible, the participant's data is anonymized, and other security measures are undertaken to prevent unauthorized access. It also underlines fair benefit-sharing through research so that results of clinical trials do not only benefit the more affluent groups but benefit the less privileged sections of society as well. The ICMR guidelines have tried to balance the ethical principles with practical considerations to achieve scientific advancement without human dignity or societal equity.

SUMMARY

India's clinical trial framework has been developed to maintain a balance between innovation, participant protection, and ethical integrity. Nonetheless, despite crating and advancing a legal ecosystem for clinical trials challenges still persist. Inconsistent enforcement across regions due to differences in regulatory capacities; procedural delays because of bureaucratic inefficiencies, understaffed ethics committees and resource constraints impact oversight mechanisms. All these factors impede the timely and effective conduct of trials, jeopardizing participant welfare and discouraging sponsors. They need to be addressed through capacity building, technological integration, funding, and making more people aware of the need to facilitate compliance. India's regulatory journey with respect to clinical trials reflects a gradual shift from an industry-driven approach to a balanced framework prioritizing participant welfare. Correcting the deficiencies by consistently updating the legal framework and encouraging transparency, accountability, and ethical rigor in conducting clinical trials will lead India towards becoming a major hub for global clinical research, where scientific advancement produces equitable benefit and protects the dignity and rights of the participant.

16. https://ethics.ncdirindia.org/asset/pdf/ICMR_National_Ethical_Guidelines.pdf

CHAPTER

27

Digital Health Promises and Challenges

INTRODUCTION

The integration of digital technologies with healthcare, known as digital health has a potential to profoundly reshape healthcare systems around the world. Digital health leverages tools like artificial intelligence (AI), telemedicine, electronic health records (EHRs), mobile health (mHealth), and health information systems, etc. enhance diagnostic accuracy, improve treatment outcomes and facilitate greater access to healthcare in underserved areas. Digital health promises to tackle some of the most persistent challenges in healthcare, such as access to services, affordability, efficiency, and quality of care. In India, where the healthcare system is characterized by both vast regional disparities and a burgeoning population, digital health holds transformative potential to revolutionize healthcare delivery, making it more equitable, timely, and patient-centred.

As one of the largest democracies in the world, India faces unique challenges in healthcare delivery. From rural and underserved areas with limited infrastructure to urban centres grappling with overcrowded facilities, there is thus an urgent need for innovative solutions that can bridge these gaps. Digital health, in this context, emerges as a powerful instrumentality to enhance the accessibility of healthcare services, ensure better distribution of medical resources, and provide high-quality care at lower costs. This chapter discusses the regulatory and policy frameworks in India's digital health ecosystem. Furthermore, it examines the challenges associated with digital health adoption in India, including issues related to digital literacy, data privacy, interoperability, and infrastructure development. Finally, the chapter presents a way forward, focusing on the steps needed to address existing barriers, scale digital health solutions, and create a robust, sustainable ecosystem that benefits all segments of society.

27.1 THE SIGNIFICANCE OF DIGITAL HEALTH IN INDIA

Digital health is a broad concept that signifies the use of digital tools and technologies to support health services, promote wellness, and improve healthcare outcomes. The integration of these technologies into healthcare systems has the potential to revolutionize the way care is delivered. It can also greatly improve both the outreach and quality of healthcare service delivery. Particularly in India, the significance of digital health cannot be overstated, as it holds the key to addressing some of the country's most pressing healthcare challenges. Some of these challenges can be outlined as follows:

- **Access to Healthcare:** With over 1.4 billion people, India's vast geographical spread makes it difficult for healthcare services to reach every citizen, especially those in remote, rural, and underserved areas. Telemedicine platforms, mobile health apps, and digital consultations can help bridge this gap, providing accessible healthcare to people regardless of their location.
- **Affordable and Efficient Care:** Digital health technologies, such as AI-driven diagnostics, electronic prescriptions, and automated healthcare systems, help streamline processes, reduce inefficiencies, and lower operational costs. These innovations can bring high-quality care within the financial reach of a larger section of the population, thus making healthcare more affordable.
- **Improved Health Outcomes:** The adoption of electronic health records (EHRs) can ensure that healthcare providers have immediate access to accurate, up-to-date patient data, which is crucial for making timely decisions. Additionally, AI and machine learning algorithms can assist doctors in diagnosing conditions at an early stage, improving patient outcomes by enabling earlier interventions.
- **Personalized Medicine:** With the help of digital tools, healthcare professionals can tailor treatment plans based on real-time data collected from wearable devices, mobile apps, and patient health records. This personalized approach enhances the effectiveness of treatments and promotes better long-term health management.

27.2 THE ROLE OF DIGITAL HEALTH IN HEALTHCARE DELIVERY

Digital health harnesses the power of information and communication technologies (ICT) to enhance healthcare services across the entire continuum of care, from prevention and diagnosis to treatment and follow-up. The integration of technology with health offers innovative solutions to traditional challenges, such as limited access, inefficiency, and fragmented and sporadic care. The integration of digital health solutions is reshaping the landscape of healthcare delivery, making services more efficient, accessible, and personalized. Some of the most widely employed digital health technologies and tools can be discussed in this light as follows:

- **Telemedicine:** Telemedicine has been a very welcome innovation in healthcare delivery, particularly in addressing the geographical and logistical barriers that often hinder access to quality healthcare. One of the ways in which telemedicine technologies bridge the access gap is by providing remote consultations between patients and healthcare professionals, telemedicine has the potential to significantly expand access to medical care in underserved regions, where traditional healthcare infrastructure is lacking. This capability became particularly evident during the COVID-19 pandemic, which saw a dramatic surge in telemedicine usage. Platforms like *eSanjeevani,* launched by the Government of India, have enabled over 100 million teleconsultations, linking rural patients to specialized doctors. Also initiatives like e-Manas for mental health support, further demonstrates the potential of telemedicine to improve healthcare access even in sensitive domains like mental health. Through telemedicine, interdisciplinary collaboration has also becomes easier since healthcare professionals from various specialties being able to consult and work together, thus improving diagnostic accuracy and care planning. This holistic approach enhances patient outcomes and makes multidisciplinary care more accessible.

Despite these advantages, the widespread adoption of telemedicine still faces several challenges. Issues such as inconsistent internet connectivity in rural areas and digital literacy gaps among both patients and healthcare providers must be addressed. Investments in infrastructure development and comprehensive digital literacy programs are critical to overcoming these barriers and ensuring that telemedicine services reach those who need them the most.

- **Electronic Health Records (EHRs):** Streamlining Care and Public Health Surveillance: Electronic Health Records (EHRs) are integral to the digitization of healthcare, enabling the seamless storage, sharing, and management of patient health data. EHRs enhance clinical decision-making by giving healthcare providers real-time access to comprehensive patient information, which reduces medical errors, improves care coordination, and ultimately leads to better patient outcomes. However, challenges persist in India, such as lack of interoperability, insufficient infrastructure, and the slow pace of adoption among healthcare providers. Beyond improving operational efficiency, EHRs play a crucial role in public health surveillance. EHR systems aggregate health data and can hence help track disease trends, monitor outbreaks, and support evidence-based public health interventions. This proactive use of EHR data enables timely responses to emerging health threats and strengthens overall healthcare resilience. For example, the Mother and Child Tracking System (MCTS)[1] uses digital records to monitor maternal and child health, ensuring that essential healthcare services are delivered in a timely manner. In addition, EHRs are invaluable for medical research. The large datasets generated by EHR systems provide insights into treatment outcomes, which can inform clinical studies and lead to the development of more effective therapies. Government initiatives like the National Digital Health Mission (NDHM) are promoting the adoption of EHRs through the Ayushman Bharat Health Account (ABHA), which consolidates medical records across different healthcare providers into a single, accessible platform.
- **Artificial Intelligence (AI):** Enhancing Diagnostics and Healthcare Efficiency: Artificial Intelligence (AI) has recently become an indispensable tool in healthcare, driving innovations in disease prediction, early detection, and personalized treatment planning. AI algorithms can process vast amounts of medical data to identify patterns and provide insights that support clinical decision-making. For example, the AI-based Pneumonia Detection System, developed in collaboration with the Ministry of Health and Family Welfare, uses AI algorithms to analyse chest X-rays, enabling healthcare providers in rural centres to detect pneumonia in children and initiate timely

1. https://apps.gov.in/apps/government/mother-and-child-tracking-system-mcts

treatment. In addition to diagnostics, AI is also improving hospital management. Predictive analytics powered by AI can optimize resource allocation, improve patient flow, and enhance operational efficiency, leading to better patient care and reduced costs. AI-driven virtual health assistants and chatbots are further enhancing patient engagement by providing health information and managing routine inquiries. However, the widespread implementation of AI in healthcare brings with it ethical concerns. Issues such as algorithmic transparency, accountability, and bias need to be carefully addressed. Ensuring that AI models are rigorously validated and that algorithms are transparent and fair is essential for preventing systemic biases and ensuring equitable healthcare outcomes.

- **Mobile Health (mHealth):** Mobile health (mHealth) solutions leverage mobile devices, applications, and wearable technologies to support health monitoring, disease management, and patient engagement. Mobile Health enables real-time health data collection, facilitates remote patient monitoring, and provides personalized health interventions. These technologies are particularly useful for managing chronic diseases, promoting preventive care, and improving medication adherence. Wearable devices, such as fitness trackers and smartwatches, are increasingly popular in mHealth. These devices provide continuous monitoring of vital signs like heart rate and blood pressure thus empowering individuals to take proactive control of their health. Integration of wearable data with Electronic Health Records (EHRs) can further enhance personalized healthcare by allowing healthcare providers to monitor patients' health remotely and make informed decisions based on real-time data. One successful example is the Aarogya Setu app, launched during the COVID-19 pandemic. This app facilitated contact tracing, self-assessment, and health status monitoring, helping track and mitigate the spread of the virus. The Reproductive and Child Health (RCH) Portal also provides mHealth services to monitor and manage maternal and child health, ensuring that timely interventions are made to improve healthcare outcomes for women and children. However, while the potential of mHealth is vast, several challenges need to be overcome. Issues related to data security, interoperability, and regulatory oversight must be addressed to build user trust and ensure that these technologies are used safely and effectively. Establishing clear guidelines on data privacy and cybersecurity is essential to protecting sensitive health information and promoting widespread adoption of mHealth solutions.

27.3 REGULATORY FRAMEWORK ON DIGITAL HEALTH IN INDIA

India's regulatory framework for digital health has been a recent introduction in the health policy landscape after a push in the National Health Policy 2017. It is designed for the purpose of facilitating safe, efficient, and ethical integration of technology into healthcare delivery. It establishes guidelines to ensure data privacy, security, and interoperability among digital health systems while promoting innovation and accessibility. The objective of such regulations is to balance the need for technological advancement with the protection of individual rights, emphasizing consent-based data sharing and accountability. Through these measures, the regulatory environment aims to create a resilient and inclusive digital health ecosystem that improves healthcare outcomes for all citizens. Some of the important constituents of India's regulatory framework on digital health have been discussed in detail below:

- **National Health Policy 2017[2]:** The National Health Policy 2017 has provided the initial impetus for advancing digital healthcare in India, emphasizing the integration of digital technologies to improve accessibility, affordability, and quality of care. It envisions leveraging information and communication technologies (ICT) to strengthen healthcare delivery, enhance disease surveillance, and streamline health information systems. By promoting the adoption of digital solutions such as telemedicine, electronic health records, and health information exchanges, the policy aims to bridge healthcare gaps, particularly in rural and underserved regions. This strategic focus on digital health aligns with the broader goal of achieving universal health coverage and improving overall public health outcomes. To realize this vision, the policy encourages the development of robust digital infrastructure, interoperability standards, and secure data management systems. It also highlights the importance of capacity building through digital literacy programs for healthcare professionals and the public in order to create an environment where technology-driven solutions can thrive. Additionally, the policy advocates for collaborative efforts between government agencies, private stakeholders, and technology innovators to drive sustainable healthcare innovations. To realize this vision, the policy encourages the development of robust digital infrastructure, interoperability standards, and secure data management systems. The National Health Policy (NHP) 2017 advocates for the extensive deployment of digital tools to improve the efficiency and outcomes of the healthcare system linking public and private health providers, ensuring continuity of care through two-way systemic linkages between various levels of care primary, secondary, and tertiary. This approach aims to create an integrated health information system that facilitates seamless data exchange and supports comprehensive healthcare services. To achieve these objectives, the NHP 2017 recommends the development of a National Health Information Network by 2025. This initiative is intended to standardize health data management, promote interoperability among diverse health information systems, and ensure the privacy and security of patient data. Overall, the policy aims to bridge healthcare gaps, particularly in rural and underserved regions, thereby contributing to the broader goal of universal health coverage and improved public health outcomes in India.
- **National Digital Health Blueprint (NDHB, 2019)[3]:** In pursuance of the policy priorities pertaining to digital health in NHP 2017, the National Digital Health Blueprint (NDHB) has been prepared as a step towards realizing a digital health ecosystem in India. It laid the groundwork for integrating healthcare systems nationwide and envisioned the development of an interoperable digital infrastructure. The NDHB emphasized the importance of Health IDs, electronic health registries, and data exchange systems that allow patients' health information to flow seamlessly between providers, thereby improving care coordination. An essential feature of the NDHB is its federated

2. https://nhsrcindia.org/sites/default/files/2021 07/National%20Health%20Policy%202017%20%28English%29%20.pdf.
3. National Digital Health Blueprint. Available at: https://abdm.gov.in:8081/uploads/ndhb_1_56ec695bc8.pdf

architecture, which acknowledges the federal structure of India and allows state and central systems to operate cohesively while respecting the autonomy of state-level healthcare services. This federated approach is crucial for ensuring that healthcare delivery is tailored to the regional needs while still conforming to national standards. The development of digital health literacy programs within the workforce has been identified as a key pillar in the blueprint, aimed at reducing the digital divide between urban and rural healthcare providers. However, challenges persist despite goals. The decentralization of the healthcare system means that states have varying levels of readiness and infrastructure to adopt digital health initiatives. This has led to fragmented implementation, where some states have made considerable strides while others lag behind. Additionally, securing consistent funding for the nationwide rollout remains a critical concern. The private sector's role is indispensable in driving innovation and providing the necessary infrastructure, but public-private collaboration remains uneven. The NDHB's emphasis on privacy and data security is vital, given the sensitive nature of health information. The guidelines outlined in the blueprint are consistent with international standards on privacy, but their practical enforcement remains a significant hurdle. Developing a robust regulatory framework to ensure compliance with these privacy standards, as well as ensuring that healthcare institutions maintain strict data protection measures, is necessary for building trust in digital health. Finally, the capacity building outlined in the NDHB, particularly through extensive digital literacy initiatives and professional development programs for healthcare workers, is critical for the long-term sustainability of the digital health infrastructure. Scaling these initiatives, however, requires careful coordination and extensive investment, both at the central and state levels.

- **Ayushman Bharat Digital Mission (ABDM, 2020)[4]:** The Ayushman Bharat Digital Mission (ABDM) is a flagship initiative aimed at transforming healthcare delivery through digital technologies. A key feature of ABDM is the creation of the Ayushman Bharat Health Account (ABHA), a unique identifier for citizens that facilitates the integration of healthcare services across India. The ABHA ensures that patients' health records are easily accessible by authorized healthcare providers, thereby enhancing the quality of care. In addition to the ABHA, the mission introduced two important components: the Health Facility Registry (HFR) and Health Professional Registry (HPR). These registries play an instrumental role in standardizing healthcare infrastructure and workforce data. By mapping healthcare facilities and professionals across the country, ABDM ensures that citizens have access to a transparent and well-regulated healthcare ecosystem.
- **The Unified Health Interface (UHI)** is another key component that facilitates interoperability across healthcare services. The UHI allows healthcare providers to share information on a secure, interoperable platform. The seamless integration of healthcare services is expected to reduce fragmentation and improve patient care outcomes, especially in remote or underserved areas. Despite its promising potential, the ABDM faces several challenges, particularly in the realm of digital literacy and

4. Ayushman Bharat Digital Mission. https://abdm.gov.in/

infrastructure development. Rural India remains underserved in terms of internet access, digital devices, and technological infrastructure. These barriers make it difficult for the average citizen to fully benefit from the digital health ecosystem, as they may struggle to access their health information, engage with digital health services, or understand how to use these technologies effectively.

Moreover, privacy and consent management are key concerns in the ABDM. The implementation of a consent-driven data exchange system is crucial to safeguard patient autonomy and prevent misuse of health information. It is essential that robust mechanisms are in place to ensure patient consent is collected, recorded, and respected throughout the entire healthcare process. Additionally, achieving widespread adoption of ABDM requires comprehensive public awareness campaigns that educate citizens on the benefits of digital health tools. Finally, addressing health disparities and ensuring that inclusive access to digital health services is a priority will be essential for the ABDM to reach its full potential. The integration of telemedicine, mobile health services, and rural healthcare delivery systems into the ABDM framework is critical for extending the benefits of digital health to all corners of the country.

- **Health Data Management Policy (2020)[5]:** The Health Data Management Policy established under the Ayushman Bharat Digital Mission (ABDM) serves as a critical guideline for ensuring the safe, secure, and ethical management of health data. Central to the policy is the principle of data minimization, which requires that only the necessary health information be collected, stored, and processed. This principle is crucial to reducing the risk of exposure of sensitive data and ensuring that personal health information is used for legitimate, predefined purposes. A key aspect of the policy is its emphasis on informed consent, requiring patients to have control over their personal health data. The policy mandates that healthcare providers ensure transparency in how patient data will be used, stored, and shared. The consent mechanism is a pivotal element in maintaining patient autonomy and maintaining trust in digital health systems. It also aligns with the broader goals of user empowerment, enabling individuals to manage their health data proactively.

  Additionally, the policy introduces federated data architecture, where health data is stored locally with the data fiduciary (e.g., a hospital or healthcare provider) while being accessible through secure channels when necessary. This decentralized approach reduces the risk of large-scale data breaches and ensures that data ownership remains with the patient or the healthcare provider. One challenge in the implementation of this policy is the enforcement of data protection measures, particularly in the private healthcare sector, where regulations are often loosely followed. To address these challenges, the government must ensure that compliance mechanisms are strengthened, with penalties for non-compliance clearly outlined. A dedicated oversight body could facilitate enforcement and maintain consistency in data management practices across public and private institutions. The policy's alignment with the broader Data Protection Laws, such as the Digital Personal Data Protection (DPDP) Act, is critical. There needs to be a harmonization between these regulations to ensure that health data management

5. https://abdm.gov.in:8081/uploads/health_management_policy_bac9429a79.pdf

aligns with the highest standards of data privacy and security. The integration of health data policies with the DPDP Act will be pivotal for ensuring comprehensive protection of personal health information.

- **Information Technology Act (2000) and IT Rules (2011):** The Information Technology Act (2000) and its accompanying IT Rules (2011) form the cornerstone of India's digital infrastructure, setting the legal framework for data security and privacy. Section 43A of the IT Act mandates that organizations handling sensitive personal data implement reasonable security practices. This includes health data, making the IT Act relevant in the context of healthcare. However, the IT Act was drafted before the proliferation of digital health technologies, and as such, it lacks provisions specific to healthcare data management. The absence of a health-specific regulatory framework limits its applicability in dealing with the complexities of digital health systems. For example, the increasing use of artificial intelligence (AI) and telemedicine in healthcare raises new concerns about data security, patient consent, and the ethical use of technology are some of the concerns that the current IT Act does not sufficiently address. The IT Rules (2011) offer greater detail on the implementation of security measures, but like the Act itself, they are general and do not specifically cater to the healthcare sector. The growing importance of AI and machine learning (ML) in healthcare also necessitates a re-evaluation of the IT Rules to ensure that they address issues related to automated decision-making and algorithmic transparency in health services. Also challenges in enforcement remain, particularly in ensuring that healthcare providers, especially small and medium-sized clinics, adhere to these regulations. Since the IT Act does not contain clear guidelines for the healthcare sector, there is a need for more focused regulations to address the risks specific to healthcare IT systems. To address these gaps, a dedicated healthcare IT regulatory framework could be developed to complement the IT Act and IT Rules. This framework would specifically focus on health data security, patient consent, AI ethics, and the broader implications of emerging technologies in healthcare.
- **Digital Personal Data Protection Act (DPDP Act)[6]:** The Digital Personal Data Protection Act (DPDP Act), passed in 2023, represents a significant step towards establishing comprehensive data protection laws in India. It introduces principles such as data minimization, purpose limitation, and accountability for data fiduciaries handling personal data, including health information. One of the main strengths of the DPDP Act is its emphasis on giving users greater control over their personal data, which aligns with the broader goals of patient-centred care in digital health.

  However, the exemptions for government entities in the DPDP Act are a contentious issue, especially when it comes to the handling of sensitive health data by public authorities. This provision could undermine the protections offered to personal health data, as it allows government bodies to bypass some of the strict data protection obligations imposed on private entities. This raises concerns about the potential for government overreach and unauthorized access to health data. To ensure that the

6. https://www.meity.gov.in/writereaddata/files/Digital%20Personal%20Data%20Protection%20Act%202023.pdf

DPDP Act fully protects sensitive health data, regulatory clarity is required regarding the roles and responsibilities of government bodies and the private sector in managing and securing health data. The need for sector-specific data protection laws that provide clear guidelines on the use of health data, including AI-driven health technologies, is essential to ensure that personal health information is handled with the utmost care and privacy. While the DPDP Act lays down robust provisions for data protection, its success in the context of healthcare will depend on effective implementation. This includes strengthening the regulatory framework, establishing independent oversight mechanisms, and ensuring that the health sector is fully integrated into the law's provisions. The integration of the DPDP Act with other healthcare-specific regulations will also play a pivotal role in the overall effectiveness of data protection in India's digital health ecosystem.

27.4 CHALLENGES IN INDIA'S DIGITAL HEALTH REGULATION

Digital Literacy

Digital literacy is one of the most significant barriers to the widespread adoption of digital health solutions in India. Both healthcare providers and patients face challenges in effectively engaging with digital health tools due to varying levels of proficiency with technology. Many healthcare professionals, particularly in rural or under-resourced areas, are unfamiliar with digital tools such as electronic health records (EHRs), telemedicine platforms, and health management apps. This lack of familiarity leads to reluctance or difficulty in utilizing these technologies, which undermines their potential to improve healthcare delivery. On the patient side, a large portion of the population, especially in rural regions and among older people, lacks the basic digital literacy skills required to access online consultations, use health monitoring apps, or navigate medical records stored electronically. This creates a digital divide where only a section of the population benefits from digital health innovations, exacerbating existing healthcare inequities. To address this gap, it is essential to launch comprehensive digital literacy programs that target both healthcare providers and the general public. For healthcare providers, training should focus on the effective use of digital tools for patient management, teleconsultation, and remote monitoring, along with the implementation of digital health policies. For patients, especially in rural areas, digital literacy initiatives should be localized, language-appropriate, and conducted in collaboration with community organizations to ensure that everyone has the capability to engage with digital health solutions.

Furthermore, enhancing digital literacy will require building trust in digital health technologies. This can be achieved by involving local communities in educational campaigns and demonstrating the real-world benefits of digital health services. Additionally, the introduction of mobile-based digital literacy programs could significantly improve reach and participation, especially among younger generations, who are more likely to adopt digital health solutions.

Infrastructure Development

While urban India may have access to adequate digital infrastructure, rural India continues to face significant challenges in accessing the tools necessary to implement and benefit from digital health solutions. The lack of reliable internet connectivity is one of the most glaring obstacles. Internet speeds in rural areas are often inconsistent or limited, hindering the seamless delivery of digital health services such as telemedicine, remote consultations, and real-time data transmission for monitoring chronic diseases. Without reliable connectivity, the potential benefits of digital health tools are limited. Furthermore, electrical grid instability is another barrier, particularly in rural or semi-urban areas where frequent power outages occur. This makes it difficult for both healthcare providers and patients to rely on digital health technologies for regular use. The absence of reliable electricity limits the potential for digital health tools to be integrated into daily healthcare delivery practices and reduces the effectiveness of existing telemedicine or health monitoring systems.

Infrastructure development must be a central focus for ensuring equitable access to digital health technologies. The government and private sector must invest in strengthening digital infrastructure, particularly in underserved areas. This includes expanding access to high-speed internet, particularly broadband and 4G/5G networks, as well as supporting the provision of reliable power to healthcare facilities and homes. Public-private partnerships (PPPs) could play a critical role in accelerating this development by sharing resources and expertise to create a more equitable digital healthcare landscape.

Additionally, mobile health solutions can serve as an intermediary in areas where fixed infrastructure is still developing. Smartphones and tablets, already widespread in India, can be leveraged for telemedicine and health data management, reducing the dependency on fixed healthcare infrastructure. However, this requires investments in mobile health applications that are specifically designed for areas with limited connectivity and resources.

Interoperability

For India's digital health ecosystem to function effectively, a seamless interoperability framework is essential. Interoperability refers to the ability of different healthcare systems, platforms, and technologies to exchange, interpret, and utilize patient data efficiently and securely. In India, the absence of standardized formats for health data exchange across the healthcare sector comprising both the public and private sectors is a significant challenge. Without interoperability, digital health tools, such as electronic health records (EHRs) and telemedicine platforms, cannot communicate effectively with each other. This creates fragmentation in the healthcare system, where patient data is siloed in different institutions, and critical health information is not shared across providers in a seamless manner. Such fragmentation results in duplicative testing, delayed diagnosis, and inconsistent treatment plans, ultimately undermining the quality of care.

To address this issue, it is crucial to establish national standards for health data exchange. The National Digital Health Blueprint (NDHB) and the Ayushman Bharat Digital Mission (ABDM) have already made some progress in promoting standards for data interoperability, particularly through the creation of Health IDs and data exchange frameworks. However, the successful implementation of these standards will depend on the collaboration of various stakeholders, including government agencies, healthcare providers, and technology vendors. Additionally, interoperability must also take into account the integration of diverse technological platforms used by healthcare providers across the country. This will require the establishment of unified protocols and application programming interfaces (APIs) that enable the secure and effective exchange of data between different systems, such as hospital information systems, EHRs, telemedicine platforms, and diagnostic tools.

In the long run, a centralized health data platform that ensures data sharing and accessibility, while adhering to privacy and security standards, will help build an integrated and efficient healthcare ecosystem that can provide timely, accurate, and coordinated care to all patients.

Data Privacy and Security

As the digital health landscape expands, data privacy and security have become paramount concerns. With the increasing amount of personal health data being collected through digital health platforms, there is a growing need to ensure that this sensitive information is protected from unauthorized access, breaches, and misuse. Health data, which often includes highly personal details about an individual's medical history, family background, and genetic information, requires the highest levels of data protection. India currently has the Information Technology Act (2000), which mandates certain data security practices, but it lacks robust provisions specifically tailored to healthcare data. The Digital Personal Data Protection (DPDP) Act, passed in 2023, aims to address some of these concerns by setting clear guidelines for data processing and the rights of individuals regarding their personal data. However, while the DPDP Act is a step in the right direction, challenges remain in ensuring its comprehensive implementation across the healthcare sector.

One of the primary concerns is the accessibility and enforcement of data protection regulations. While large, urban healthcare institutions may have the resources to implement data encryption, firewalls, and other security mechanisms, smaller clinics and healthcare providers in rural areas may not have the infrastructure or capacity to meet these standards. Furthermore, the complexity of managing and securing health data, particularly when shared across multiple entities, increases the likelihood of breaches if not handled with the utmost care.

To ensure data security, healthcare providers must implement robust security measures including data encryption, secure data storage, and access control mechanisms. Training healthcare professionals to understand the importance of data privacy and how to safeguard patient information is essential. Moreover, cybersecurity awareness campaigns must be conducted at both institutional and public levels to ensure all stakeholders are vigilant in maintaining the security of sensitive health data. Compliance mechanisms should be put in place to hold healthcare institutions accountable for adhering to privacy laws and ensuring the ethical use of health data. The creation of an independent regulatory body dedicated to overseeing health data privacy and security could be a right step in this direction to ensure that breaches are reported and rectified promptly, fostering public trust in the digital health system.

SUMMARY

Digital health presents a transformative opportunity for India's healthcare sector, promising enhanced accessibility, affordability, and quality of care. With strategic policy implementation, robust regulatory frameworks, and inclusive digital infrastructure, India can bridge healthcare disparities and realize the goal of Universal Health Coverage. A synchronized effort involving stakeholders across the public and private sectors is essential to build a sustainable, patient-centric digital health ecosystem that safeguards rights, ensures equity, and fosters innovation. To fully realize the potential of digital health in India, a holistic and collaborative approach is essential. This involves significant investments in infrastructure, particularly ensuring reliable internet connectivity and access to digital devices in rural areas, which can be facilitated through public-private partnerships. Concurrently, a nationwide digital literacy campaign must be launched to equip both healthcare professionals and the general public with the skills to navigate digital health tools, ensuring informed healthcare decisions. Strengthening data privacy and security laws, aligned with global standards, will be crucial for building trust and safeguarding sensitive health information. Also innovation through partnerships between academic institutions, research organizations, and technology companies will drive the development of solutions tailored to India's healthcare needs, with an emphasis on AI-based diagnostics, remote care, and predictive analytics.

QUESTIONS FOR PART VII

Q.1 How do legal frameworks around abortion in India balance women's reproductive rights with ethical and societal concerns?

Q.2 Discuss the legal and ethical issues surrounding sex determination and female foeticide in India.

Q.3 What are the legal regulations governing surrogacy in India, and how do they address ethical concerns?

Q.4 Discuss the legal and ethical challenges surrounding the legalization of euthanasia in India.

Q.5 How does the concept of a living will empower individuals in making end-of-life decisions?

Q.6 What are the ethical considerations in conducting clinical trials, especially in developing countries like India?

Q.7 How can regulations on clinical trials ensure the protection of vulnerable populations while fostering medical innovation?

Q.8 Discuss the challenges faced by non-binary individuals in accessing appropriate healthcare and the steps that can be taken to improve inclusivity in health systems.

Q.9 What is digital health? How can it improve healthcare service delivery for the poor and marginalised communities?

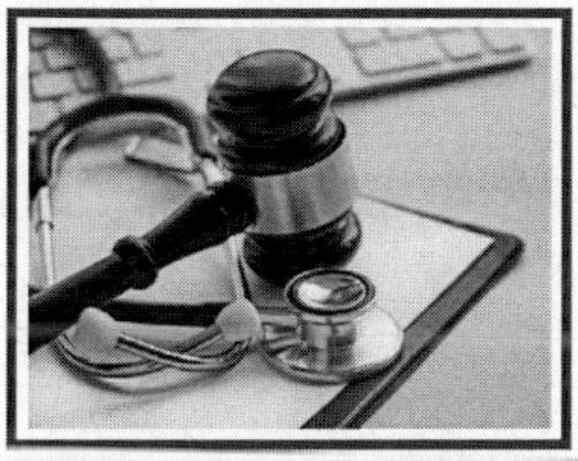

Bibliography

Books

1. Austin, G., 1966. *The Indian Constitution: Cornerstone of a Nation*. Oxford University Press.
2. Basu, D.D., 2022. *Introduction to the Constitution of India*. LexisNexis.
3. Seervai, H.M., 1996. *Constitutional Law of India*. Universal Law Publishing.
4. Chandrachud, A., 2017. *Republic of Rhetoric: Free Speech and the Constitution of India*. Penguin Random House India.
5. Sathe, S.P., 2002. *Judicial Activism in India: Transgressing Borders and Enforcing Limits*. Oxford University Press.
6. De, R., 2018. *A People's Constitution: The Everyday Life of Law in the Indian Republic*. Princeton University Press.
7. Noorani, A.G., 2002. *Constitutional Questions in India: The President, Parliament, and the States*. Oxford University Press.
8. Nariman, F., 2013. *The State of the Nation: In the Context of India's Constitution*. Hay House Publishers India.
9. Bhatia, G., 2019. *The Transformative Constitution: A Radical Biography in Nine Acts*. HarperCollins India.
10. Iyer, V.R.K., 2020. *Social Justice: Sunset or Dawn*. Edition 2020, EBC.
11. Herring, J., 2020. *Medical Law and Ethics*. Oxford University Press.
12. Gostin, L.O., 2014. *Global Health Law*. Harvard University Press.
13. Faden, R.R., and Powers, M., 2008. *Social Justice: The Moral Foundations of Public Health and Health Policy*. Oxford University Press.
14. Meyer, I.H., and Northridge, M.E., 2007. *The Health of Sexual Minorities: Public Health Perspectives on Lesbian, Gay, Bisexual, and Transgender Populations*. Springer.
15. Vincent, B., 2018. *Transgender Health: A Practitioner's Guide to Binary and Non-Binary Trans Patient Care*. Jessica Kingsley Publishers.

16. Pearce, R., 2018. *Understanding Trans Health: Discourse, Power, and Possibility.* Policy Press.
17. Poretsky, L., and Hembree, W., 2020. *Transgender Medicine: A Multidisciplinary Approach*. Springer.
18. Beitz, C.R., 2001. *Political Theory and International Relations*. Princeton University Press.
19. Bayer, R., Caplan, A.L., and Daniels, N., eds., 1983. *In Search of Equity: Health Needs and the Health Care System, The Hastings Center Series in Ethics*. Plenum Press.
20. Institute of Medicine, 1988. *Future of Public Health.* National Academy Press.
21. Pogge, T., 2013. *World Poverty and Human Rights*. Polity Press.
22. Geertz, C., 1977. *The Interpretation of Cultures*. Basic Books.
23. Benhabib, S., 2006. *The Rights of Others: Aliens, Residents and Citizens*. Cambridge University Press.
24. Carens, J.H., 2008. *Aliens and Citizens: The Case for Open Borders*. Paragon House.
25. Rawls, J., 2005. *Political Liberalism.* Columbia University Press.
26. Dworkin, R., 1977. *Taking Rights Seriously*. Harvard University Press.
27. World Health Organization (WHO), 1981. *Global Strategy for Health for All by the Year 2000.* WHO.
28. Bayer, R., Caplan, A.L., and Daniels, N., eds., 1983. *In Search of Equity: Health Needs and the Health Care System, The Hastings Center Series in Ethics*. Plenum Press.
29. Institute of Medicine, 1988. *Future of Public Health.* National Academy Press.
30. Farmer, P., 2010. *Pathologies of Power: Health, Human Rights, and the New War on the Poor*. University of California Press.
31. Gostin, L.O., 2014. *Global Health Law*. Harvard University Press.
32. Prainsack, B., and Buyx, A., 2017. *Solidarity: Normative Approaches*. Cambridge University Press.
33. Mann, J.M., Tarantola, D.J.M., and Netter, T.W., eds., 1992. *AIDS in the World.* Harvard University Press.
34. Basu, S.K., ed., 1993. *Tribal Health in India*. Manak Publications.
35. Chaudhuri, B., 1990. *Culture and Environmental Dimensions on Health*. Inter India Publication.
36. Chauhan, S.R., and Chauhan, N.S., 2006. *International Dimension of Human Rights* (Vol. 2). Global Vision Publishing House.
37. Mann, J.M., Gruskin, S., and Grodin, M.A., eds., 1999. *Health and Human Rights*. Routledge.
38. Farmer, P., Kim, J.Y., Kleinman, A. and Basilico, M., 2013. *Reimagining global health: an introduction* (Vol. 26). Univ of California Press.
39. Friedman, L.M., Furberg, C.D., DeMets, D.L., Reboussin, D.M. and Granger, C.B., 2015. *Fundamentals of clinical trials*. Springer.
40. Benatar, S. and Brock, G. eds., 2011. *Global health and global health ethics*. Cambridge University Press.

41. Gostin, L.O. and Sridhar, D., 2014. Global health and the law. *New England Journal of Medicine*, 370(18), pp. 1732–1740.
42. Packard, R.M., 2016. *A history of global health: interventions into the lives of other peoples*. JHU Press.
43. Azam, M., 2016. *Intellectual property and public health in the developing world* (p. 348). Open Book Publishers.
44. Li, P., 2013. *Health technologies and international intellectual property law: A precautionary approach.* Routledge.
45. Ragavan, S. and Vanni, A. eds., 2021. *Intellectual property law and access to medicines: TRIPS agreement, health, and pharmaceuticals.* Taylor & Francis.
46. Yarbrough, E., 2018. *Transgender mental health.* American Psychiatric Pub.
47. Kawachi, I. and Wamala, S. eds., 2006. *Globalization and health.* Oxford University Press.
48. Cohen, I.G., 2013. *The globalization of health care: legal and ethical issues.* Oxford University Press.
49. Sloan, F.A. and Chepke, L.M., 2008. *Medical malpractice* (pp. 302–03). Cambridge, MA: Mit Press.

Journal Articles

1. Held, D., McGrew, A., Goldblatt, D., and Perraton, J., 2000. 'Global Transformations: Politics, Economics and Culture.' *Politics at the Edge*, pp. 14–28. doi:10.1057/9780333981689_2.
2. Vernon, R., 2009. 'Is There a Global Harm Principle?' *Critical Review of International Social and Political Philosophy*, 12(1), pp. 1–18. doi:10.1080/13698230902738510.
3. Heyd, D., 2007. 'Justice and Solidarity: The Contractarian Case Against Global Justice.' *Journal of Social Philosophy*, 38(1), pp. 112–130. doi:10.1111/j.1467-9833.2007.00369.x.
4. Dawson, A., and Jennings, B., 2012. 'The Place of Solidarity in Public Health Ethics.' *Public Health Reviews*, 34(1). doi:10.1007/bf03391656.
5. Brody, H.E., 2009. 'Medicine's Duty to Treat Pandemic Illness: Solidarity and Vulnerability.' *The Hastings Center Report*. Accessed May 12, 2024. Available at: https://pubmed.ncbi.nlm.nih.gov/19213194/.
6. Rauprich, O., 2012. 'Principalism'. *Encyclopedia of Applied Ethics* (Second Edition). Available at: https://www.sciencedirect.com/science/article/abs/pii/B9780123739322002441.
7. Seepersad, D.-M., 2011. 'Wolfgang Friedmann and the Major Developments in International Law: 1945-1964.' *E-International Relations*. Available at: https://www.e-ir.info/2011/02/24/wolfgang-friedmann-and-the-major-developments-in-international-law-1945-1964/.
8. Kleger, H., and Mehlhausen, T., 2013. 'Indisputable and Still Disputed–European Solidarity during the Euro Crisis.' Available at: https://publishup.uni-potsdam.de/frontdoor/index/index/docId/35367.

9. Gruskin, S., Mann, J., and Tarantola, D., 1998. 'Past, Present, and Future: AIDS and Human Rights.' *Health and Human Rights*, 2(4).
10. Lakoff, A., 2010. 'Two Regimes of Global Health.' *Humanity: An International Journal of Human Rights, Humanitarianism, and Development*, 1(1), pp. 59–79.
11. Marmot, M., and Commission on Social Determinants of Health, 2007. 'Achieving Health Equity: From Root Causes to Fair Outcomes.' *Lancet*, 370(9593).
12. McMichael, A.J., and Butler, C.D., 2006. 'Emerging Health Issues: The Widening Challenge for Population Health Promotion.' *Health Promotion International*, 21(Supplement 1).
13. Thompson, A.K., Faith, K., Gibson, J.L., and Upshur, R.E.G., 2006. 'Pandemic Influenza Preparedness: An Ethical Framework to Guide Decision-Making.' *BMC Medical Ethics*, 7(1).
14. Baylis, F., Kenny, N.P., and Sherwin, S., 2008. 'A Relational Account of Public Health Ethics.' *Public Health Ethics*, 1(3).
15. Boozary, A.S., Farmer, P.E., and Jha, A.K., 2014. 'The Ebola Outbreak, Fragile Health Systems, and Quality as a Cure.' *JAMA*, 312(18).
16. Dawson, A., and Jennings, B., 2012. 'The Place of Solidarity in Public Health Ethics.' *Public Health Reviews*, 34(1).
17. O'Neill, J., 2016. 'Antimicrobial Resistance: Tackling a Crisis for the Health and Wealth of Nations.' *The Review on Antimicrobial Resistance*. Wellcome Collection.
18. Prainsack, B., and Buyx, A., 2017. 'Solidarity: Normative Approaches.' *Solidarity in Biomedicine and Beyond.*
19. Smith, M.J., and Upshur, R.E.G., 2015. 'Ebola and Learning Lessons from Moral Failures: Who Cares About Ethics?' *Public Health Ethics*, 8.
20. Giubilini, A., 2018. 'Vaccination and Herd Immunity: Individual, Collective, and Institutional Responsibilities.' *Springer eBooks*.
21. Viens, A.M., and Littmann, J., 2015. 'Is Antimicrobial Resistance a Slowly Emerging Disaster?' *Public Health Ethics*, 8.
22. Remais, J.V., Zeng, G., Li, G., Tian, L., and Engelgau, M.M., 2012. 'Convergence of Non-communicable and Infectious Diseases in Low- and Middle-income Countries.' *International Journal of Epidemiology*, 42(1).
23. Satyanarayana, K. and Srivastava, S., 2007. Poverty, health & intellectual property rights with special reference to India. *Indian Journal of Medical Research*, 126(4), pp. 390–406.
24. Guan, W., 2016. IPRs, public health, and international trade: an international law perspective on the TRIPS amendment. *Leiden Journal of International Law*, 29(2), pp. 411–440.
25. Winter, S., Diamond, M., Green, J., Karasic, D., Reed, T., Whittle, S. and Wylie, K., 2016. Transgender people: health at the margins of society. *The Lancet*, 388(10042), pp. 390–400.

26. Seelman, K.L., Colón-Diaz, M.J., LeCroix, R.H., Xavier-Brier, M. and Kattari, L., 2017. Transgender noninclusive healthcare and delaying care because of fear: connections to general health and mental health among transgender adults. *Transgender health*, 2(1), pp. 17–28.
27. Reisner, S.L., Poteat, T., Keatley, J., Cabral, M., Mothopeng, T., Dunham, E., Holland, C.E., Max, R. and Baral, S.D., 2016. Global health burden and needs of transgender populations: a review. *The Lancet*, 388(10042), pp. 412–436.
28. Meyer, I.H., 2001. Why lesbian, gay, bisexual, and transgender public health? *American Journal of Public Health*, 91(6), p. 856.
29. Forman, L., 2017. Human Rights Treaties Are an Important Part of the" International Health Instrumentariam": Comment on" The Legal Strength of International Health Instruments—What It Brings to Global Health Governance?". *International Journal of Health Policy and Management*, 7(5), p. 467.
30. Dibaba, S.D., 2021. The Human Right to Health: In International, Regional and National Legal Instruments. *GSJ*, 9(6).
31. Cornia, G.A., 2001. Globalization and health: results and options. *Bulletin of the World Health Organization*, 79, pp. 834–841.
32. Brundtland, G.H., 2003. The globalization of health. *Seton Hall J. Dipl. & Int'l Rel.*, 4, p.7.
33. Oyebode, F., 2013. Clinical errors and medical negligence. *Medical Principles and Practice*, 22(4), pp. 323–333.
34. Bryden, D. and Storey, I., 2011. Duty of care and medical negligence. *Continuing Education in Anaesthesia, Critical Care & Pain*, 11(4), pp. 124–127.
35. Mohanty, K.C., 2005. Influence of guidelines in determining medical negligence. *BMJ: British Medical Journal*, 330(7499), p. 1086.
36. Rayamane, A.P., Nanandkar, S.D. and Kundargi, P.A., 2016. Profile of medical negligence cases in India. *Journal of Indian Academy of Forensic Medicine*, 38(2), pp. 144–148.
37. Madan, R., Das, N., Patley, R., Nagpal, N., Malik, Y. and Math, S.B., 2024. Consequences of medical negligence and litigations on healthcare providers—A narrative review. *Indian Journal of Psychiatry*, 66(4), pp. 317–325.
38. Agrawal, A., 2016. Medical negligence: Indian legal perspective. *Annals of Indian Academy of Neurology*, 19(Suppl 1), pp. S9-S14.
39. Vogel, D., 1998. The globalization of pharmaceutical regulation. *Governance*, 11(1), pp. 1–22.
40. Rago, L. and Santoso, B., 2008. Drug regulation: history, present and future. *Drug benefits and risks: International textbook of clinical pharmacology*, 2, pp. 65–77.
41. Agarwal, N.B. and Karwa, M., 2018. Pharmaceutical regulations in India. In *Pharmaceutical Medicine and translational clinical research* (pp. 215–231). Academic Press.
42. Keshri, V.R., Sriram, V. and Baru, R., 2020. Reforming the regulation of medical education, professionals and practice in India. *BMJ Global Health*, 5(8), p. e002765.

43. Bhat, R., 1996. Regulation of the private health sector in India. *The International journal of health planning and management*, 11(3), pp. 253–274.

44. Srihita, R.H., Goli, G. and Rajya laxmi, M., 2024. Legal and Regulatory Consideration in Healthcare Industry of India. In *Healthcare Industry Assessment: Analyzing Risks, Security, and Reliability* (pp. 171–200). Cham: Springer Nature Switzerland.

45. Mayra, K., Padmadas, S.S. and Matthews, Z., 2021. Challenges and needed reforms in midwifery and nursing regulatory systems in India: Implications for education and practice. *PLOS one*, 16(5), pp. 251–331.

46. Tiwari, S.K., Kalyan, G., Silpa, K., Murry, L.L. and Joshi, P., 2024. National Nursing and Midwifery Commission Act, 2023 in India: Issues and the Way Forward. *Policy, Politics, & Nursing Practice*, 25(3), pp. 189–198.

47. Timmons, S., Evans, C. and Nair, S., 2016. The development of the nursing profession in a globalised context: A qualitative case study in Kerala, India. *Social Science & Medicine*, 166, pp. 41–48.

48. Umali-Deininger, D. and Sur, M., 2007. Food safety in a globalizing world: opportunities and challenges for India. *Agricultural Economics*, 37, pp. 135–147.

49. Yang, H., 2019. Food safety in India: status and challenges. *Gates Open Res*, 3(1043), p. 1043.

50. Kohli, C. and Garg, S., 2015. Food safety in India: an unfinished agenda. *MAMC Journal of Medical Sciences*, 1(3), pp. 131–135.

51. Dhara, D., Biswas, S., Das, S. and Biswas, O., 2021. Status of food safety and food security in India in the perspective of FSSAI. *Indian J Anim Health*, 60(2), pp. 167–173.

52. Blumstein, J.F., 1989. Government's role in organ transplantation policy. *Journal of health politics, policy and law*, 14(1), pp. 5–39.

53. Mathiharan, K., 2011. Ethical and legal issues in organ transplantation: Indian scenario. *Medicine, Science and the Law*, 51(3), pp. 134–140.

54. Agarwal, S.K., Srivastava, R.K., Gupta, S. and Tripathi, S., 2012. Evolution of the Transplantation of Human Organ Act and law in India. *Transplantation*, 94(2), pp. 110–113.

55. Capoor, M.R. and Bhowmik, K.T., 2017. Current perspectives on biomedical waste management: Rules, conventions and treatment technologies. *Indian journal of medical microbiology*, 35(2), pp. 157–164.

56. Babu, B.R., Parande, A.K., Rajalakshmi, R., Suriyakala, P. and Volga, M., 2009. Management of biomedical waste in India and other countries: a review. *Journal of International Environmental Application & Science*, 4(1), pp. 65–78.

57. Mastorakis, N.E., Bulucea, C.A., Oprea, T.A., Bulucea, C.A. and Dondon, P., 2010. Environmental and health risks associated with biomedical waste management. *Develop Energy Environ Economics*, 2010, pp. 287–94.

58. Kutner, L., 1968. Due process of euthanasia: the living will, a proposal. *Ind. LJ*, 44, p. 539.

59. Emanuel, E.J. and Emanuel, L.L., 1990. Living wills: past, present, and future. *The Journal of Clinical Ethics*, 1(1), pp. 9–19.

60. Kurfees, J.F. and Th, M., 1987. On Living Wills. *Journal of Biblical Ethics in Medicine*, 2(1), p. 6.
61. Abrams, P., 2015. The bad mother: stigma, abortion and surrogacy. *Journal of Law, Medicine & Ethics*, 43(2), pp. 179–191.
62. Mallik, R., 2003. *'Negative Choice'sex Determination and Sex Selective Abortion in India*. Centre for Enquiry and Allied Themes.
63. Katz, J., 2017. Human experimentation and human rights. In *Human Experimentation and Research* (pp. 225–272). Routledge.
64. Bansal, N., 2012. The opportunitics and challenges in conducting clinical trials globally. *Clinical Research and Regulatory Affairs*, *29*(1), pp. 9–14.

Online Reports and Documents

1. United Nations, 2024. 'In Larger Freedom: Towards Development, Security and Human Rights for All: Report of the Secretary-General - United Nations and the Rule of Law.' Available at: https://www.un.org/ruleoflaw/blog/document/in-larger-freedom-towards-development-security-and-human-rights-for-all-report-of-the-secretary-general/.
2. United Nations, 2024. 'Report of the Independent Expert on Human Rights and International Solidarity.' Available at: https://digitallibrary.un.org/record/690228?ln=en.
3. United Nations, 2024. 'UN Charter.' Available at: https://www.un.org/en/about-us/un-charter.
4. United Nations, 2024. 'Universal Declaration of Human Rights.' Available at: https://www.un.org/en/about-us/universal-declaration-of-human-rights.
5. United Nations, 2024. 'International Covenant on Economic, Social and Cultural Rights–Main Page.' Available at: https://legal.un.org/avl//ha/icescr/icescr.html.
6. United Nations, 2024. 'International Law, Codification, Legal Affairs, Commission, ILC, Instruments and Reports, Yearbook.' Available at: https://legal.un.org/ilc/guide/6_3.shtml.
7. United Nations, 2024. 'Preamble to the United Nations Universal Declaration of Human Rights.' Available at: https://www.humanrights.com/what-are-human-rights/universal-declaration-of-human-rights/preamble.html.
8. Global Centre for the Responsibility to Protect, 2021. 'The Responsibility to Protect: Report of the International Commission on Intervention and State Sovereignty, 2001.' Available at: https://www.globalr2p.org/resources/the-responsibility-to-protect-report-of-the-international-commission-on-intervention-and-state-sovereignty-2001/.
9. United Nations, 2024. 'A/RES/60/1 2005 World Summit Outcome.' Available at: https://www.un.org/en/development/desa/population/migration/generalassembly/docs/globalcompact/A_RES_60_1.pdf.
10. United Nations, 2024. 'Draft Articles on the Protection of Persons in the Event of Disasters.' Available at: https://legal.un.org/ilc/texts/instruments/english/draft_articles/6_3_2016.pdf.

11. United Nations, 2024. 'Draft Articles on the Responsibility of International Organizations.' Available at: https://legal.un.org/ilc/texts/instruments/english/draft_articles/9_11_2011.pdf.
12. Evans, G., 2024. 'The Responsibility to Protect: From an Idea to an International Norm.' Available at: https://gevans.org/speeches/speech202.html.
13. World Health Organization, 2015. *Tracking universal health coverage: first global monitoring report.* World Health Organization.
14. World Health Organization, 2019. *It's time to walk the talk: WHO Independent High-level Commission on Noncommunicable Diseases-final report.* World Health Organization.
15. World Health Organization, 2015. *WHO global strategy on people-centred and integrated health services: interim report* (No. WHO/HIS/SDS/2015.6). World Health Organization.
16. World Health Organization, 2014. *Report: 8th FAO/WHO joint meeting on pesticide management and 10th session of the FAO panel of experts on pesticide management, 14-17 October 2014, Rome* (No. WHO/CDS/NTD/WHOPES/2014.6). World Health Organization.
17. World Health Organization, 2015. *Trends in maternal mortality: 1990–2015: estimates from WHO, UNICEF, UNFPA, world bank group and the United Nations population division.* World Health Organization.
18. World Health Organization, 2010. *Monitoring the building blocks of health systems: A handbook of indicators and their measurement strategies.* World Health Organization.
19. World Health Organization, 2020. Coronavirus disease 2019 (COVID-19): Situation report, 73.
20. World Health Organization, 2013. *WHO report on the global tobacco epidemic, 2013: enforcing bans on tobacco advertising, promotion and sponsorship.* World Health Organization.
21. World Health Organization, 2020. *Global status report on preventing violence against children* 2020.
22. World Health Organization, 2019. *Nutrition Landscape Information System (NLIS) country profile indicators: interpretation guide.*
23. World Health Organization, 2021. *Primary health care on the road to universal health coverage*: 2019. Global monitoring report.

Index